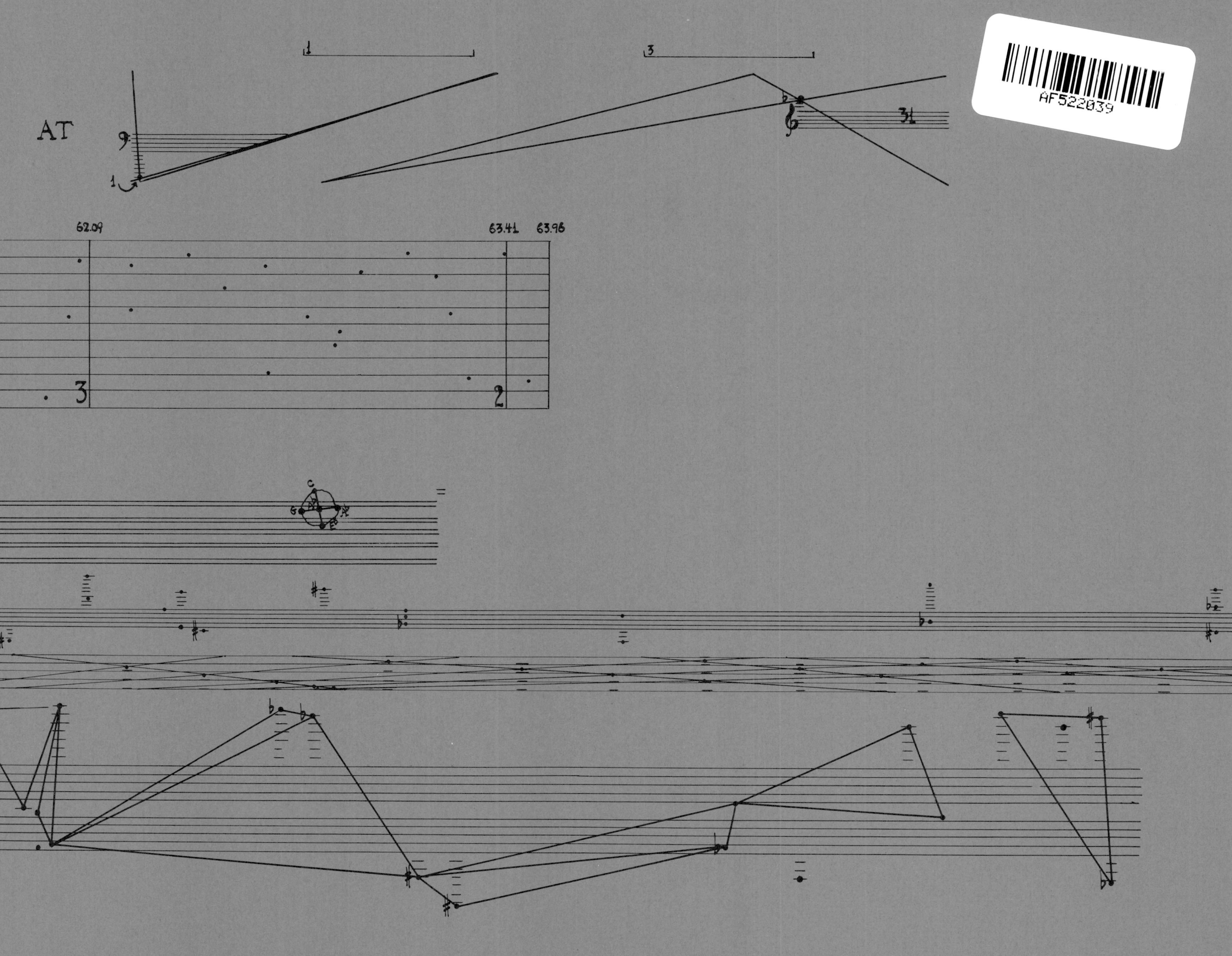
AT
1
3
31
62.09
63.41
63.96
3
2
G
C
Eb

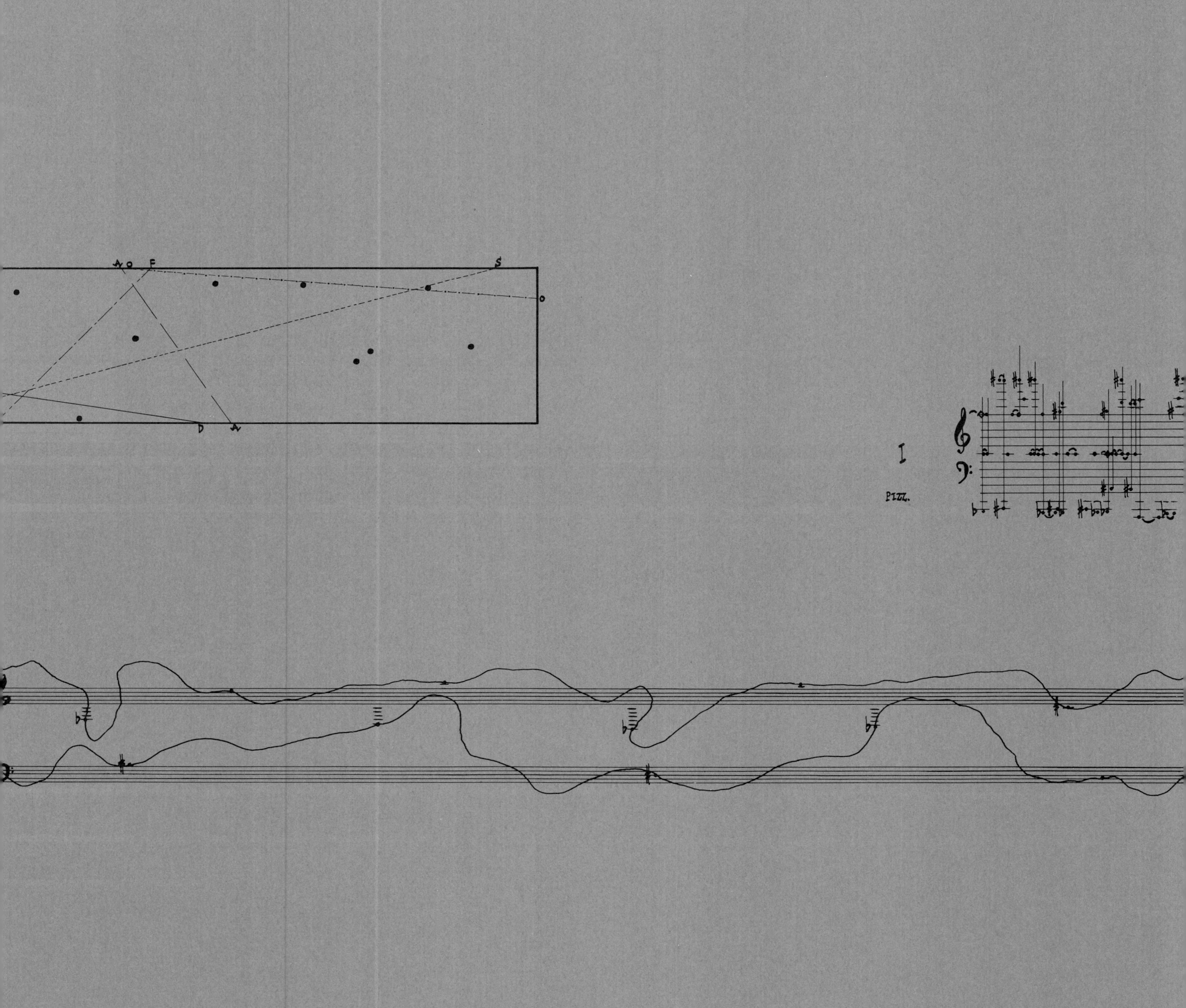
A
O
F
S
O
D
A
I
pizz.

JOHN CAGE WAS

for Carolyn

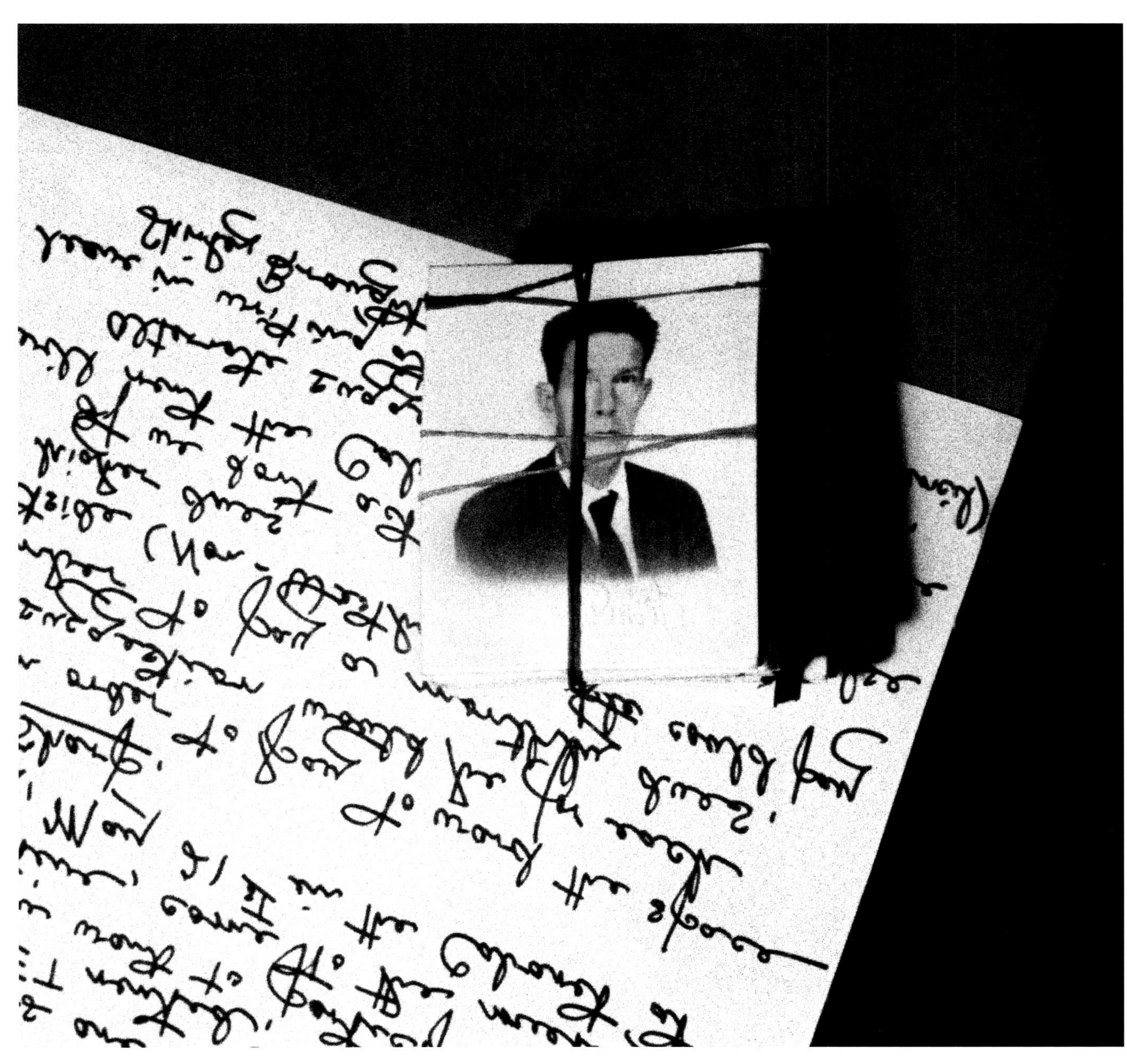

JOHN CAGE WAS

PHOTOGRAPHS BY JAMES KLOSTY

Wesleyan University Press, Middletown, Connecticut

I look for something I haven't yet found.
My favorite music is the music I haven't yet heard.
I don't hear the music I write.
I write in order to hear the music I haven't yet heard.

— John Cage, from "An Autobiographical Statement"

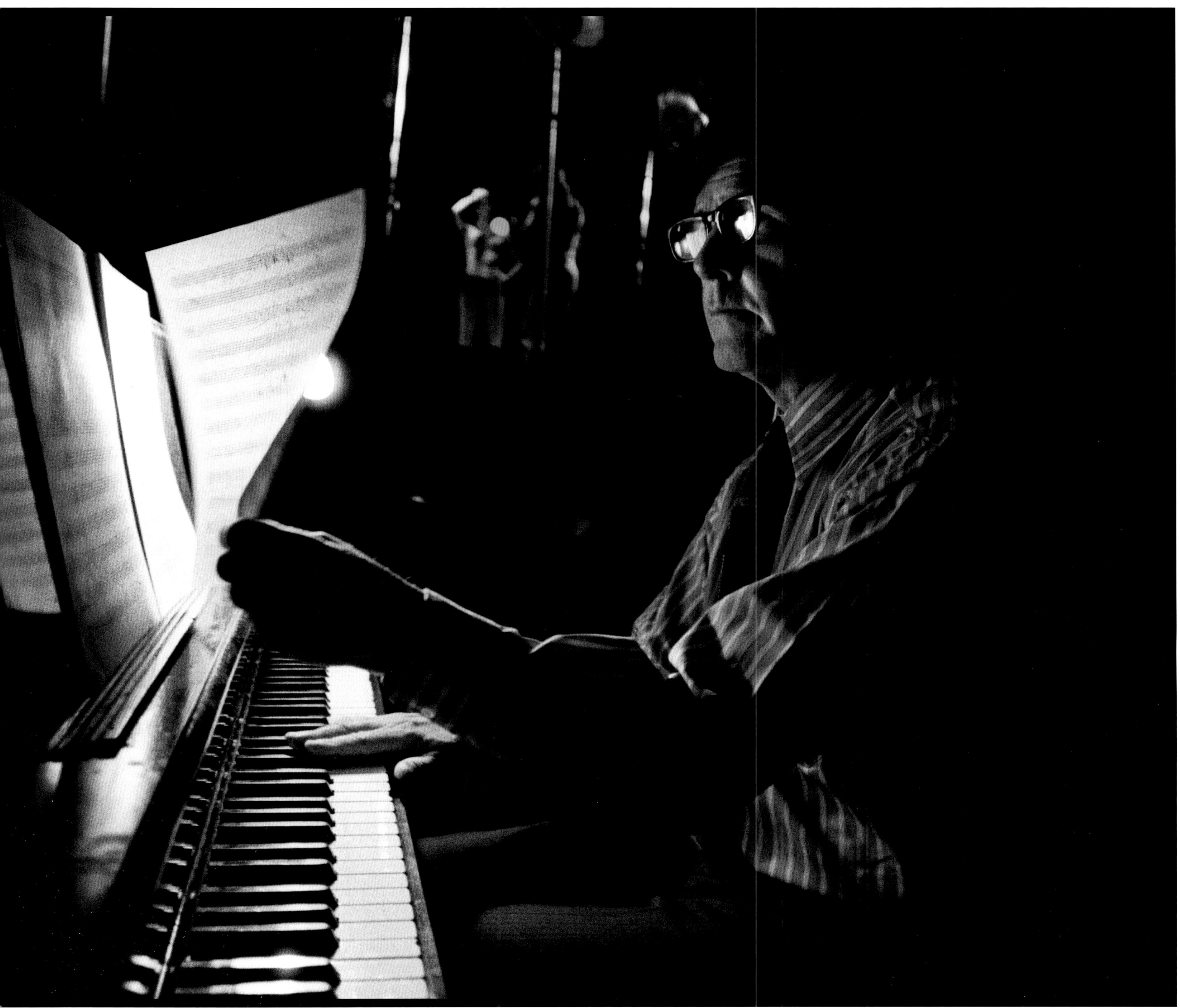

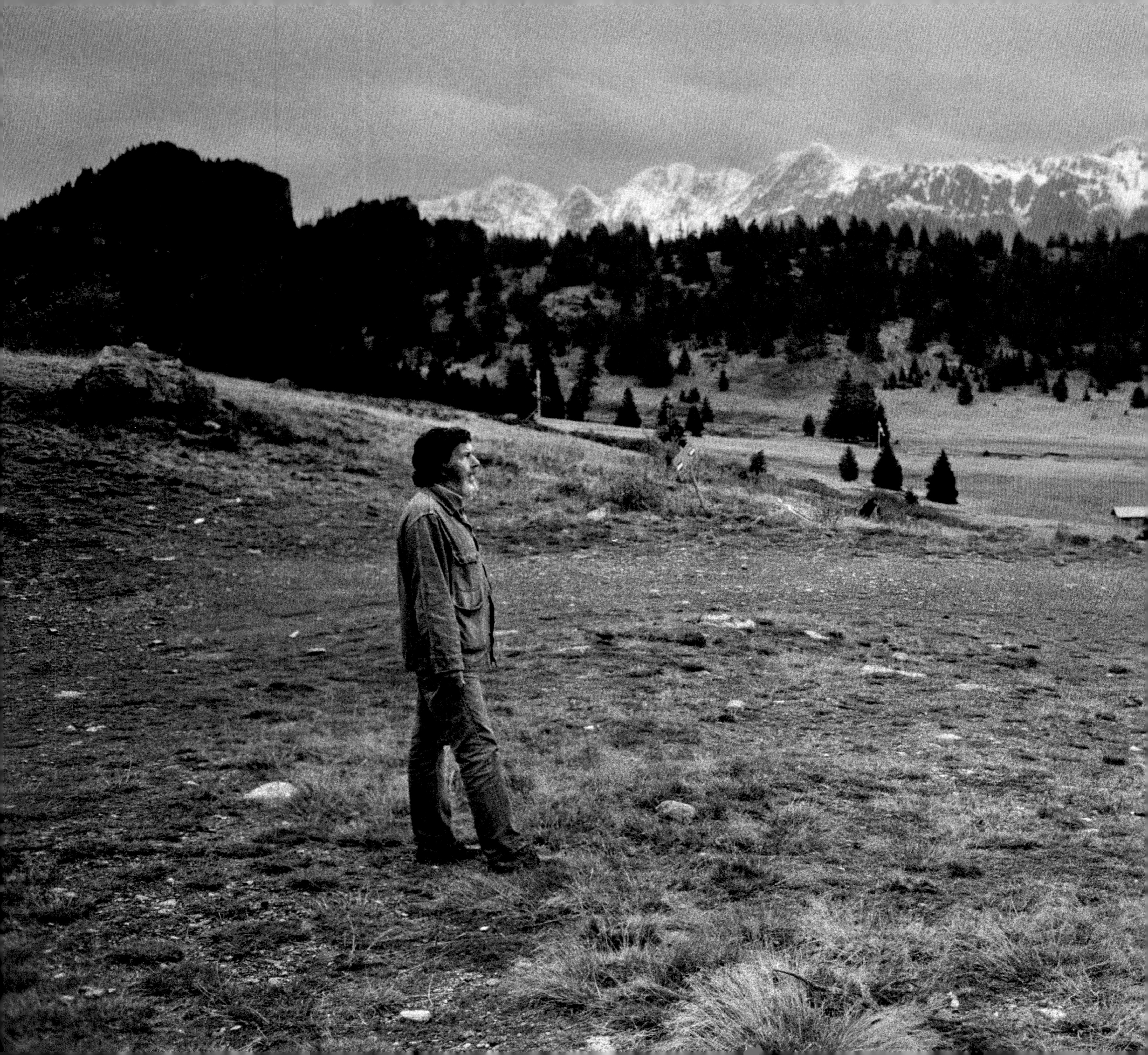

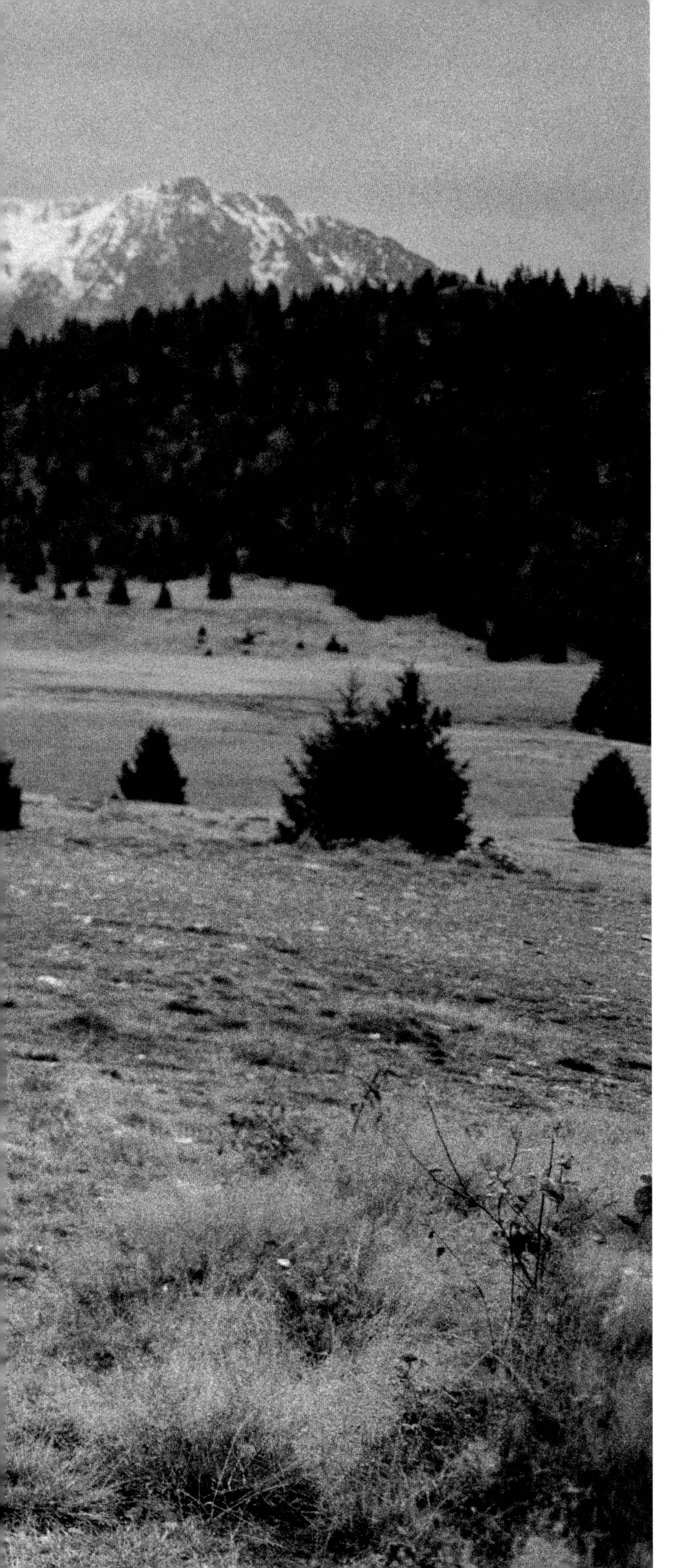

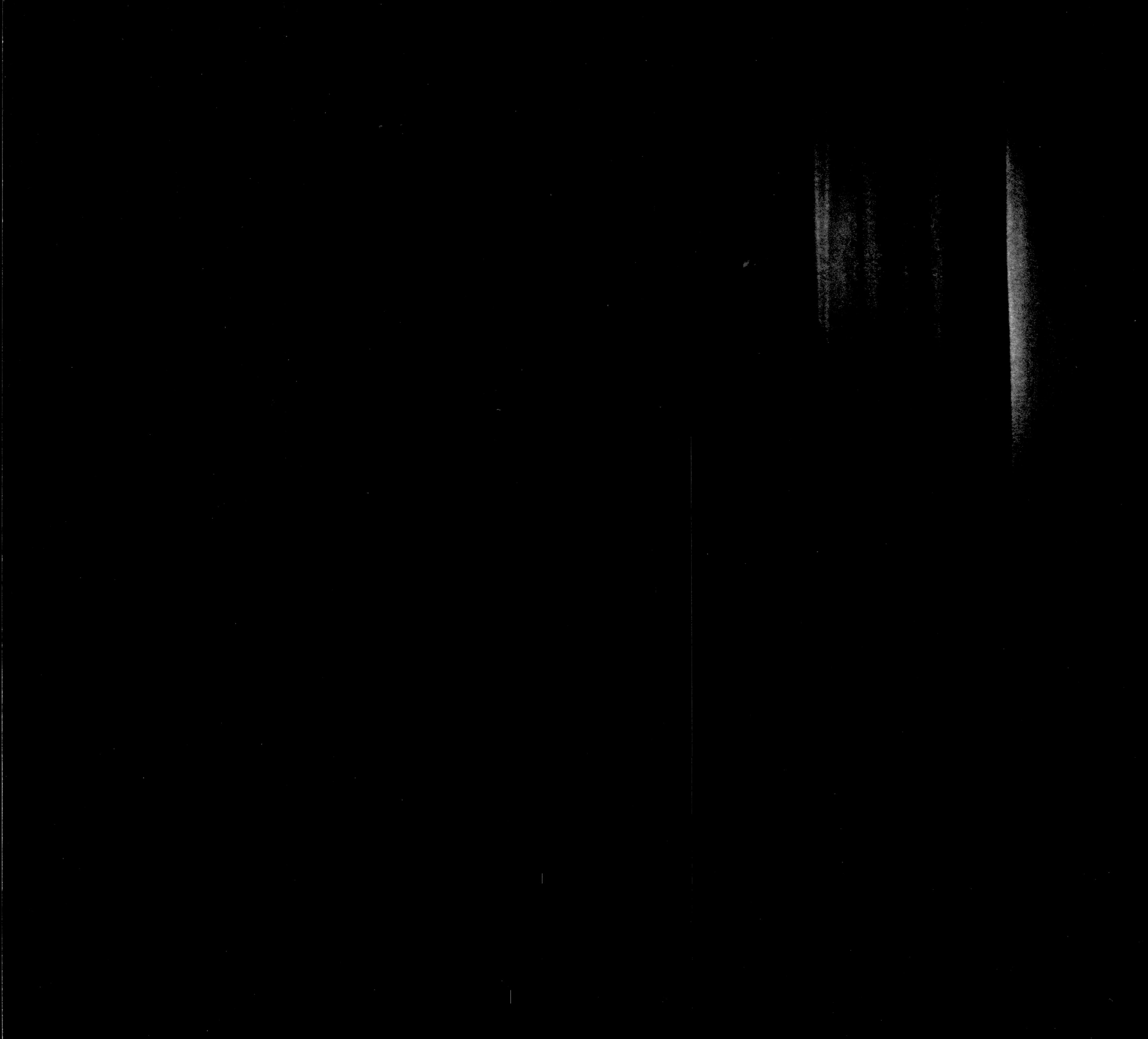

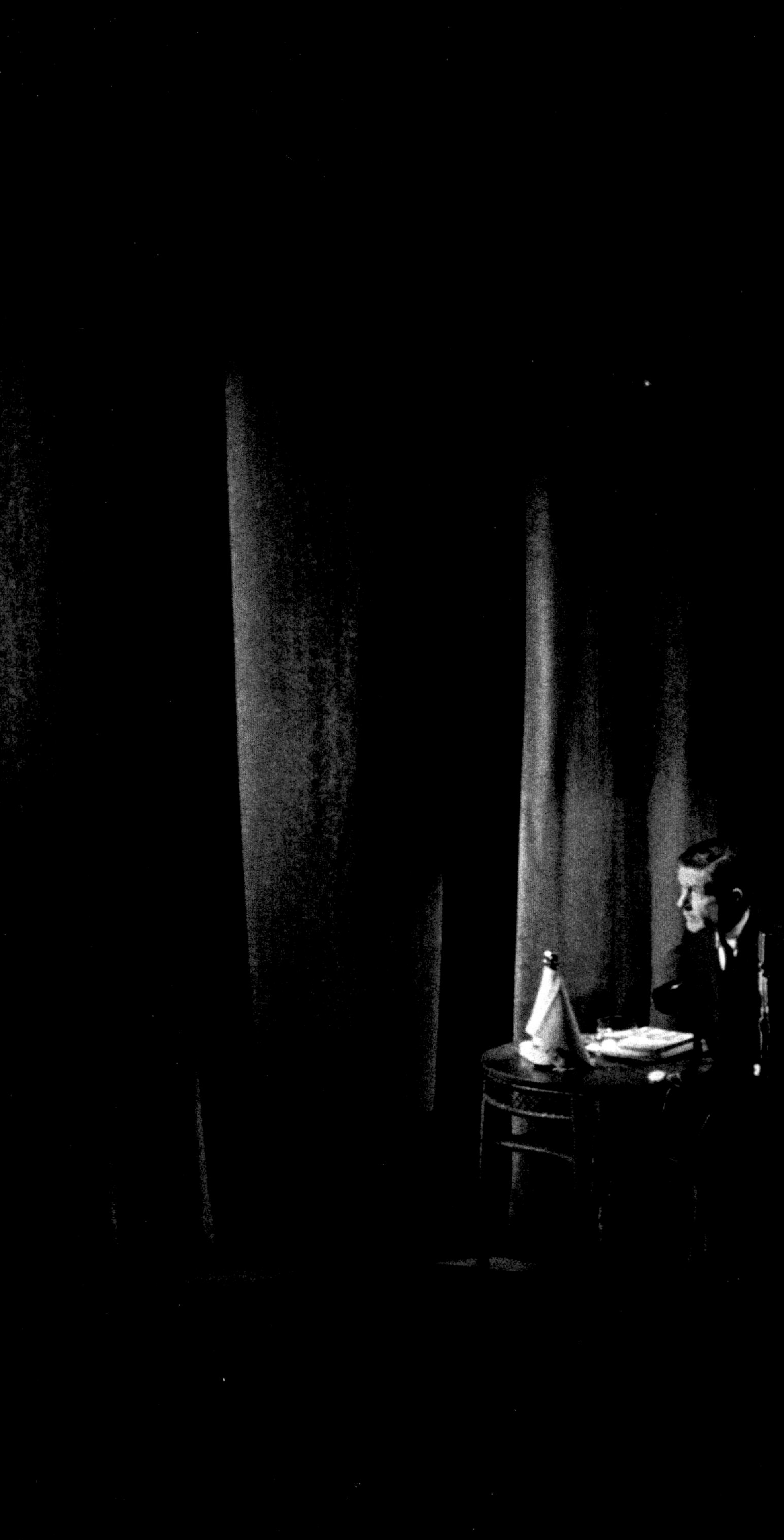

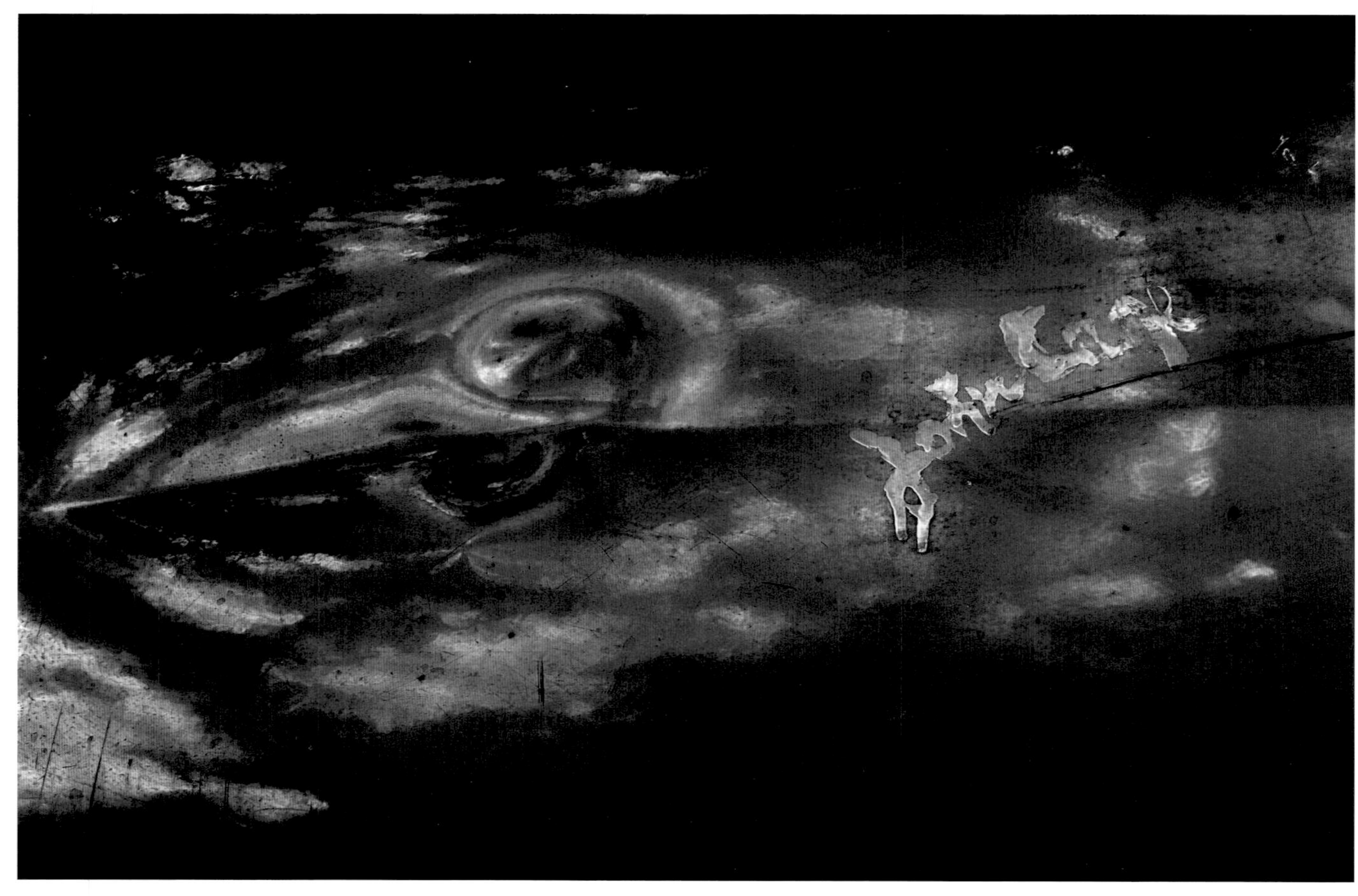

I asked him to sign the dent. He happily agreed.

JOHN CAGE WAS

Perhaps an atypical teenager, I didn't care one whit about Elvis Presley or the imminent arrival of the Beatles. I adored the music of Stravinsky and Mahler: Mahler, obsessed with composing the strivings of the human soul; Stravinsky, convinced music was about nothing beyond the syntax of music. An odd pairing of enthusiasms, although "enthusiasm" may actually be too mild a term considering that on Stravinsky's birthday I insisted the back window of our family car display the painted cardboard proclamation:

HAPPY BIRTHDAY IGGY!

So I suppose it's not all that surprising I cofounded our high school music club—although I remember few of those afterschool meetings other than the wonderful afternoon that Nina Totenberg, an enthusiastic member, brought her father Roman Totenberg to play his violin for us. Math teacher Joel Forbes, the club's faculty advisor, happened also to be the drivers' ed. instructor. The profound significance of that seemingly unimportant coincidence completely escaped me—until writing this introduction some fifty years later. Although Joel did his best to make us aware of less obvious trends in contemporary music—he once led an expedition to the Five Spot Cafe in the bowels of the East Village to hear Thelonious Monk—I recall no discussions of John Cage's *4'33"*, whose controversial first performance had taken place only eight years earlier. Nor do any contemplations of the allure of chance processes glitter, prophetically, among the shards of my hazy memories of those meetings.

As if to make amends for that vacancy, John Cage entered my life with a bang five or six years later, in typically disarming fashion, with an unexpected—and very concrete—demonstration of aleatoric principals. This is where the significance of Joel Forbes's drivers' ed. class becomes paramount. If John had taken Joel's class—Joel was a very good instructor—this book might not exist!

The texts in this book make clear that John Cage was many things to many people, but I can attest that a good parallel parker he was not. Attempting to park on Third Avenue in the fall of 1966 he backed into my beloved Sunbeam Alpine as I was driving by in the stream of northbound traffic. Two years before, in the fall of 1964, I had been in London on leave of absence from college. Barbara Newman—now a dance writer residing in London but then a close friend from high school—had told me that if I ever had the opportunity to see the Merce Cunningham Dance Company I should take it. Lo and behold, there it was! Critical acclaim from London's many dance critics had extended the company's one-week engagement at the Sadler's Wells Theatre to several weeks at the Phoenix Theatre in the West End, which is where I first laid eyes on them and where I became immediately enthralled by what struck me as the most compelling theater I had ever seen. I attended as many remaining performances as I could, even abandoning a performance of *Coriolanus* at first intermission to dash down Charing Cross Road and sneak in to what remained of the Cunningham matinee. I began plying the musicians in the pit, John Cage, Gordon Mumma, and David Tudor, with questions. So, two years later, when John Cage sheepishly emerged from his car to assess the damage, I instantly recognized him. Anger dissolved into delight. I asked him to sign the dent. He happily agreed.

A month or two later the Cunningham Dance Company gave a performance at my alma mater, Brandeis University. Cunningham performances in the United States being criminally rare events in those years, I probably would have attended anyway, but I arrived brandishing a small can of green paint. The residual impression of our encounter was duly signed. When eventually I sold the Sunbeam I kept the door with its aleatoric, arty-fact dent.

The gravitational pull of the Cunningham Company became stronger in the next few years. It seemed the closest thing to the heady mix of groundbreaking artistic endeavors of Diaghilev's Ballets Russes that we in our essentially cultureless country could hope to see. But Merce received scant critical notice in America in those years and what there was seemed misguided. I hoped my 1975 book, *Merce Cunningham*, would bring more attention to his work. That was its sole purpose. Although it was not wonderfully printed, Leo Castelli, that dear man, and subsequently the International Center of Photography, inexplicably presented exhibitions of the photographs, so my photographer's soul was assuaged.

The introduction I wrote for *Merce Cunningham* was a quite different affair than this and had a very different purpose. Because it was the first book to appear on Merce—those that exist now were years in the future—I felt it necessary to explain the essential aesthetic principals that were the foundation of the company. No similar responsibilities weigh on me here. It is no mean trick, in fact, merely to keep track of all the volumes about John that have appeared in the last two decades. His work and his influence have been dissected, disparaged, lauded, complained about, explained, and wondered over from points of view ranging from purely musical to philosophical to spiritual. I feel absolved from any need to add a word. What I offer instead are a few simple facts about the contents of this book.

The rules for the texts I commissioned were simple but strict:

– one hundred words or less

– must somewhere contain the phrase "John Cage was"

The exceptions herein are from Robert Wilson and Octavio Paz. Trying to count the number of words in Mr. Wilson's piece was beginning to give me a headache, so I stopped. It seems quite clear it exceeds the limit. I am happy to have it. Octavio Paz's poem "On Reading John Cage" was written many years ago and I wanted very much to include it here in a translation by Monique Fong that has not heretofore been published. Alberto Ibargüen gave me four choices. I've included more than one. And then there is Mary Bauermeister, who cheated, but so charmingly, that I have looked the other way.

As for the photographs, all were taken in the five years, from 1967 to 1972, when I was working on *Merce Cunningham*. John, Merce's partner in life as in art, was, needless to say, almost always around. Is it a vast oversimplification to posit the principal difference between Merce and John as this: Merce worked on steps—the limitations, real dangers, and potential epiphanies of bodies moving in space—and John on incorporeal ideas? Somewhat. It is *not* an oversimplification to say that Merce, at least in those days, did not enjoy having photographs taken, either of the work or of himself. In fact, he disliked being photographed intensely. John adored it. Merce concocted. John connected. Nevertheless, there was never a moment, outside of meals or the search for mushrooms and wild edibles, when I saw John *not* working—whether composing, writing, editing, performing, or making graphic art.

Unless he was playing chess. Shortly before I began photographing him, John had become devoted to the game. His passion for chess was fueled not merely by the fact that, as a discipline, it was the polar opposite of his devotion to chance processes, but, more important, chess was the door to friendship with Marcel Duchamp, whom John had always revered. Cage did not know Duchamp well nor was he a real chess player before screwing up his courage to ask, late in Duchamp's life, if Duchamp would teach him the game. Duchamp agreed. As Cage amusingly explained to Calvin Tomkins in *Duchamp: A Biography*, Marcel's method of teaching was to sit nearby, observing or not, while John played against his wife, Marcel stirring himself every now and then to comment on how badly John was playing. Originally the game was less important to John than the opportunity to spend time with Marcel, but with Duchamp's death in 1968 John continued playing with his widow. Alexina Duchamp, universally known as "Teeny," had formerly been married to Pierre Matisse, son of Henri Matisse. In the next decade she and John spent increasing hours over the chessboard. For John this was as much an ongoing homage to Duchamp as it was a testimony to his ever deepening love for the game. Chess had been central to Marcel and Teeny's relationship. Now it drew Teeny and John together as well, with the inevitable result that Teeny grew extremely close to both John and Merce.

Some of the photographs in this book may seem posed, or set up, or carefully lit. Not the case. John was so open to life that he was fully available to the intrusion of the camera at any moment. After *Merce Cunningham* was published, I abandoned my enlarger—in fact, photography in general. The basement space that served as my darkroom was rededicated, and seems to be enjoying its new role as wine cellar. John would have approved. However, as a consequence, I have had to scan all my old negatives into a computer in order to make this book. I am deeply mistrustful of Photoshop and have tried to avoid the cornucopia of tricks it permits. In any case, a Luddite by nature, my technical abilities in the digital realm are so limited that I have done little that I would not have done in the darkroom: basic dodging, burning, etc. The only "tricky" image, "watersmoke," was created back in the darkroom days when, for the first and only time in my life, I made a sandwich of two unrelated negatives—one of John and his cigarette holder and one of water in a stream at Lake Minnewaska—and printed them together as one. My wonderful designer, Yolanda Cuomo, is far stricter about Photoshop chicanery than I. As of this writing I do not know if the one or two photos in which I allowed myself to play with certain "artistic filters" and "curves" will be allowed in these pages. If she has her way, they will not.

I feel blessed as a photographer that those five brief years between 1967 and 1972 coincided with John's progress through the entire gamut of his physical avatars—from the clean shaven, seemingly respectable businessman in suit and black tie to the denim-clad, shaggily bearded mountain man of his Thoreau years, who emerged to take pride of place in the spring of 1971.

I was, indeed, lucky. I could leave it at that, but I shall risk being presumptuous: I admit to hoping that those interested in John Cage will find in these photographs not merely representations of an influential composer, performer, writer, mycologist, artist, and philosopher, but also, here and there, glimpses into an always searching, unfailingly playful, uniquely beautiful spirit.

— James Klosty
Millbrook, New York

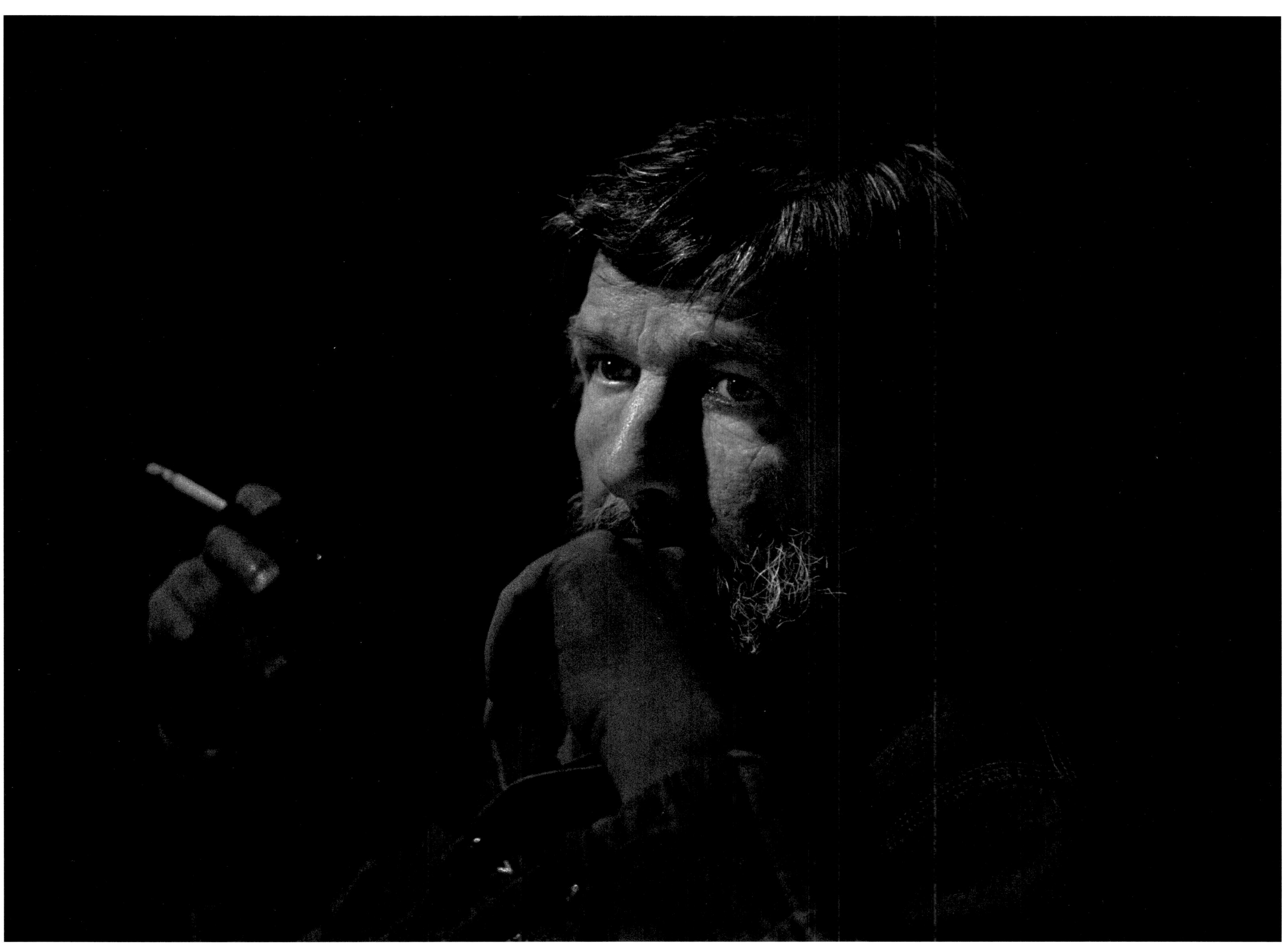

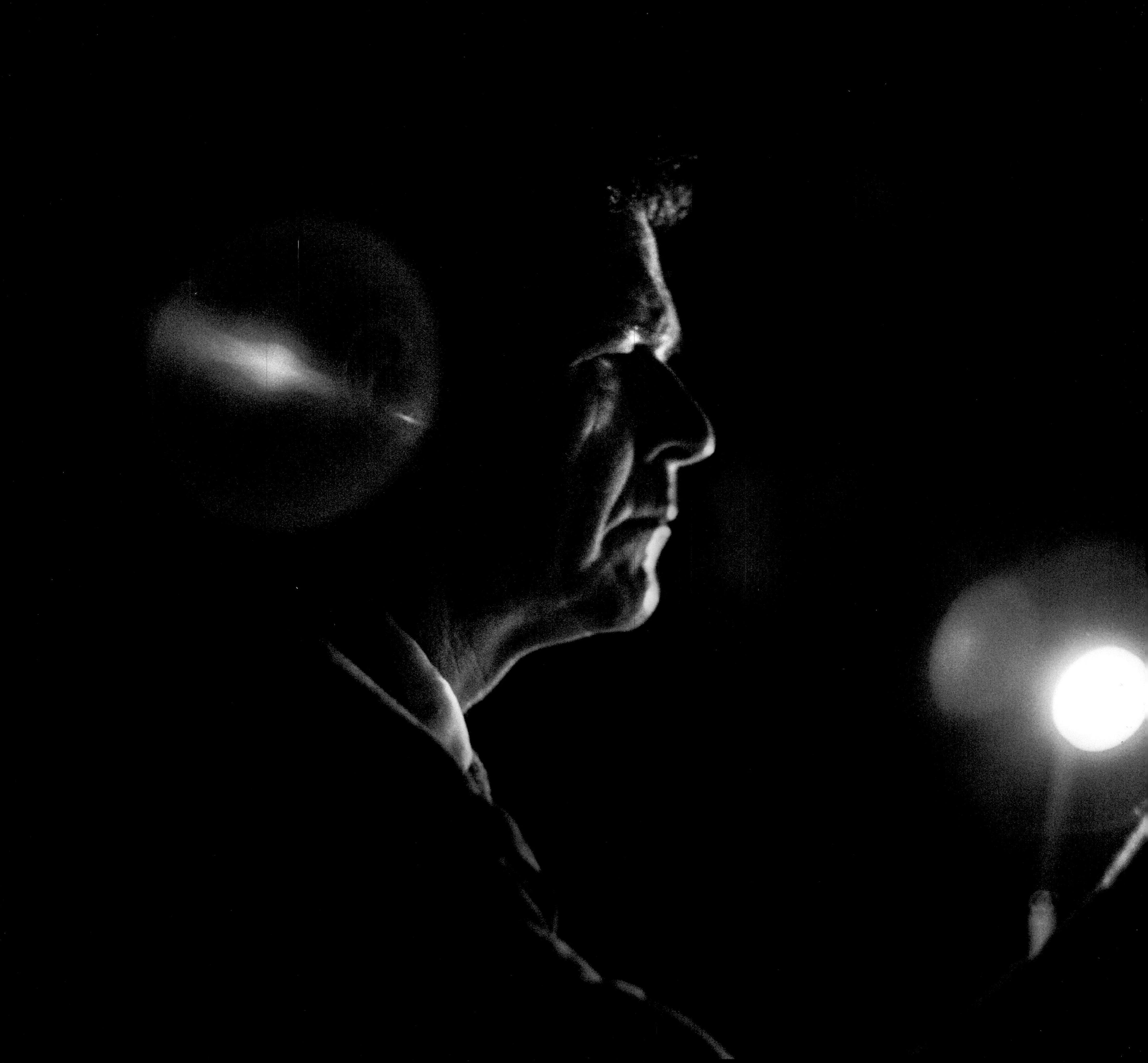

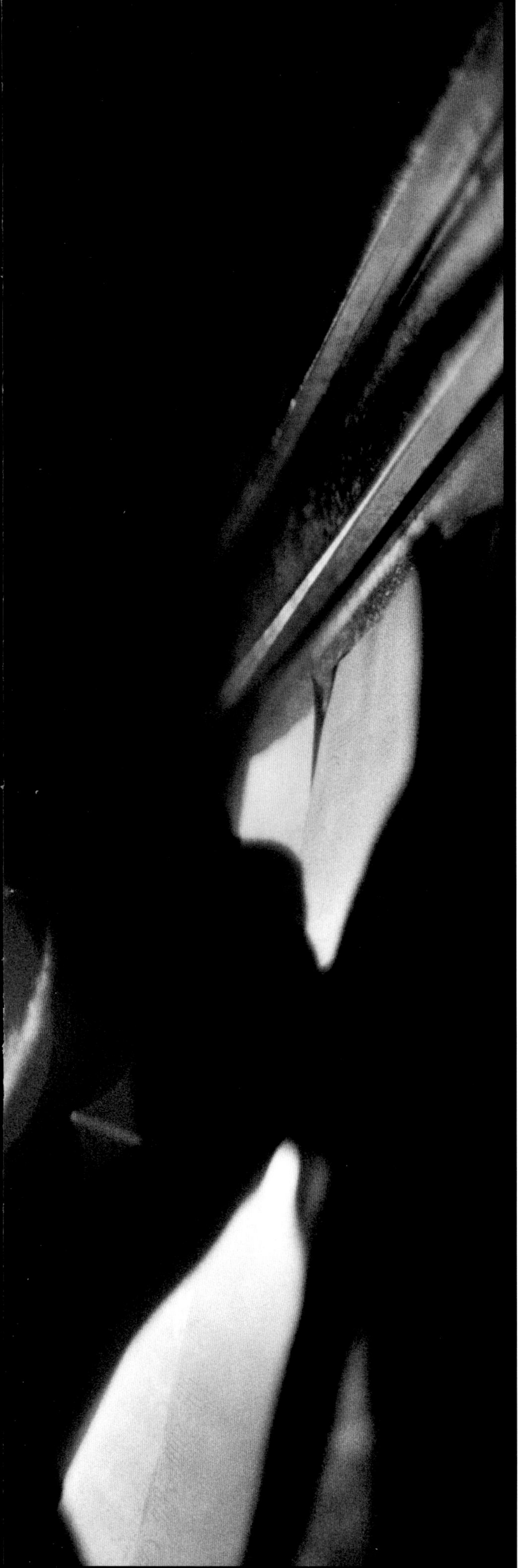

At first, the mind of John Cage
was a mystery to me.
Like so many people in the 1960s,
I believed that he was a charlatan, not a composer.
When he coached a performance of *Amores*,
however, his deep sensitivity to sound and phrase
convinced me that his unusual ideas
rested on a foundation of true musicality.
From then on, his unorthodox goals made sense.
As my ears gradually opened
to his vastly enlarged world of sonic surprises,
I experienced a stretching of my mind
that has colored all my subsequent work
as a pianist, composer, and teacher.

— Joel Sachs

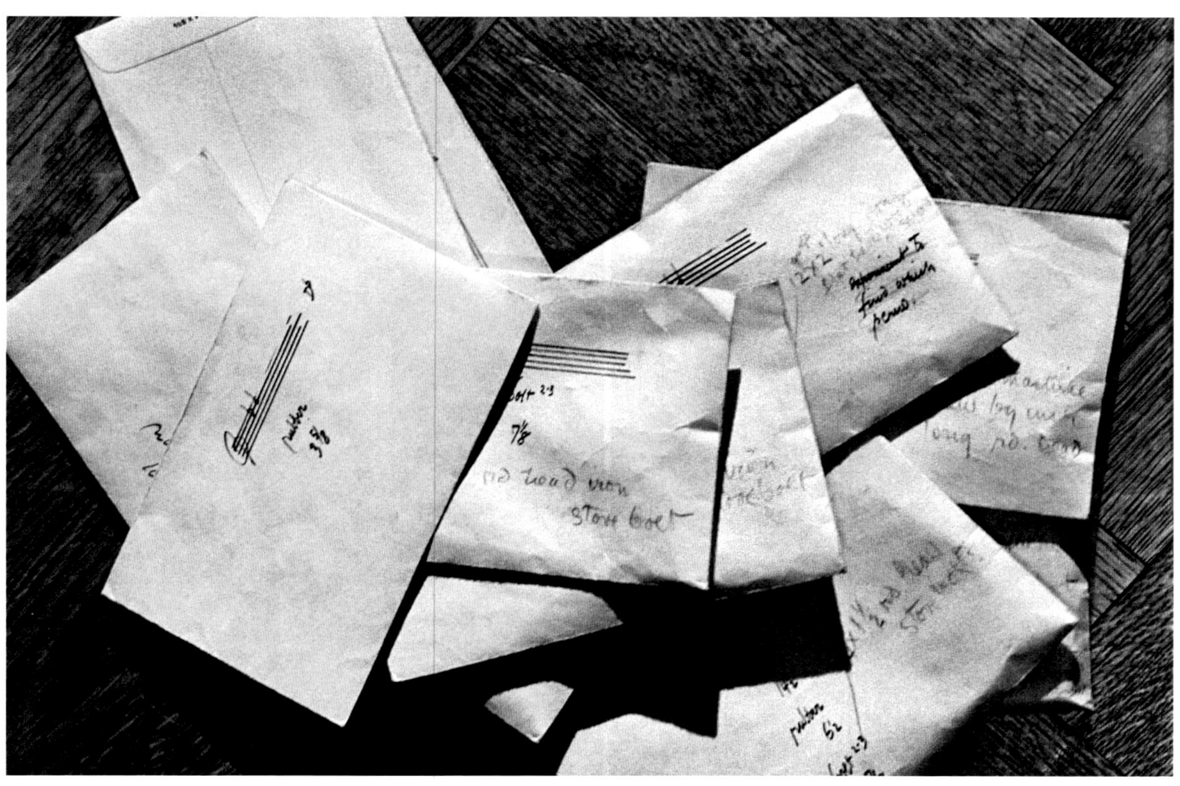

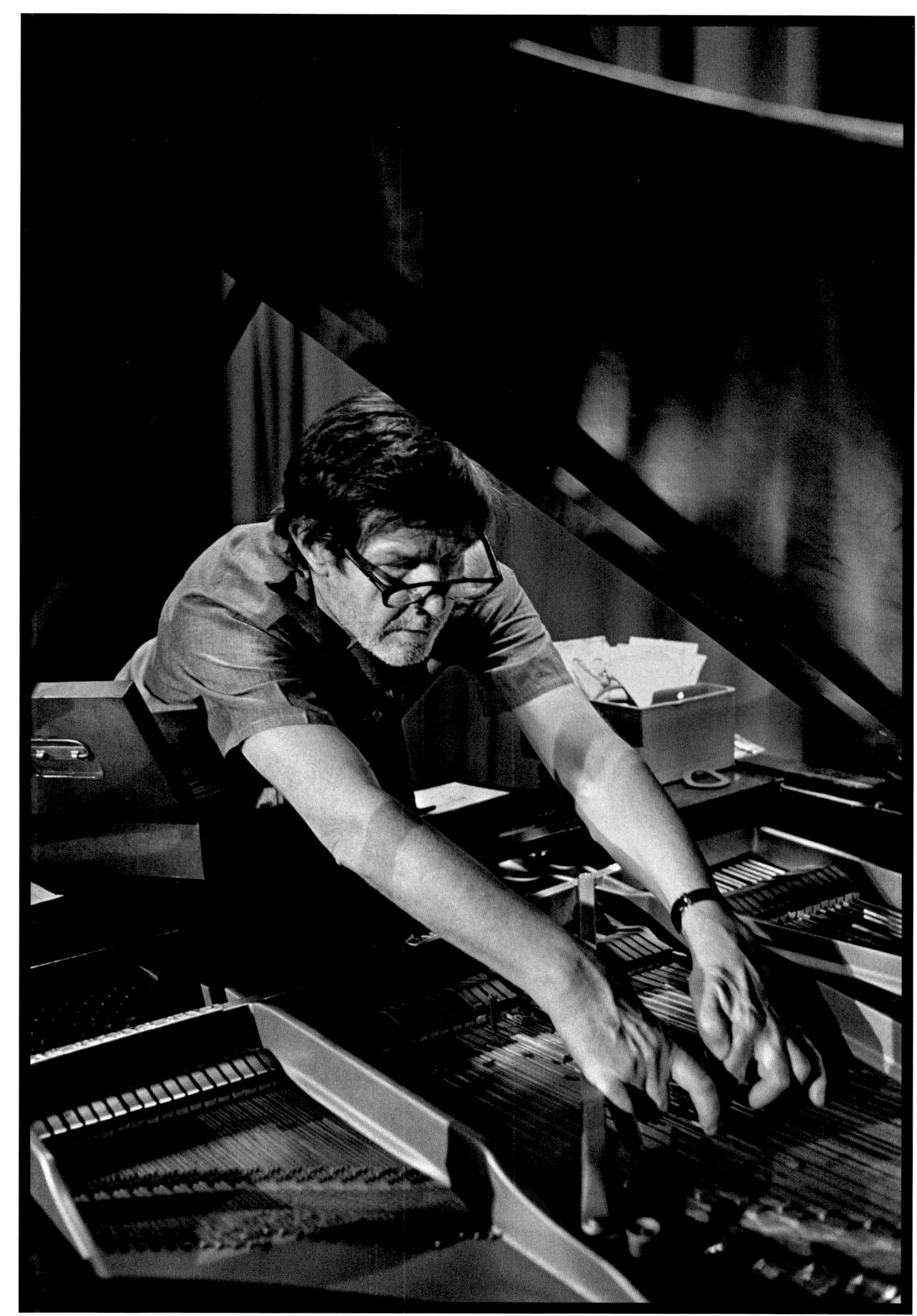

John Cage était un génie . . .

transformateur de pianos à queue en longues guitares horizontales . . .

premier poète américain zen à introduire le Hasard et l'Indétermination dans la composition musicale . . .

généreux et créatif . . .

il a fait partager ses joies à Marcel Duchamp et beaucoup d'autres . . .

Equivalent du Fou au jeu d'échecs, champion des diagonales, des martingales . . .

aviateur sans avion, amateur de champignons . . .

ses misères . . .

quelle belle entourloupette pour vivre . . .

grâce au rire . . .

Cage n'est mort, le bienheureux, d'aucune maladie.

John Cage was a genius

. . . transforming grand pianos into long horizontal guitars

. . . the first American Zen poet to introduce Chance and Indeterminacy into musical composition

. . . generous and creative

. . . he shared his joys with Marcel Duchamp and many more

. . . Bishop in the game of chess, master of diagonals, of martingales

. . . an airman without airplane, mushroom lover

. . . his troubles

. . . what a great trick for living

. . . with the help of laughter

Blessed Cage who died of no illness.

— Alain Jouffroy

Translation by Monique Fong

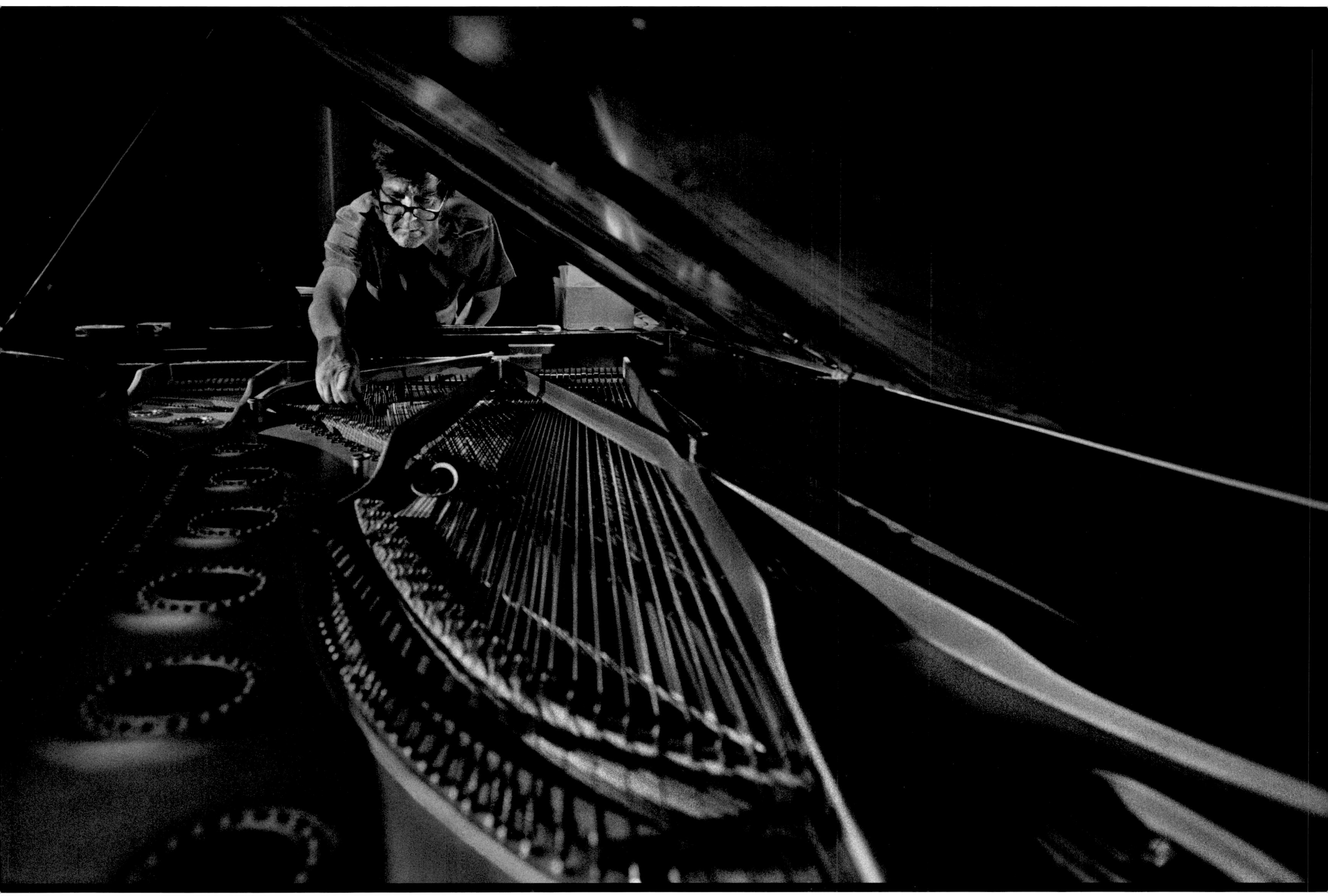

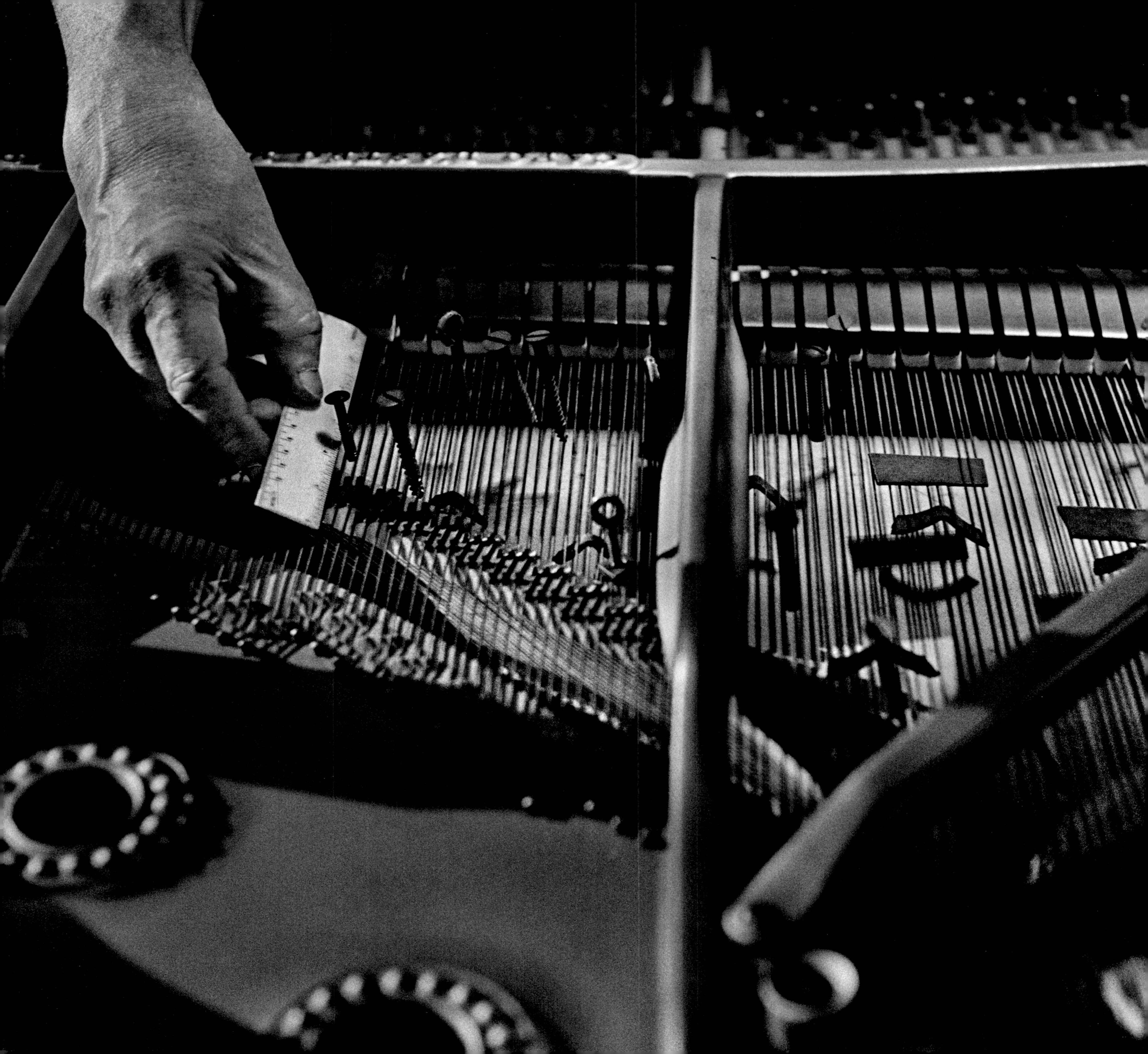

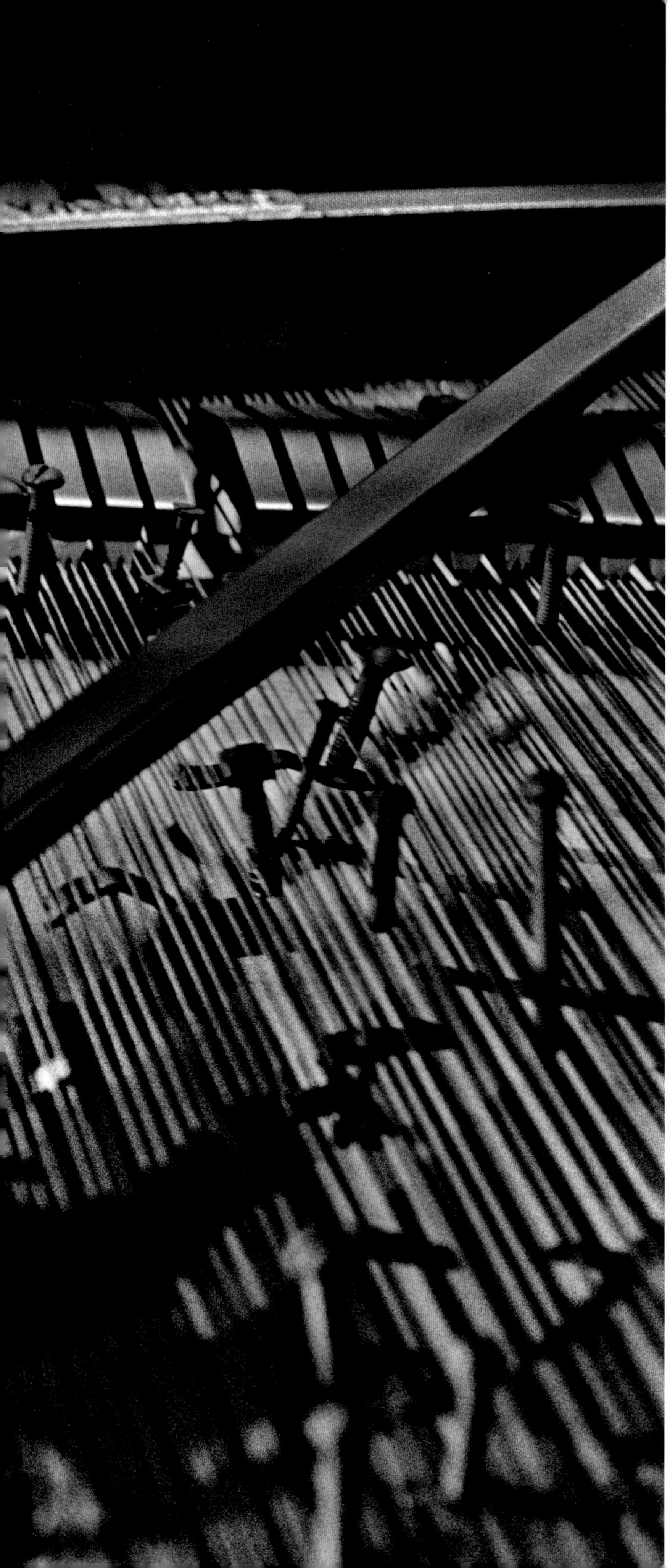

John Cage was not terribly useful or influential for my own work, but I did indeed use a prepared piano to imitate Oriental sounds when I played the first song I'd written for <u>Pacific Overtures</u> for my collaborators, most of whom were unfamiliar with Cage and thus much impressed with my inventiveness.

—Stephen Sondheim

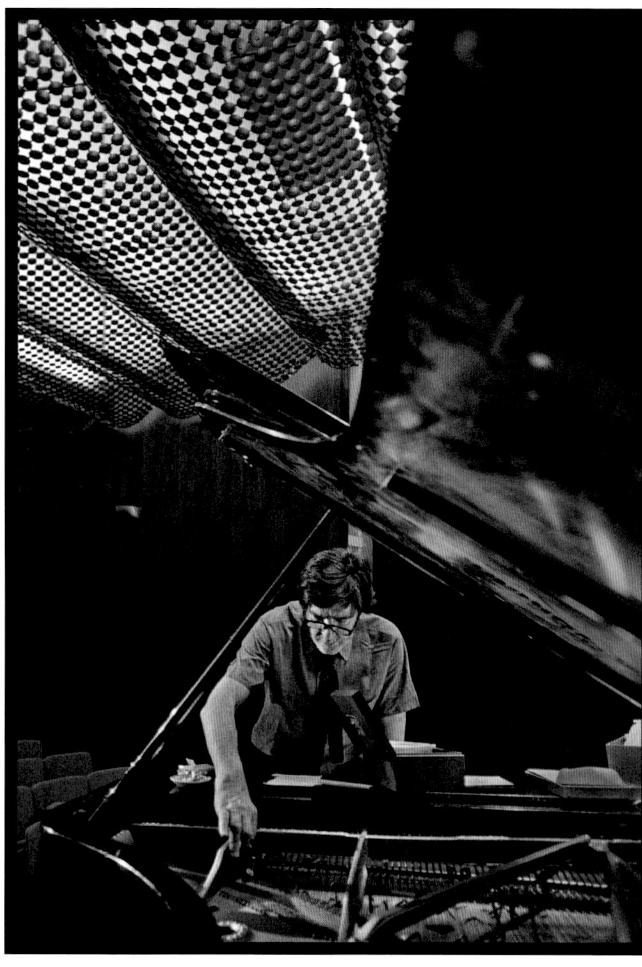

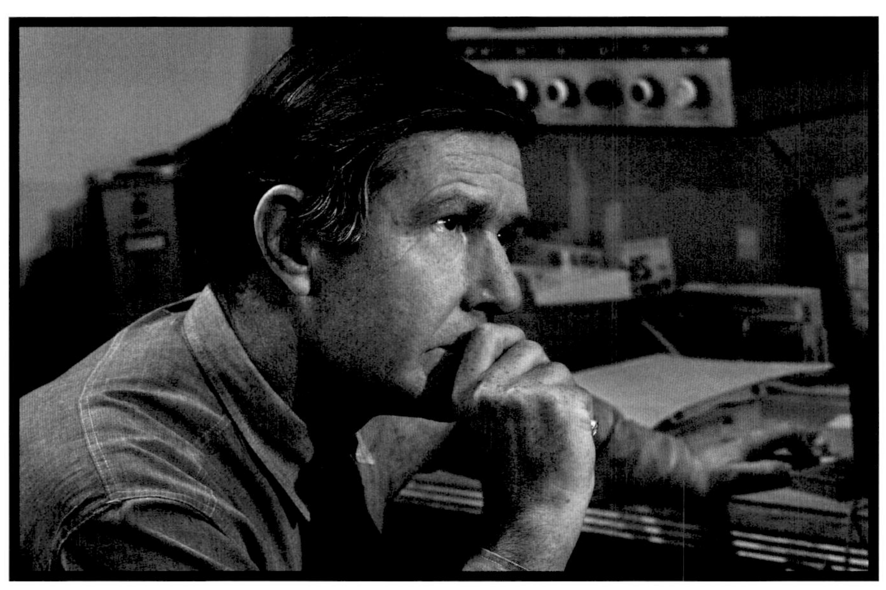

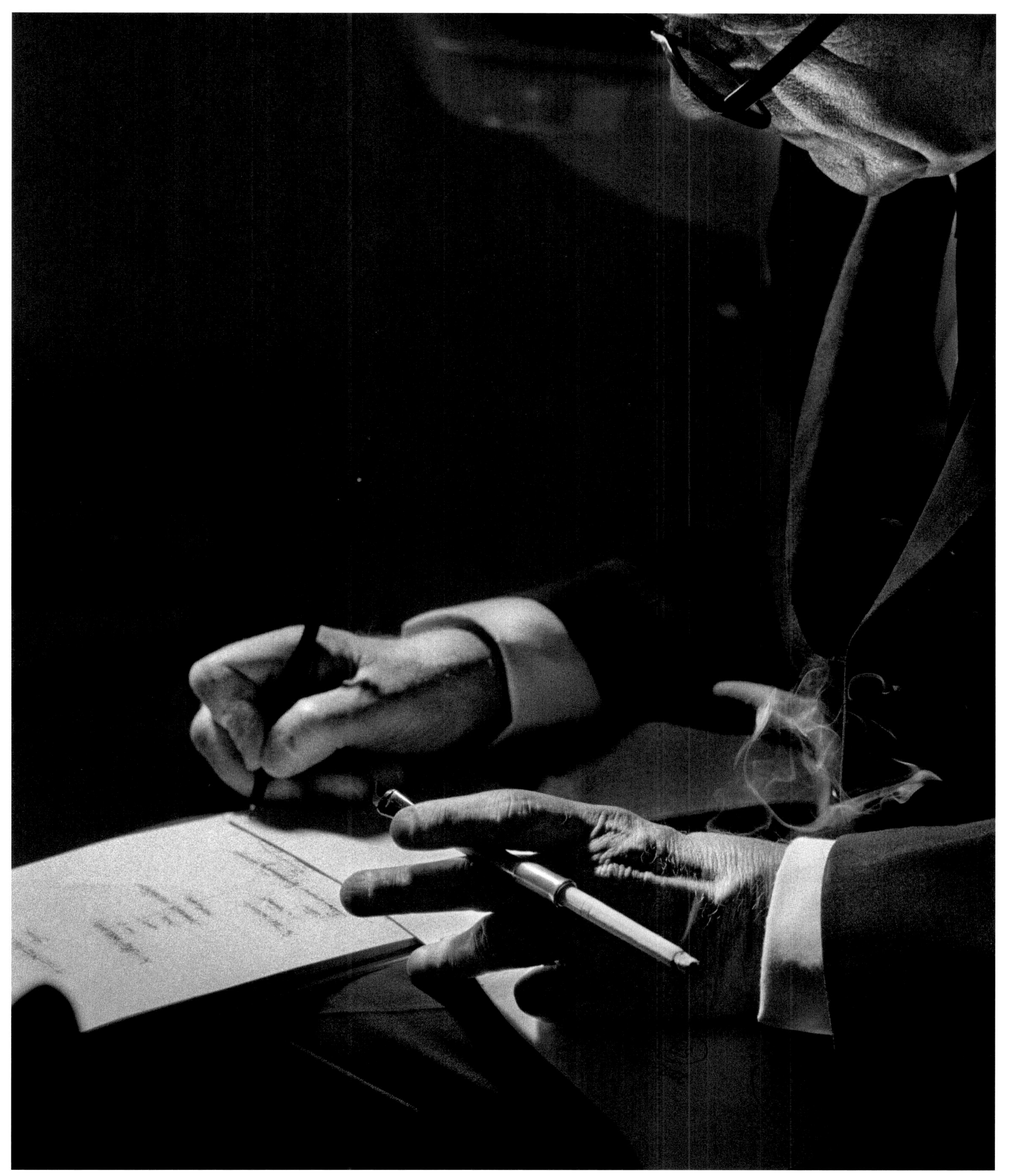

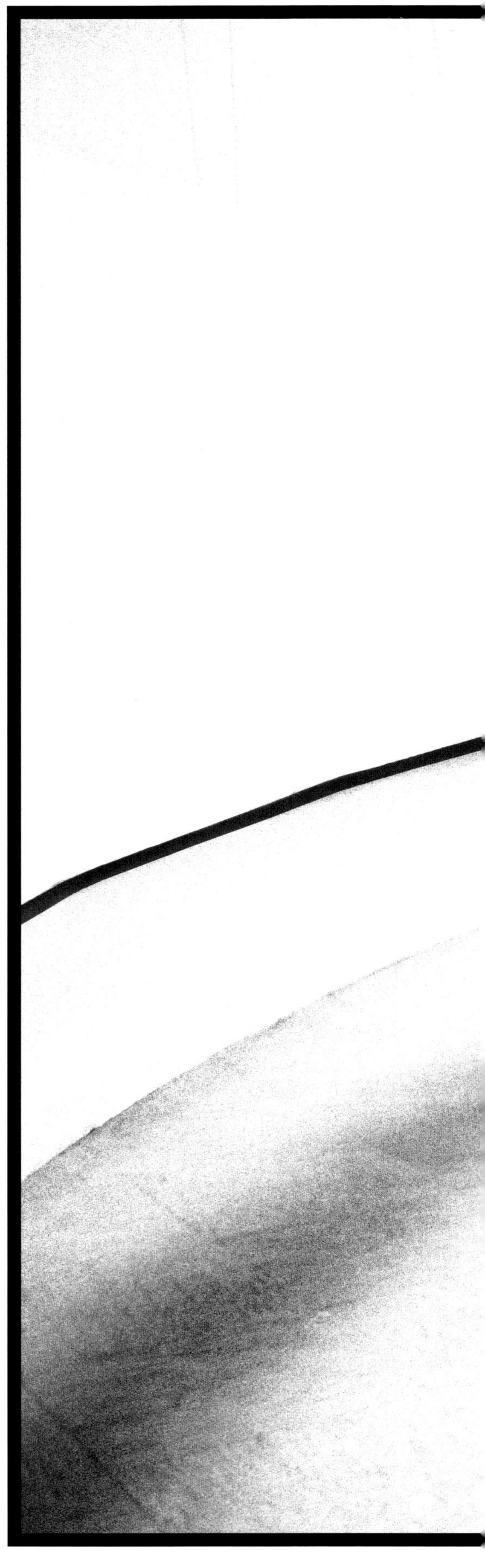

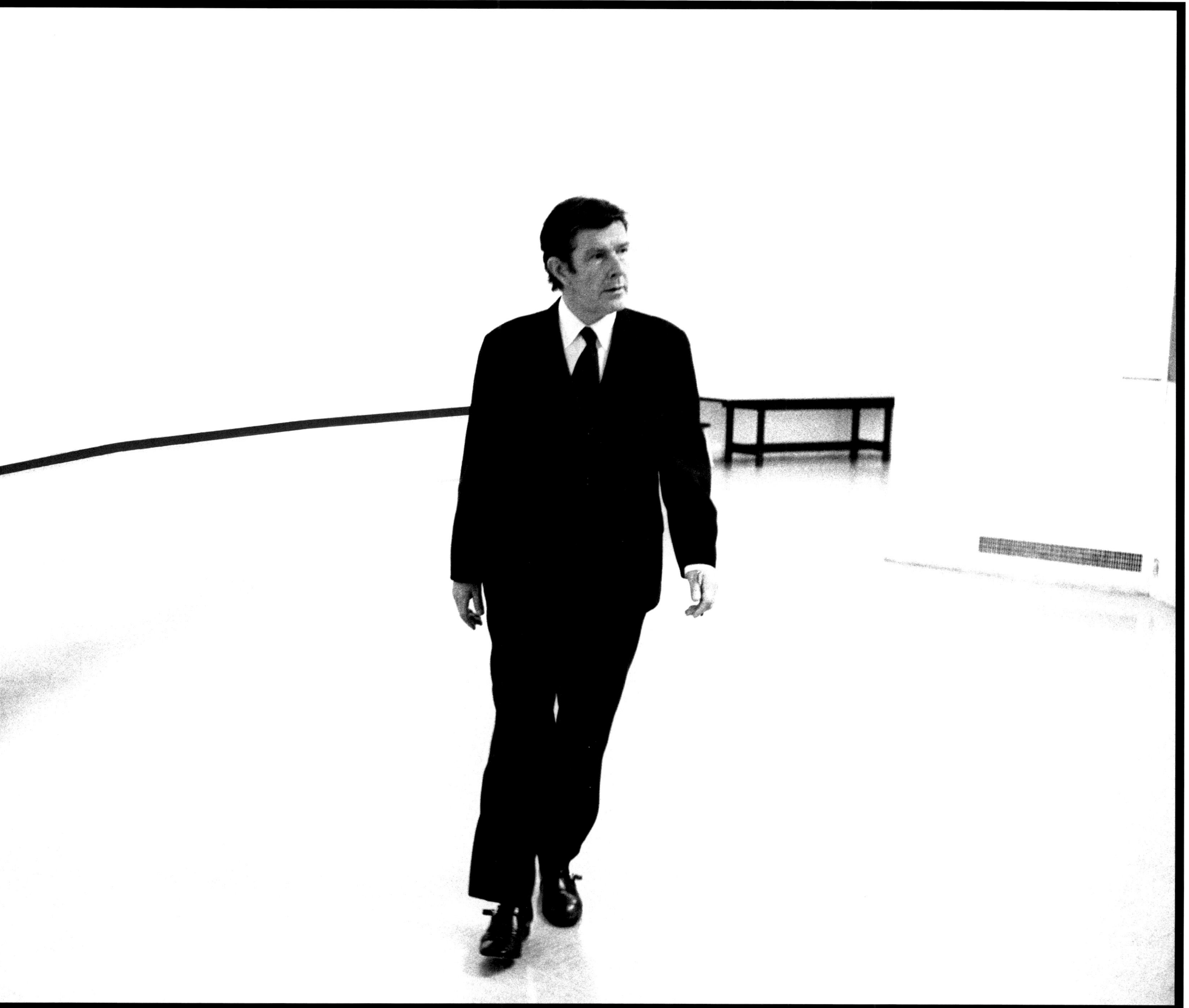

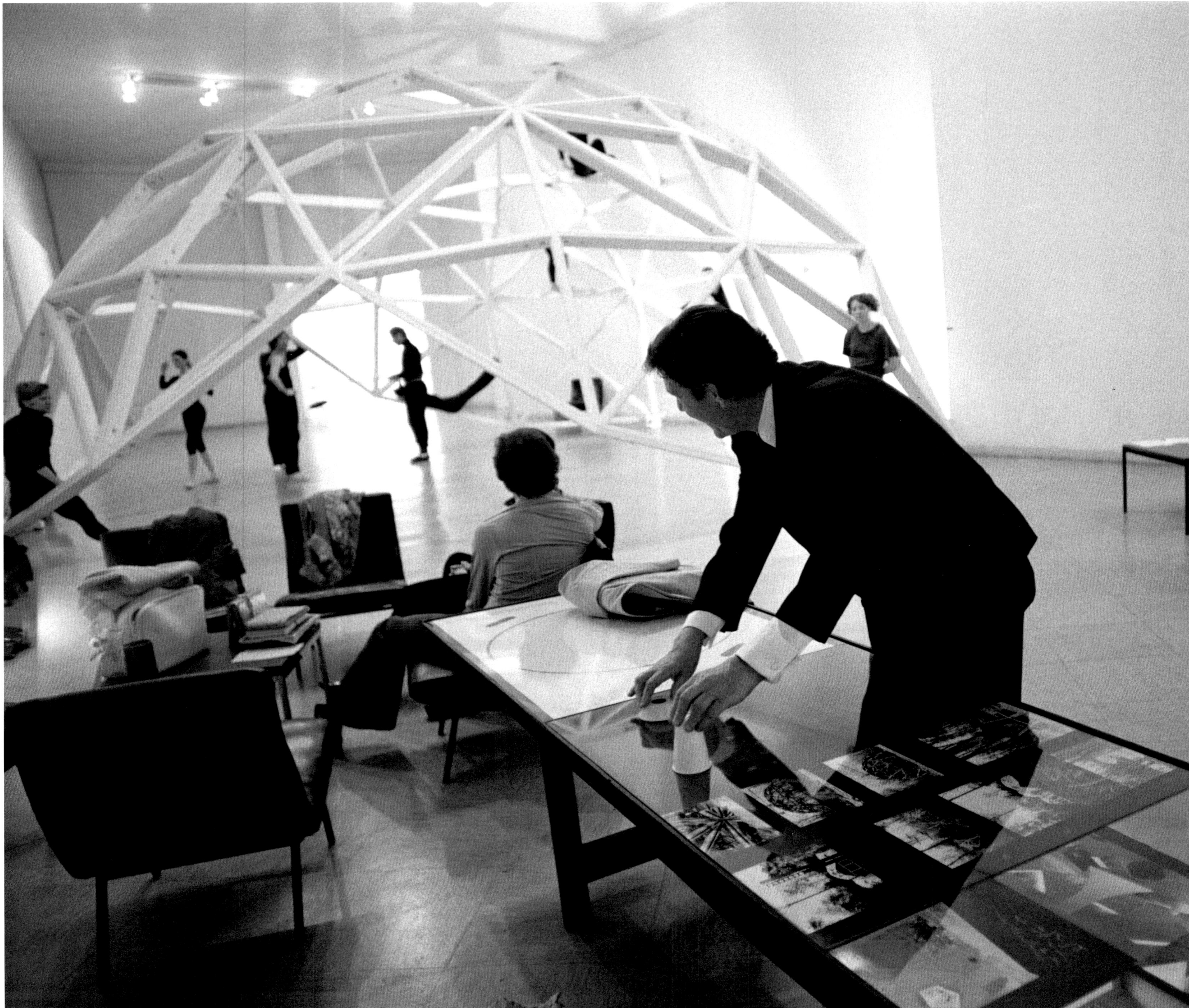

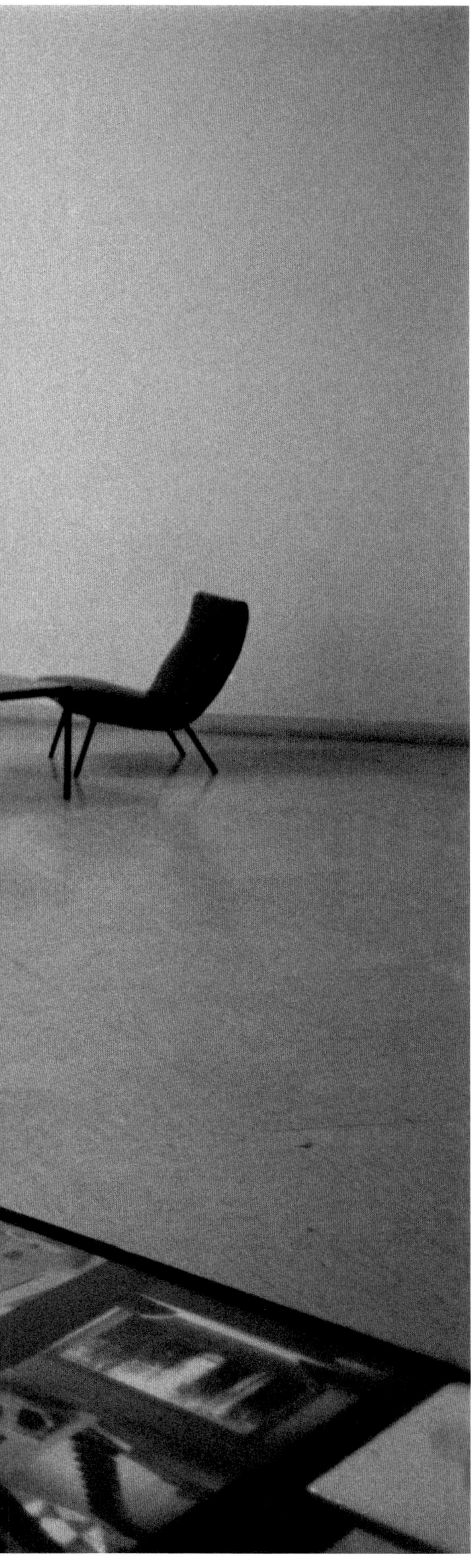

John Cage was
an original.
He lived a musical journey
unlike any before or after him.
At first his concerns were
the creation of music
in which every sound
was exquisitely
chosen and arranged.
But he went beyond this idea.
He imagined
that pieces
and the process
of playing them
could be doorways
for performers
and listeners
to a different way
of thinking about music.
He invites us
to be his partner
in the process of creation.
That can be a
transforming
experience.

— Michael Tilson Thomas

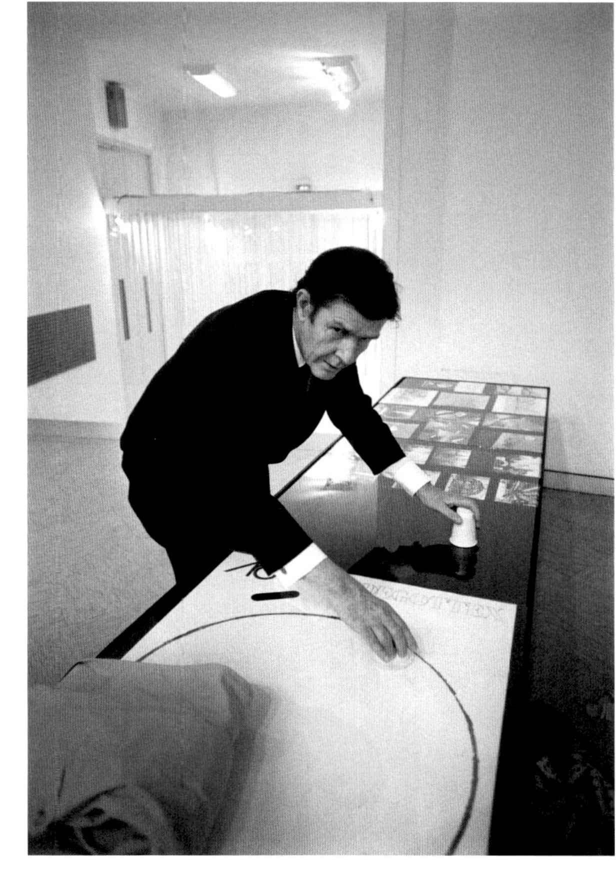

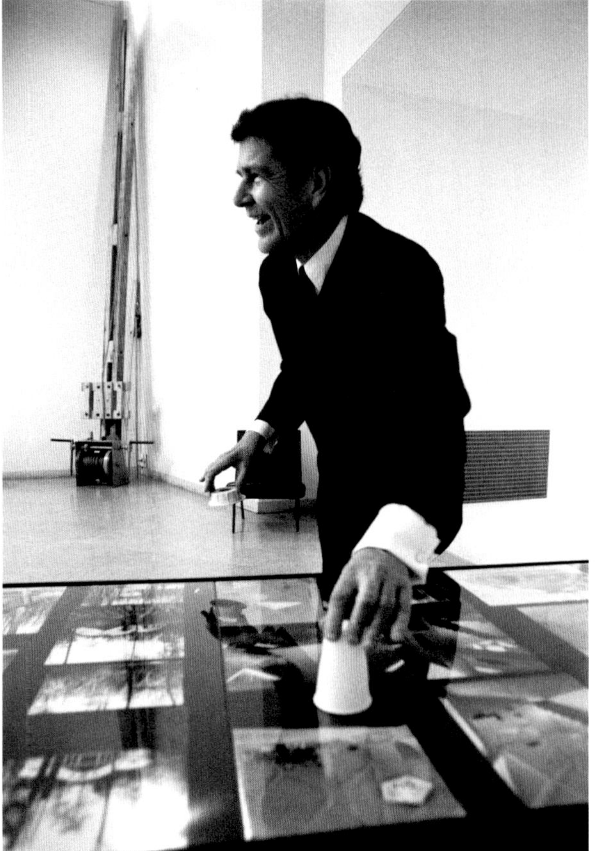

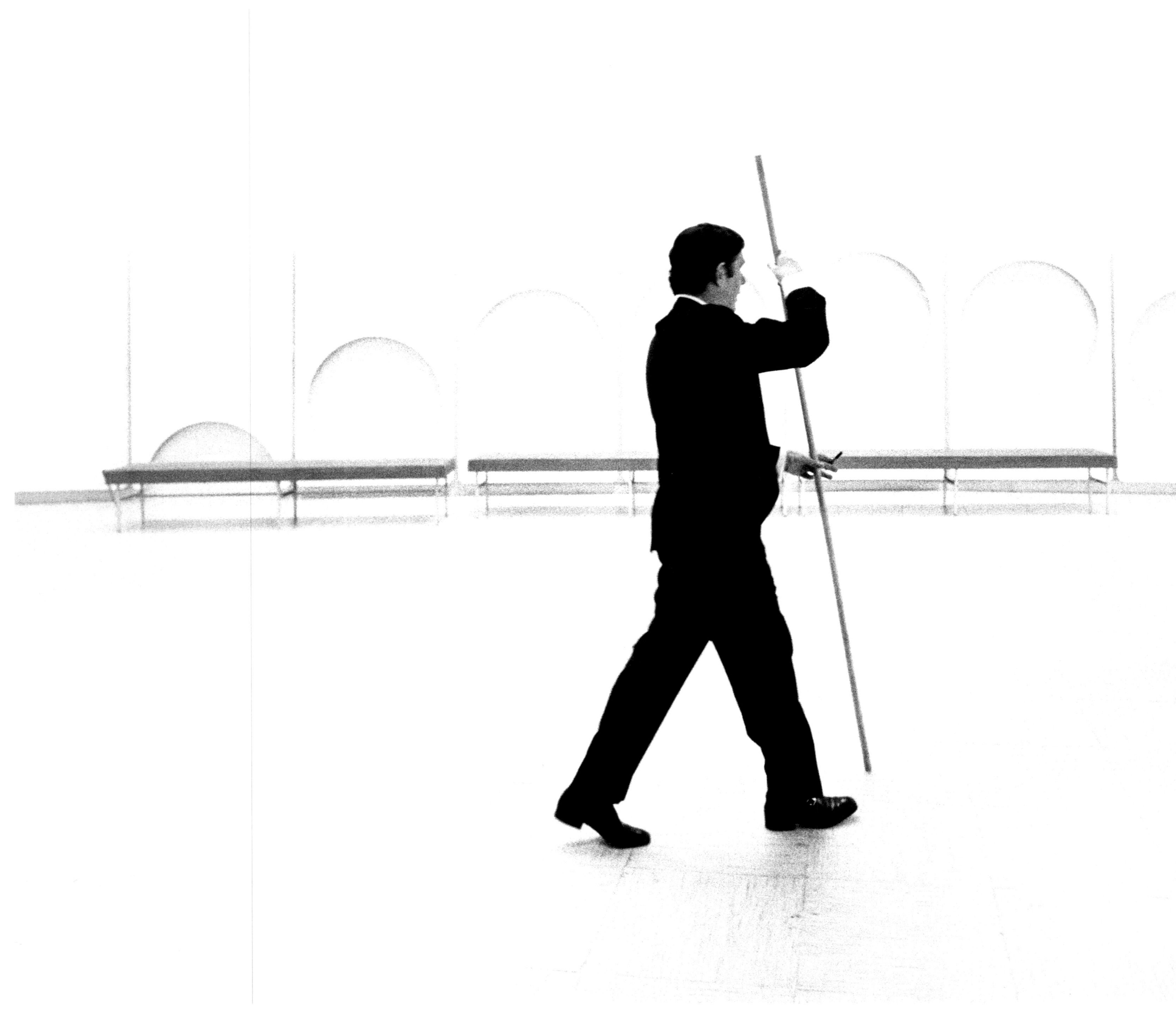

John Cage was the figure who,
for thousands of musicians,
opened the door to the world beyond rationality.
By introducing us to the I Ching,
and showing us how to use it both artistically and practically,
he made it seem safe and creative and irresistible
to explore not only Eastern thought and Buddhism,
but astrology, Tarot, Jungian theory,
and any discipline based in an ineffable synchronicity.
He freed us to not understand what we were doing,
and making art has been more interesting ever since.

— Kyle Gann

I never understood John Cage until I learned, from neuroscience and everyday experience, that true silence does not exist—except perhaps through highly disciplined meditation. Rare is the moment when I don't hear a motor whirring, a bird chirping, music in my head, or tinnitus in E♭. Even during external silence, the brain is alive with spontaneous activity. Speech-related brain circuits may be active without speech. Silence has intrigued thinkers through the ages, from the ancient Indian philosophers to Thoreau. John Cage was the modern liberator of silence in Western music. I now understand him. — Jamshed Bharucha

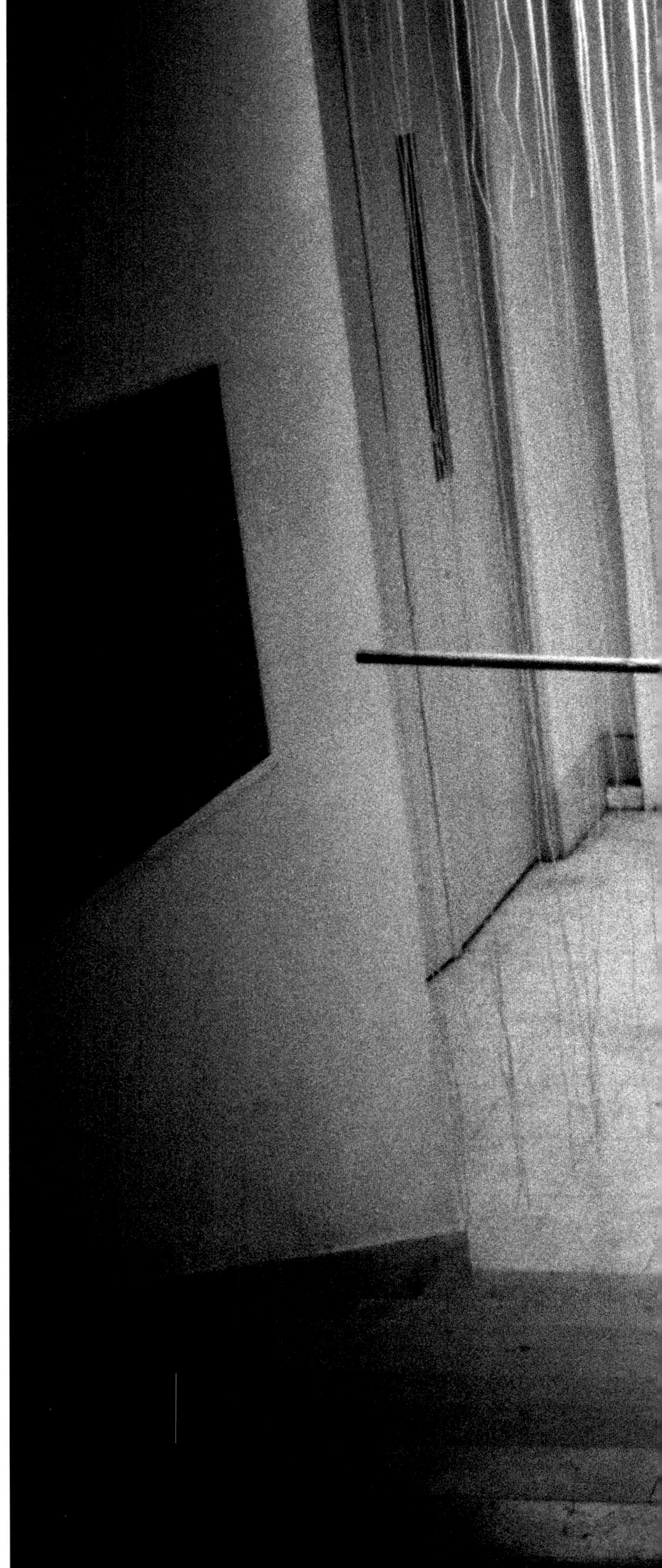

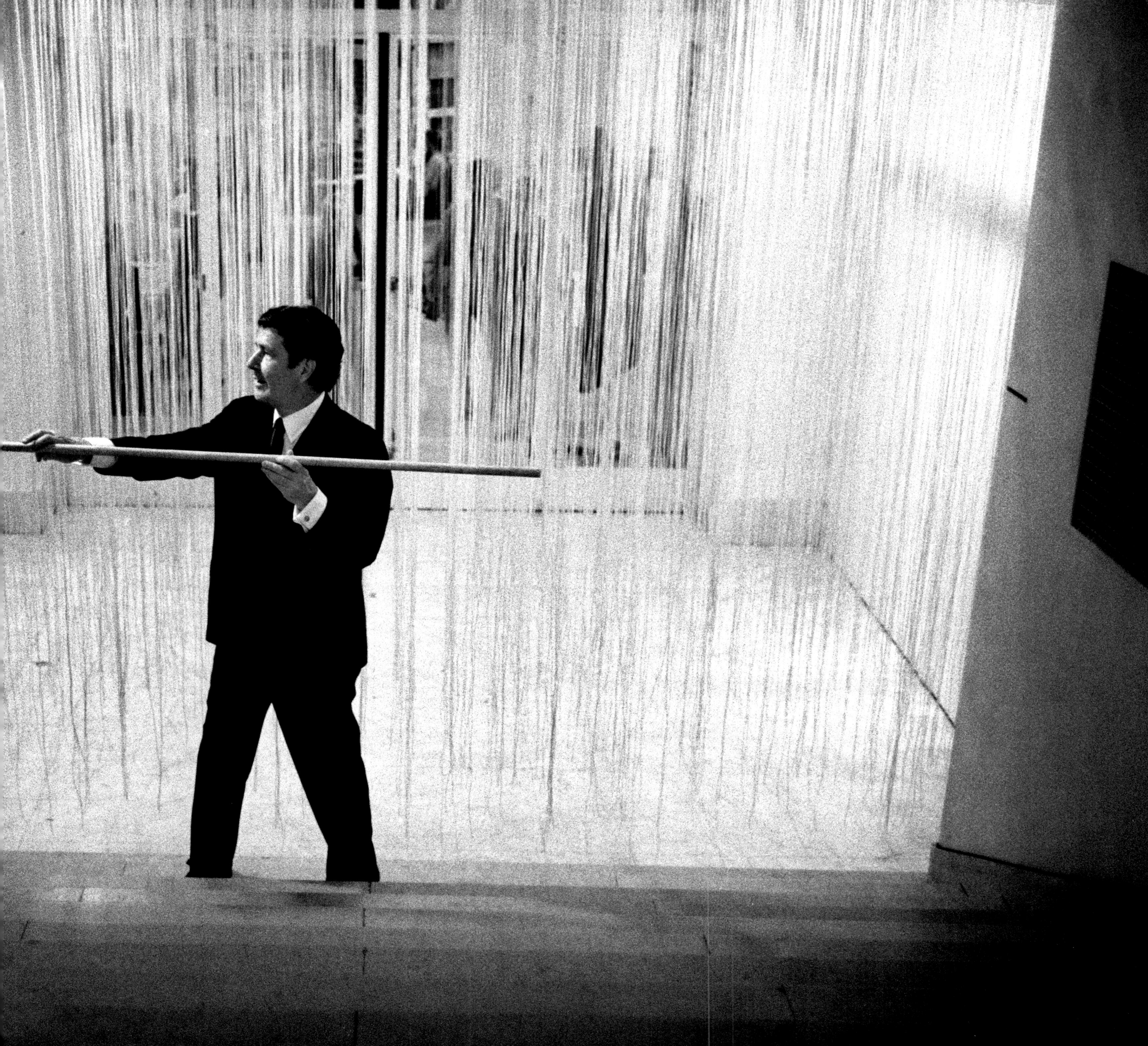

Under the Sun

John Cage
was a new or
short or longer
pause suppliant.
John Cage was
a friend to
brains of two
sexes, to
Buddha, to eat
him, destroy
him. John Cage
as John Cage
was, sat down.
Rest not,
Tetrapod!
John Cage was
for us as
poetics arrived
in pure
perfection,
turned and
never
stammered to
listen, John
Cage was
metabolic twin
listener. Dark
doom that
never rides. But
he does. John
Cage was a
founder.
Surprise is
never barren, all
over the
timing world.
John Cage was a
culture, gaps in
the cave to know
Neanderthal.
Hours with
him, a boon.

— Anne Waldman

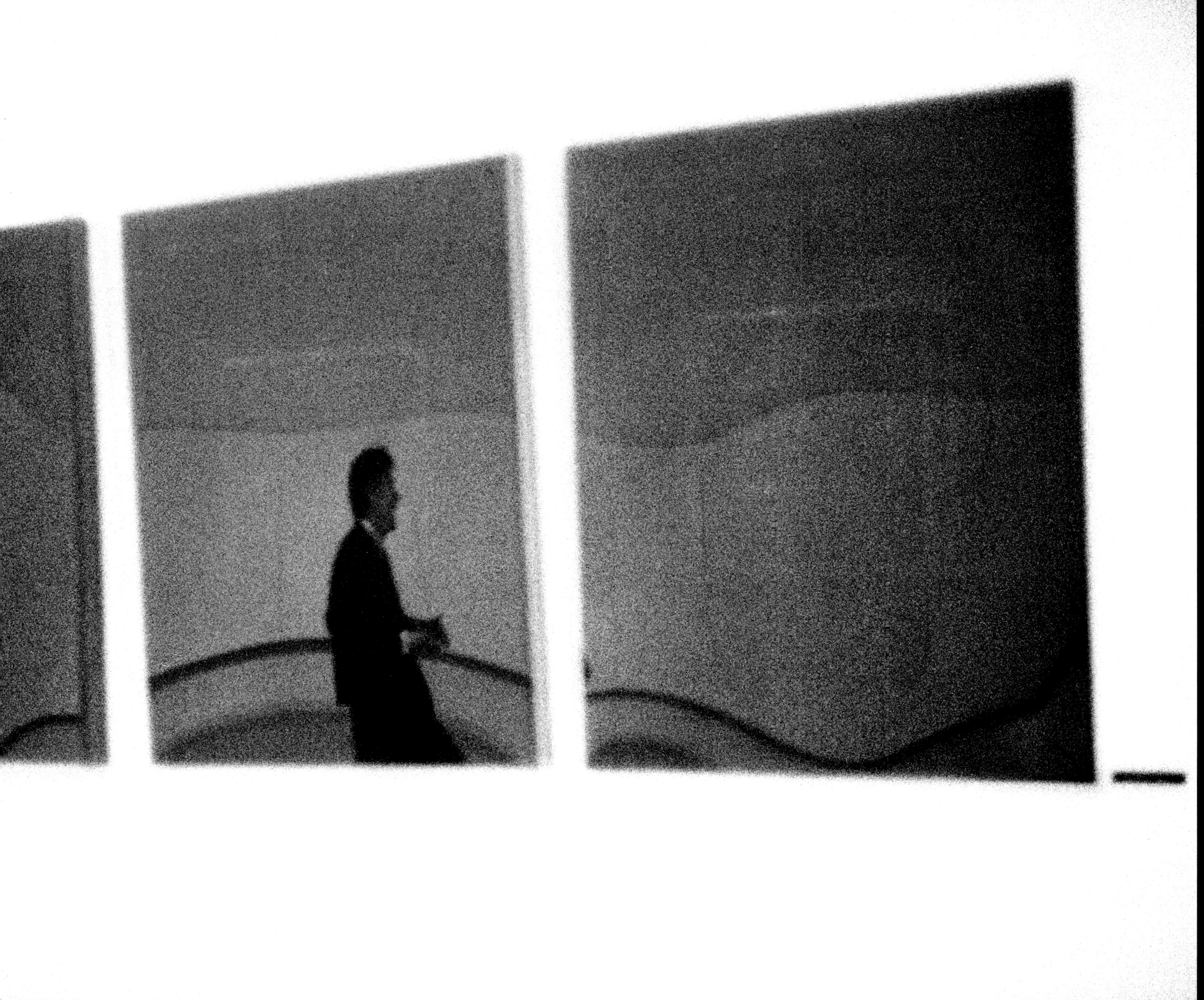

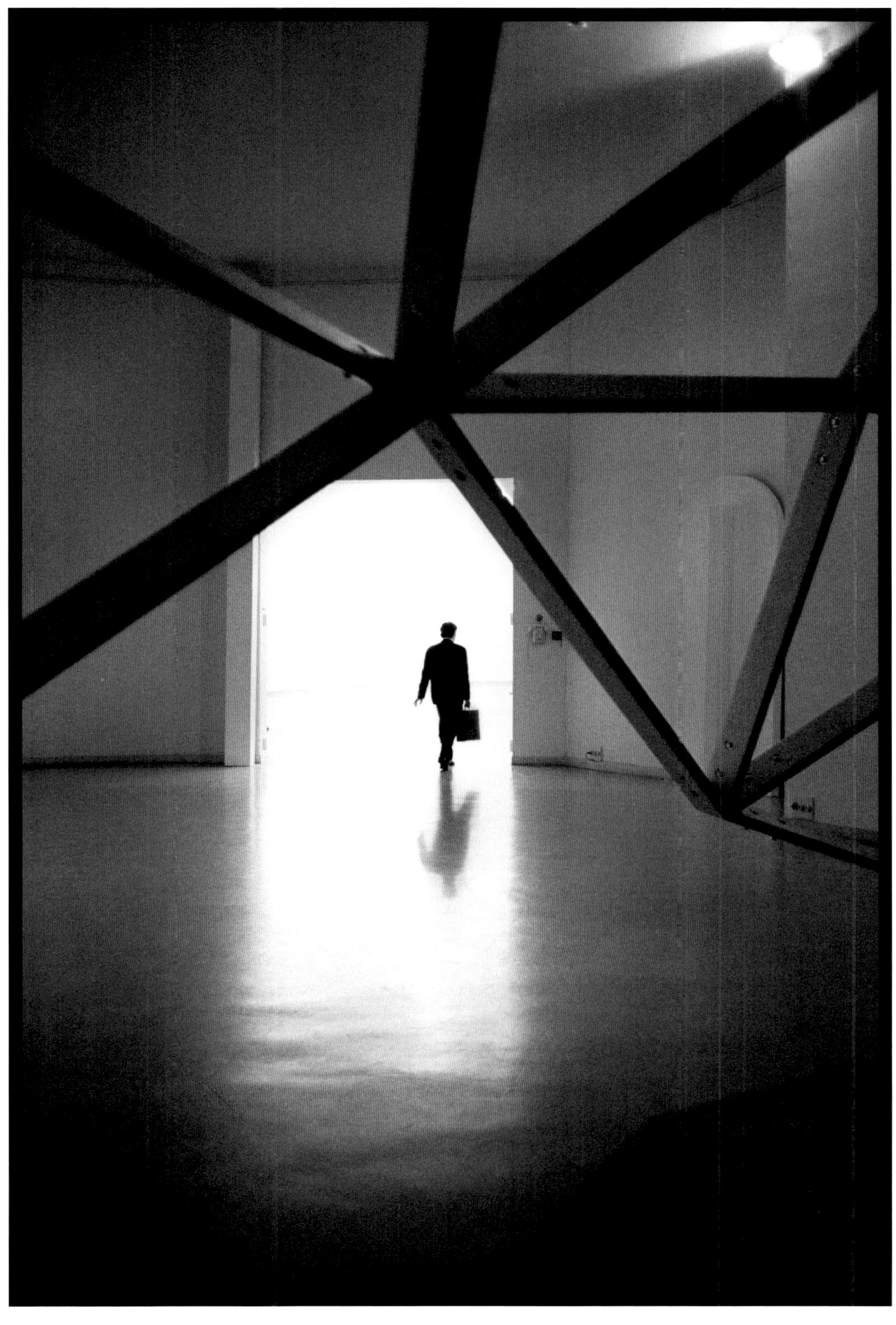

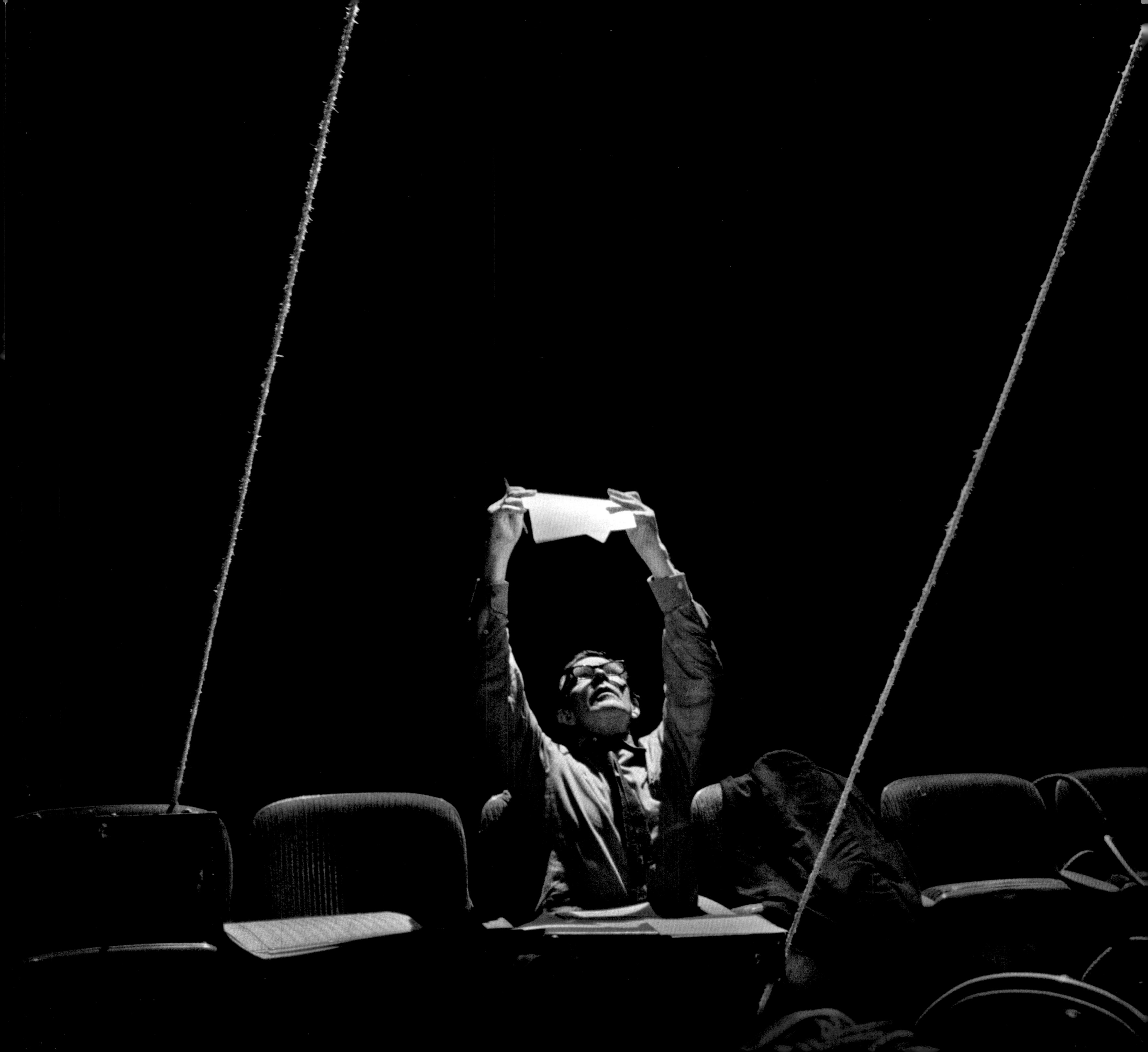

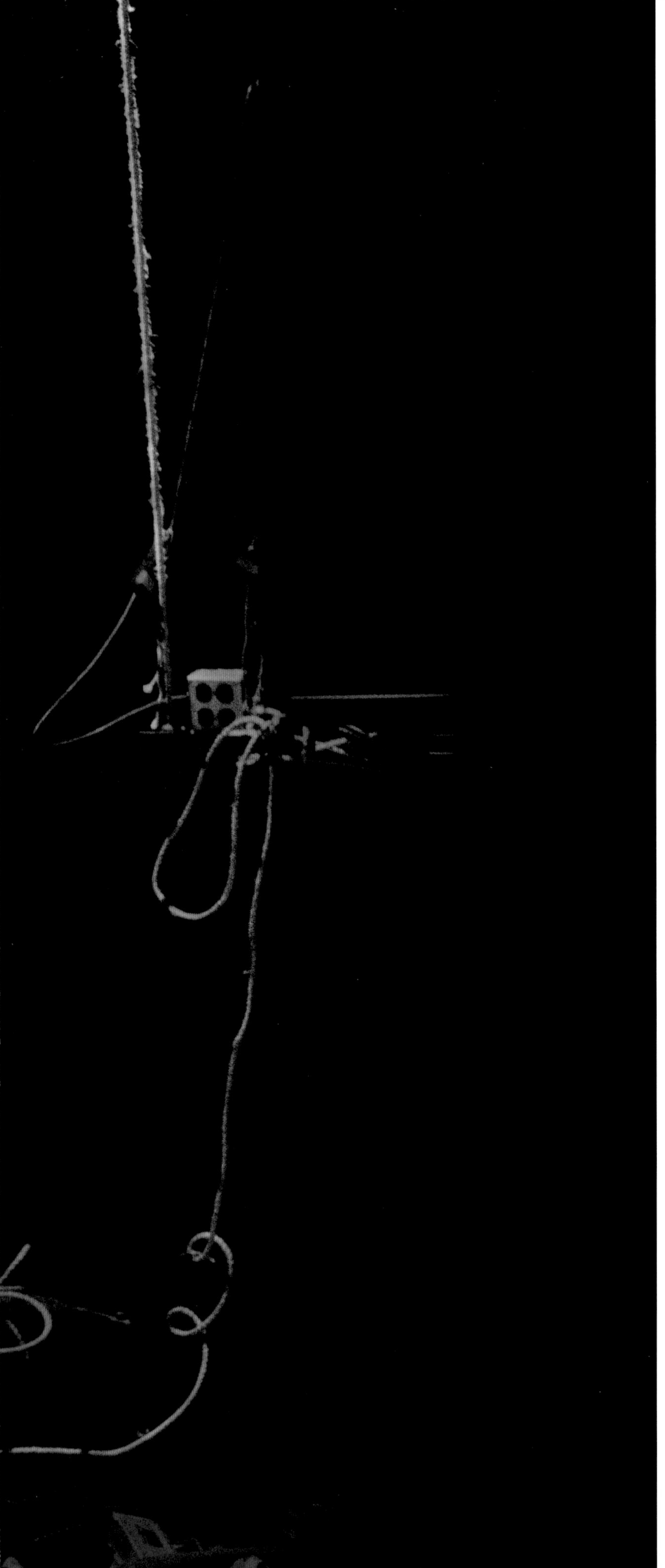

John Cage was a gift from the Gods. — Laura Kuhn

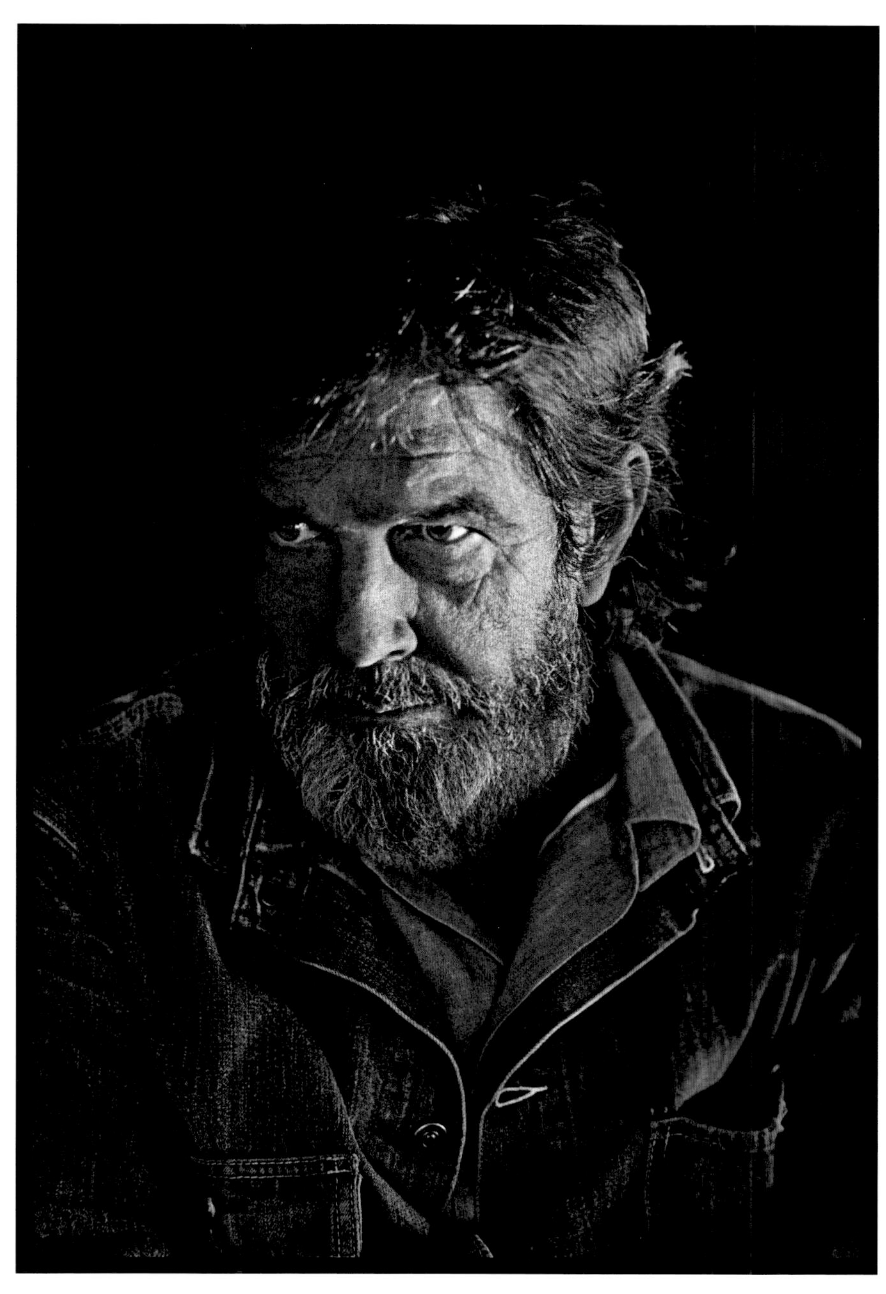

John Cage was like a big sunflower with a thousand seeds. He created his own energy like the sun, very generous, never thinking of himself but always true to himself.

He loved everything and nothing.

His laughter was irresistible and broke through any barriers.

He liked to be occupied to the hilt: chess while driving, cooking for us all. Eating from the earth wild plants.

The mushrooms grew for him even out of season.

And suddenly he left us. We can't forget.

We don't ever want to forget.

— Teeny Duchamp

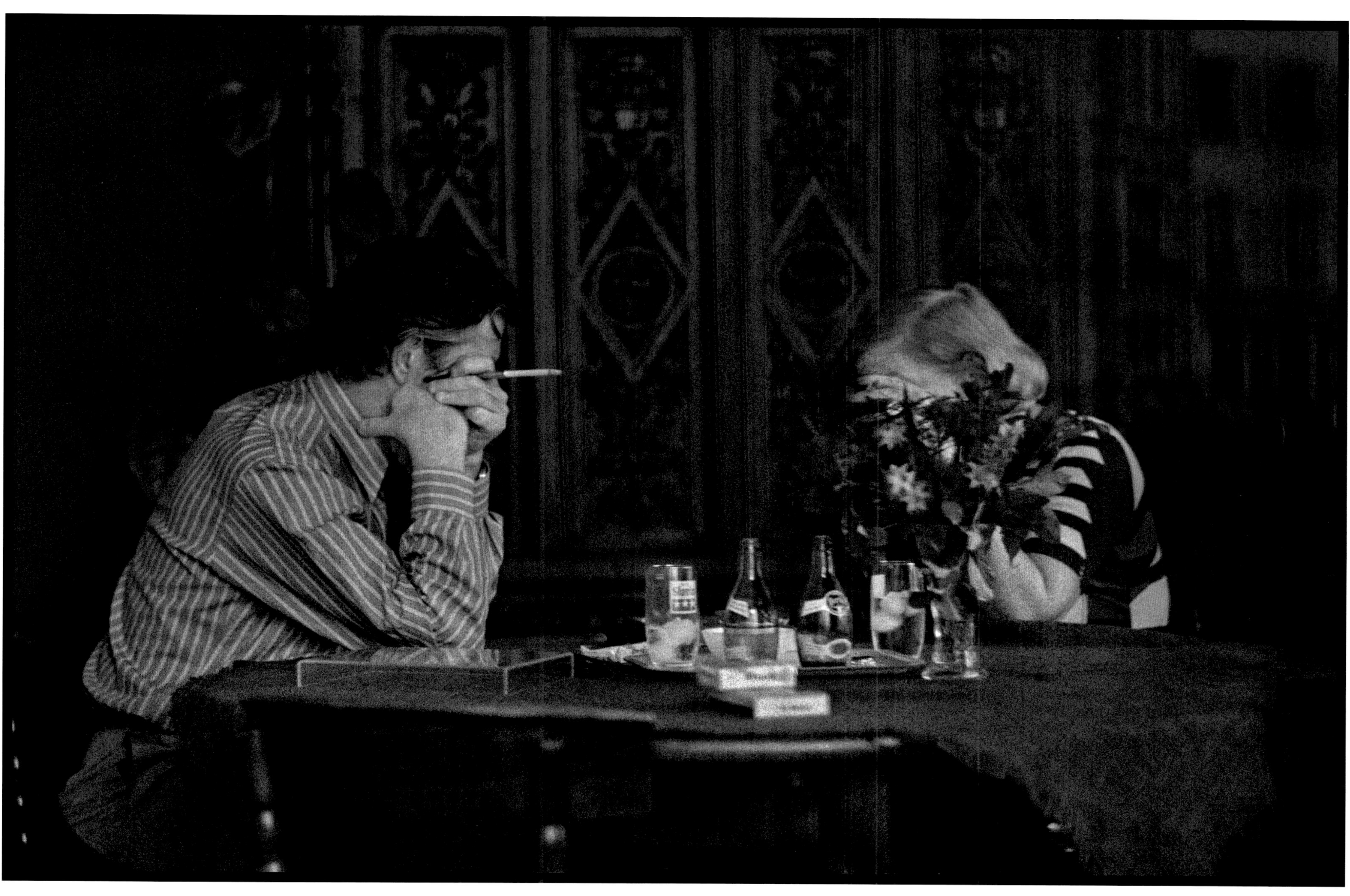

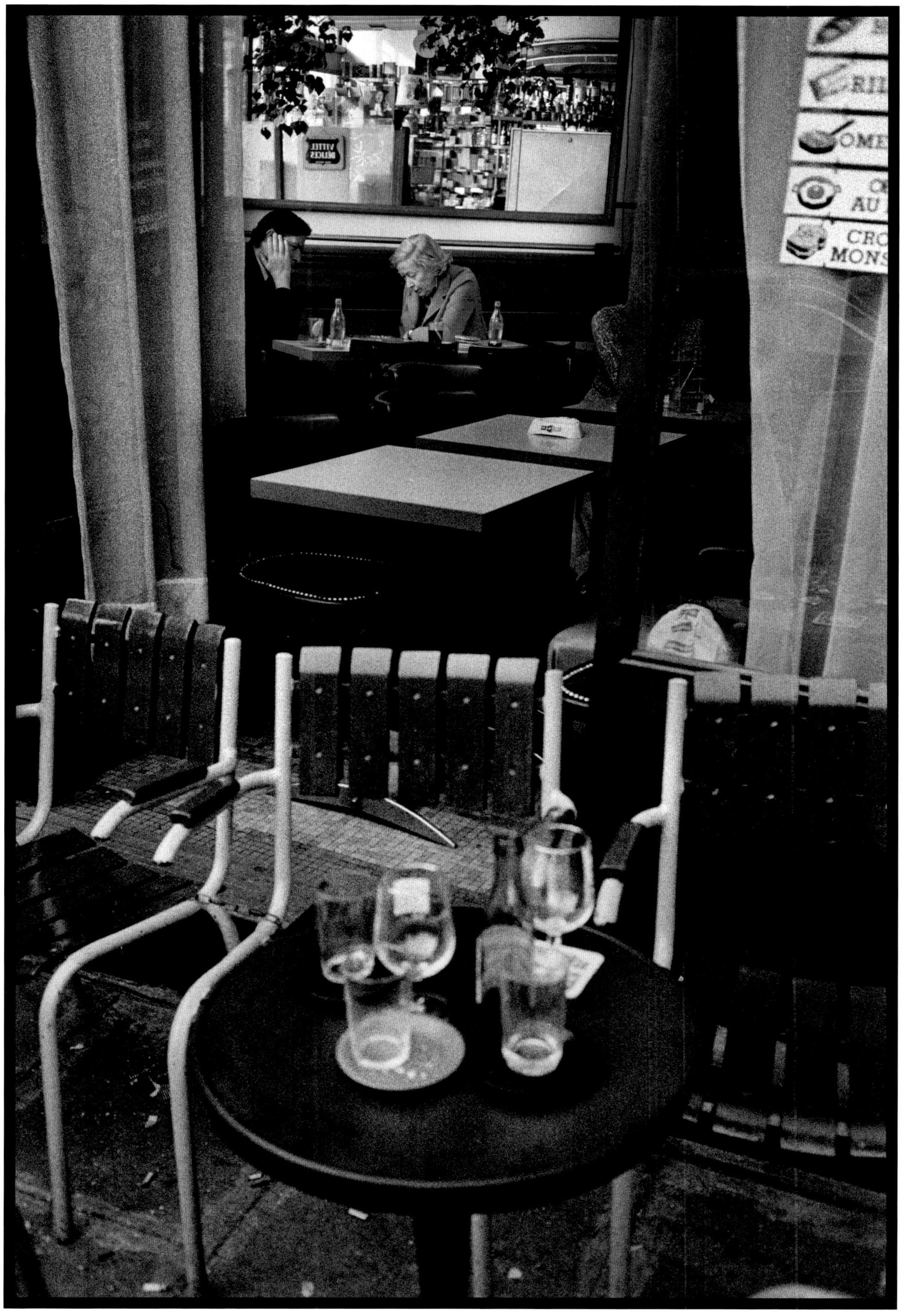

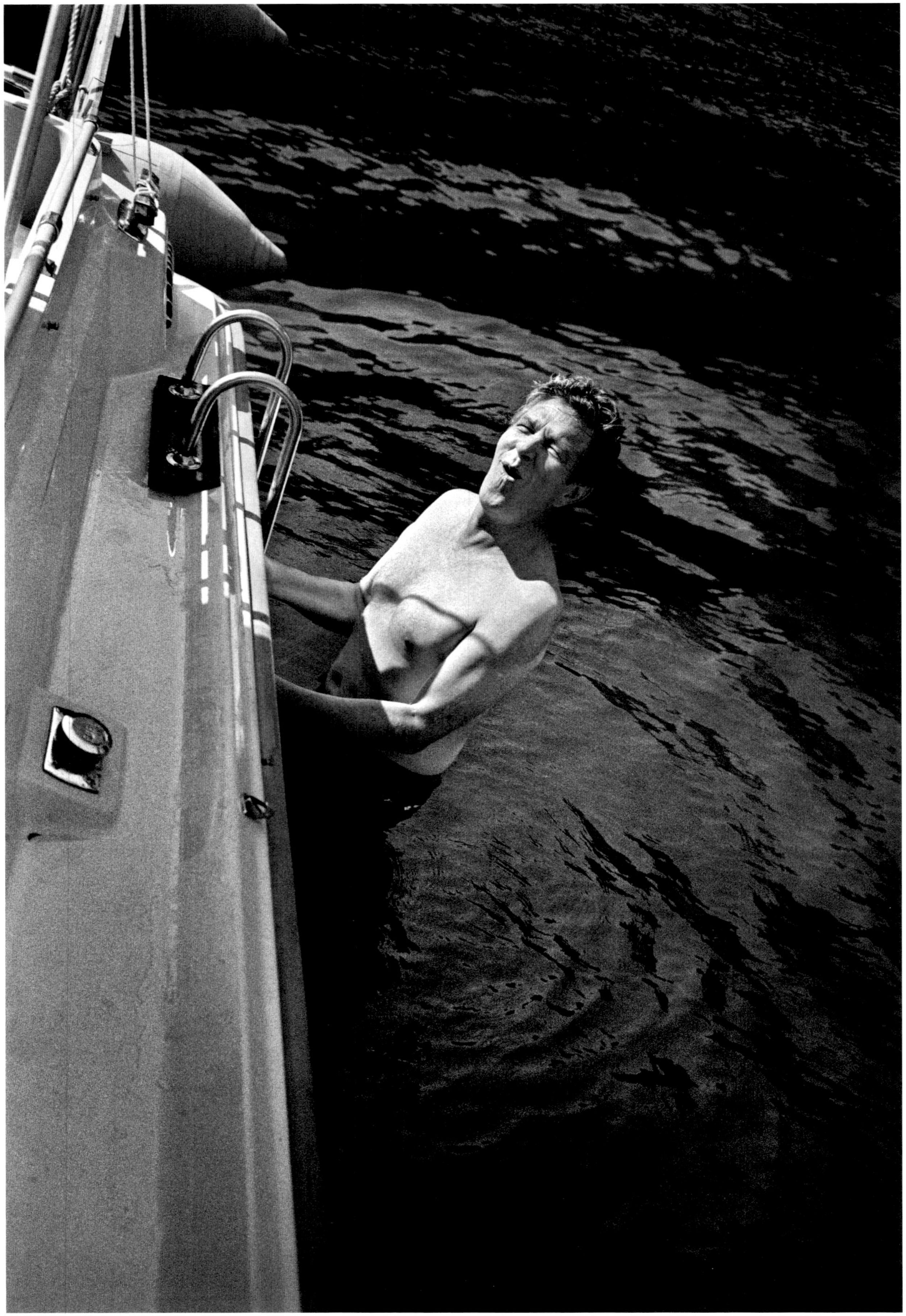

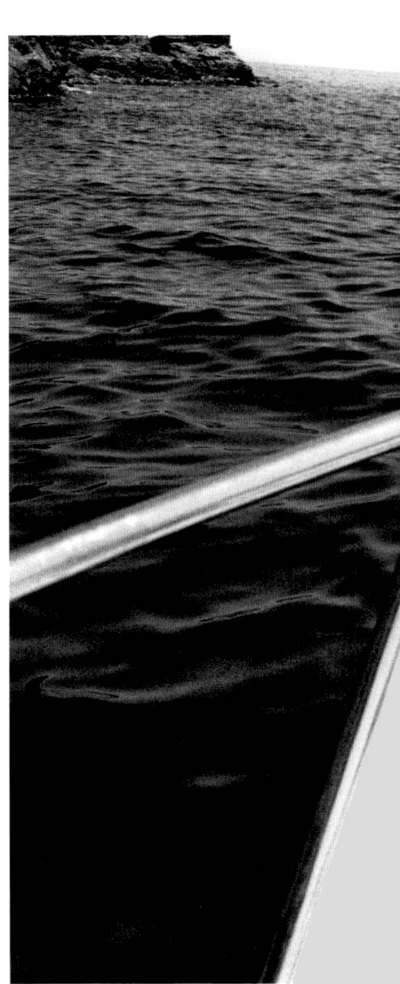

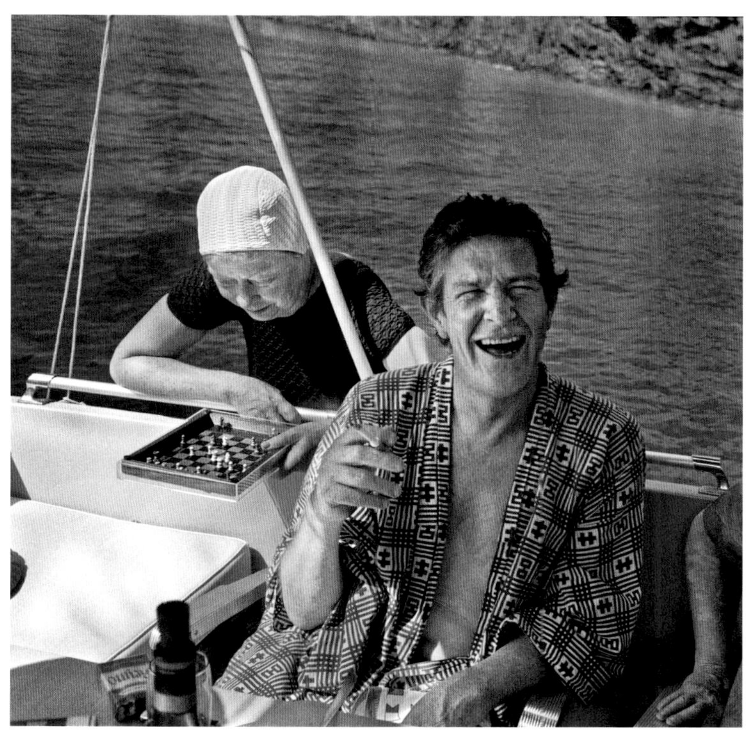

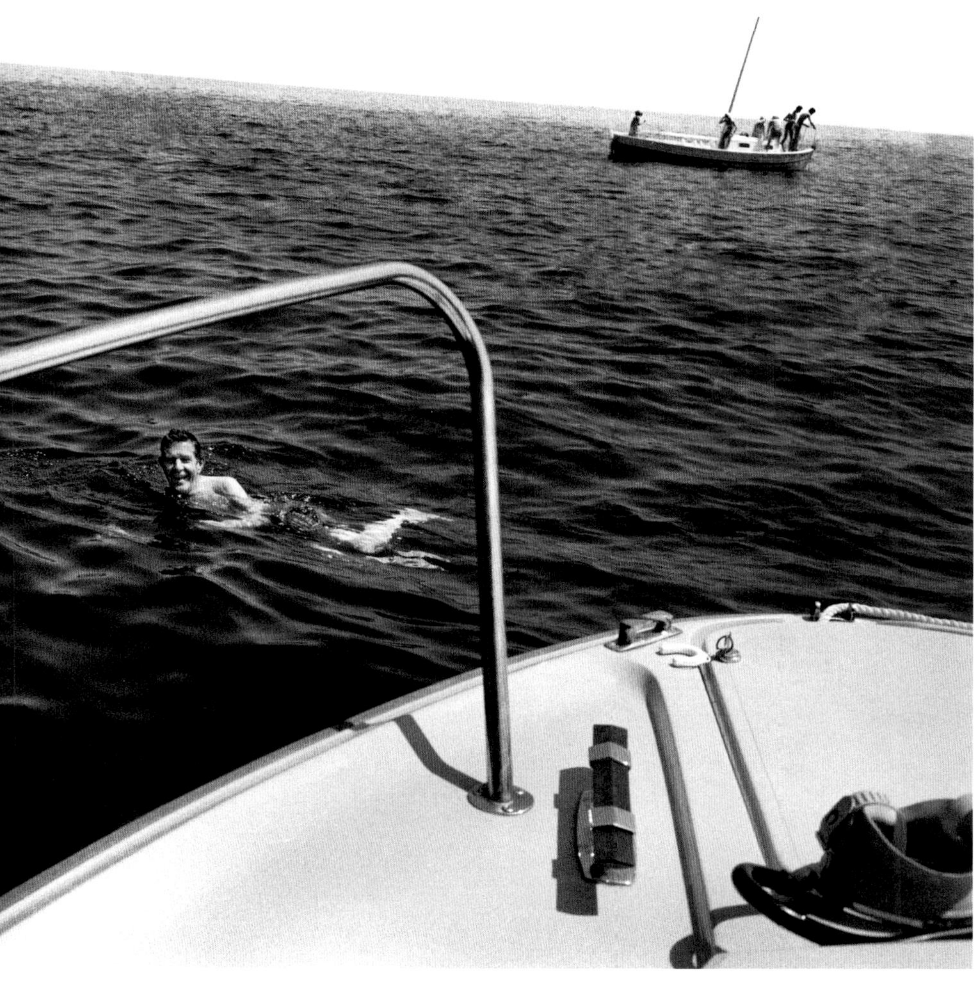

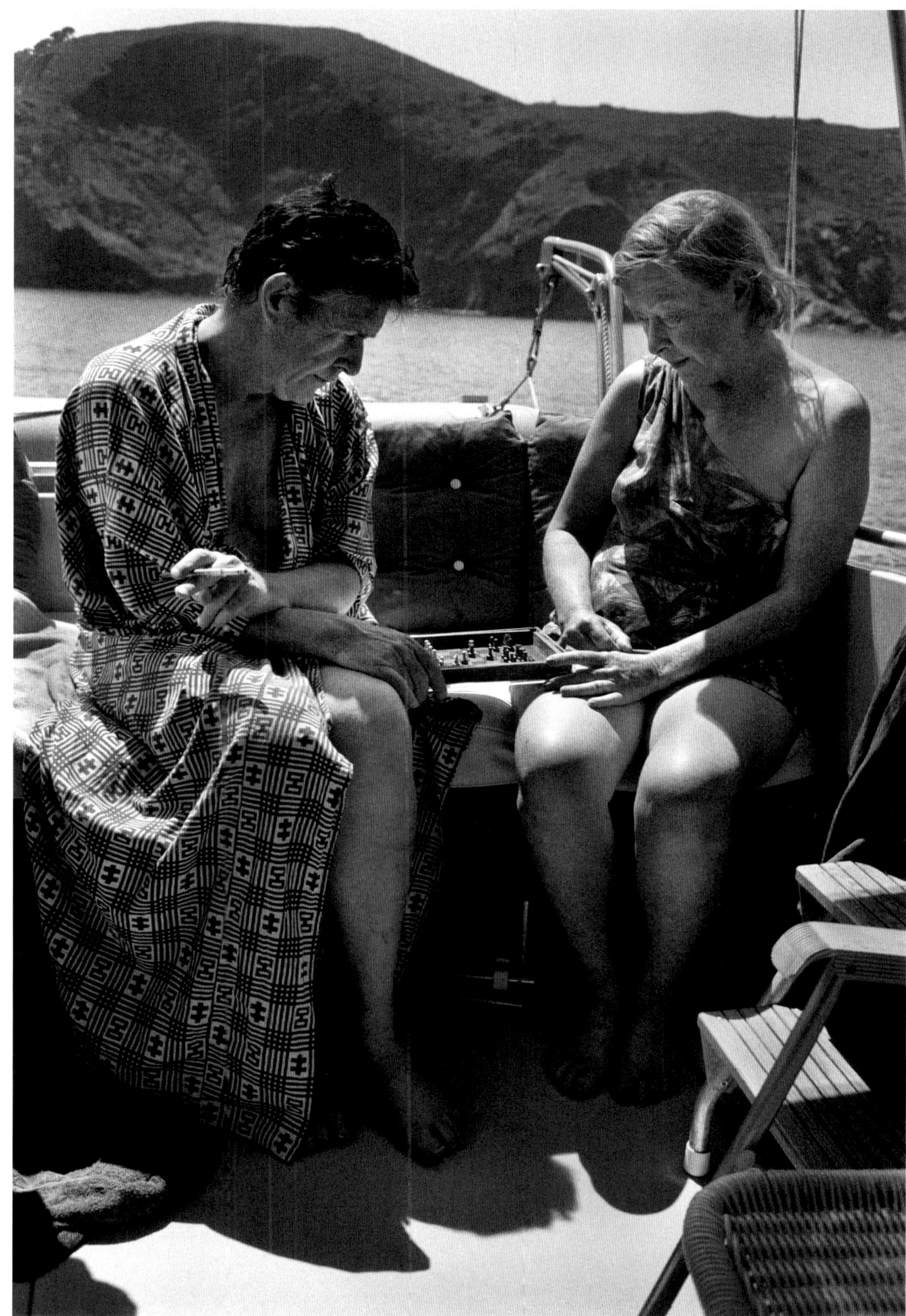

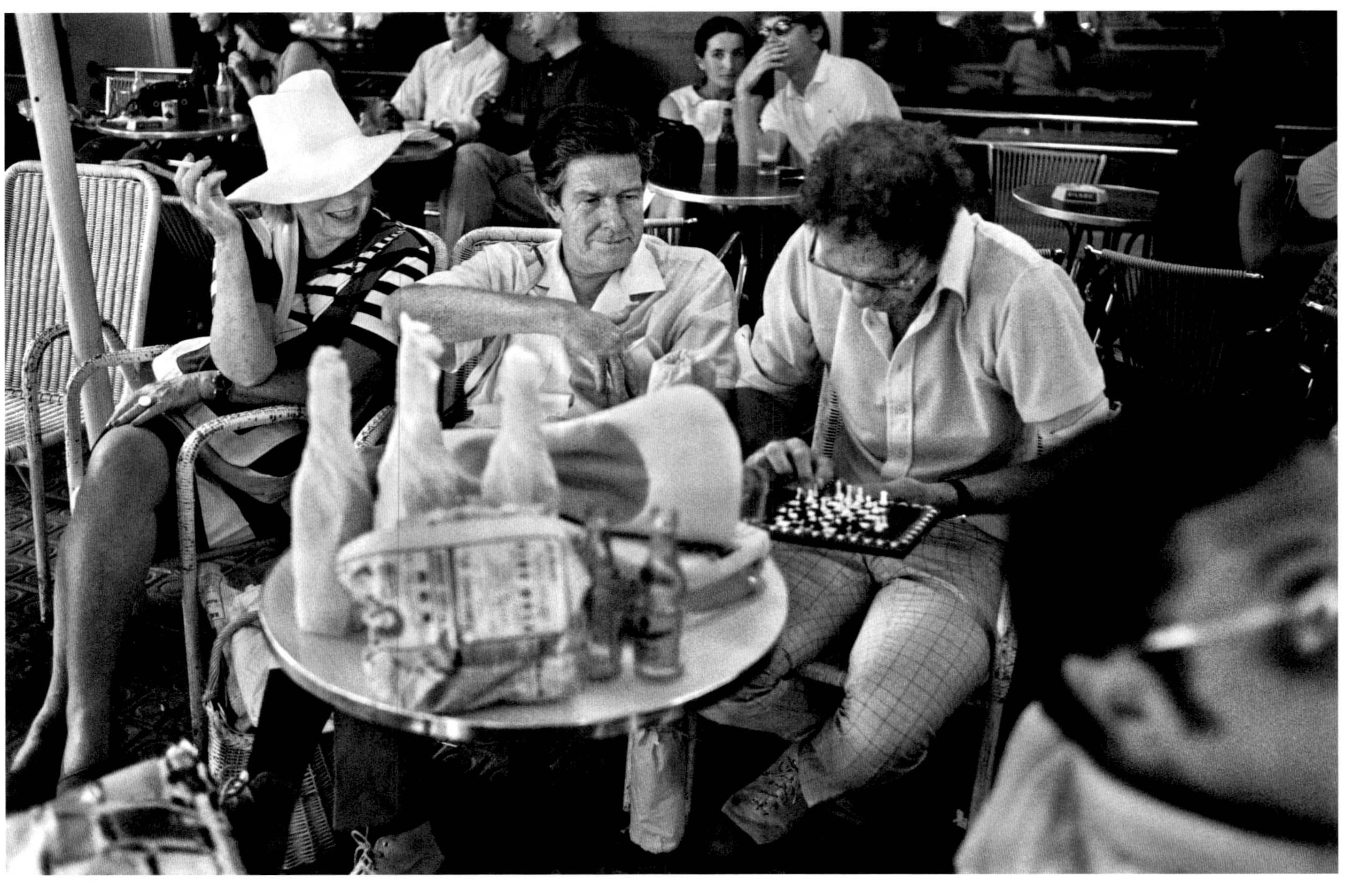

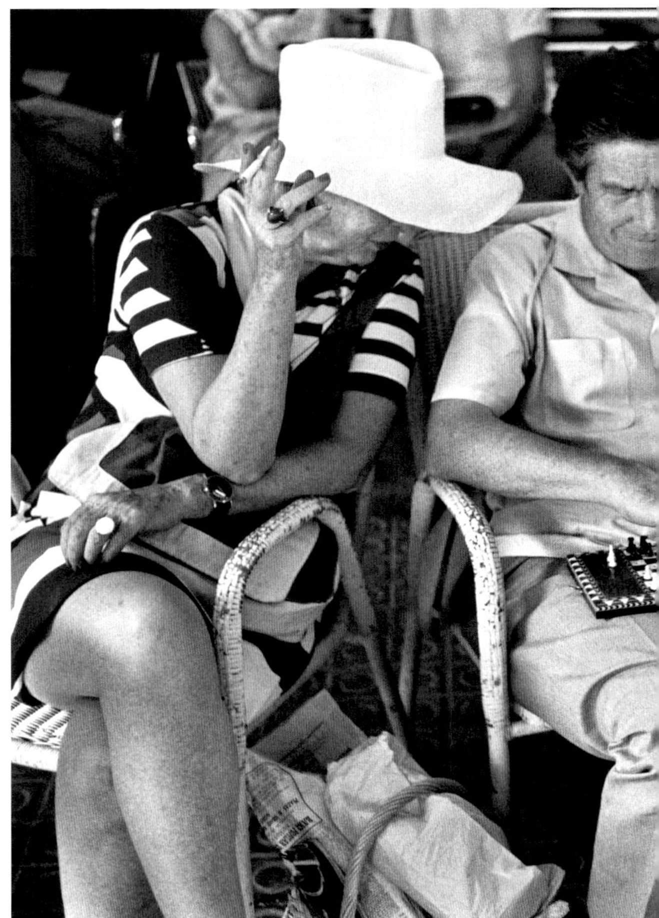

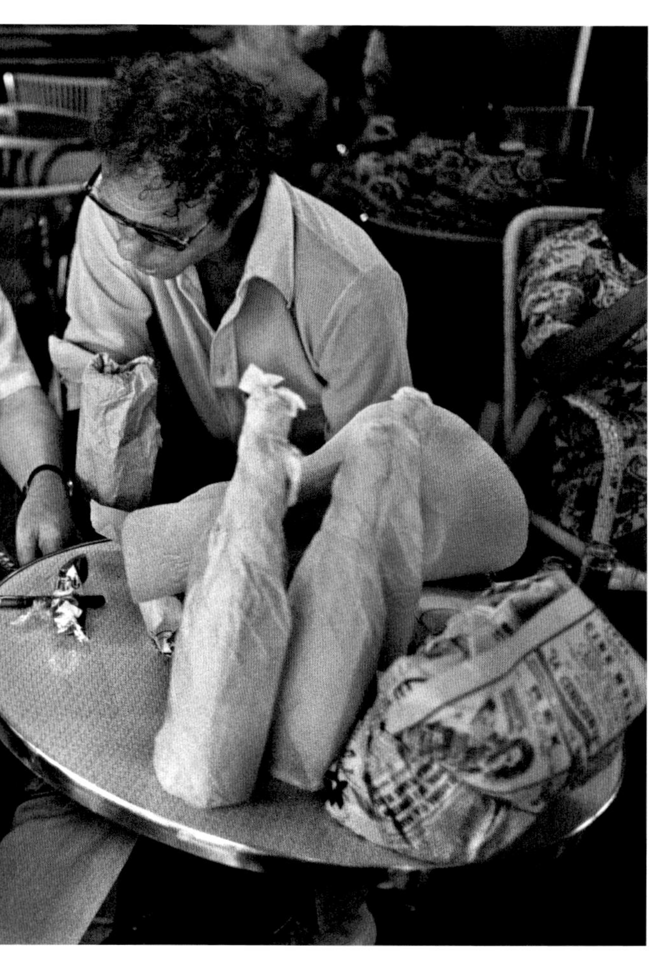

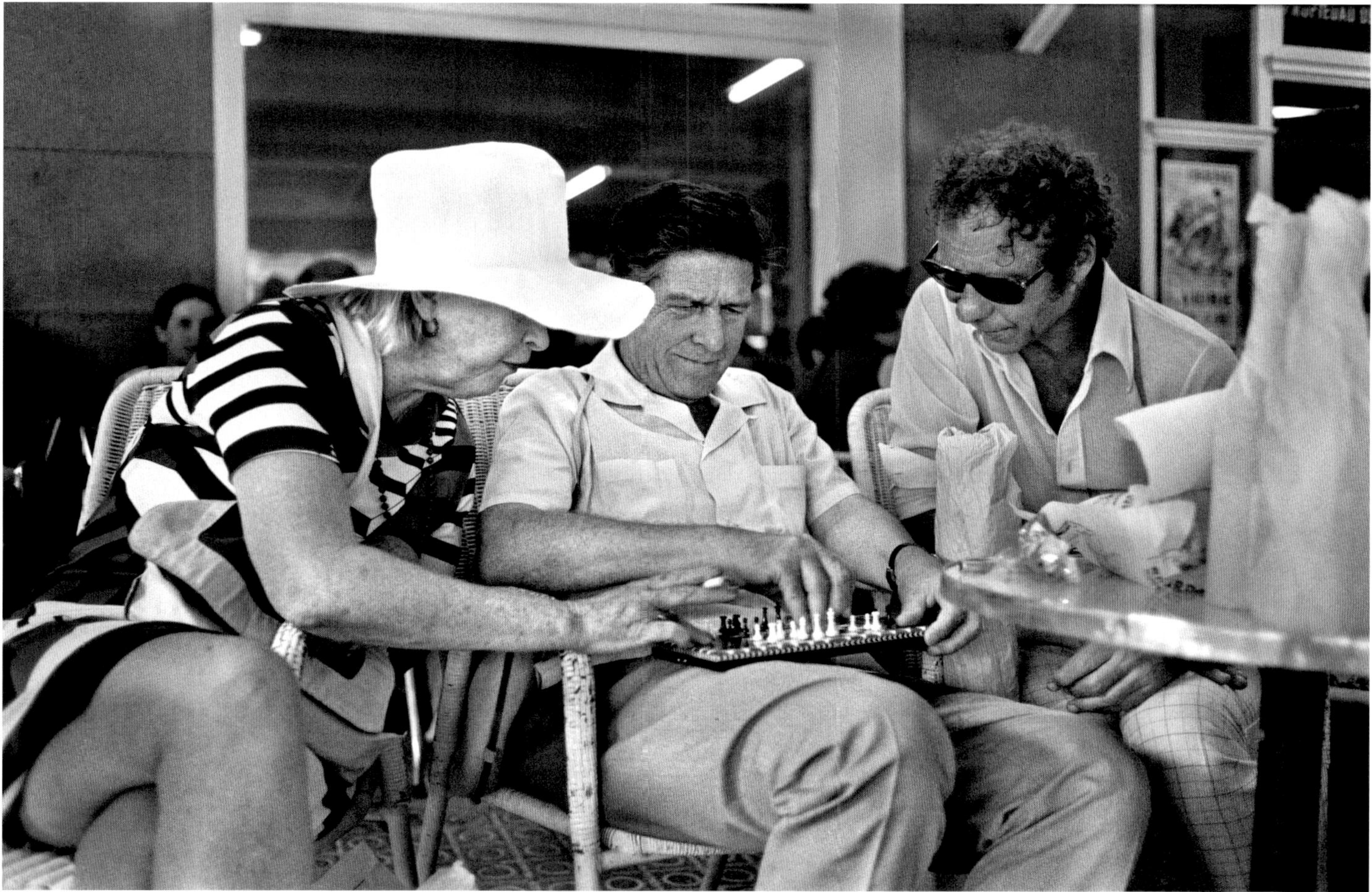

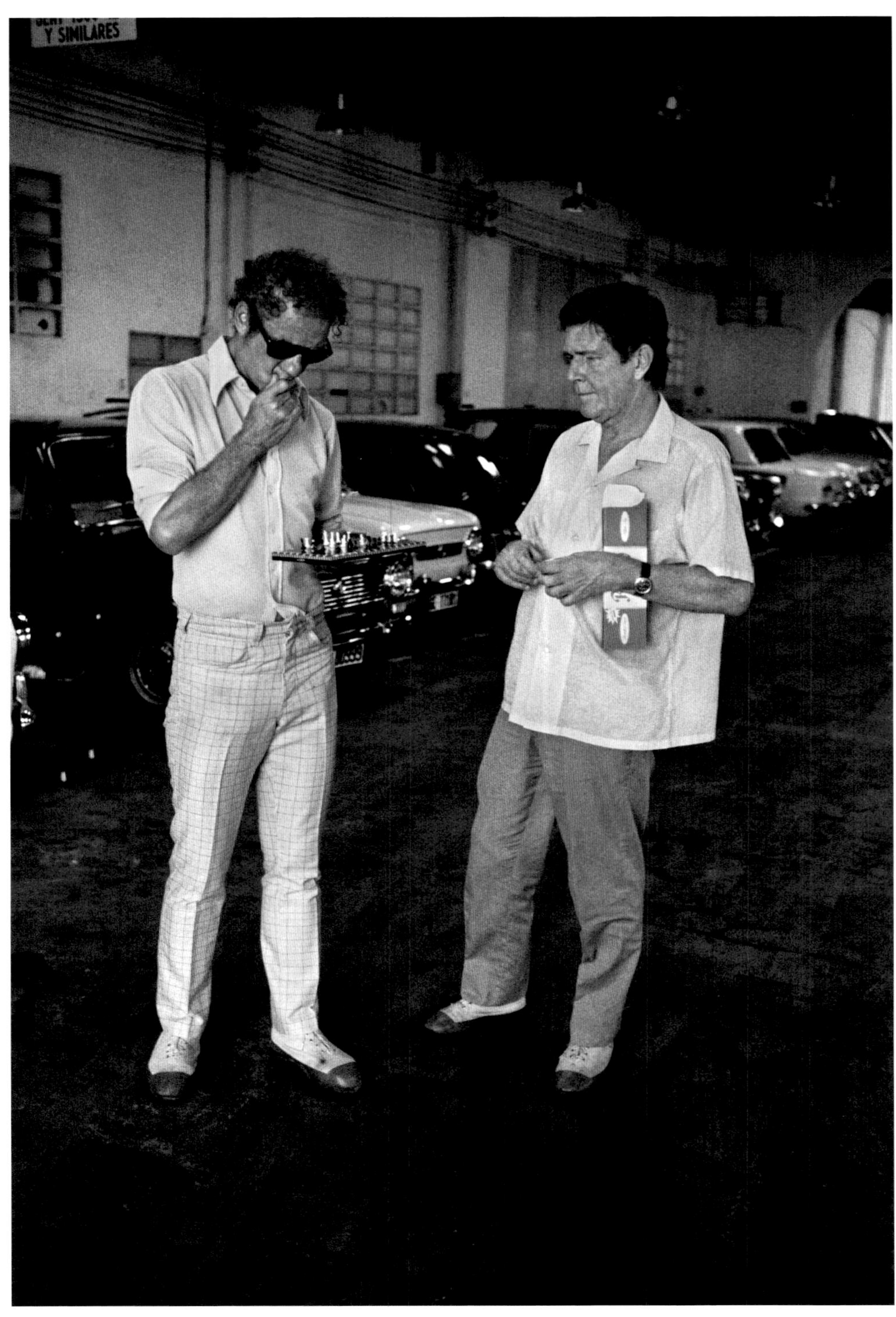
Y SIMILARES

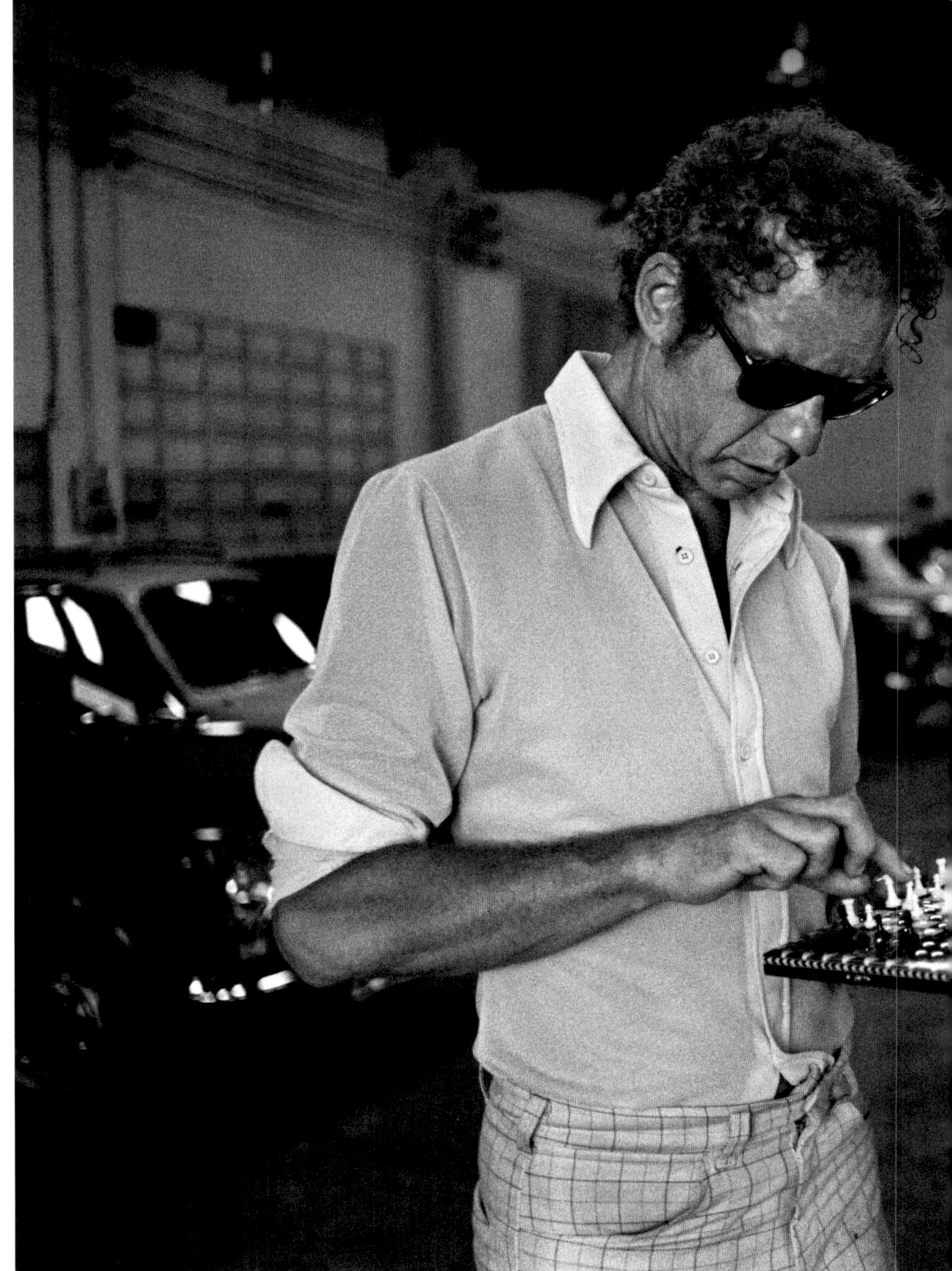

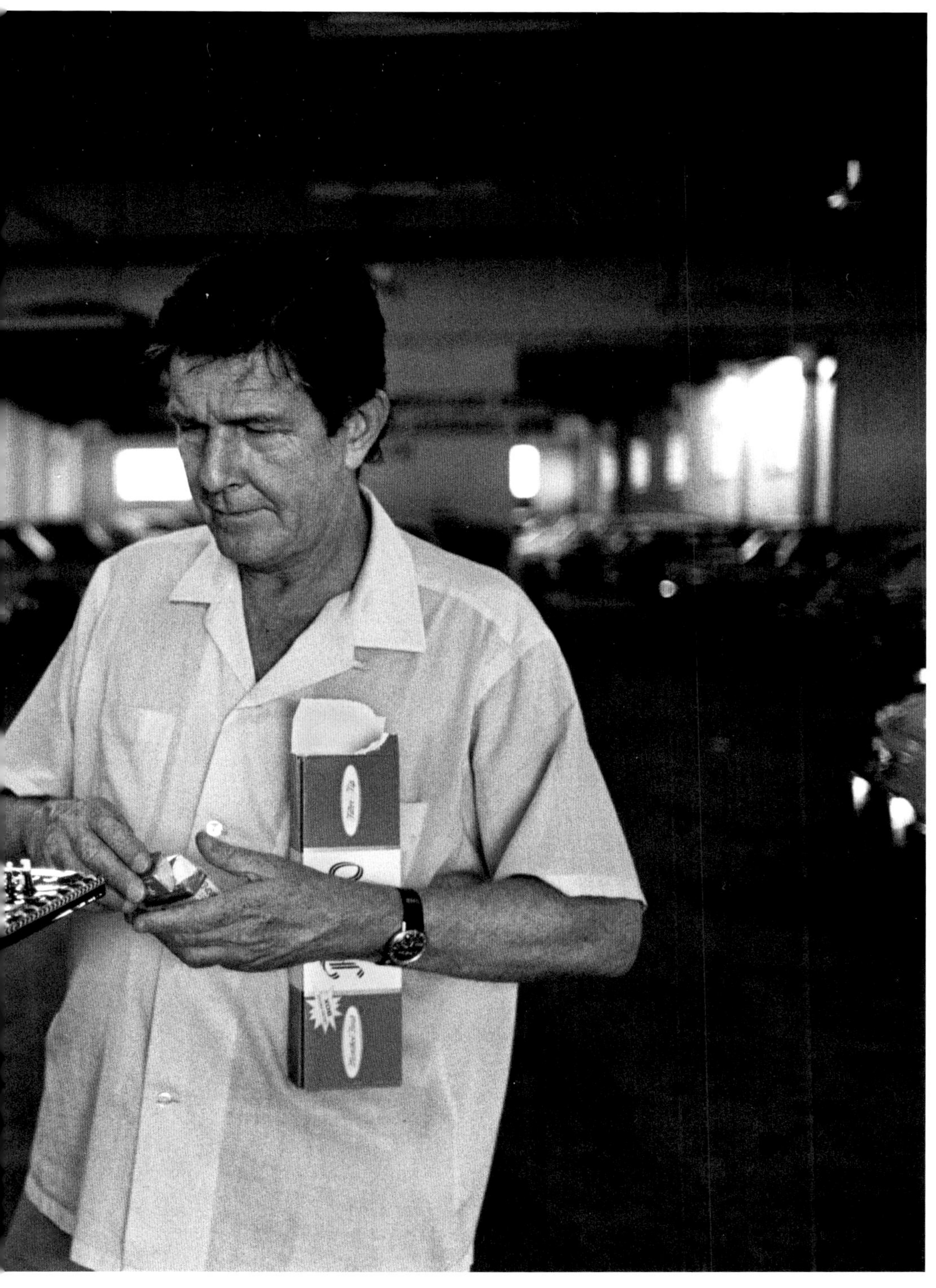

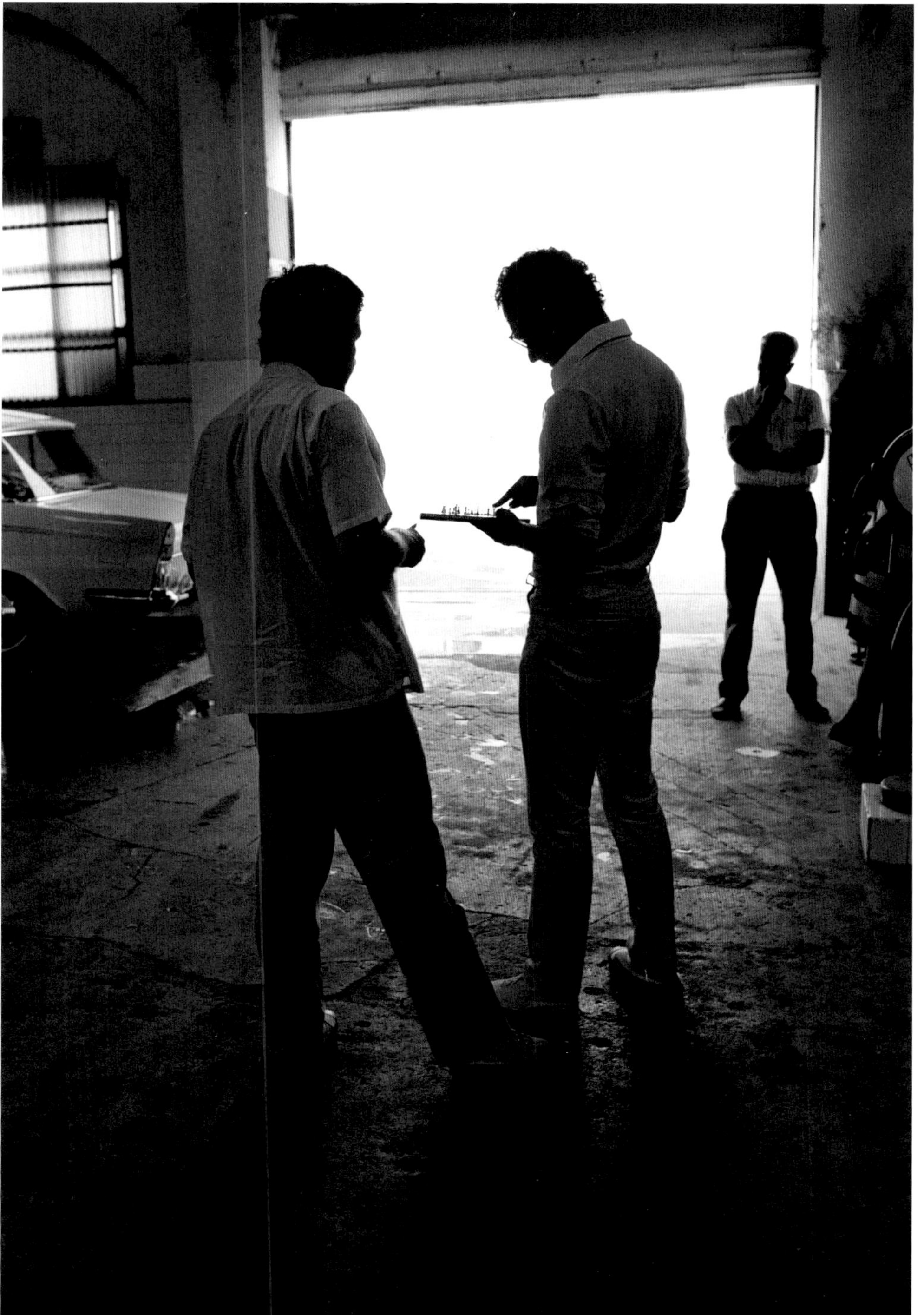

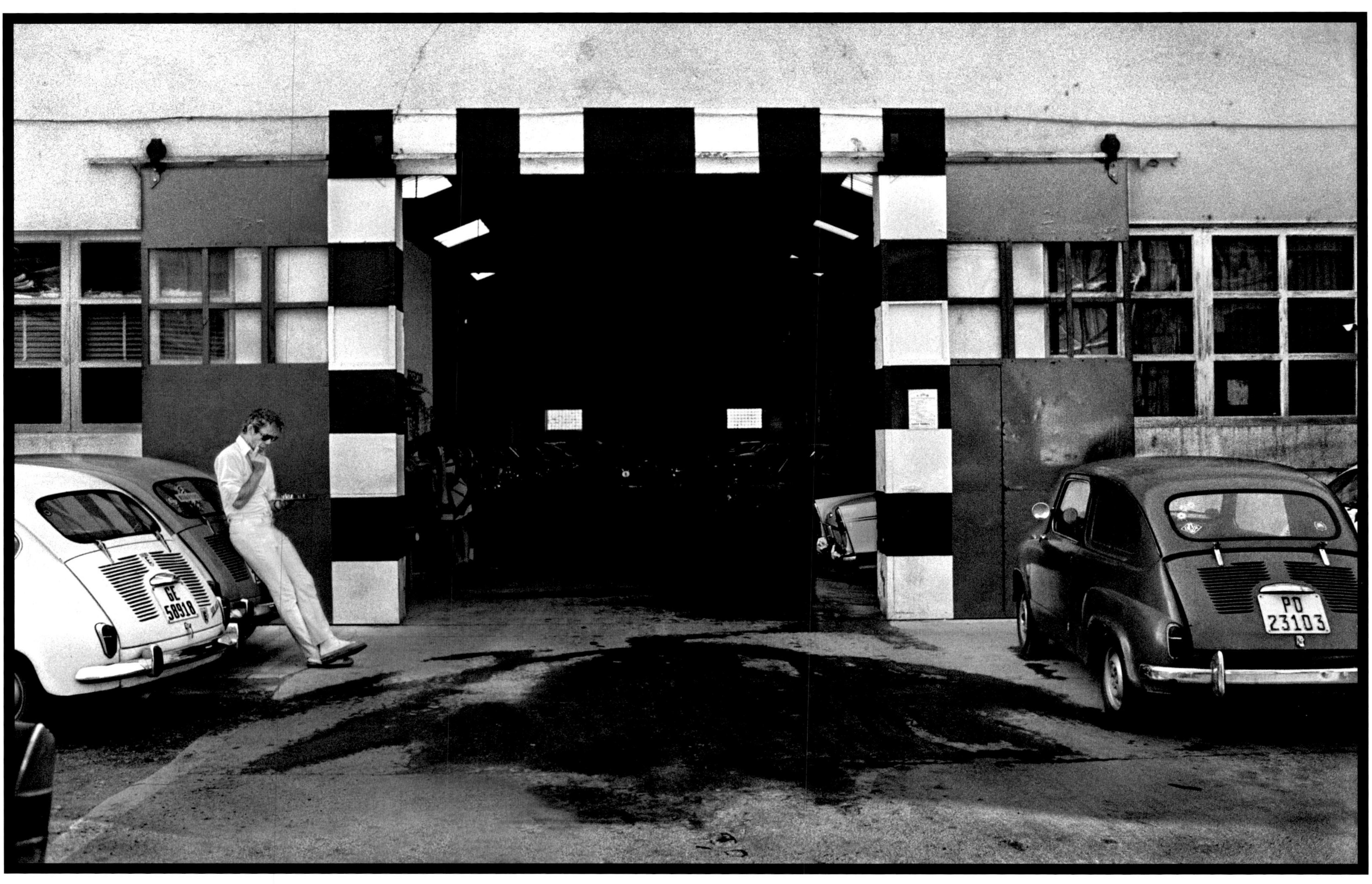
GE
58918
PD
23103

John Cage was

Once asked in a local magazine

He probably didn't care for,

Nor frequently read, *Why Are We Here?* To which, observing a

Cagean brevity,

A Cagean resistance, he replied, *No why, just here.*

God, what a *perfect* comeback, so perfect it's possible he didn't

Even say it. Maybe Merce said it. Or maybe it

Was an idea that orbited around out there in the ether,

An advertisement for emptiness, an answer that

Satisfied in resisting *satisfaction.* An idea to take up or cast off as needed.

— Rick Moody

At Merce's memorial, someone asked me,

"What did John Cage teach you?"

I answered, "John Cage was the man who taught me to say *yes*."

"What did you say before?"

"I said *no*. I'm French."

I learned from John that

saying *yes* could enrich my life

more than saying *no*

could ensure its integrity.

— Monique Fong

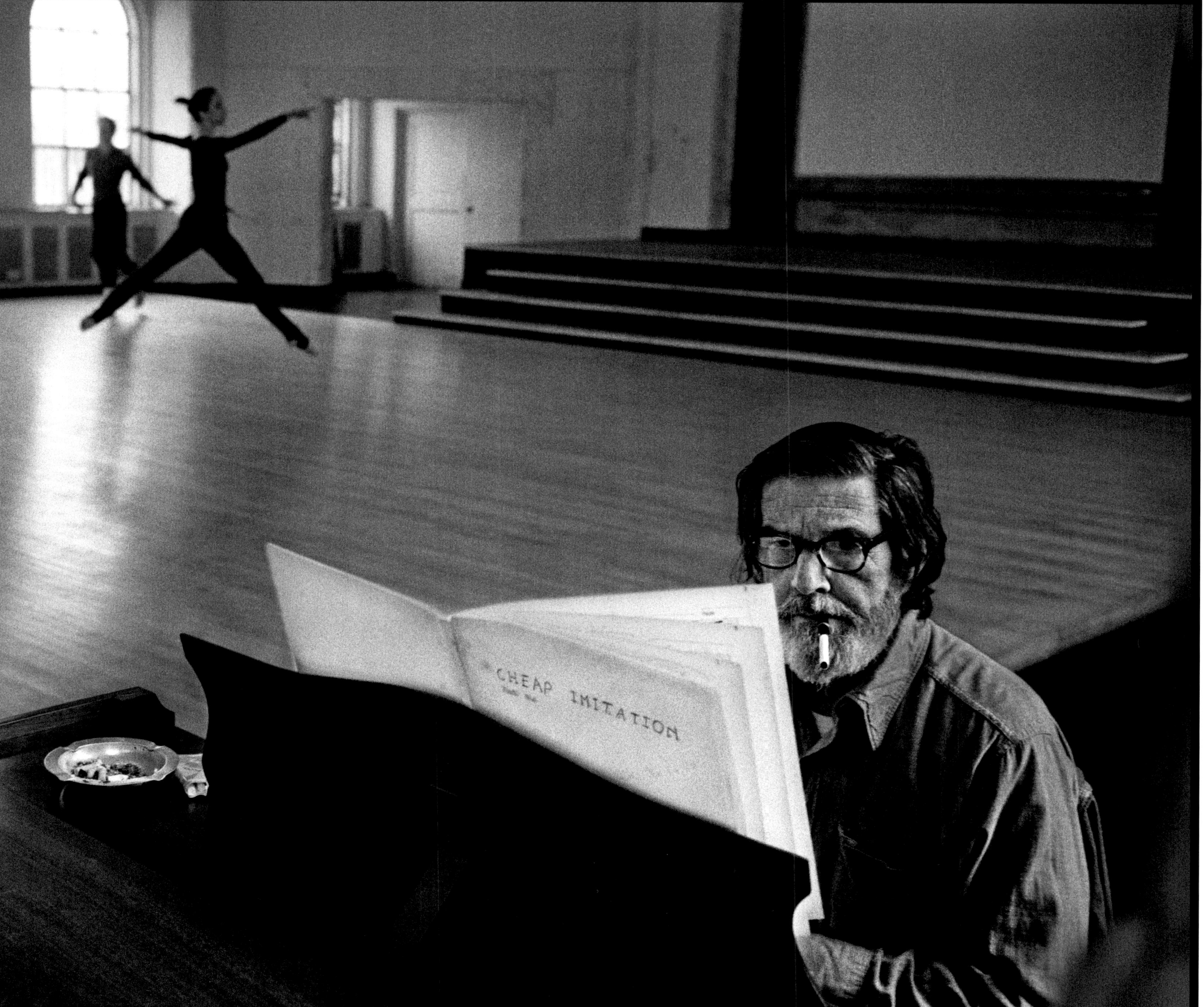
CHEAP IMITATION

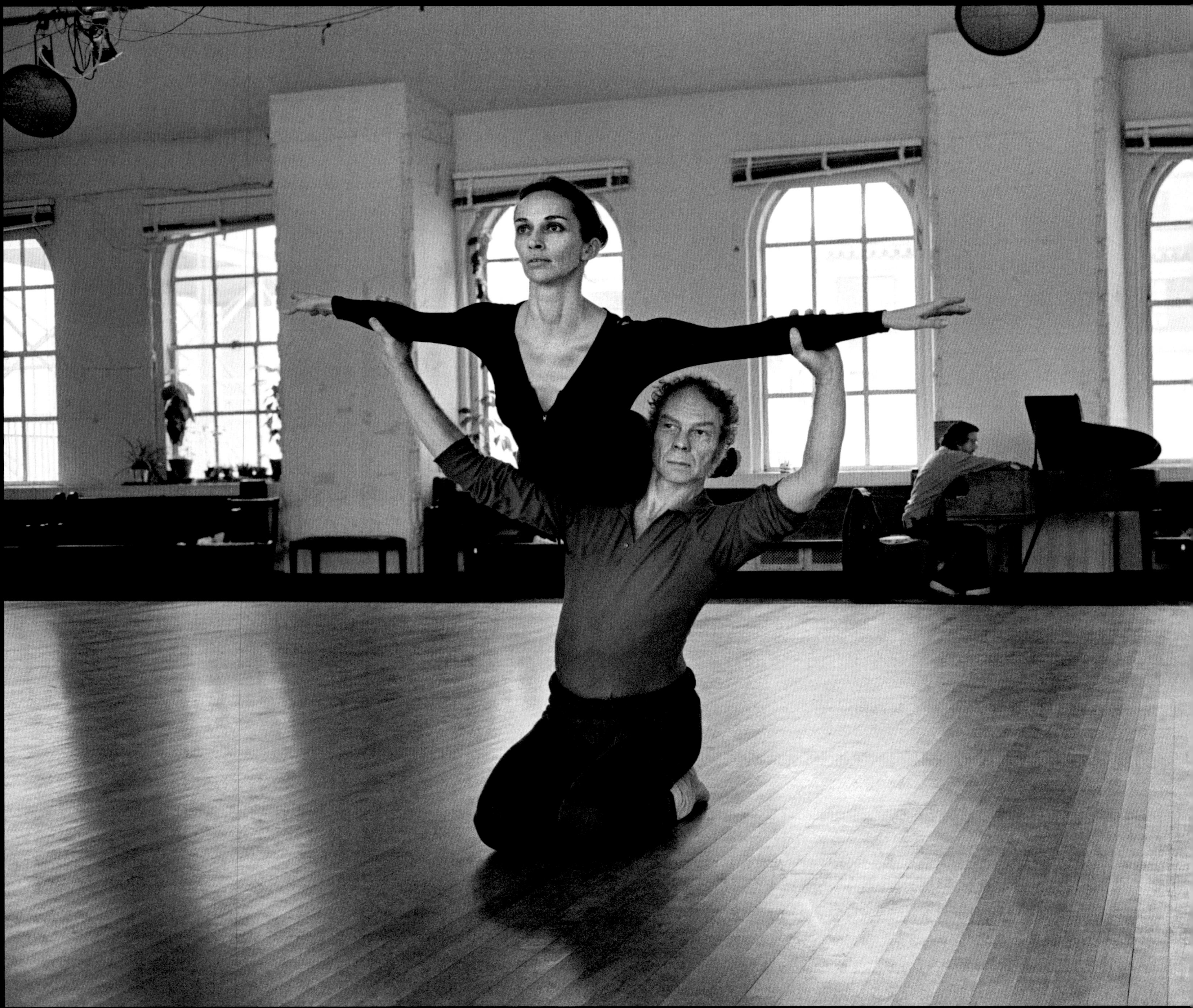

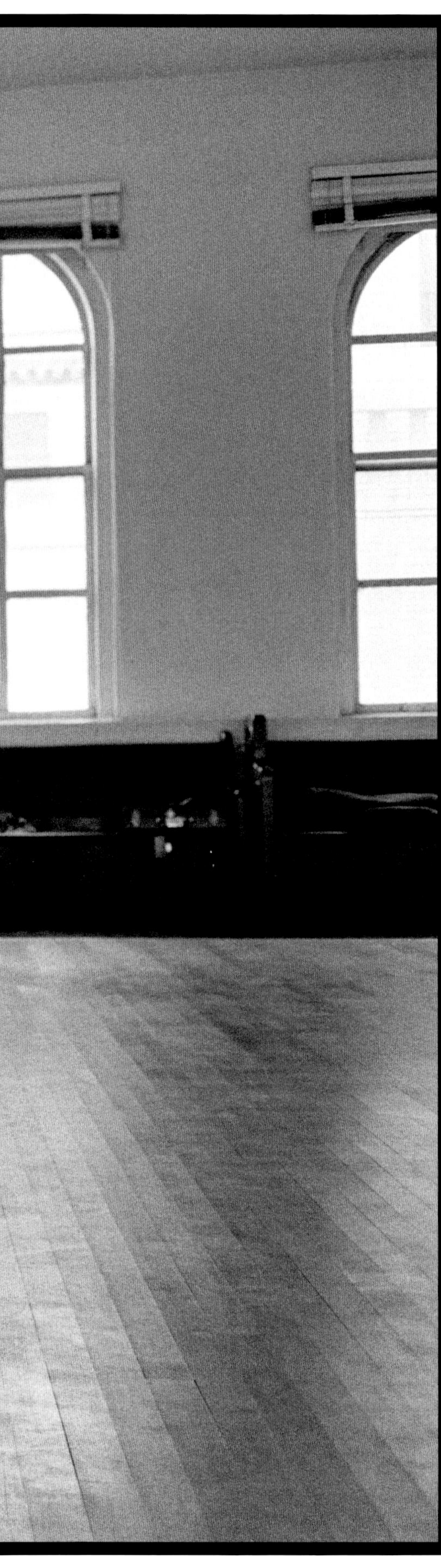

John Cage was
one of the two most important artists of the twentieth century.
It was seeing the Cunningham Dance Company,
just when I had abandoned a life in improvised music,
that opened my mind to what was possible in art,
and I decided that this was what
I wanted to spend the rest of my life doing.
Later I worked with John and experienced his generosity,
both personal and intellectual.
Unlike with other master/acolyte relationships,
John's followers never sound anything like him.
Anything goes, provided—as he would always say—that you take
"nothing" as the base.

— Gavin Bryars

It's not just that John Cage was gracious enough to eat the worst macrobiotic muffins ever—their affinity, perhaps, with recent gifts of rocks . . . ?

His presence—open, radiant.

Coexistence
  Dissonance
    Hopi creation myths
      I Ching
        Merce
          Mushrooms
            Ryoan-ji gardens
              Silence
                Sound
                  Space
                    Time
                      Zen Buddhism . . .

The adventure of that first conversation—cosmic pinball:
disparate ideas, dazzling possibilities exploding like Roman candles.

Multiplicity.

Interdependencies discovered, uncovered, serendipitously.

My sense, at twenty, of life's processes elementally challenged—forever transformed.
Sensibilities intensified, awakened. Freed.
Liberated from linearity, preconceptions, causality.
Exhilarated by the potency, poetry of collaboration.

— Melissa Harris

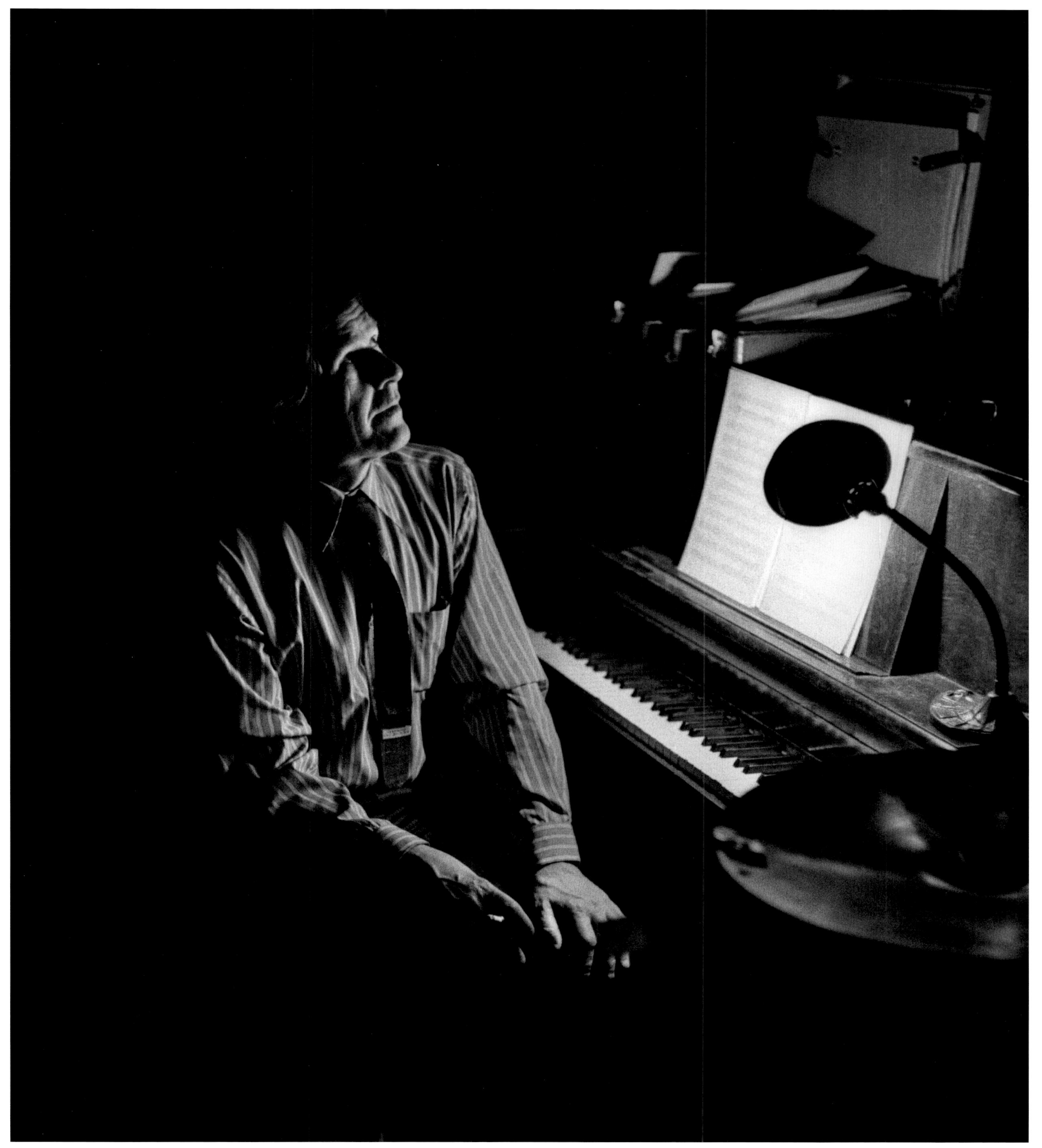

1. John Cage was a composer, a performer of "electronic music," and a different kind of thinker. In 1965, in the brownstone Methodist chapel at Wesleyan University, he rolled ball bearings down metal planks and microphones picked up and broadcast the plink/plank sounds. It was music. I was there and my epiphany was that we were only bound by the blinders we allowed to be placed on our imagination. He opened me to ideas and made me receptive to contrary thinking. As president of a foundation, I could wish for no better start.

2. John Cage was willful and calming. He had to be. He lived with Merce when men together were rejected, and he made music that most didn't accept or understand. He willed their lives together, he influenced a generation of artists' thinking, and he made art. When he died, the MCDC lost its balance for some years because the level had been John. He smiled and prodded and no one crossed him; he had Merce's back and it worked. In managing complex organizations of creative people, diversity in personalities and styles is crucial.

3. At dinner with Merce and Laura Kuhn one night, Merce said he and John were once poor and looking for a place to live. They had found nothing. Merce was desperate, John Cage was funny and a man used to beginning again. He said "if we don't find a place soon, we'll move to Bolivia." Right about then, someone told them about an apartment near 6th Avenue, the Avenue of the Americas, with all the hemisphere's flags. They saw it and looked out the window and saw the Bolivian flag. They never moved.

4. John Cage was sitting just in front of me in the first row at a concert of his music for trombone and prepared piano on the Saturday night before he died. We were at MoMA, which presented Cage music every weekend that summer in the sculpture garden to honor his eightieth. Merce sat next to him. The trombone played a long note and a car horn on 54th Street serendipitously called back. John turned to Merce, beaming. True to the end, for John, every sound was music and magical.

— Alberto Ibargüen

My first John Cage encounter, in 1950, was the LP recording of Maro Ajemian performing his *Sonatas and Interludes for Prepared Piano.* I bought it with a week of my sophomore high school lunch money.

We connected, performed, talked, and ate together from 1960 onwards. John Cage was always generous and nourishing with ideas and resources.

My deepest memories are of our performing together and sharing ideas. Those Cage experiences were significant in adjusting my ability to focus on the activities at hand, away from old habits, eroding distractions, and anxieties. For us both, even our few disagreements were liberating.

— Gordon Mumma

John Cage was born one hundred years ago and he is still cheering us up, like an English cup of tea.

To honor his life I made a concert program of seventy-nine minutes, one minute for each year lived. In Poland

it started well, but then people began to leave. (Surprising what we do for a living.) At the end, those

who stayed gave us a big cheer, standing in a show of solidarity. It went much better in Germany:

only a few came, but they all stayed.

Now John Cage has fallen silent, and we are the ones left cheering.

— Paul Hillier

JOHN CAGE WAS
ONE OF THE MOST INDEPENDENT AND INFLUENTIAL ARTISTS
OF THE CENTURY BUT WHENEVER HE AND I MET,
WE ALWAYS TALKED ABOUT MUSHROOMS,
NOT MUSIC.
IT WAS, HE WOULD SAY IN HIS GENTLE, DETACHED WAY,
A DIFFICULT YEAR FOR MORELS . . .
BUT THAT'S THE WAY IT GOES WITH MORELS.
AND BESIDES, MUSHROOM COMES BEFORE MUSIC IN THE DICTIONARY.
OF COURSE, I WOULD AGREE.
FIVE DANCES,
MY UNLIKELY ARRANGEMENTS OF CAGE KEYBOARD PIECES
WERE PREMIERED AT THE 2008 BARD CAGE FESTIVAL;
"UNLIKELY"
BECAUSE ARRANGING
PREPARED PIANO MUSIC FOR STRINGS
WAS AN IDEA IN ITSELF,
QUITE ECCENTRIC ENOUGH FOR JOHN.

— ERIC SALZMAN

When I met him in 1951 John Cage was (also) graphic designer for The Living Theater. As I was taken with his creativity and without a real budget, we at Larsen hired him to design our graphics, particularly the greetings and move announcements, which were handcrafted by the Cunningham troupe and are now in the MoMA collection. I can think of few people as influential in shaping our aesthetics in the second half of the twentieth century as John. He was also a pragmatic visionary.

— Jack Lenor Larsen

John knew me as an artist using sound.
This developed from my interest in beans as a primary food
but also as a percussion instrument when housed in paper.
John's cooking always involved beans and rice.
Even in this realm John Cage was not interested in improvisation.
We layered ingredients in a bamboo steamer:
Fish on top, vegetables beneath catching the drippings.
Summer 1968 . . . employing chance operations,
the I Ching,
three pennies,
and help from a bottle of Campari,
we structured the book *Notations*.
One penny fell.
I scrambled under the piano to see if it was heads or tails.

— Alison Knowles

“Humans, as a part of nature, have changed over time,” I began.
John gave me a sharp glance.
“Humans and nature are different things,” he said.
His rebuke established a gap.
John may have tried to mend it.
We met last after my showing of the *Goldberg Variations* in California.
John came up.
I knew his antipathy to Bach;
it had drawn my attention to Bach’s music.
Listening to these *Variations* was not a pleasure for him.
But he came.

John Cage was aiming to “stretch our ears.”
That sounds like evolution to me.
He would probably think otherwise.

— Steve Paxton

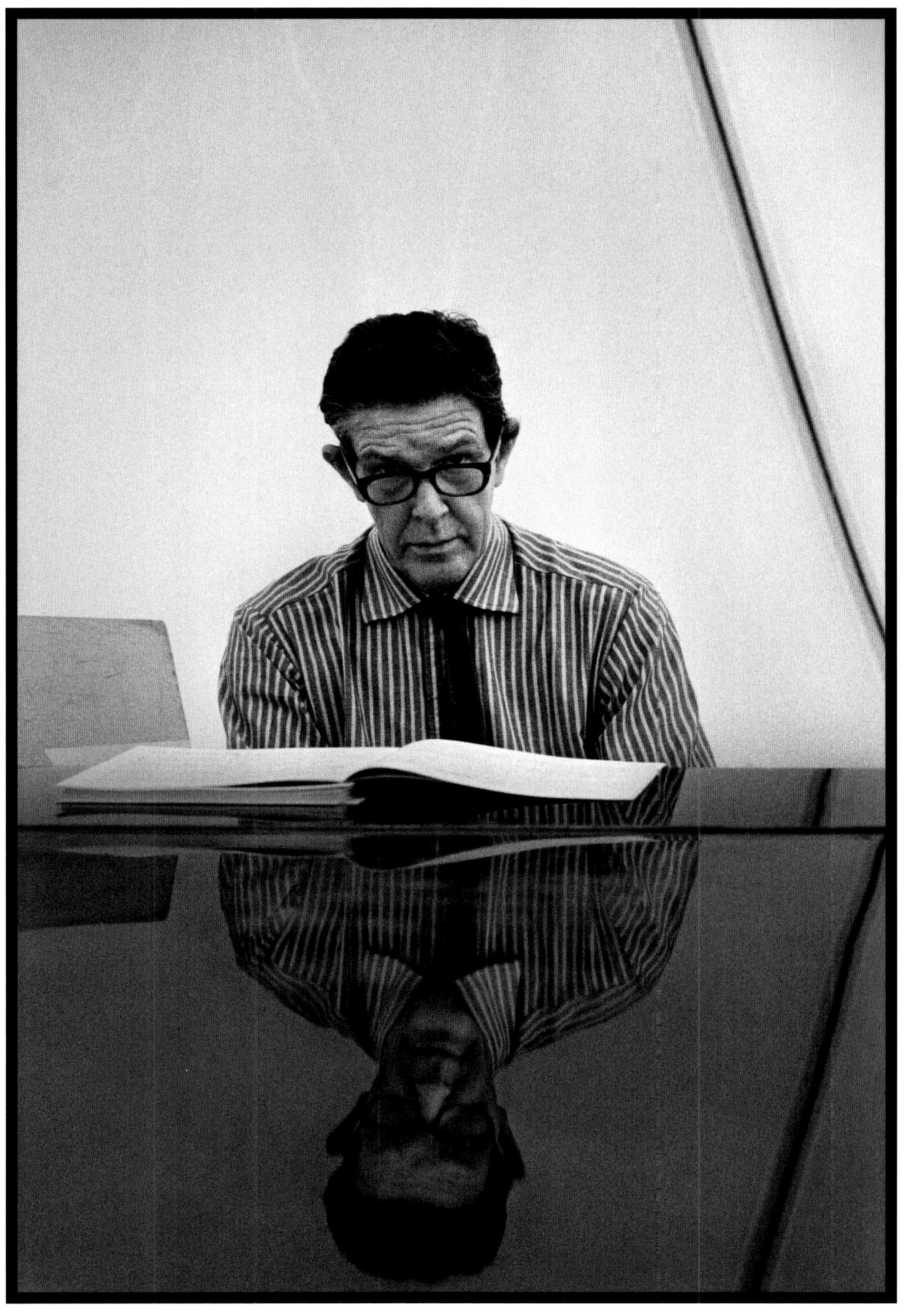

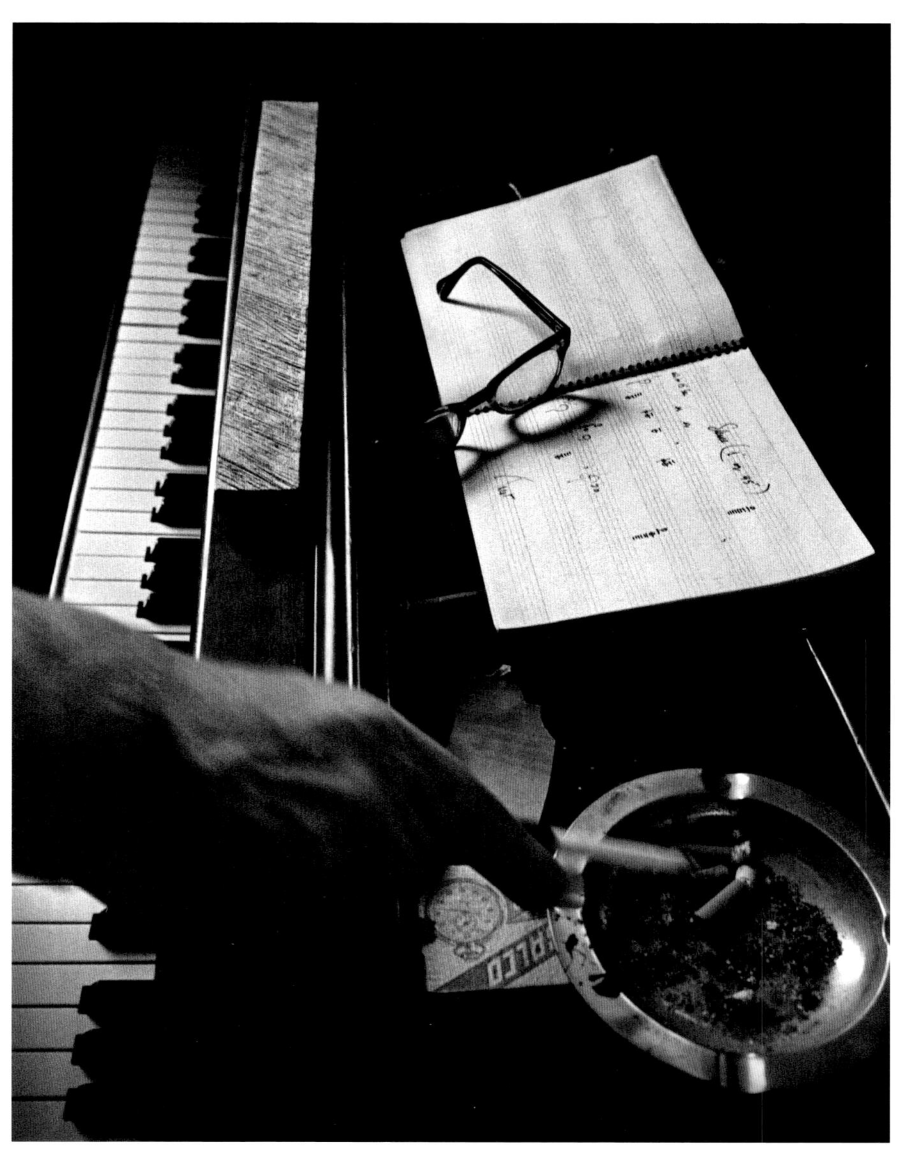

John Cage was one of the few authentic human beings I met in life.

(1958/59) I experienced him as an inspiration to the postwar avantgarde music-art-scene in Germany, felt encouraged by him in my own research: indeterminacy, chance operation, Art as result of conception versus expression of taste. (47)

(1960) we performed his music in my Lintgasse studio in Cologne, the "counterfestival" opposing the official IGNM concerts. Paiks "hommage" with cutting John's tie was the climax of our anarchistic activities. (78)

(1964) I dedicated an art work object to him titled "don't defend your freedom with poisoned mushrooms or hommage a John Cage" ... (97) words

[One word left - so please write the following in one word without intermission]

In the early seventies I visited a lecture by John at Wesleyan University. The students were revolting, one of them had unplugged the electricity, so John could not go on reading. I went to the stage, put the plug in again, went to his desk, embraced him with the words, here is the light back; he wondered: ~~where from~~ heaven's sake are you coming from? These were the last words we exchanged.

JOHN CAGE WAS—ACTUALLY, IS—A PRESENCE IN MY HEAD. AN EXTRAORDINARY EXAMPLE OF DEVOTION, TO OTHERS—AND TO MYSELF; TO WORK, MOSTLY, IN MY EXPERIENCE, MUSICAL (9 MONTHS TO MAKE THE 4¼-MINUTE TAPE PIECE *WILLIAMS MIX*!); ALSO TO THE FINDING, IDENTIFICATION, AND USE (COOKING AND EATING) OF MUSHROOMS; AND TO THE PURSUIT OF IDEAS, ESPECIALLY AS THEY RELATED TO A POSSIBLY GOOD LIFE. INFLUENCE? MORE THAN THAT: HE CREATED A SPACE WHERE I (AND OTHERS) FELT FREE TO DO WHAT WAS NEW, TO DISCOVER FREELY AND REALIZE IT. AND HE MADE ME UNDERSTAND THAT MUSIC WAS SOCIAL.

— CHRISTIAN WOLFF

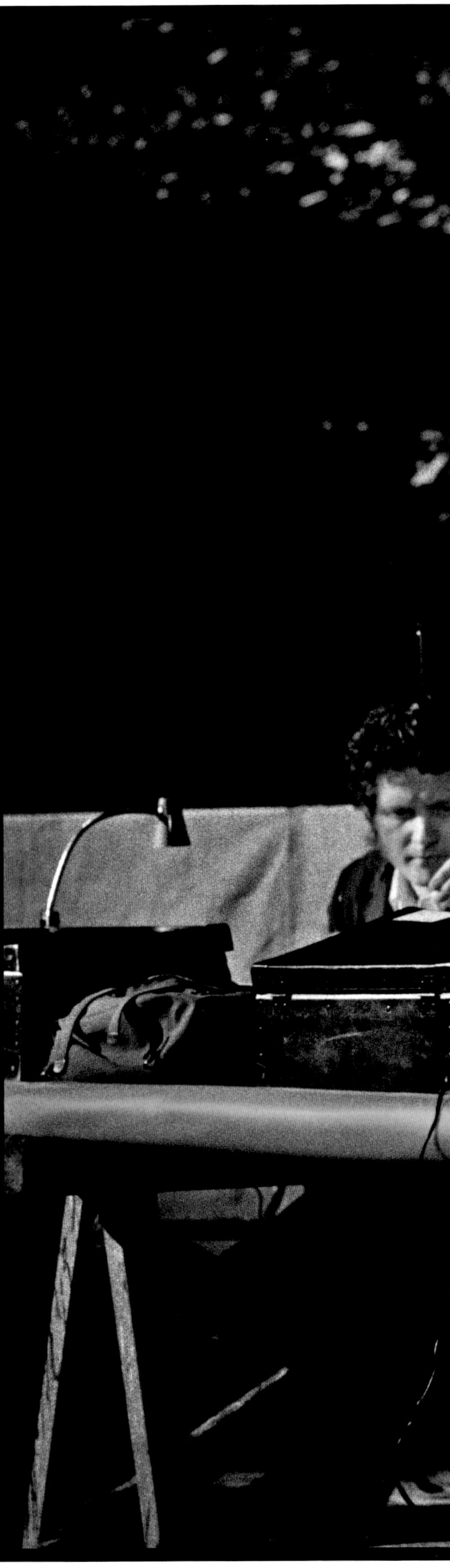

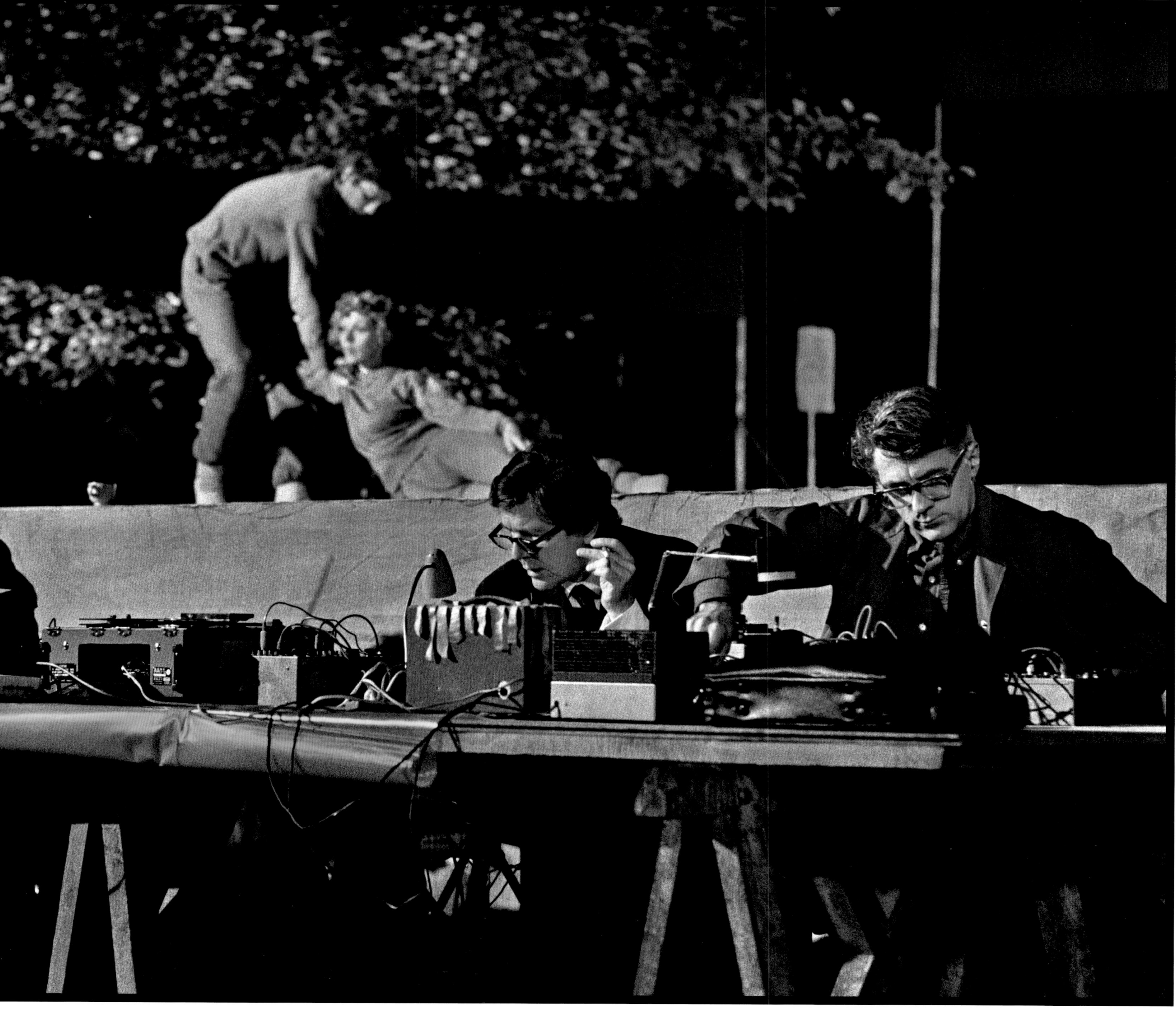

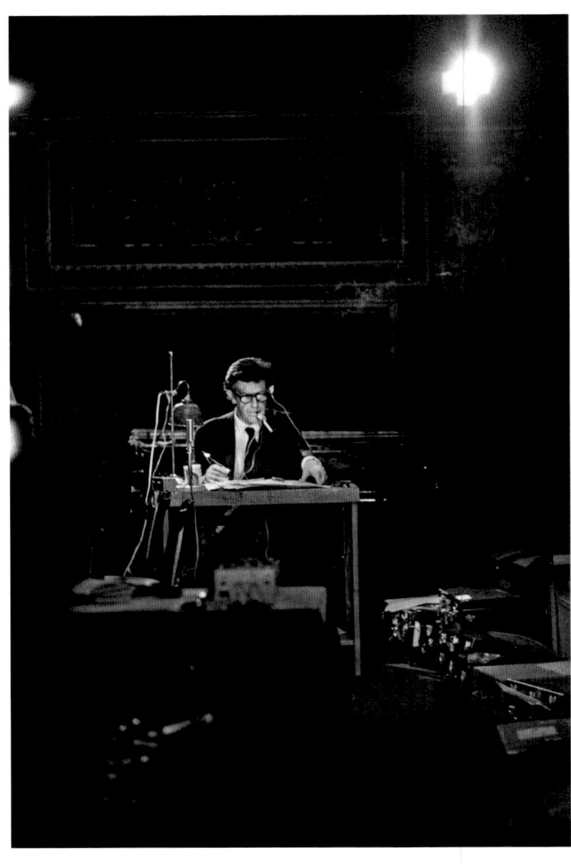

15. My first composition lesson.
Francis Simon sat down at the piano and played *4′33″*,
putting me in contact with John Cage.
Isolated in Miami,
I bought all his books and my universe exploded.
John showed up to the first ever BoaC* insisting
—generous to other artists as always—
he buy his ticket.
Whenever I reach a boundary I can't seem to get over
I think of John writing at a table wired with contact mikes.
It always opens up.
John Cage was father to so many ideas
we are still processing them.
We will be for a long time.

—Michael Gordon

*Bang on a Can

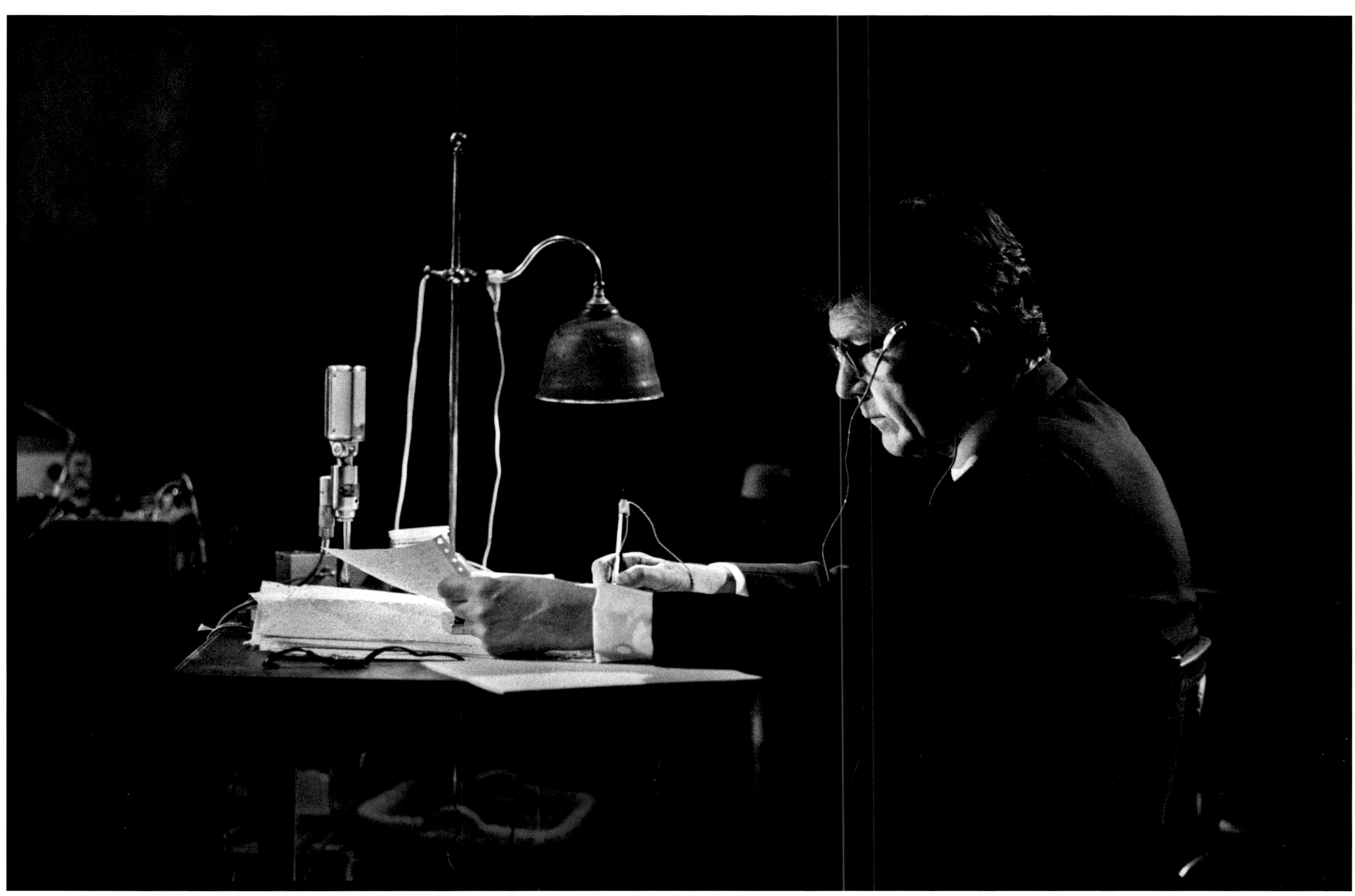

When young, working in a new way, my reaction to John Cage was

his direction was clearly not my own.

My impression of his contribution is that his early percussion and prepared piano pieces will survive best.

Some suggest Cage's early pieces laid the groundwork for my music of the 1960s and early '70s.

In that Cage's pieces were structured rhythmically rather than harmonically,

a technical affinity exists even if they had no conscious influence on my music.

I value a distinct voice.

Talent, technique alone, without vision, seem increasingly irrelevant.

John Cage had a vision and followed it.

— Steve Reich

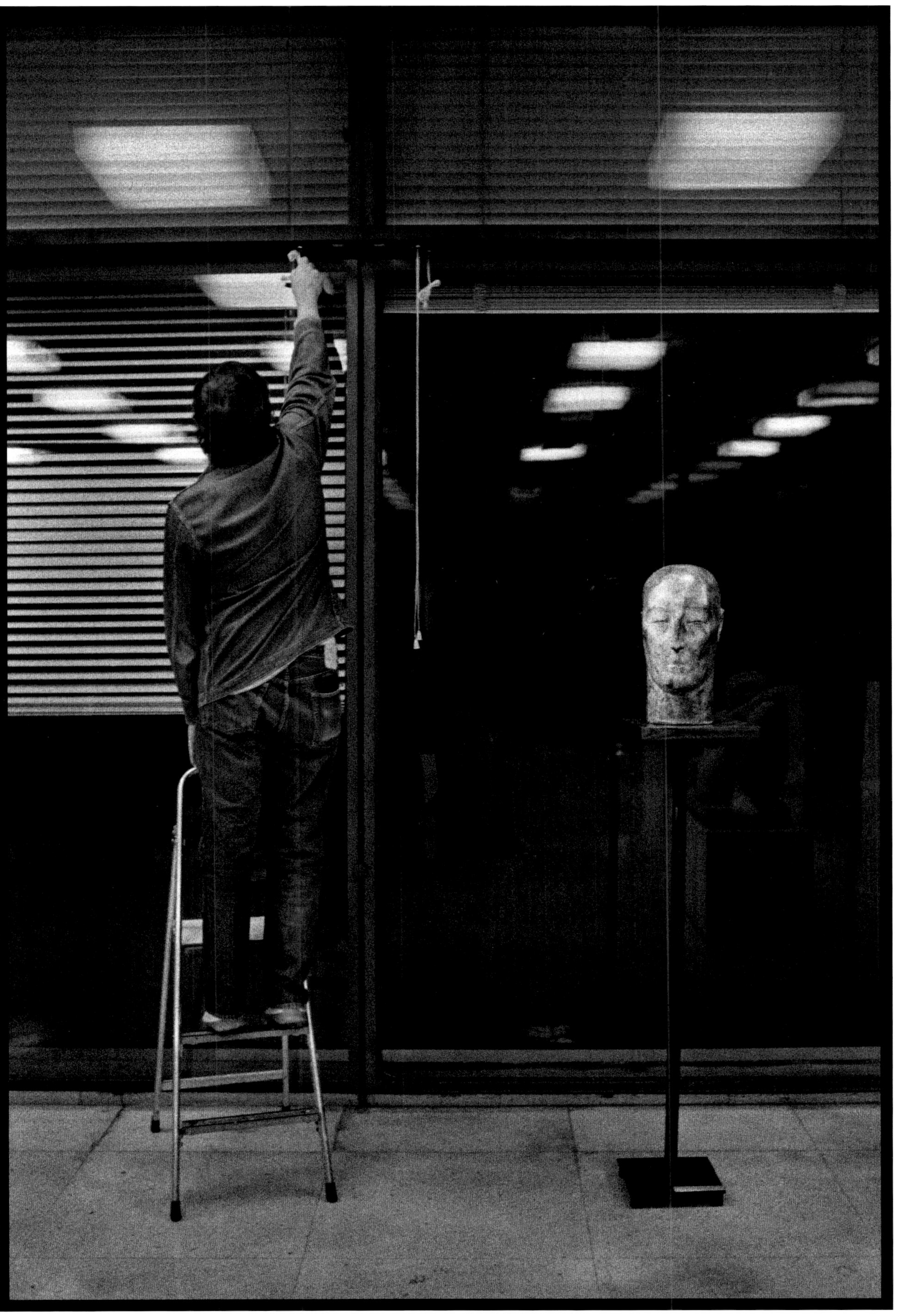

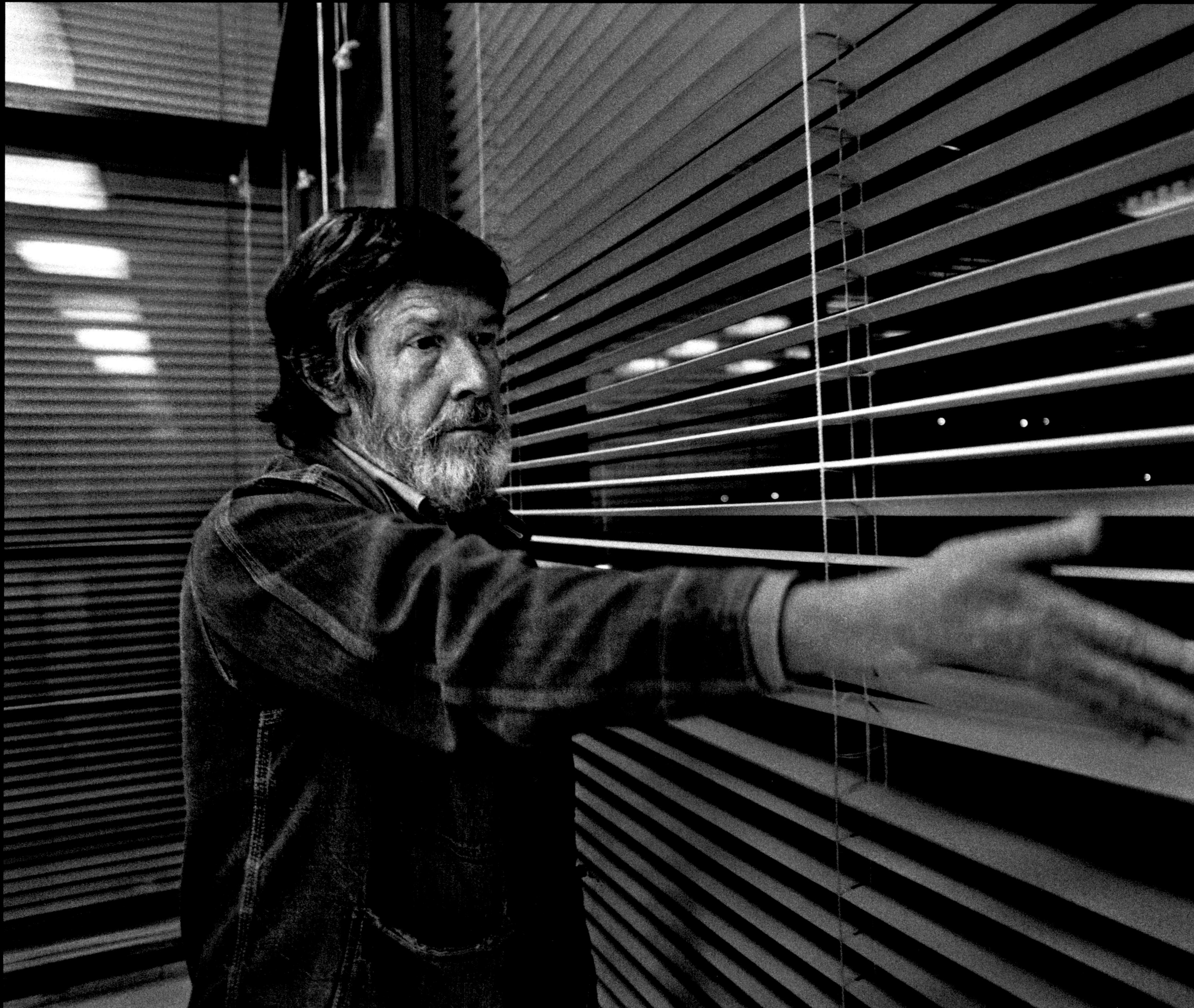

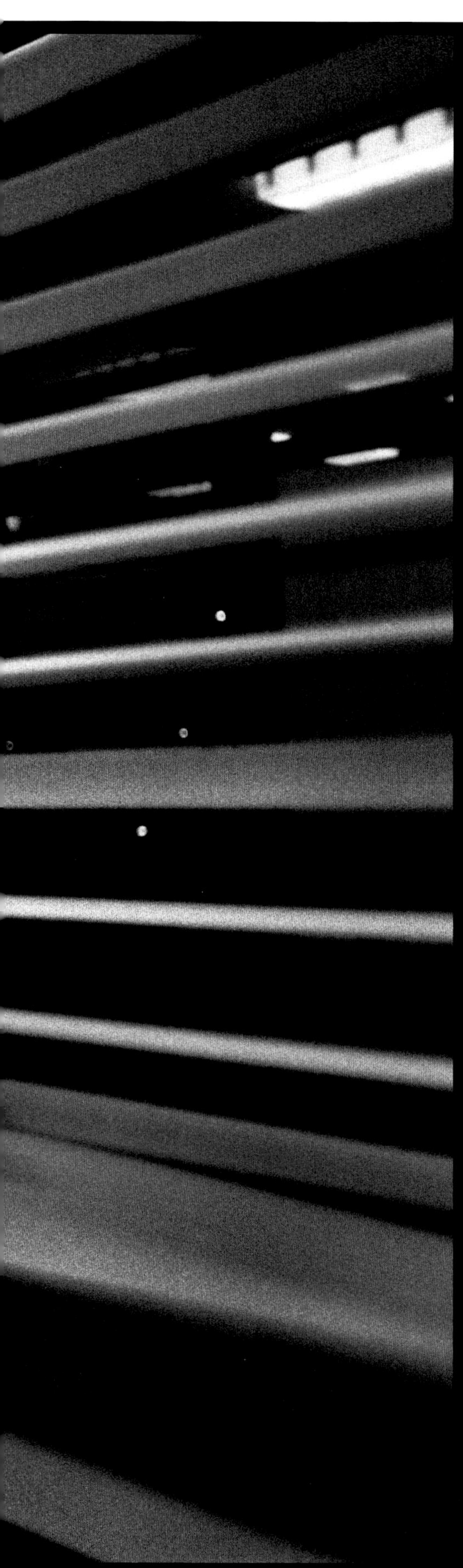

John Cage was almost eighty and what I really wanted to know was whether he thought things were getting better or worse. But it seemed like such a stupid question that I was afraid to ask so I talked around it for ten minutes about information theories and evolutionary developments and finally Cage said, "Um, exactly what are you trying to say?" So I asked him my real question. He stopped only for a moment and said, "Oh better. Much better. I'm sure of that. It's just that we can't see it. It's just that it happens so slowly." — Laurie Anderson

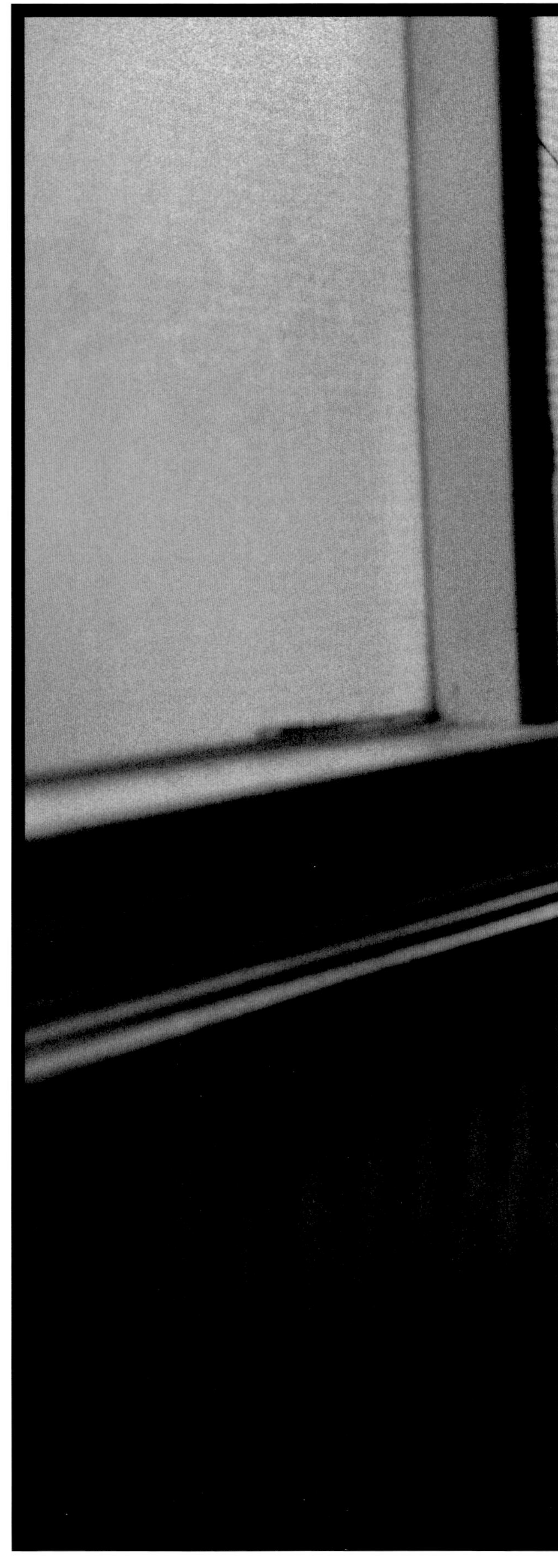

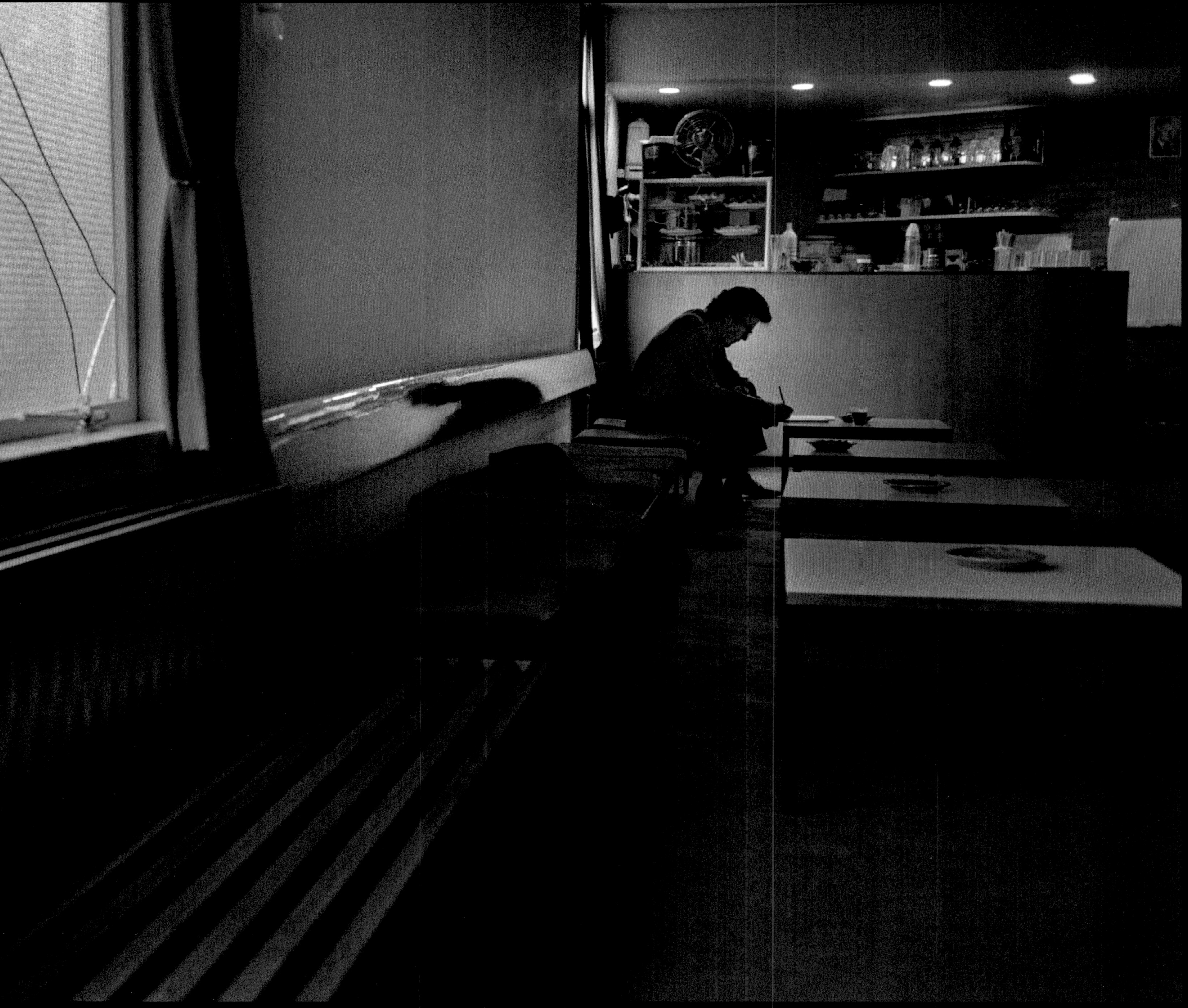

John Cage was a liberator of words.

He taught us that,

like sound, all language can be poetry

if we only had the eyes to read it.

By treating all language as equal,

he sought to eradicate meaning,

realizing that words as they are

have enough meaning

without our needing to do

anything else to them.

In this attitude, he precedes

and predicts today's writing environment:

how we move information

(move being both physical as well as emotional)

is more important

than the content of which we are moving.

— Kenneth Goldsmith

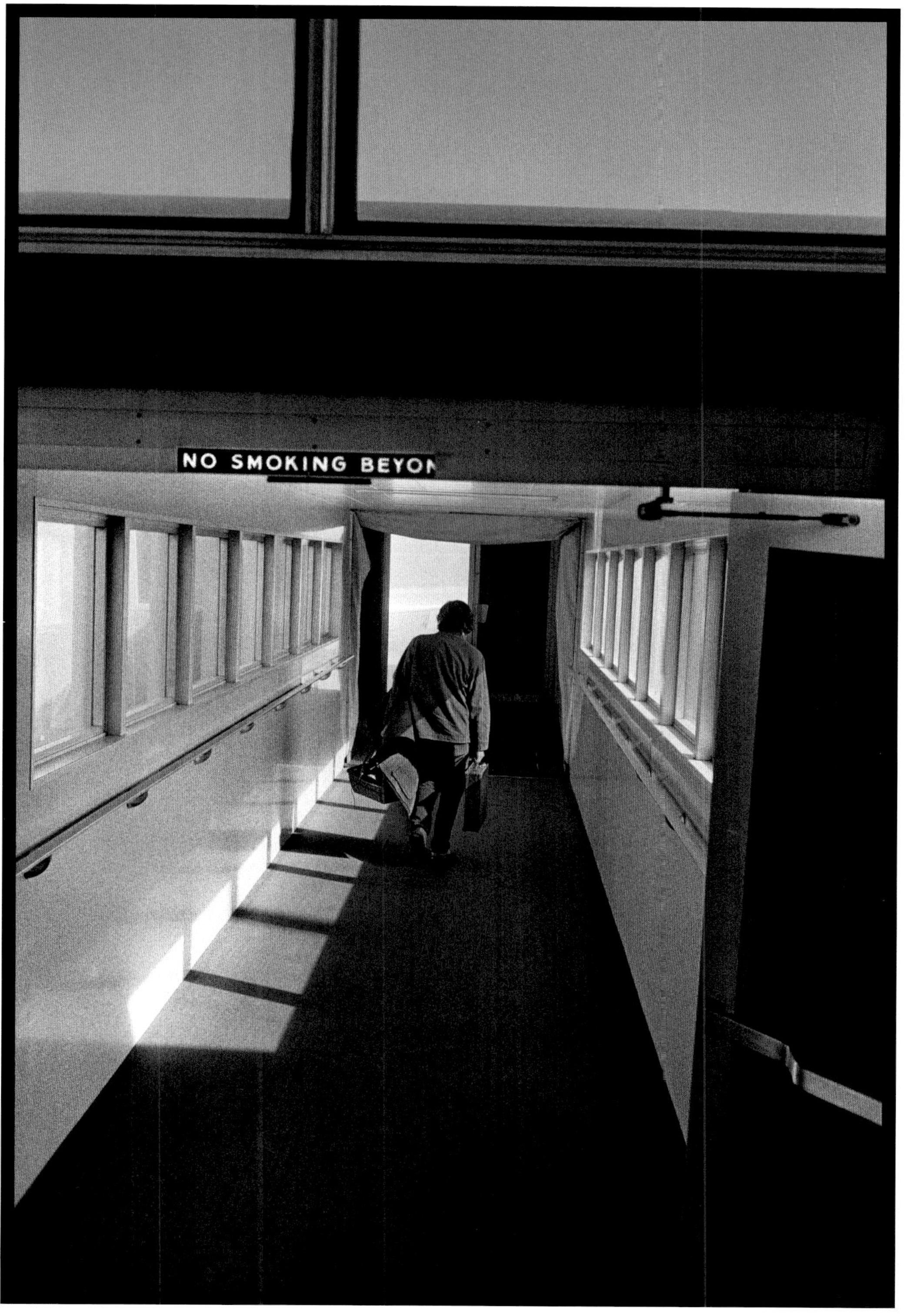
NO SMOKING BEYON

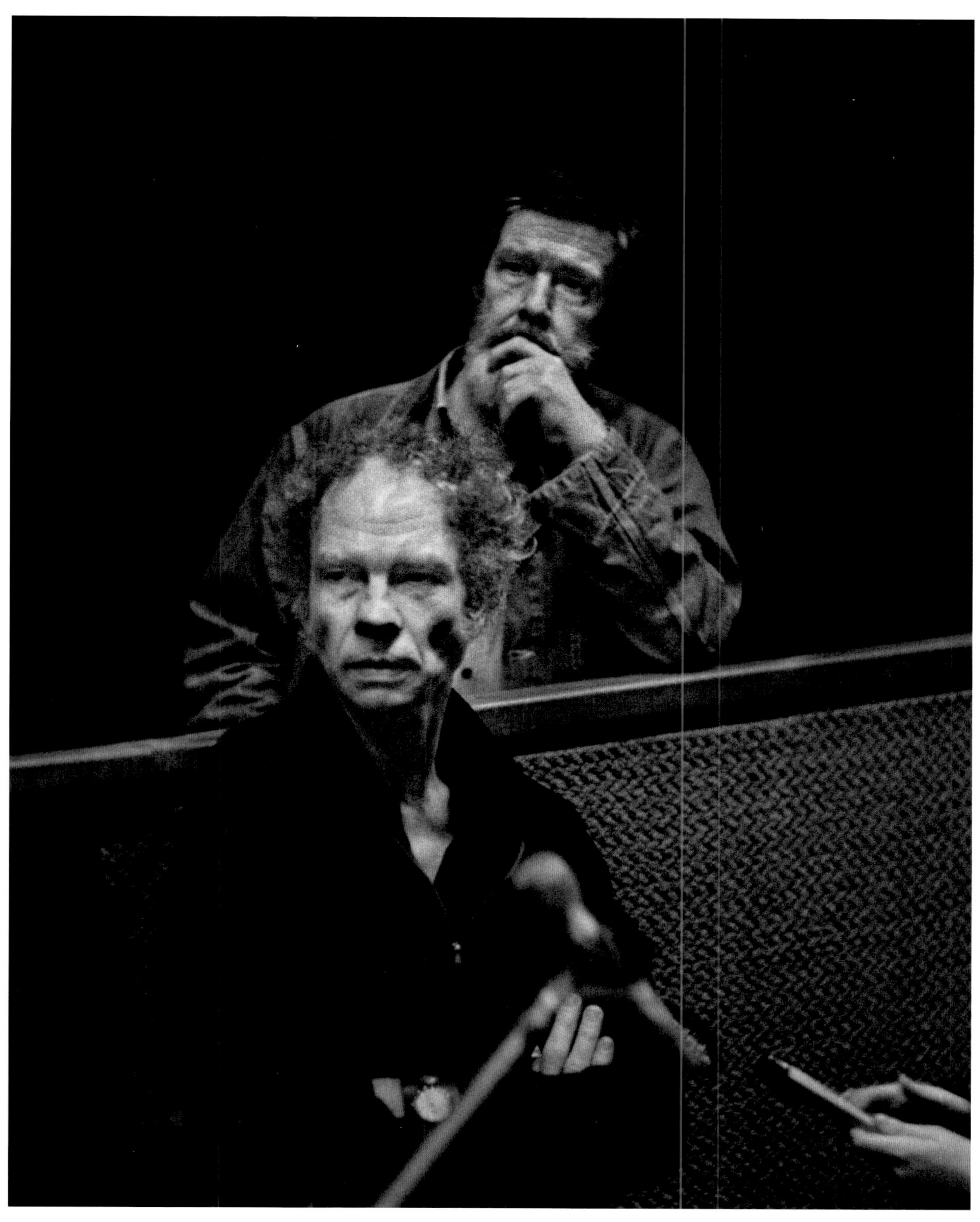

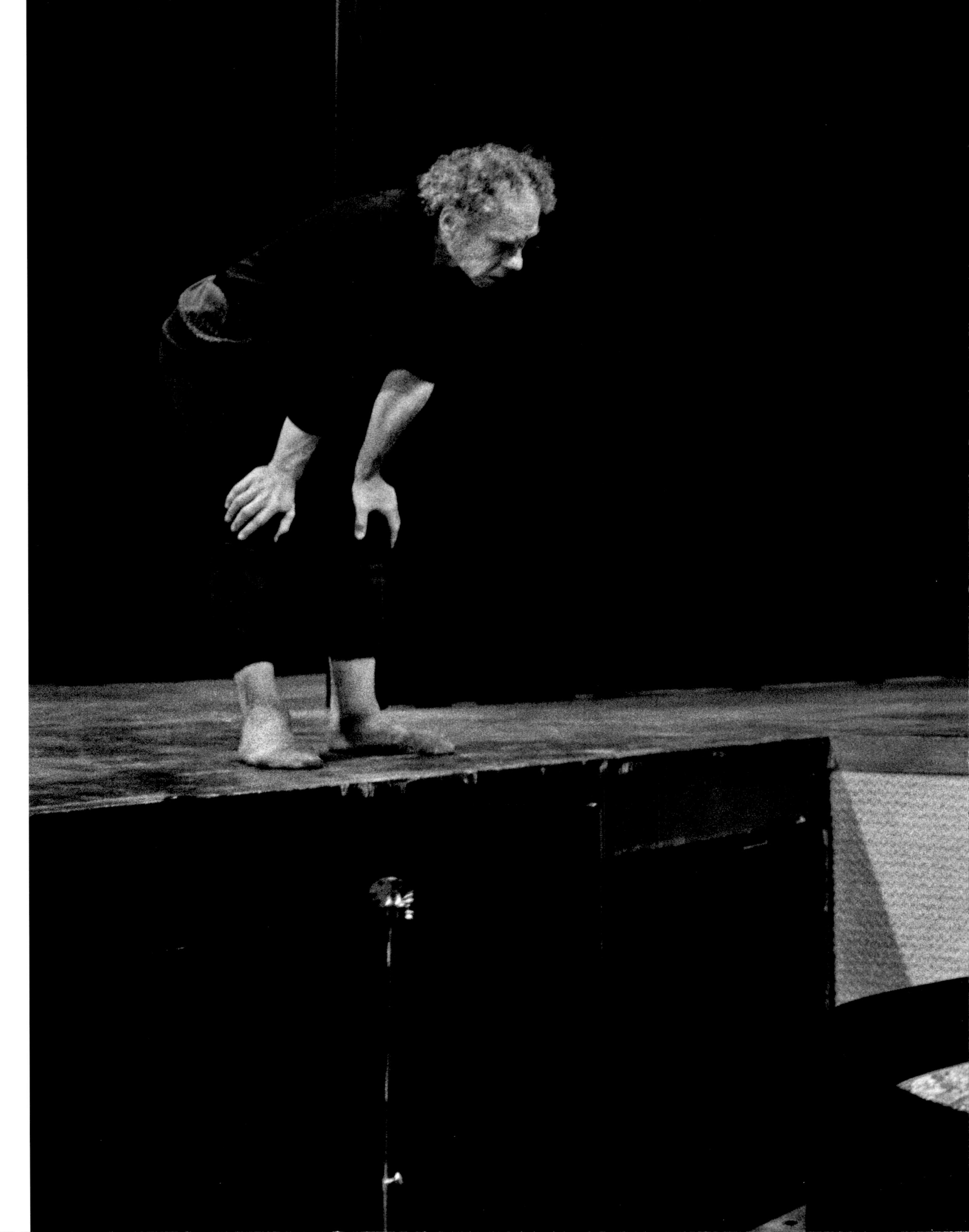

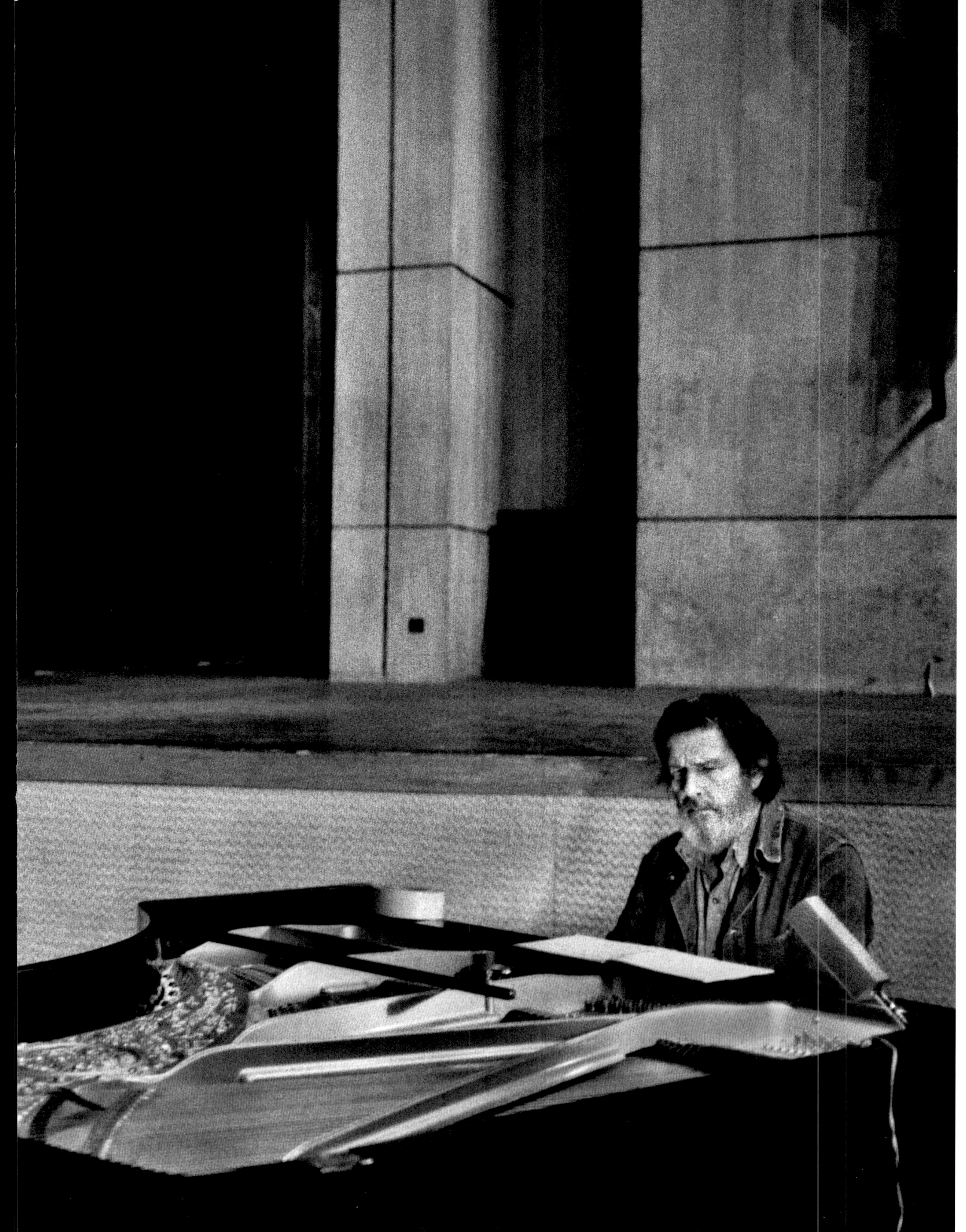

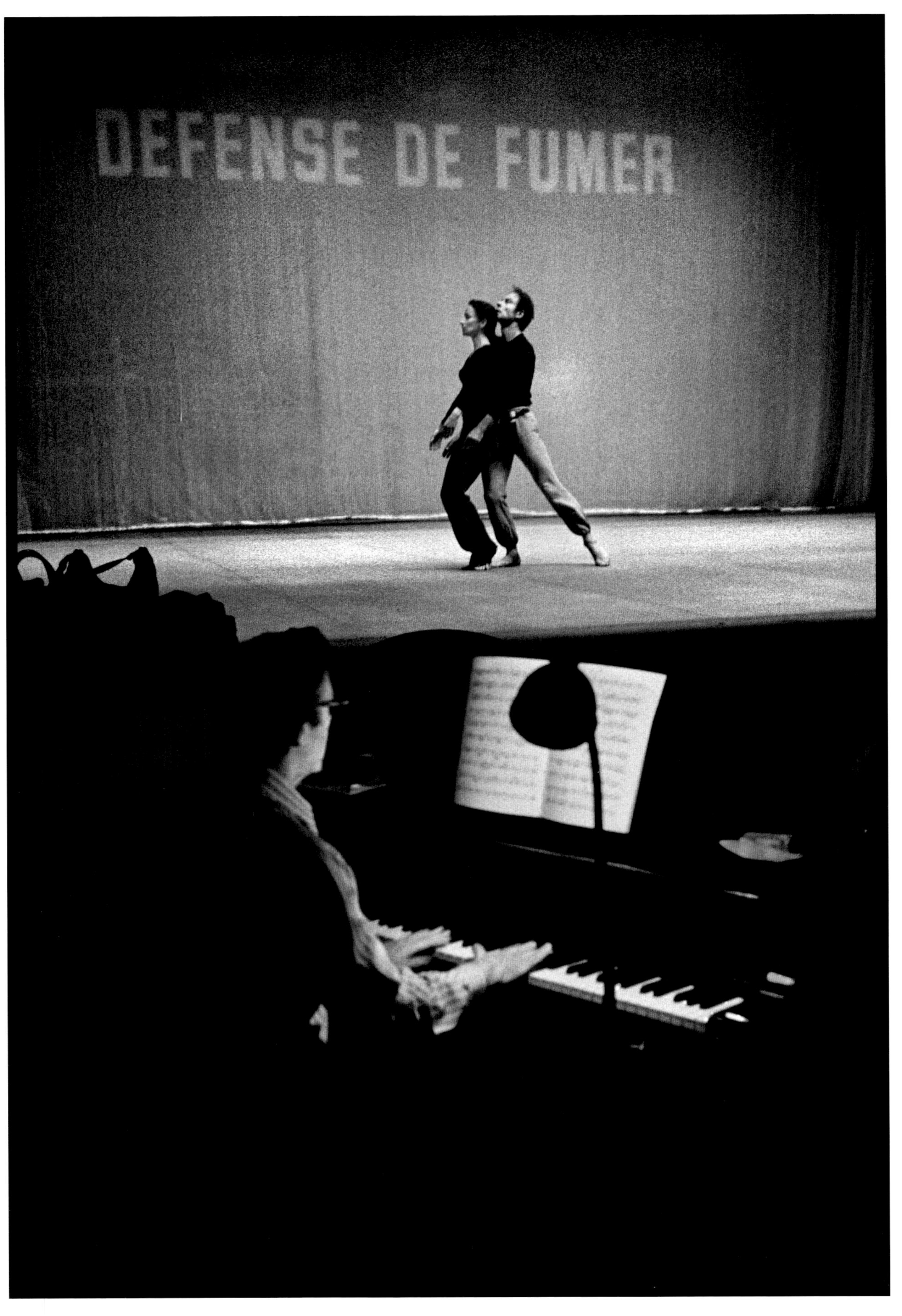
DEFENSE DE FUMER

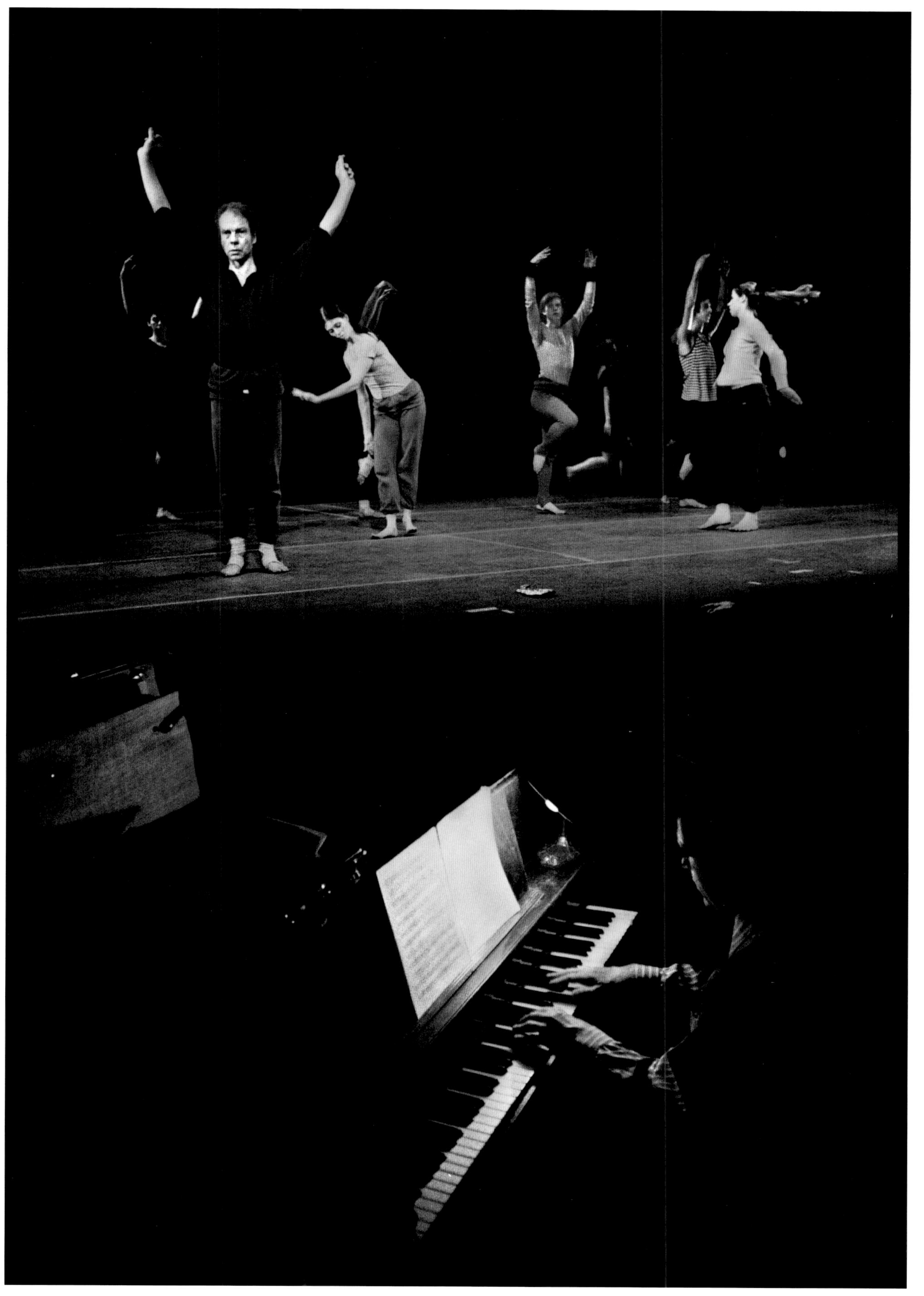

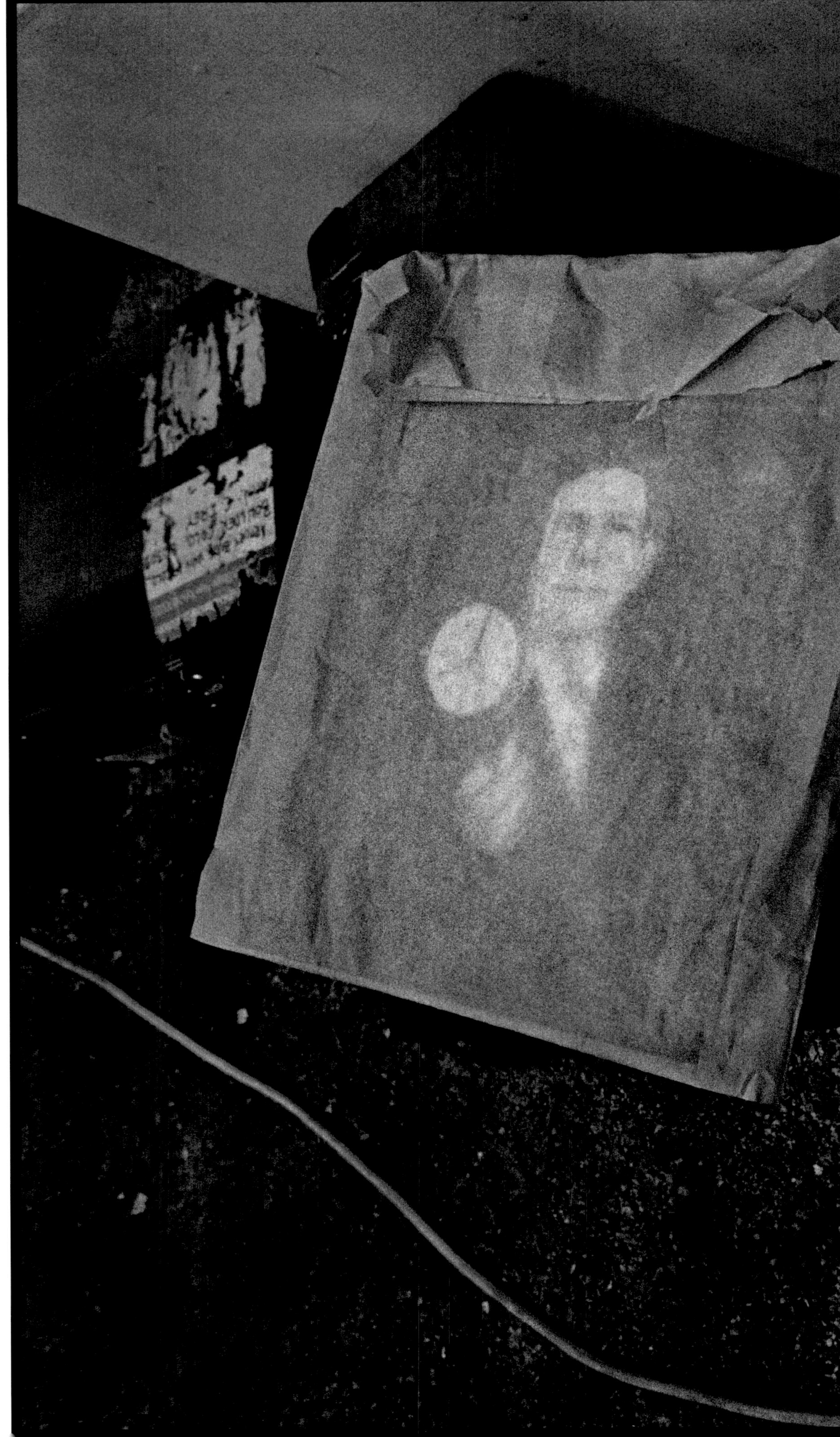

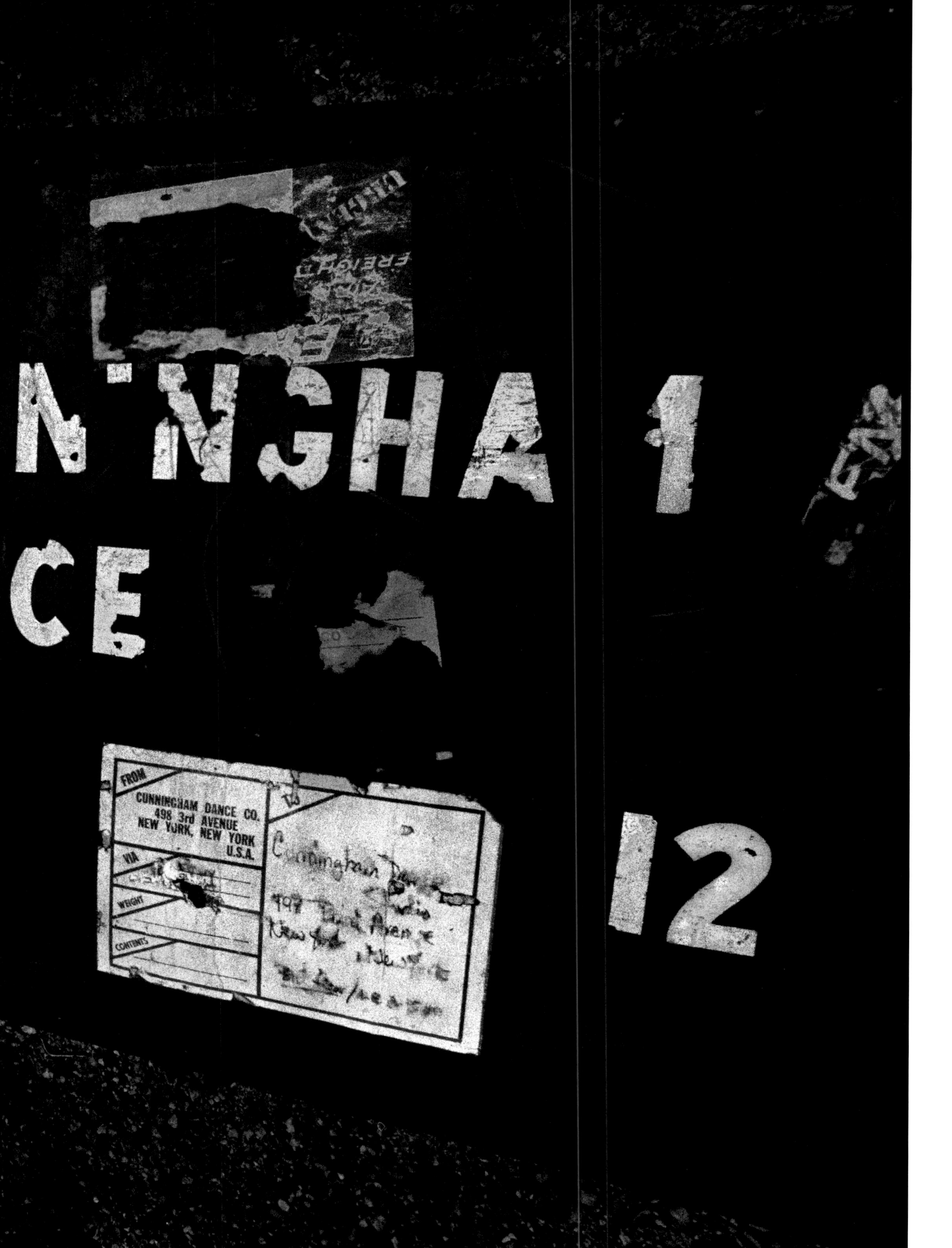
FROM
CUNNINGHAM DANCE CO.
498 3rd AVENUE
NEW YORK, NEW YORK
U.S.A.
VIA
WEIGHT
CONTENTS
TO
12

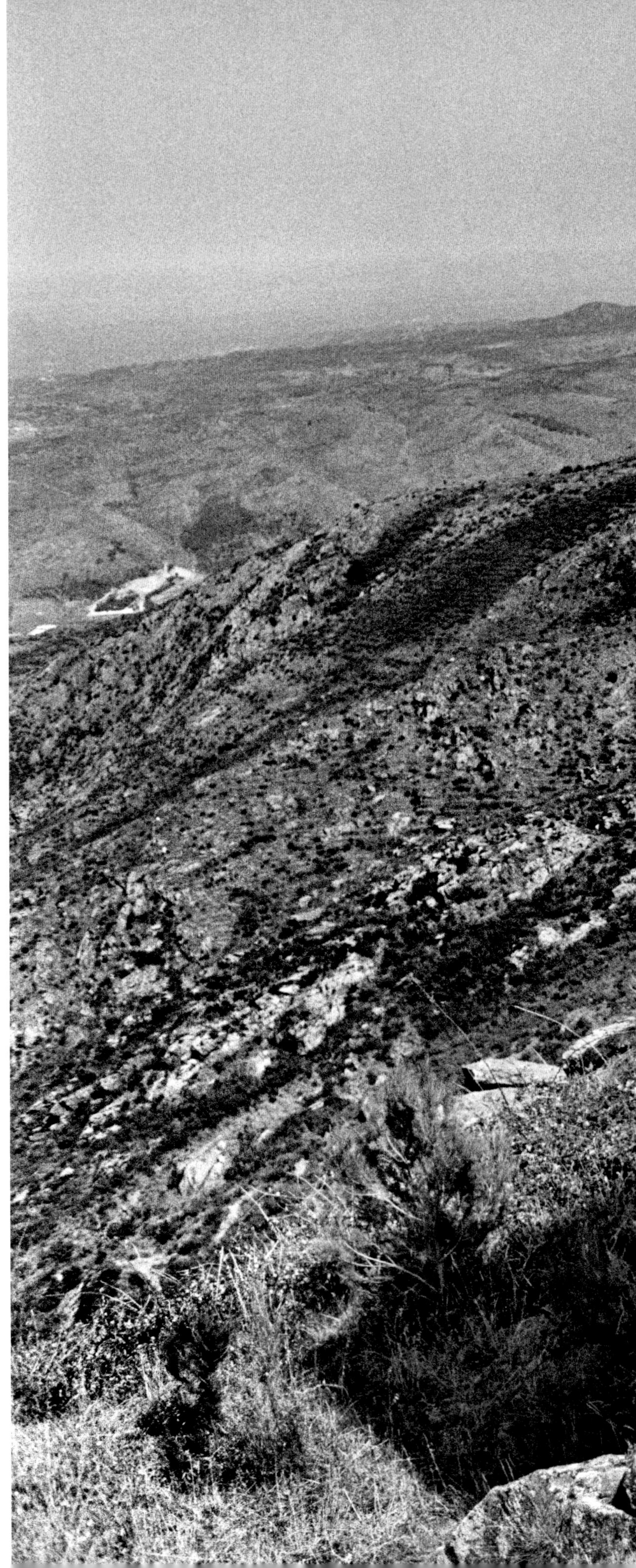

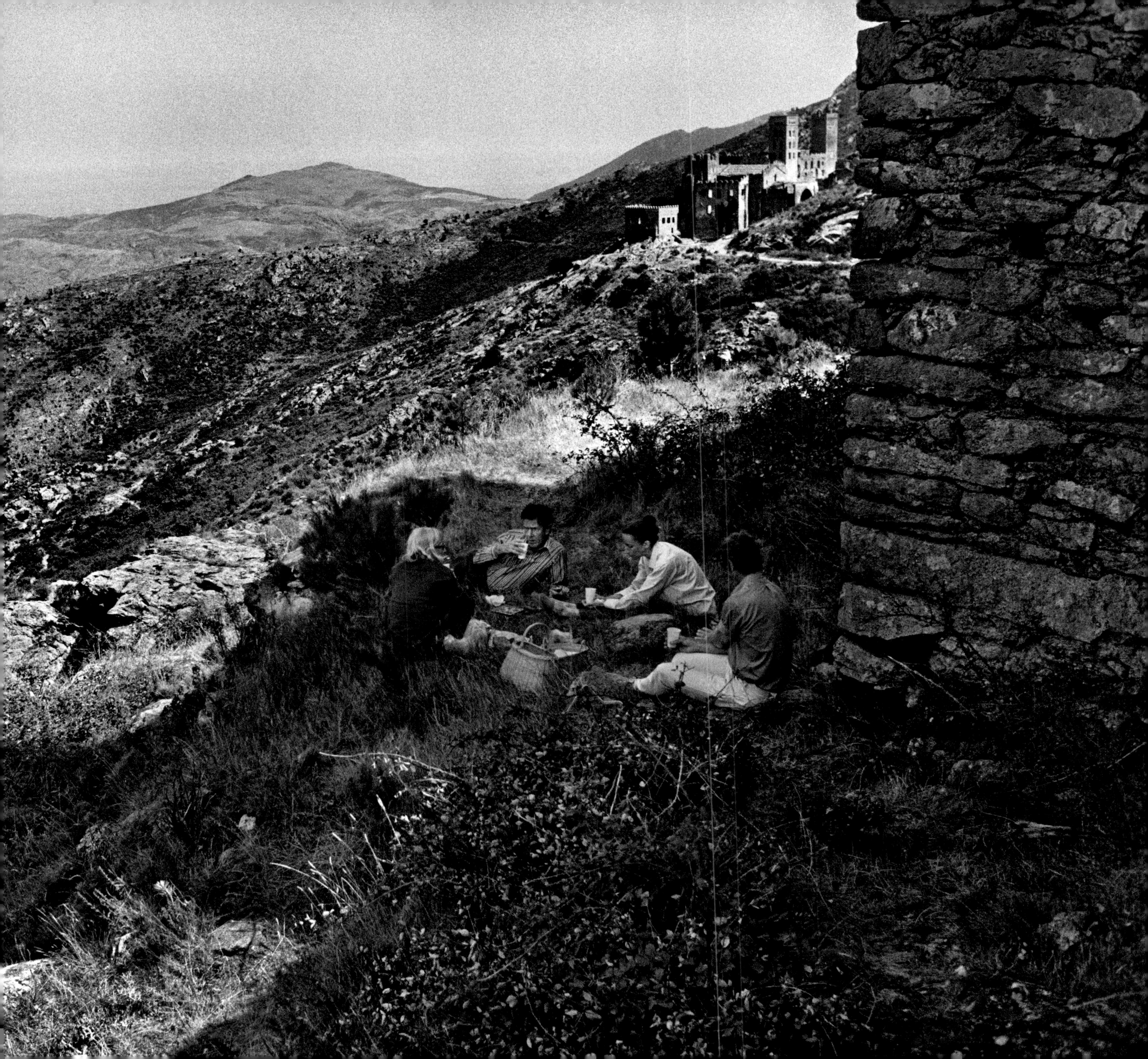

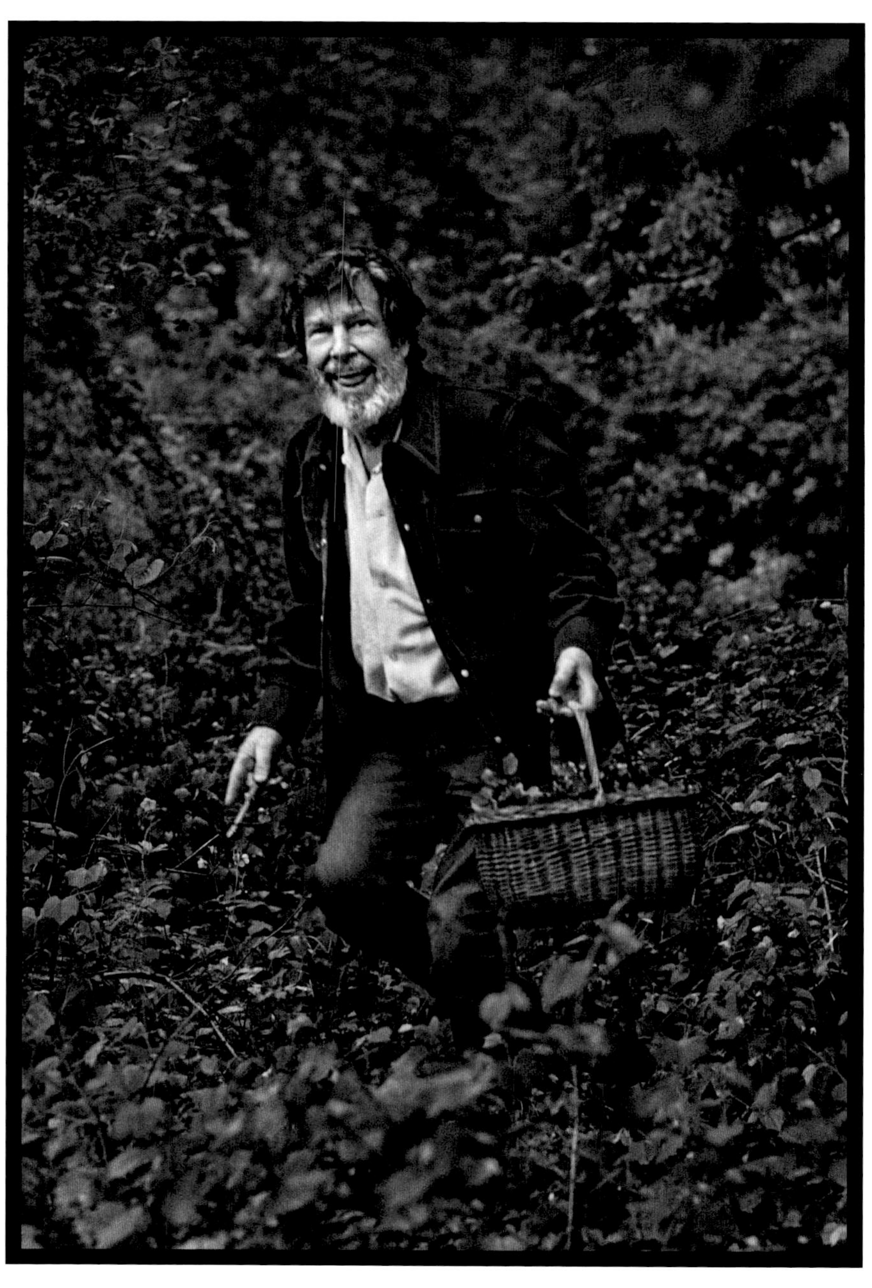

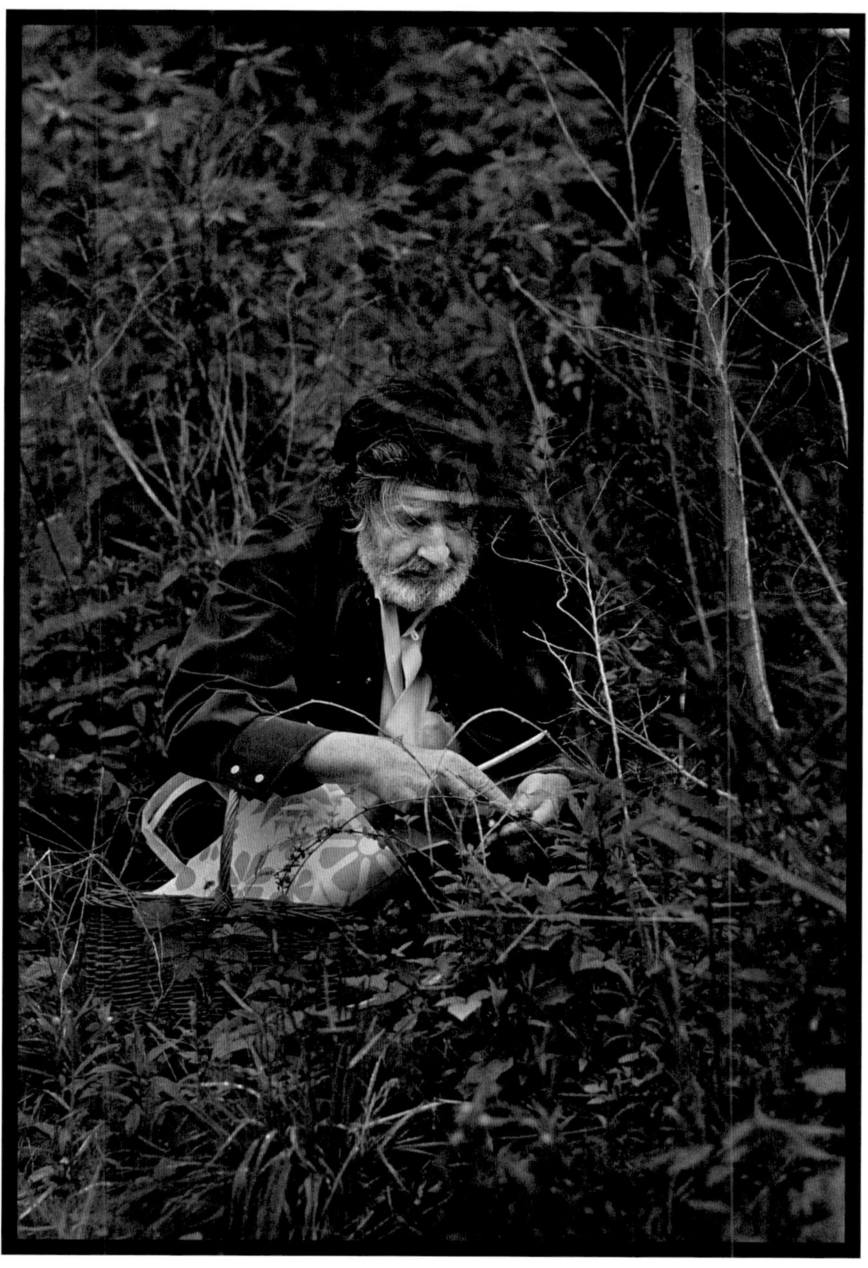

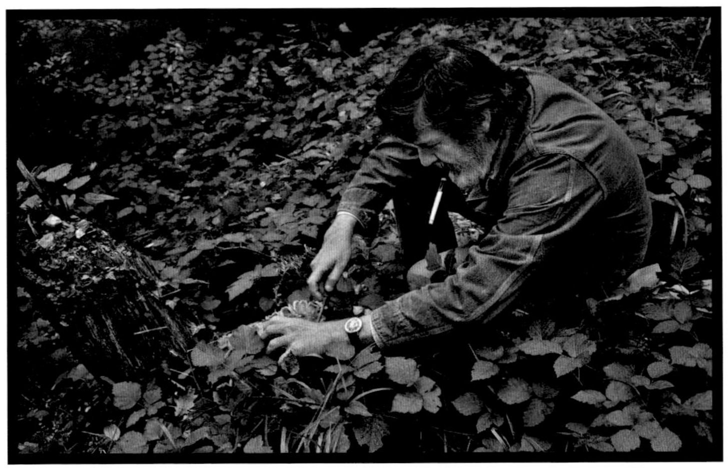

John and I were good friends
and performed one another's works
but did not truthfully influence each other—
the look and feel of our work
shared similarities
but the results were quite different.
John Cage was
an exceptionally friendly
and creative man,
in fact, uniquely so,
considering he was not only
a musician but a painter and a theorist.
His passion for mycology
brought him to
my aunt's house where,
preparing for an Italian TV game show,
we rehearsed
the Latin names of mushrooms.
He won,
and purchased a car
for the trips of Merce Cunningham
and his dance company.

— Sylvano Bussotti

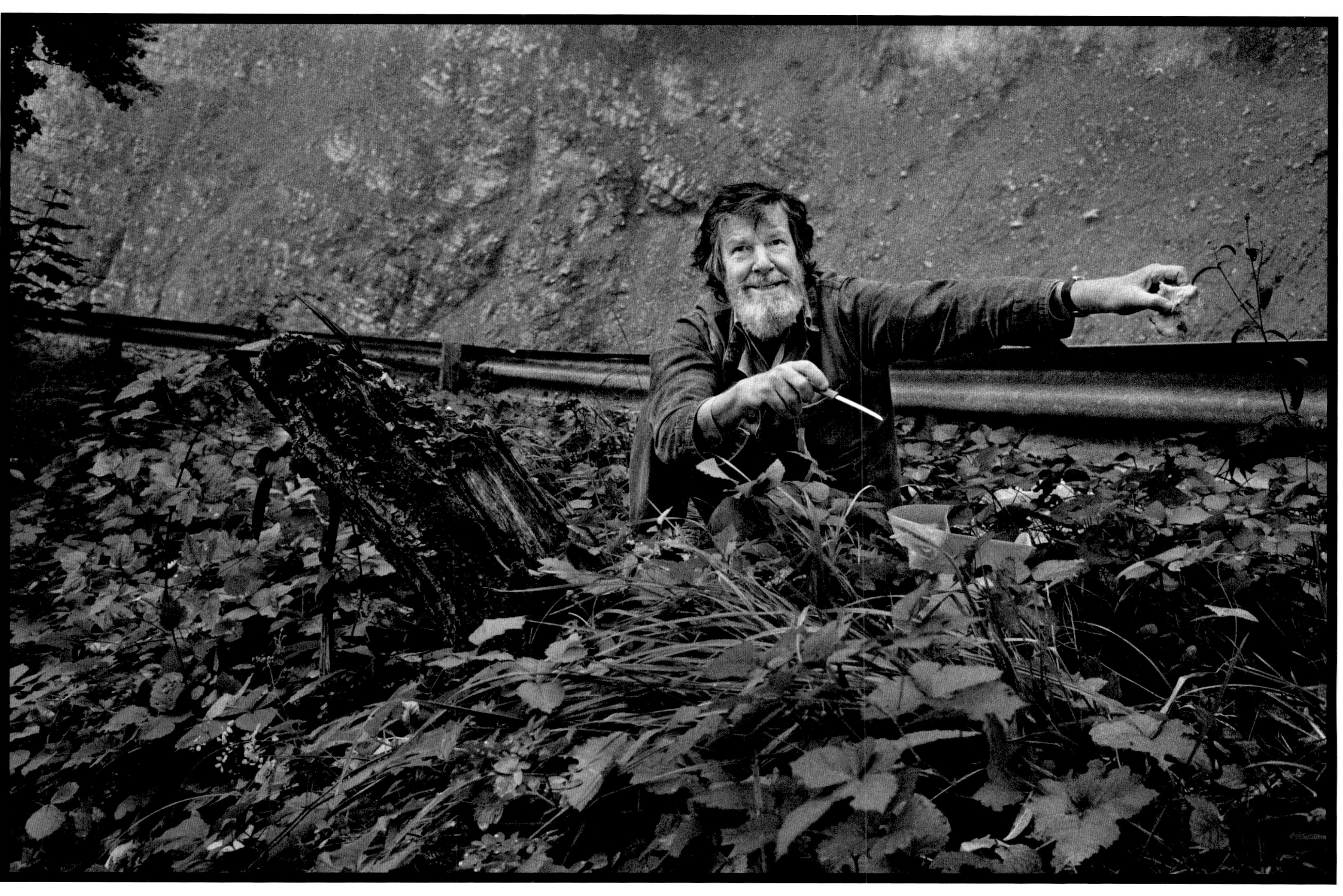

John Cage was at Jacob's Pillow and so was I.

In the Tea Garden, he was interviewed for awhile and then

took questions from a small, rapt crowd.

The final question was a simple, yes/no one that had to do with mushrooms.

Mr. Cage sat, alert for what seemed one hour (but was probably more like one minute).

After listening to nothing in particular: music from dance classes, kitchen clatter, birds, bees,

wind in the trees, gravel crunched under tires, typewriting, distant shouting,

dancers' footfalls, murmuring of passersby, airplanes, coughing, telephones ringing,

I heard his soft reply:

"No."

— Mark Morris

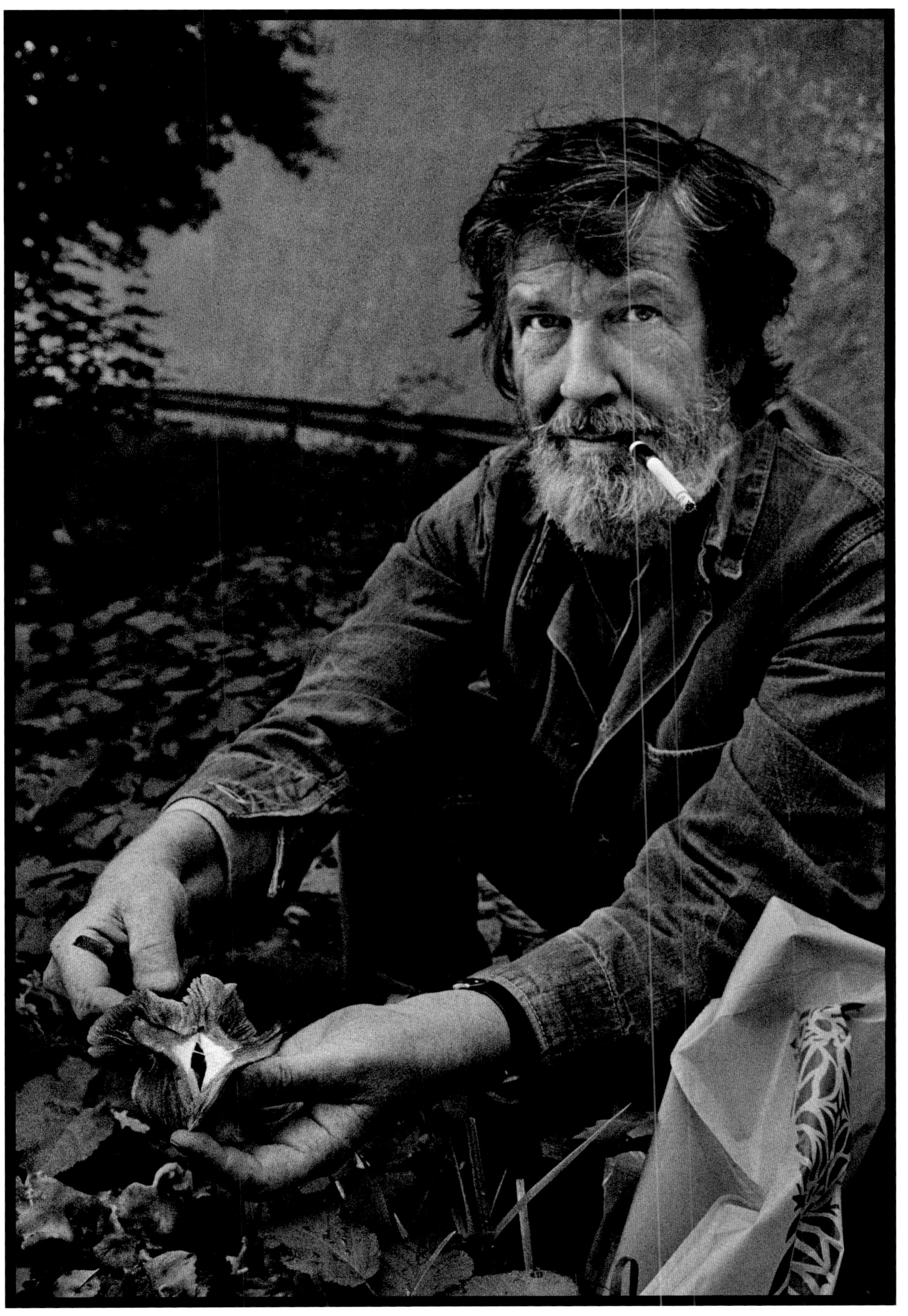

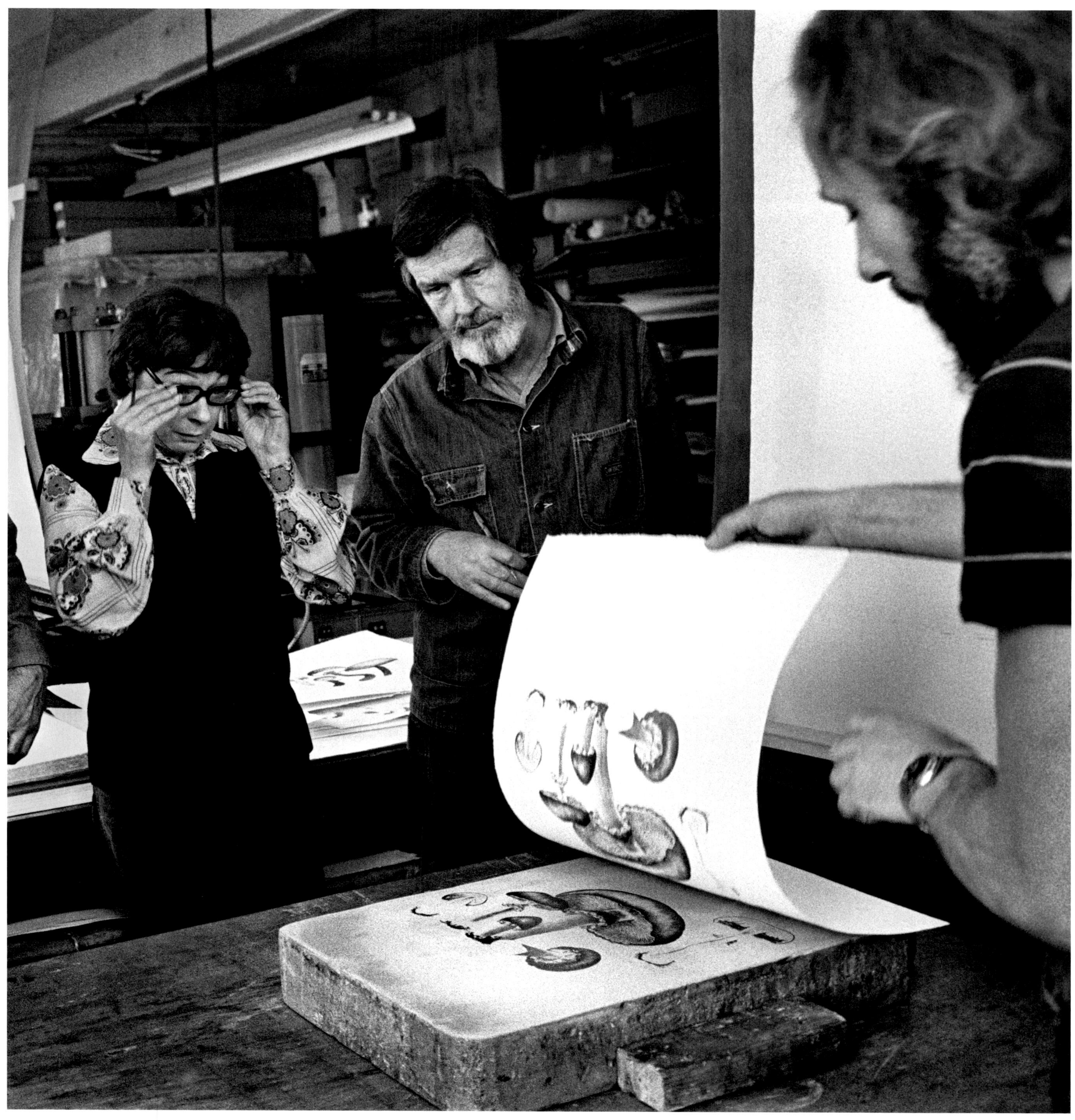

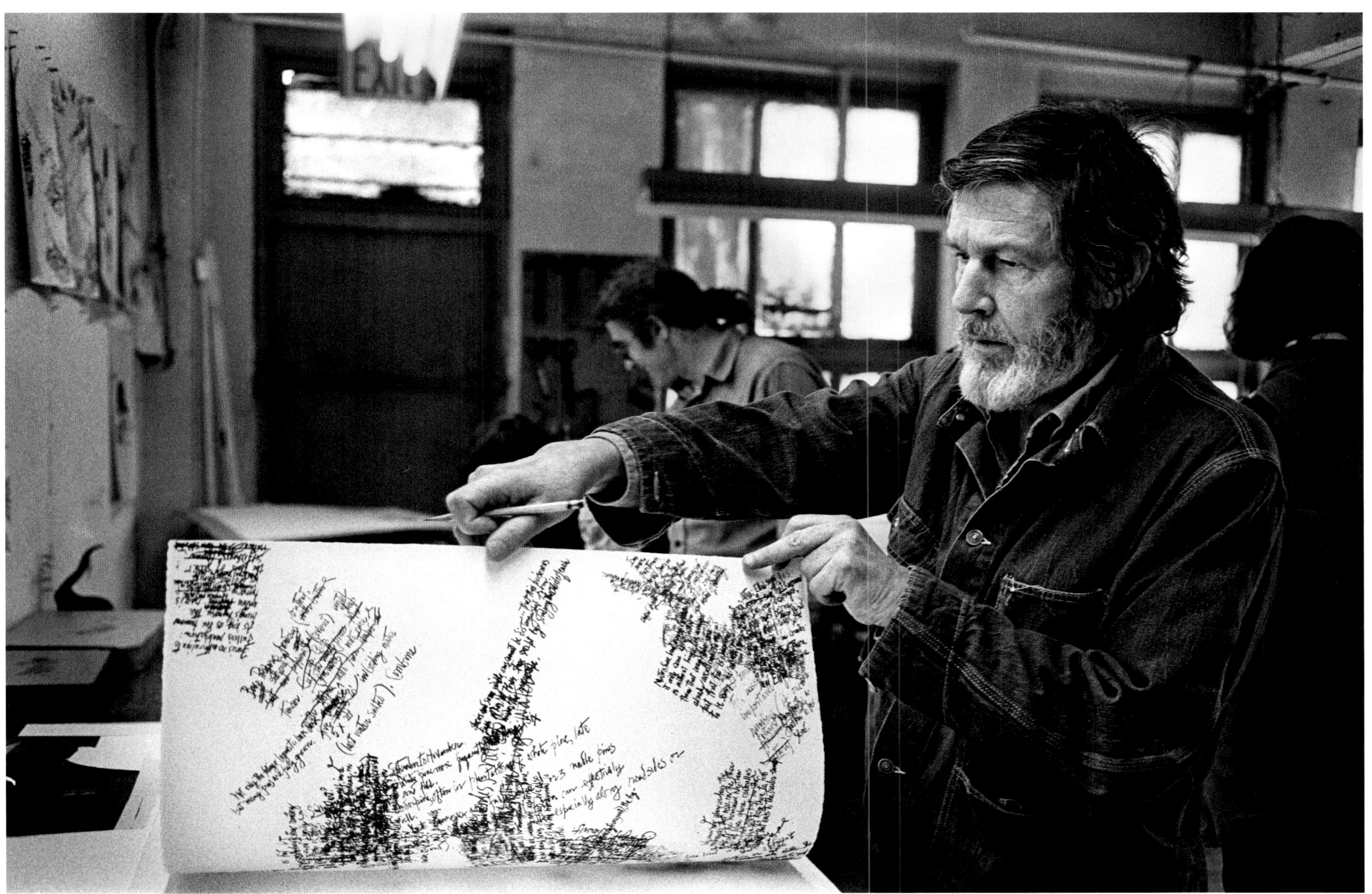

John Cage was a maverick,
an unbranded range animal he followed Susan Sontag's rubric:
do not seek society's kiss on your forehead,
and Steve Jobs: stay restless stay hungry,
far far away and long long before they uttered these suggestions.
He suffered perhaps not a bit.
Every glance was an invention. He thought different.
We died to know what he thought.
To be close to the glow helped.
The guessing the disagreement with solutions or answers was stunning.
"I have nothing to say and I'm saying it"
Yes he was and did in Silence.

— Elizabeth Streb

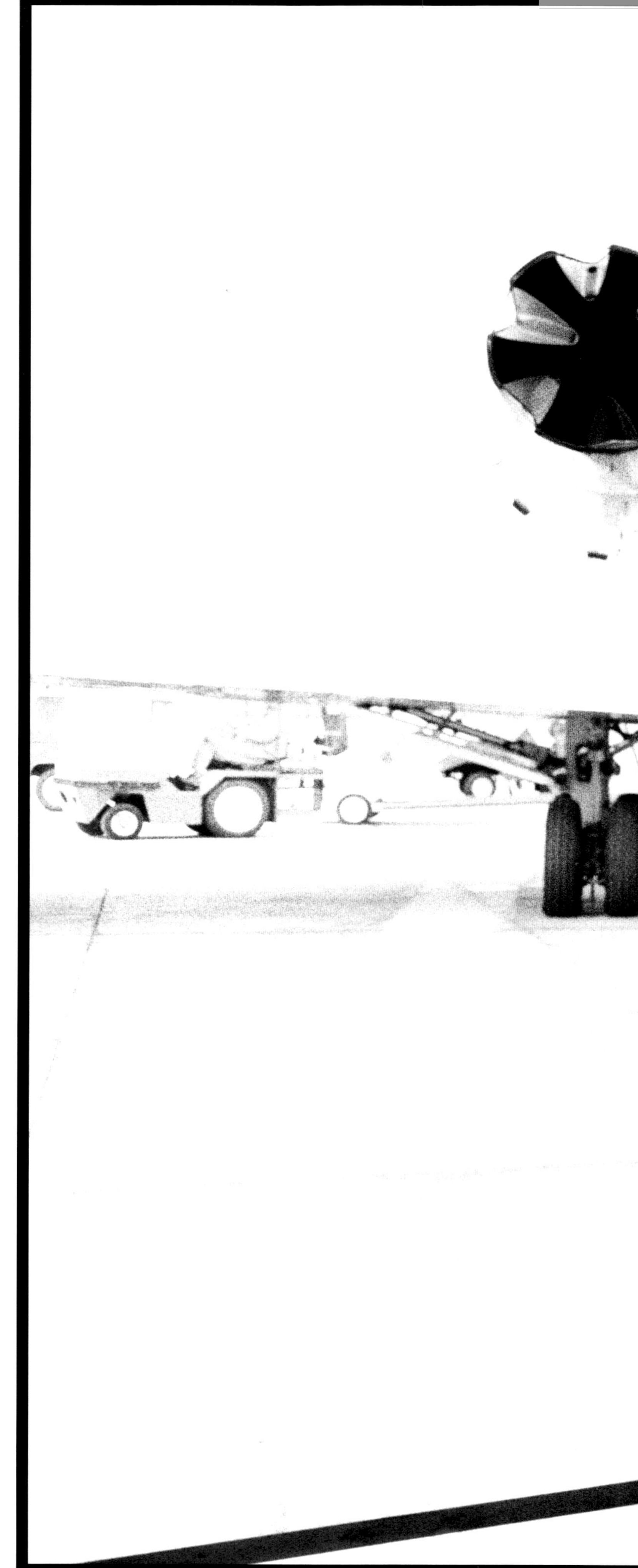

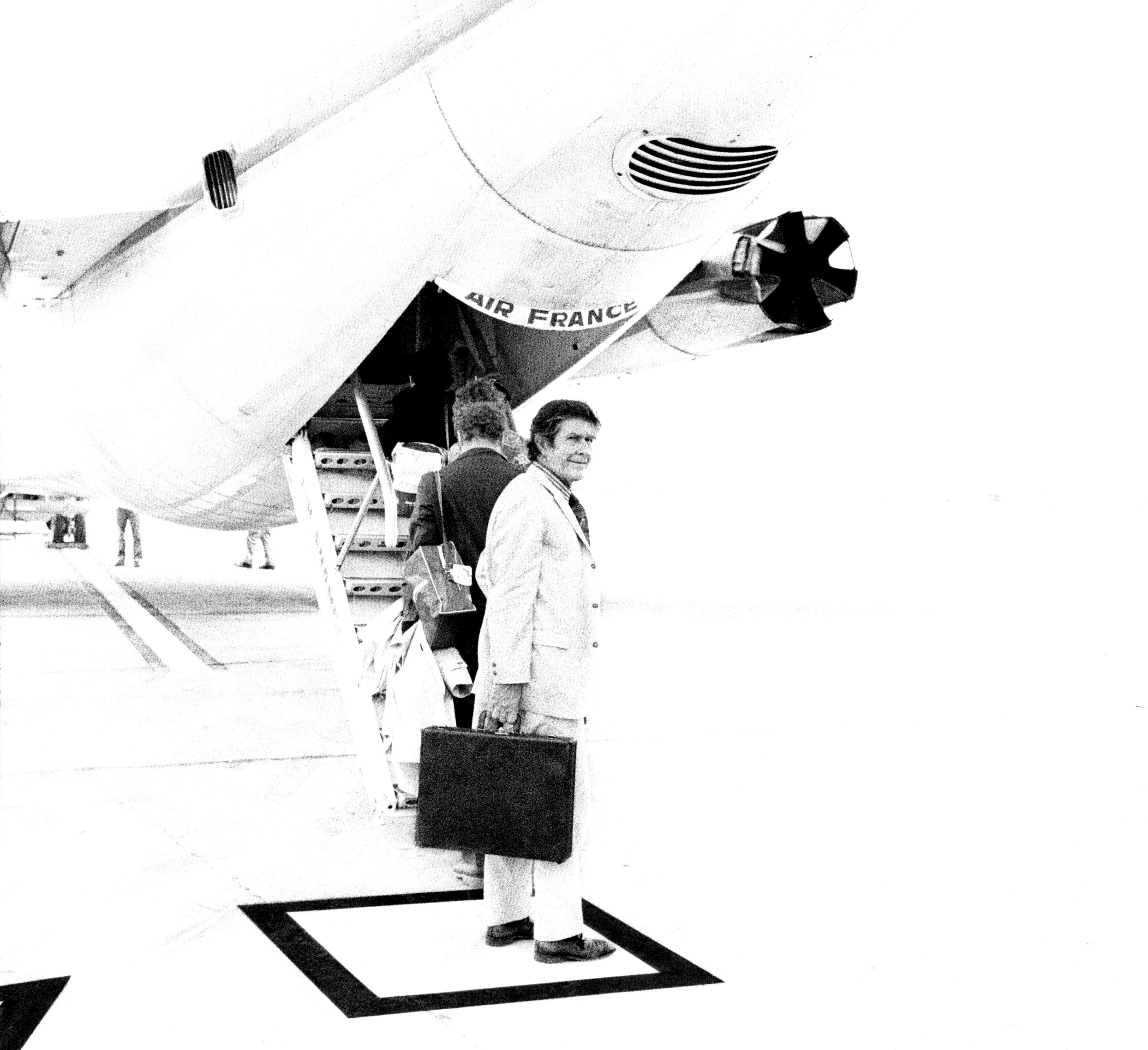
AIR FRANCE

John Cage was not going to Washington. I asked him why not.

I was going to Washington where Merce Cunningham was to be a recipient of the Kennedy Center Honors and his company would dance from *Native Green*. I thought that my going could be an expression of my support and affection for Cunningham and his work.

"Why are you not going, John?"

"I might have to be photographed with a politician."

— Jasper Johns

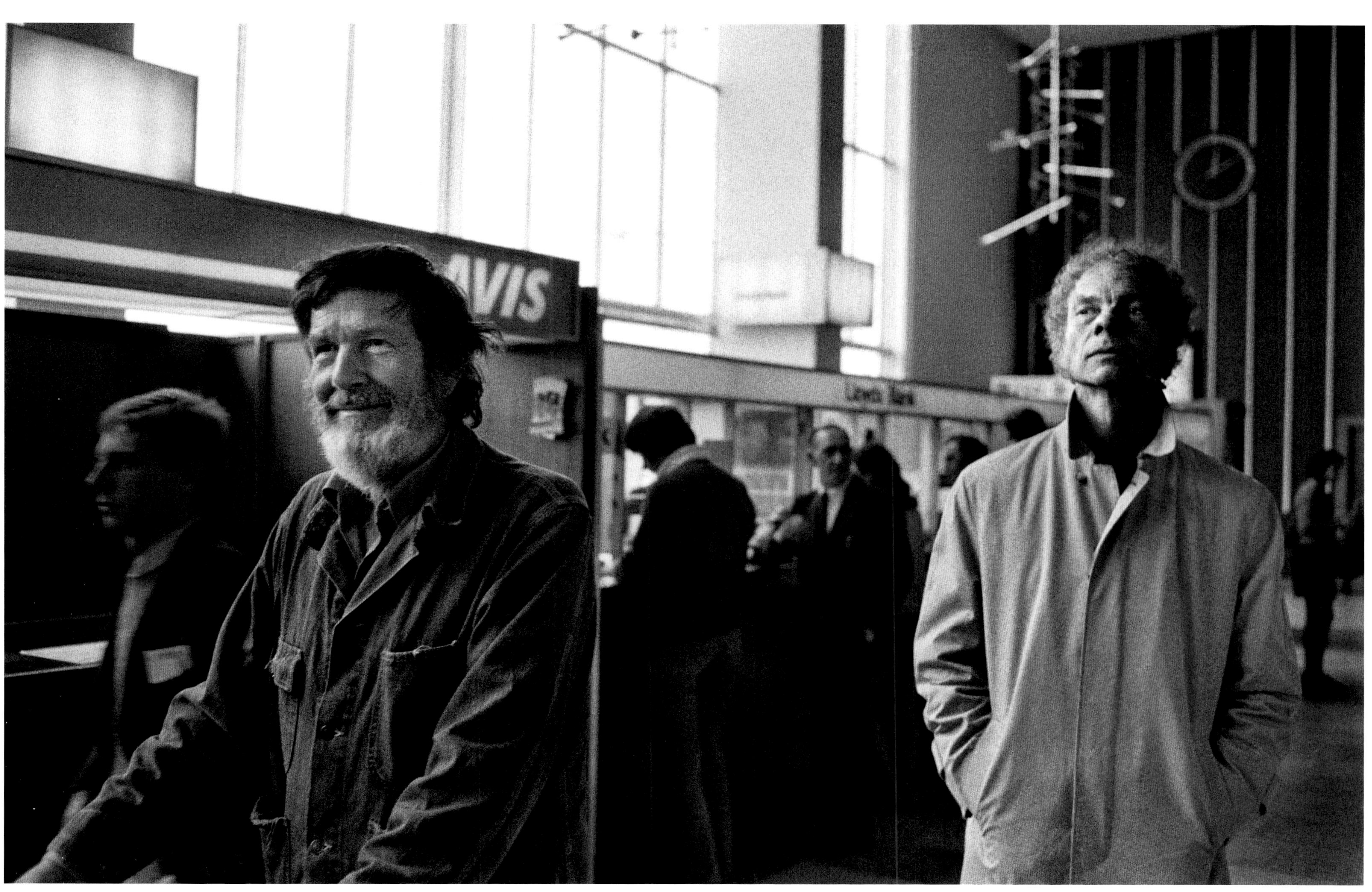
AVIS

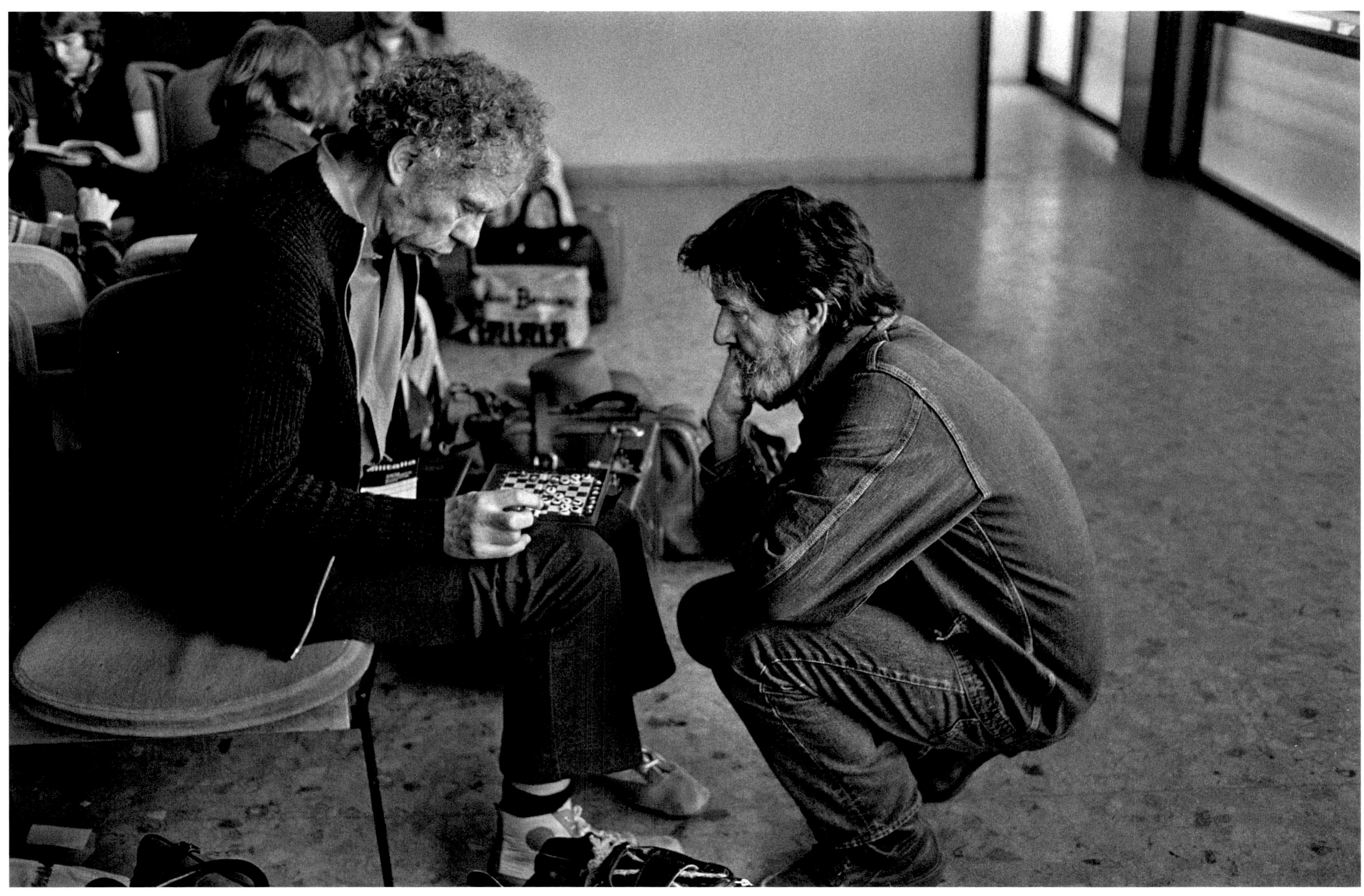

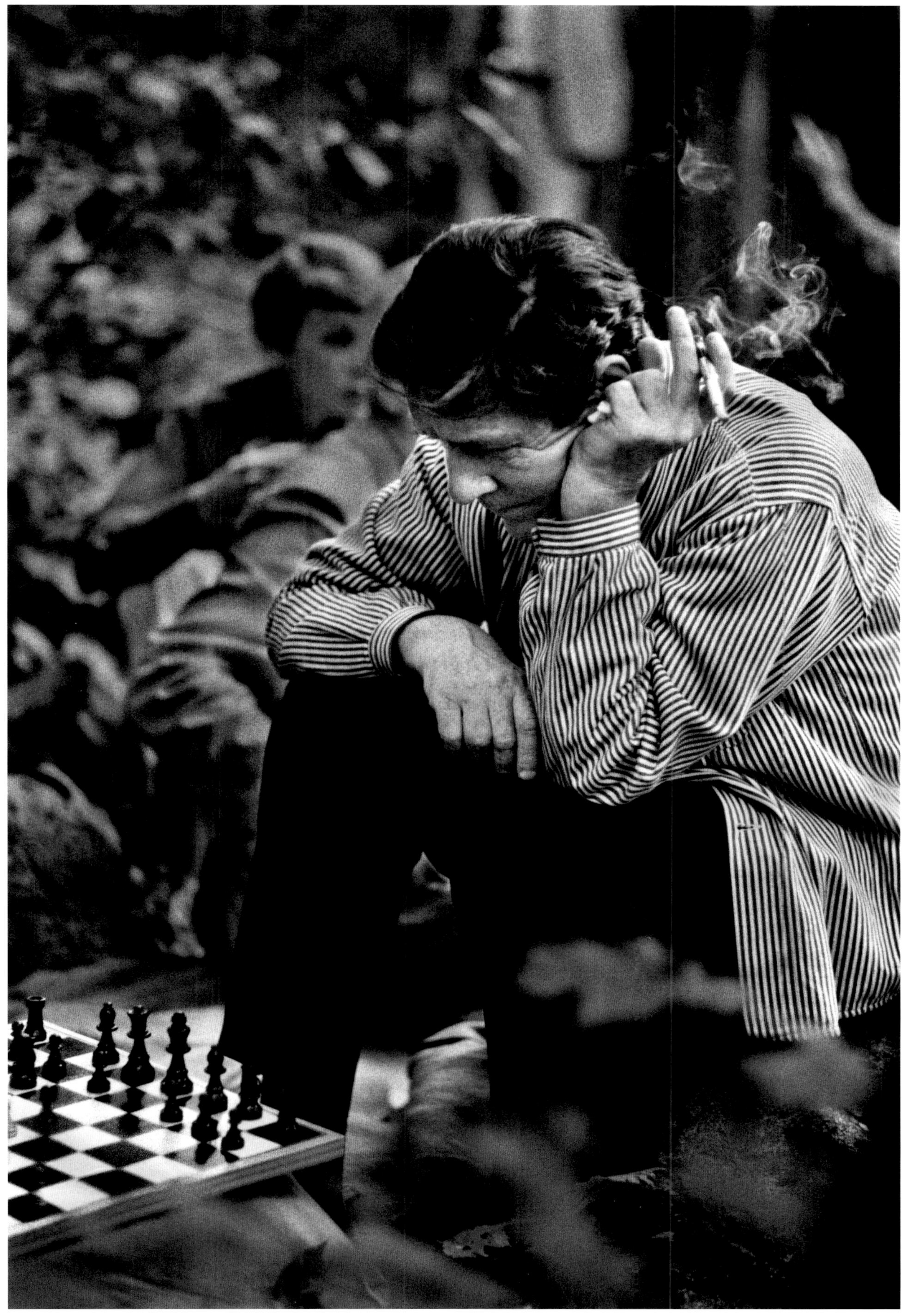

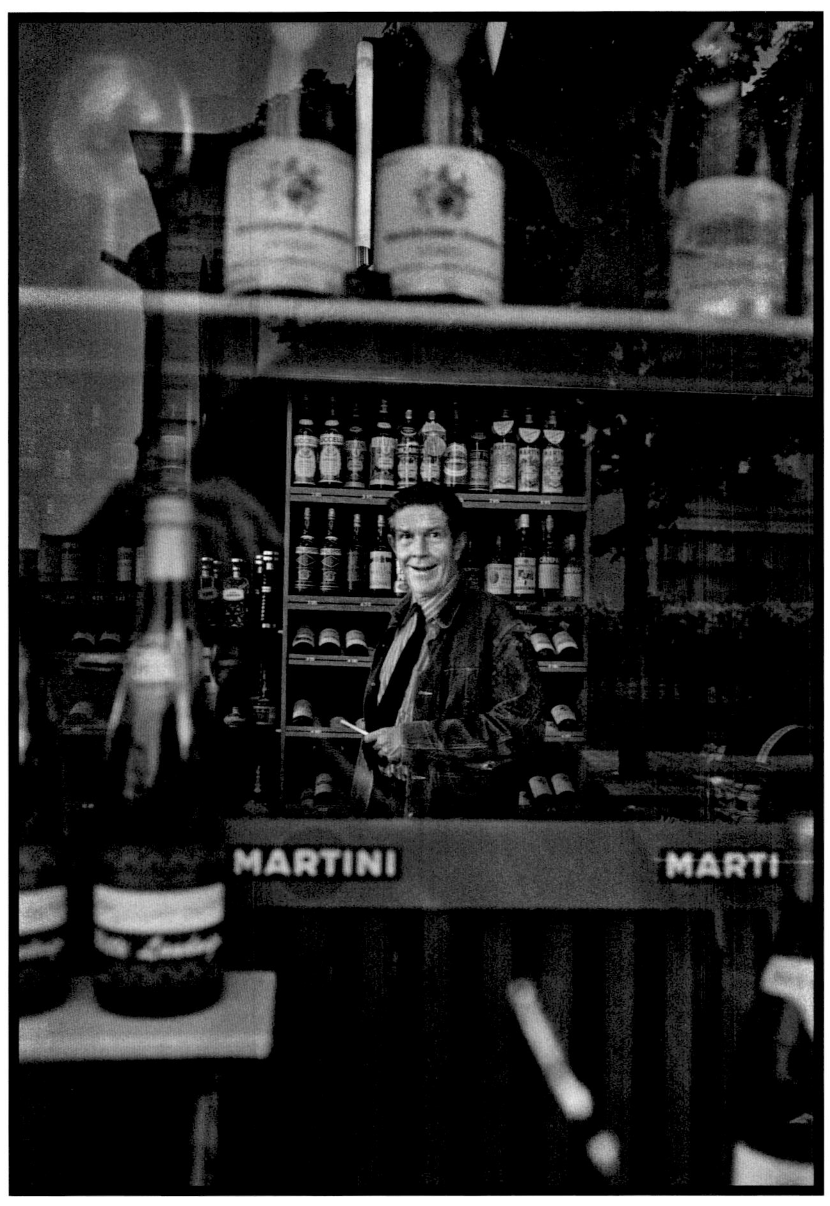

John Cage was
a mischievous,
ever present sub-text,
influence,
and provocation
for me.
Much as I tried to evade
and counter his influence,
I finally had to admit
that without John's laughing face
and Till Eulenspiegel–like utterances,
I would not have developed,
for better or for worse,
into the artist I became.
I see his laugh,
tongue lurking on his lower lip,
eyes atwinkle
with the sheer pleasure
of pronouncing his conundrums.
He could be indignant
when dismissed,
but was one of the
most impassioned artists
I've ever met,
serious to a fault,
even when harmonizing
his blenders.

— Yvonne Rainer

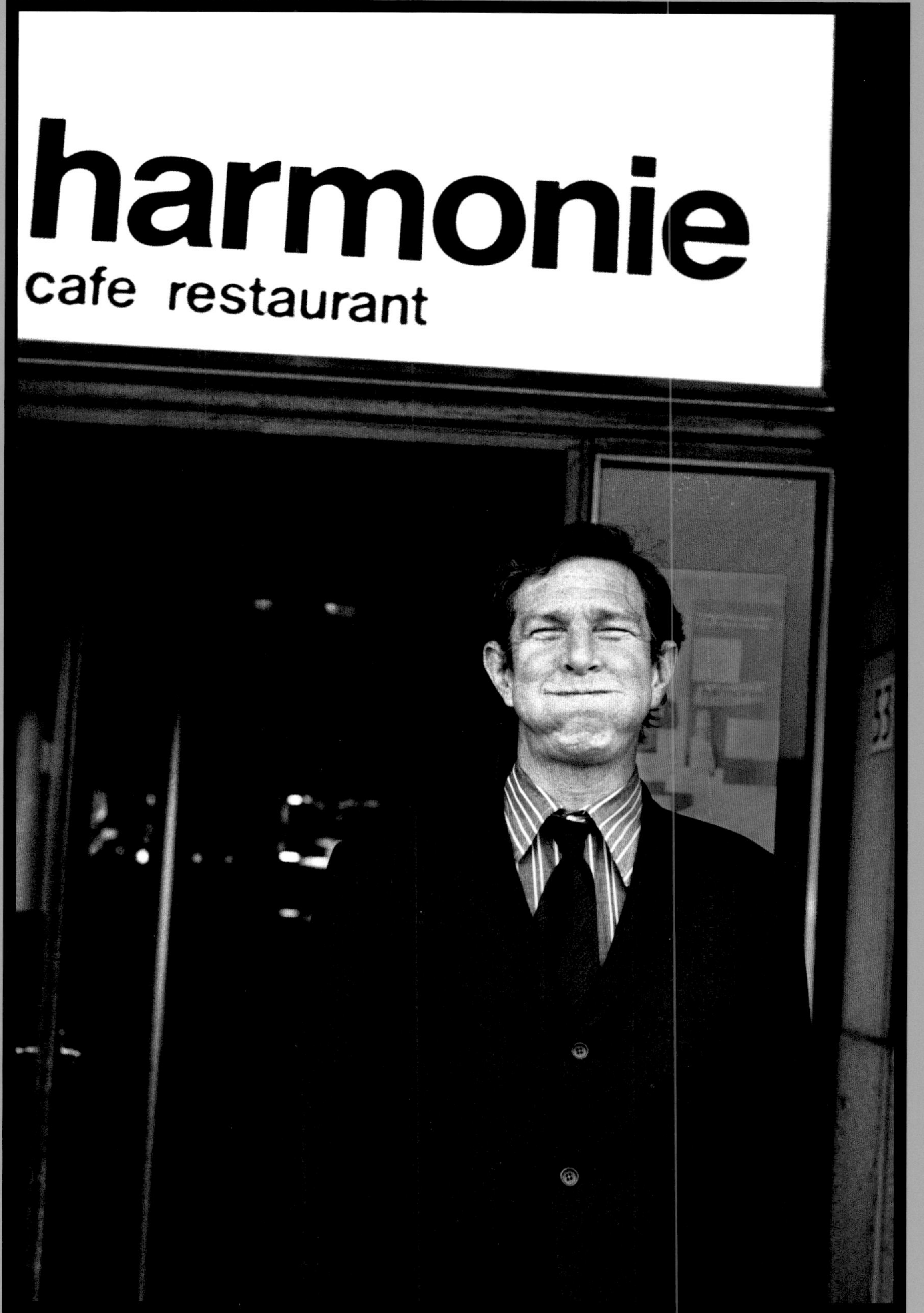
harmonie
cafe restaurant

In the 1950s I was a teenager in the Deep South
where even classical music was an alien world.
I then discovered someone who dared proclaim all sounds music! John Cage
was my liberator, musical freedom fighter,
a loveable anarchist anyone would want
as their wild and crazy uncle.
He was the nicest famous composer I ever knew.
He inspired me by his leadership, courage, and support
to dash into the fray without being afraid.
Even now, what greater comfort is there than knowing
no matter how radical the idea or musical plan,
he's still out there taking the hardest hits.

— Stephen Montague

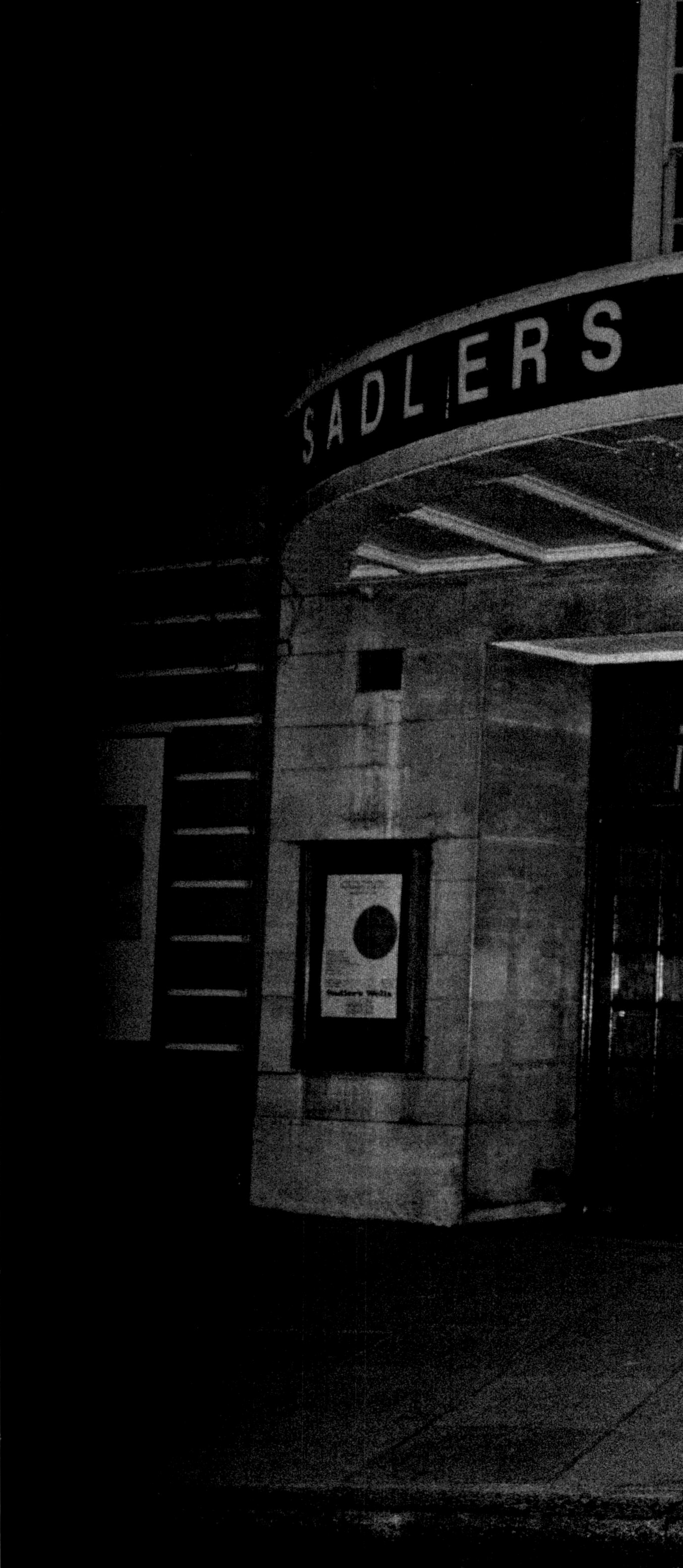

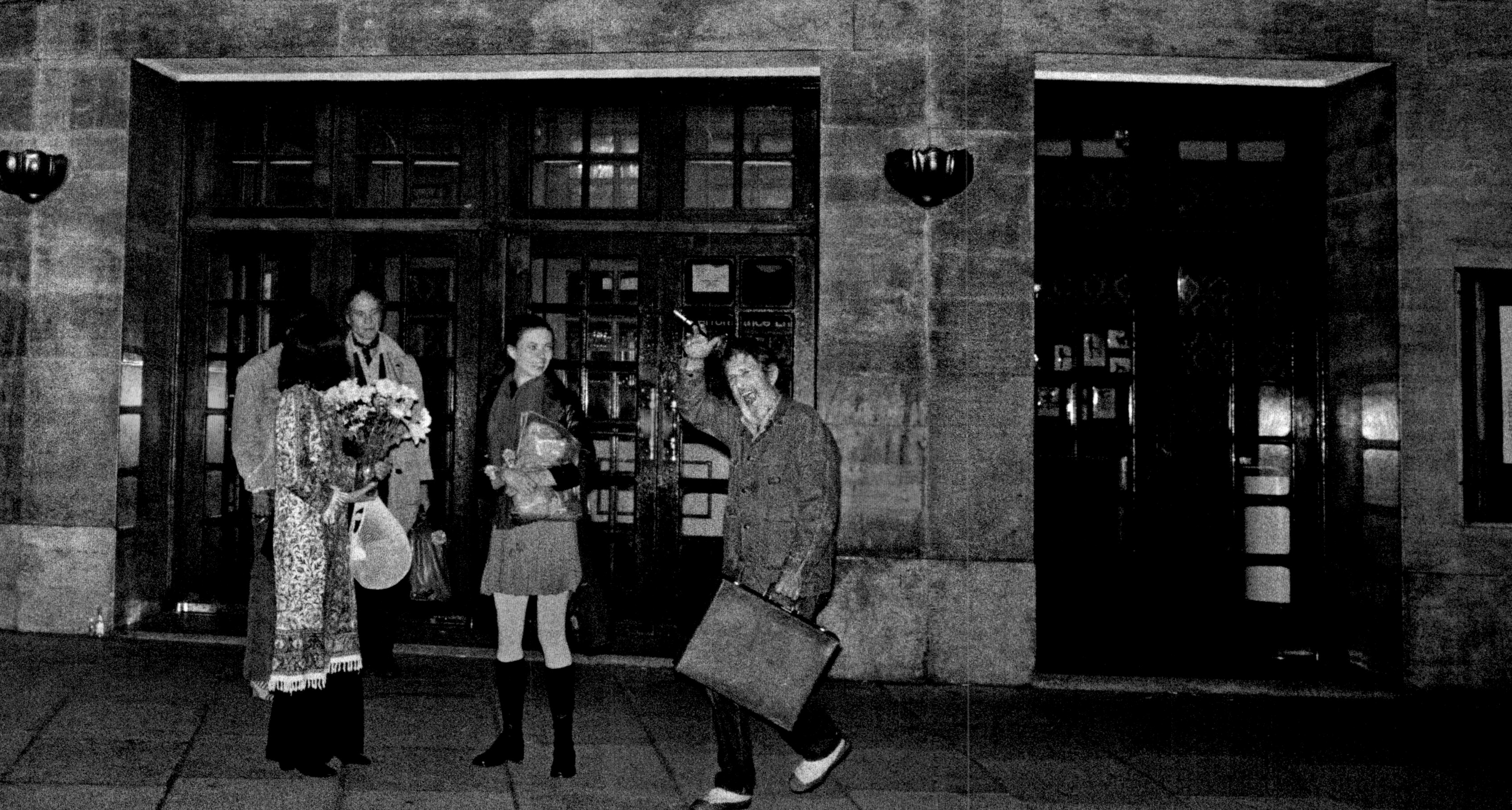
ELLS THEATRE

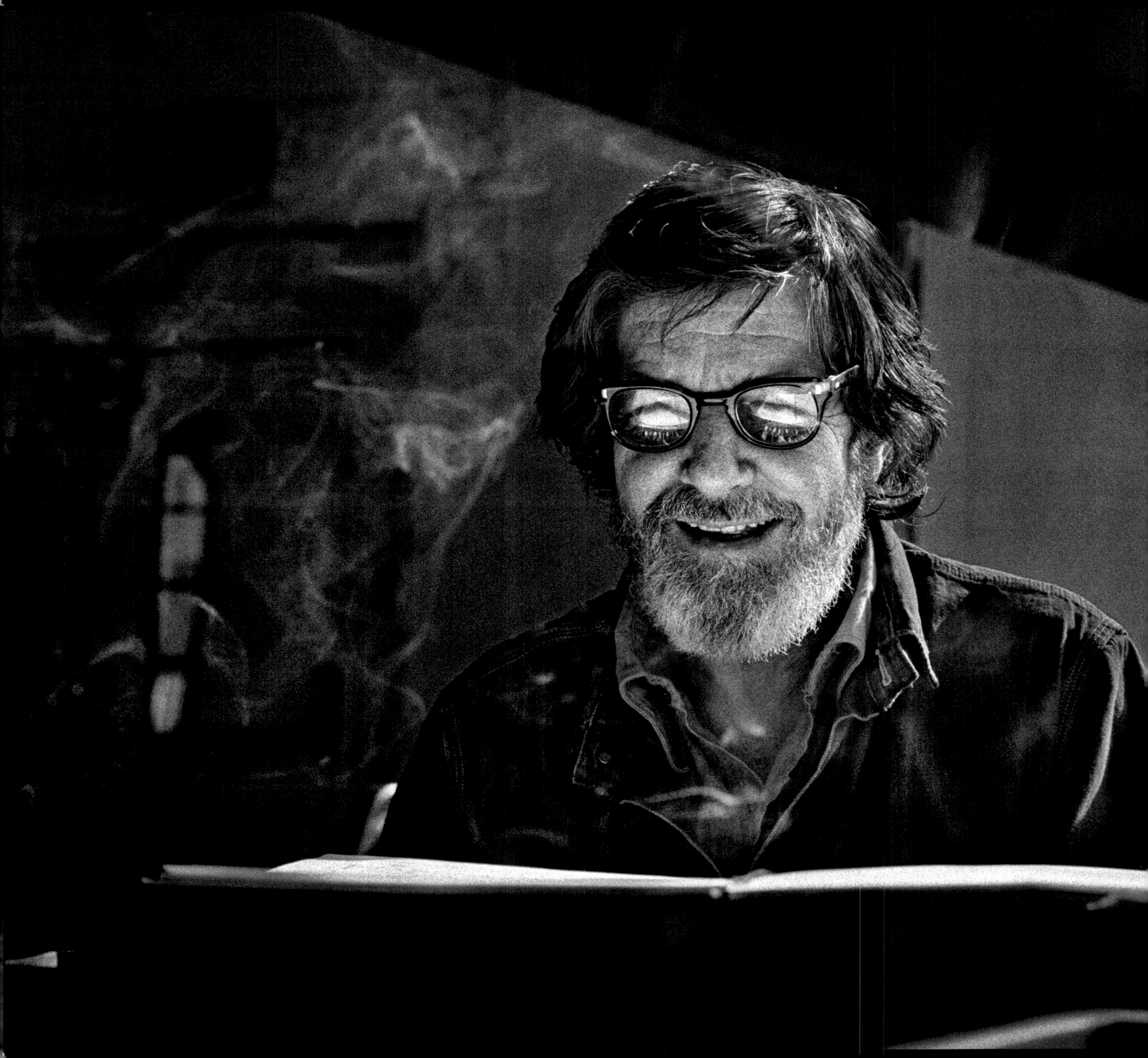

The first thing
I liked about John Cage
was the combination of his artistic freedom
and his last name.

The second thing
I liked was how difficult his music could be
and how easy he could be.

The third thing
was that he was a composer
and I was a poet,
and so I could get energy from his work
without seeming to owe him much.

The fourth thing
was that he allowed me to laugh more, invisibly.

The fifth thing
was that I knew John Cage was great
and he made me feel
I didn't have to know why.

— Ron Padgett

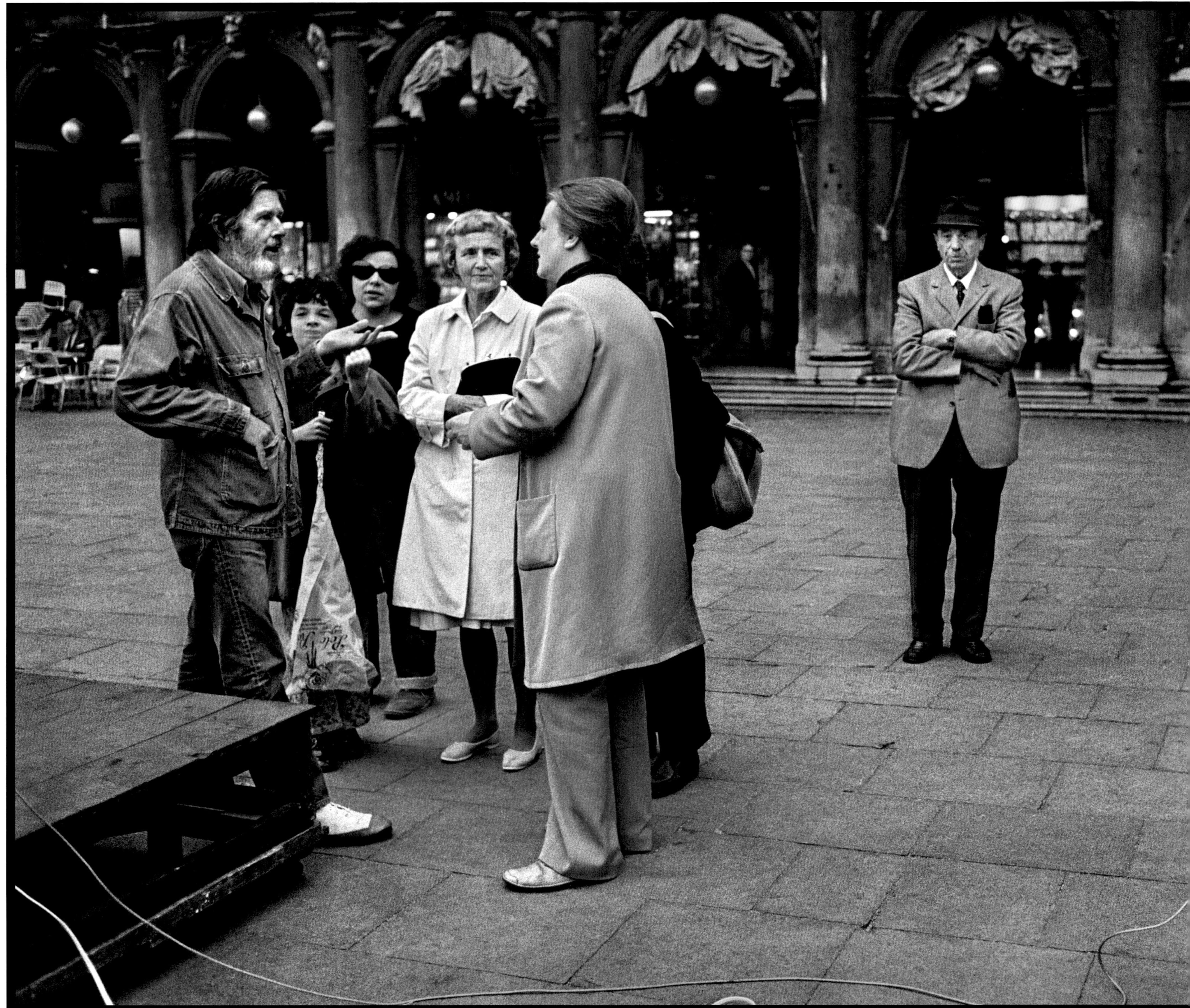

I met him by chance. he'd already been dead for
some years.
Now, when I find a particular material or object I see
its possibilities
as something quite different than before. The simple
has become
complex and the opposite too. He reminds me that
playfulness
is a serious business and chance an invaluable kind
of alchemy.
Every time I bump into him I'm struck by the clarity
and generosity
of his ideas. Then I realize how little I know or
understand.
What an invaluable position to be in. Nothing to say
and still saying it.
John Cage was John Cage.

— Alex Julyan

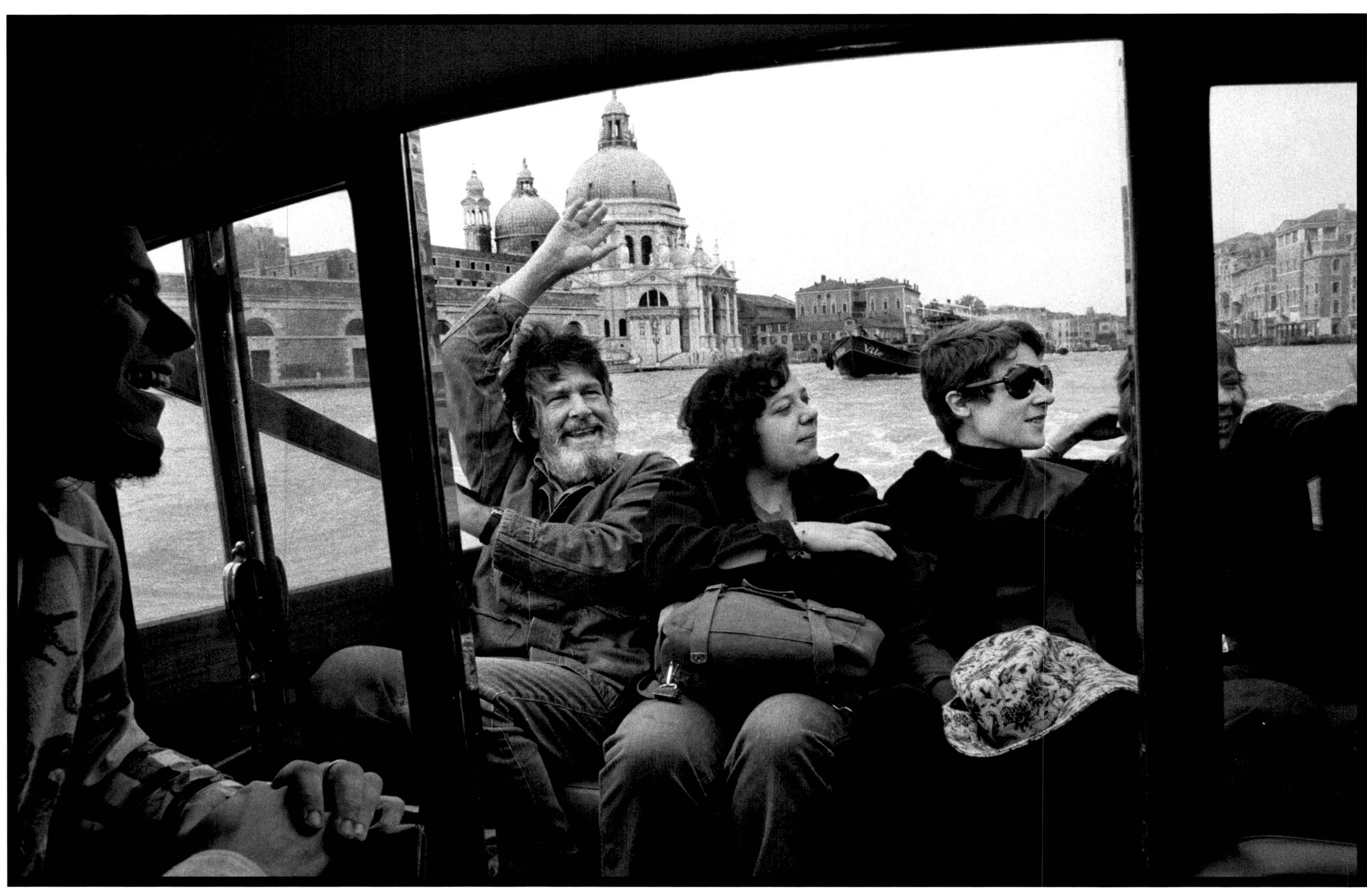

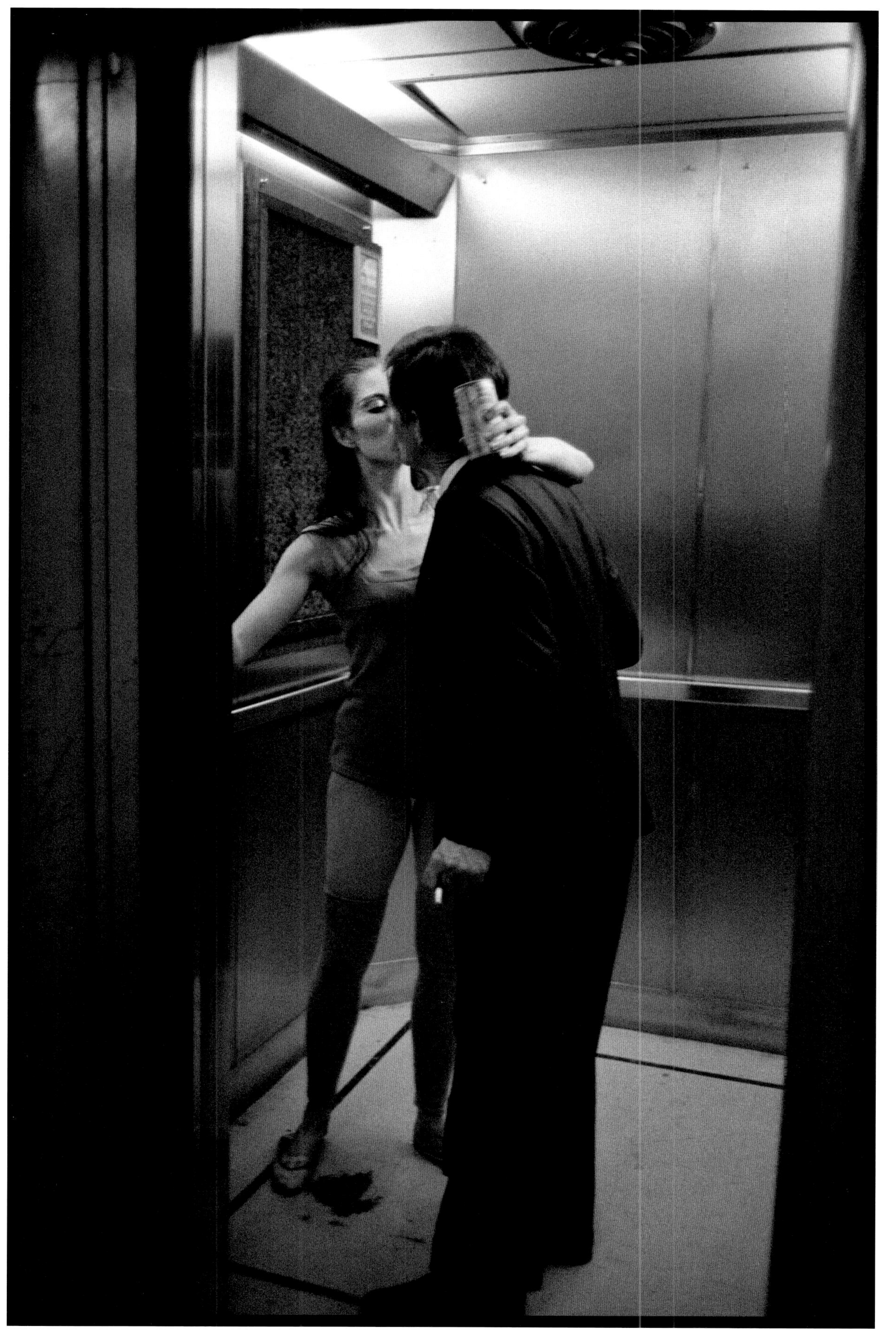

John Cage was delightful and profound. Over the years I had the joy and privilege of sharing time with him; singing some of his music; cooking meals together. To be with him, even for a few minutes, was always an inspiration. When John would enter a room, the energy would immediately change—a liveliness and vibrancy would become palpable. His curiosity, immediacy, and playfulness were infectious. His life was a reminder that we can continue to grow, change, and live in the moment for our entire lives.

— Meredith Monk

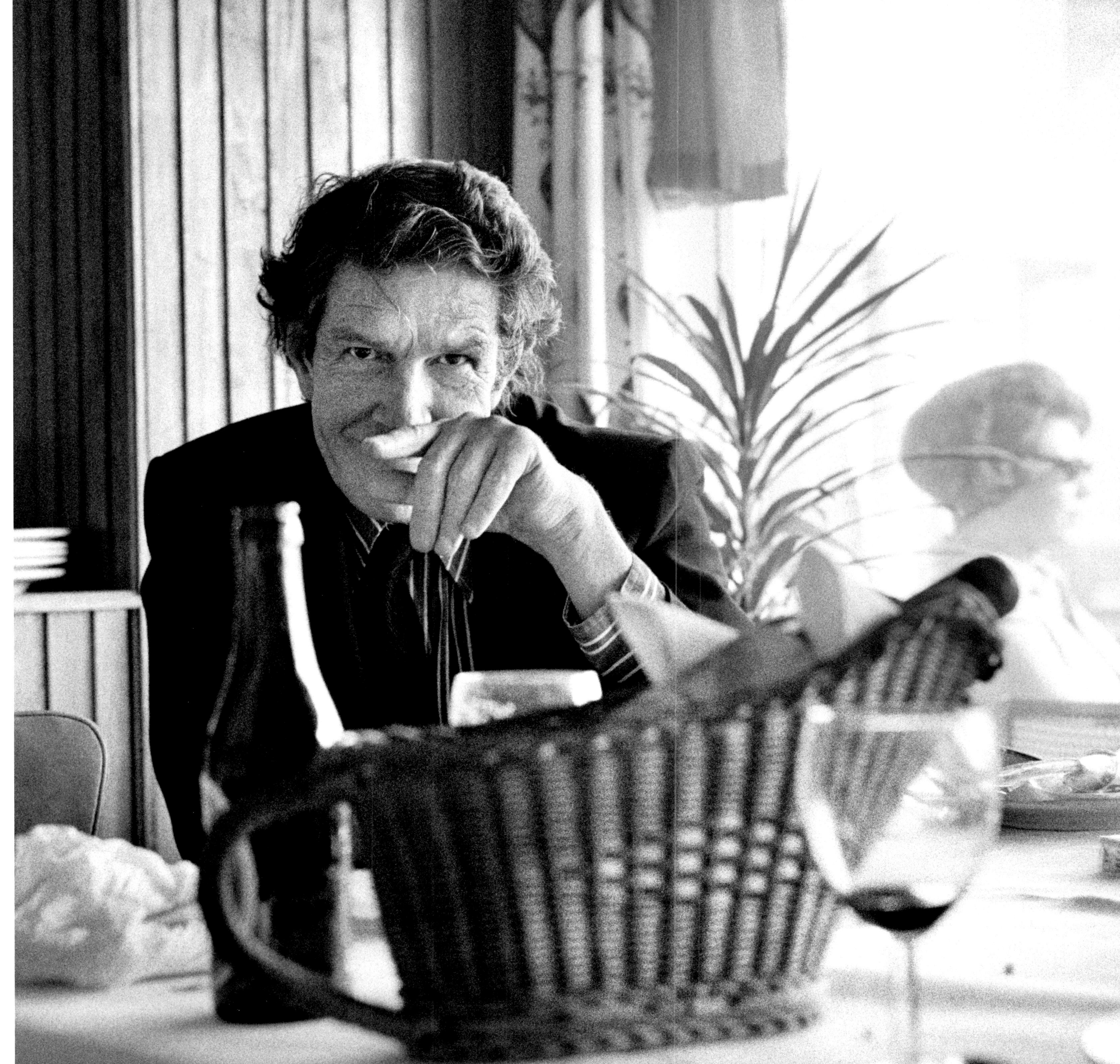

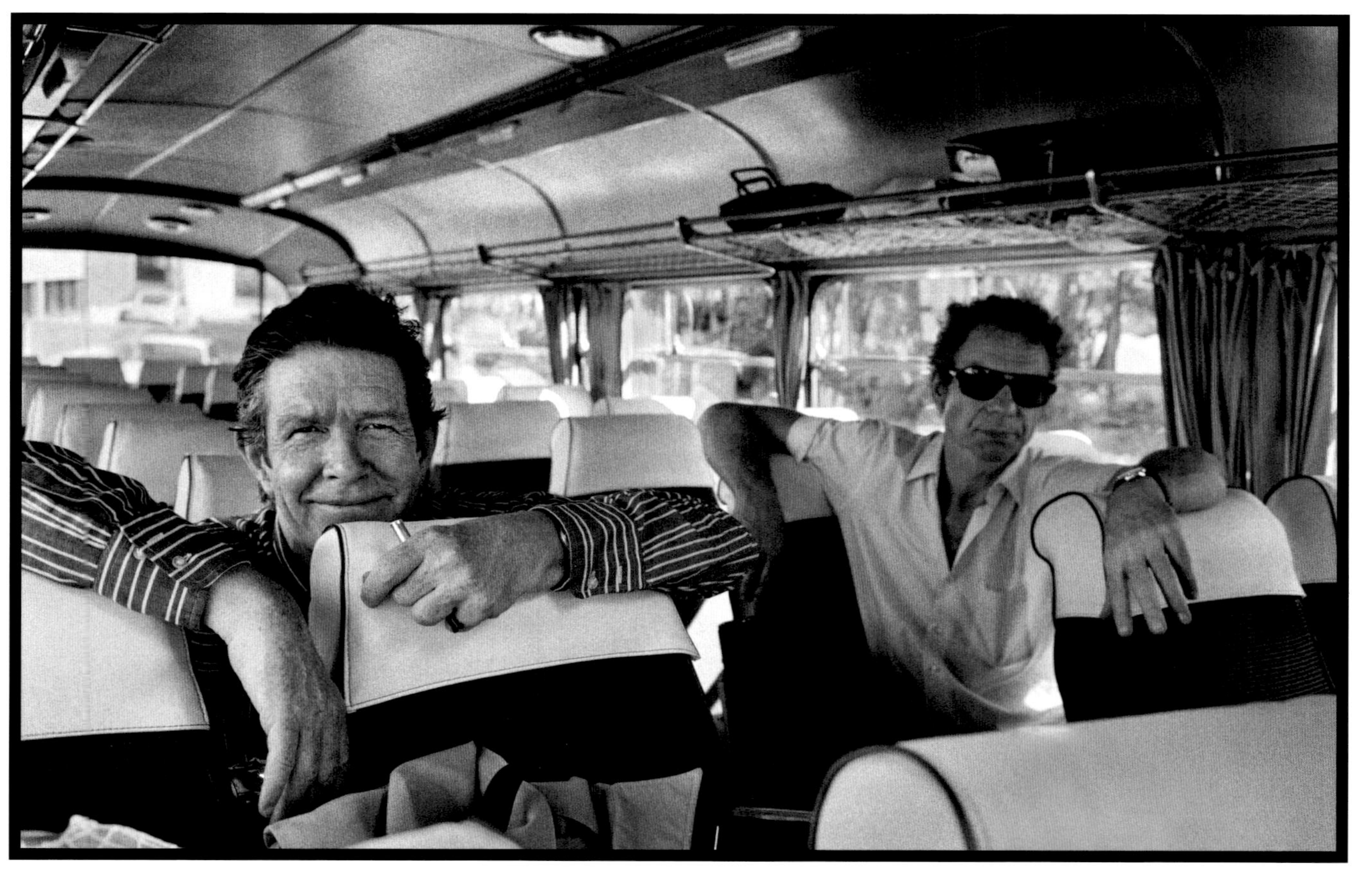

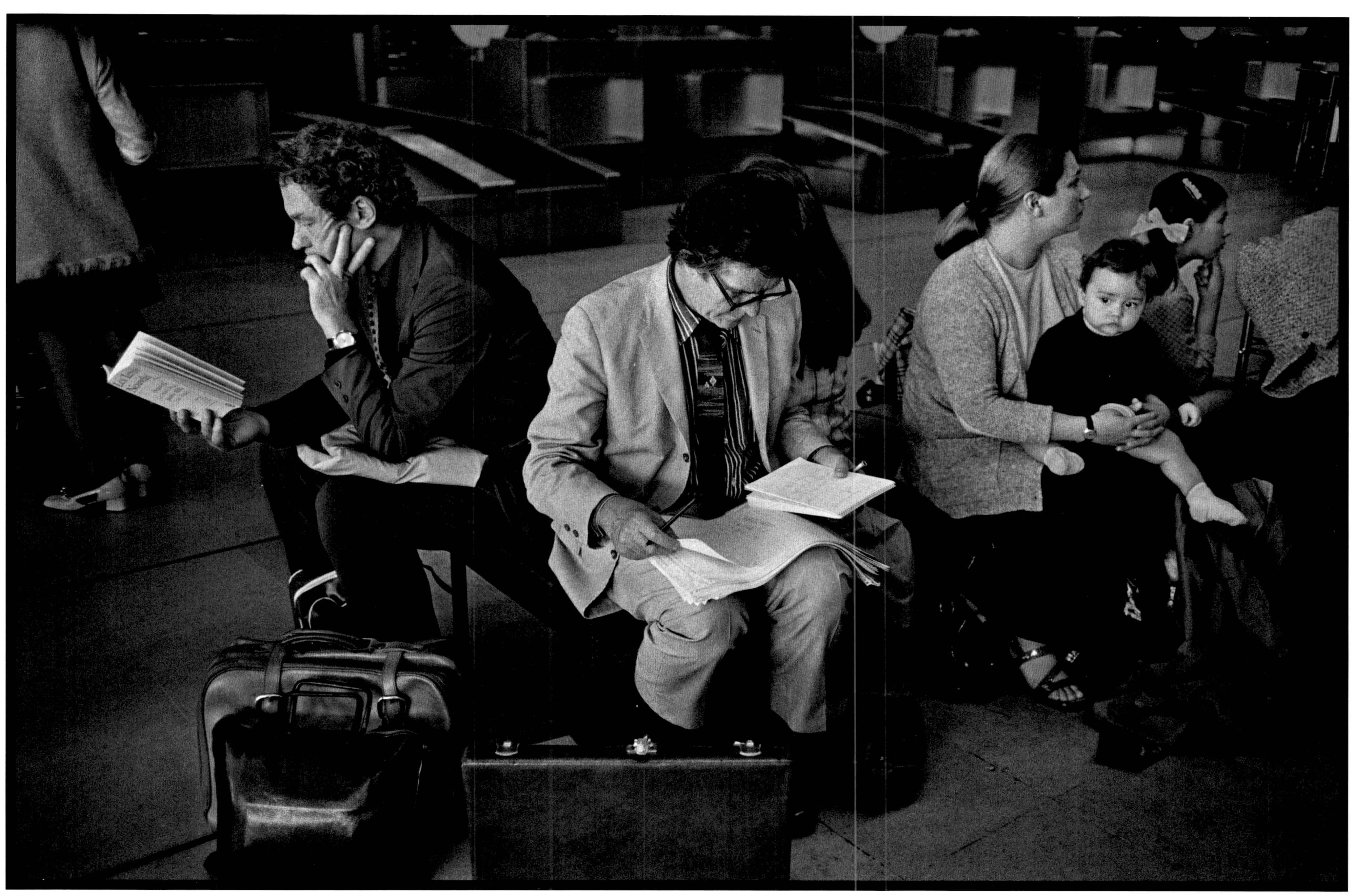

Marcel Duchamp's retrospective exhibition
at the Philadelphia Museum in 1973 was a grand occasion,
a black tie event.
Only Philadelphia could assemble
the entire oeuvre around his immovable masterpieces
La mariée mise à nu par ses célibataires, même and *Étant donnés*.

Black ties have no place in my wardrobe
so I wore the standard Levi jeans and jacket.
Looking down from the landing of the imperial staircase
in the entrance hall I saw a figure
resplendent in blue denim.
John Cage was ascending towards me through the crush
to offer his greeting,
"I knew I could depend on you, Richard."

—Richard Hamilton

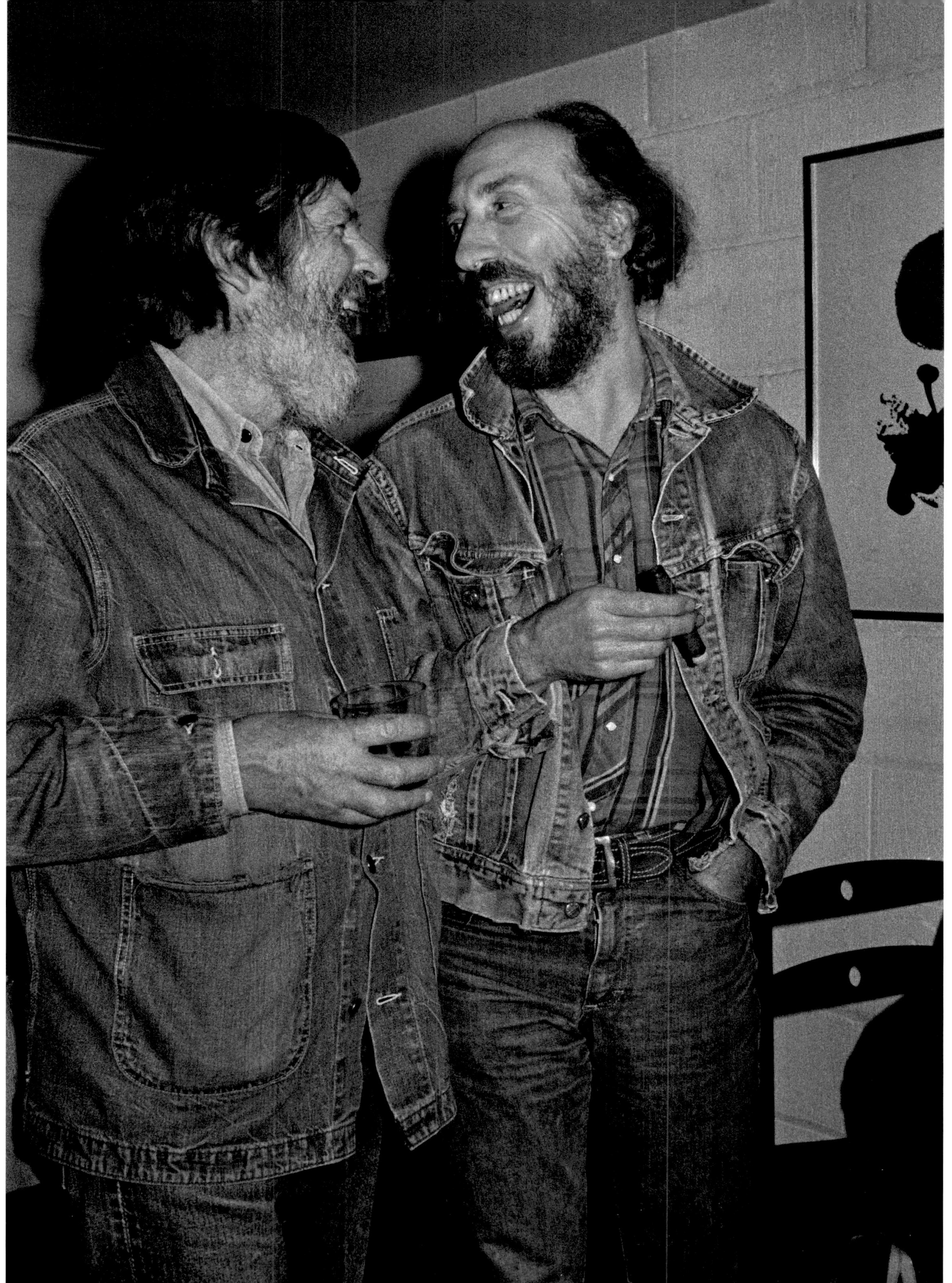

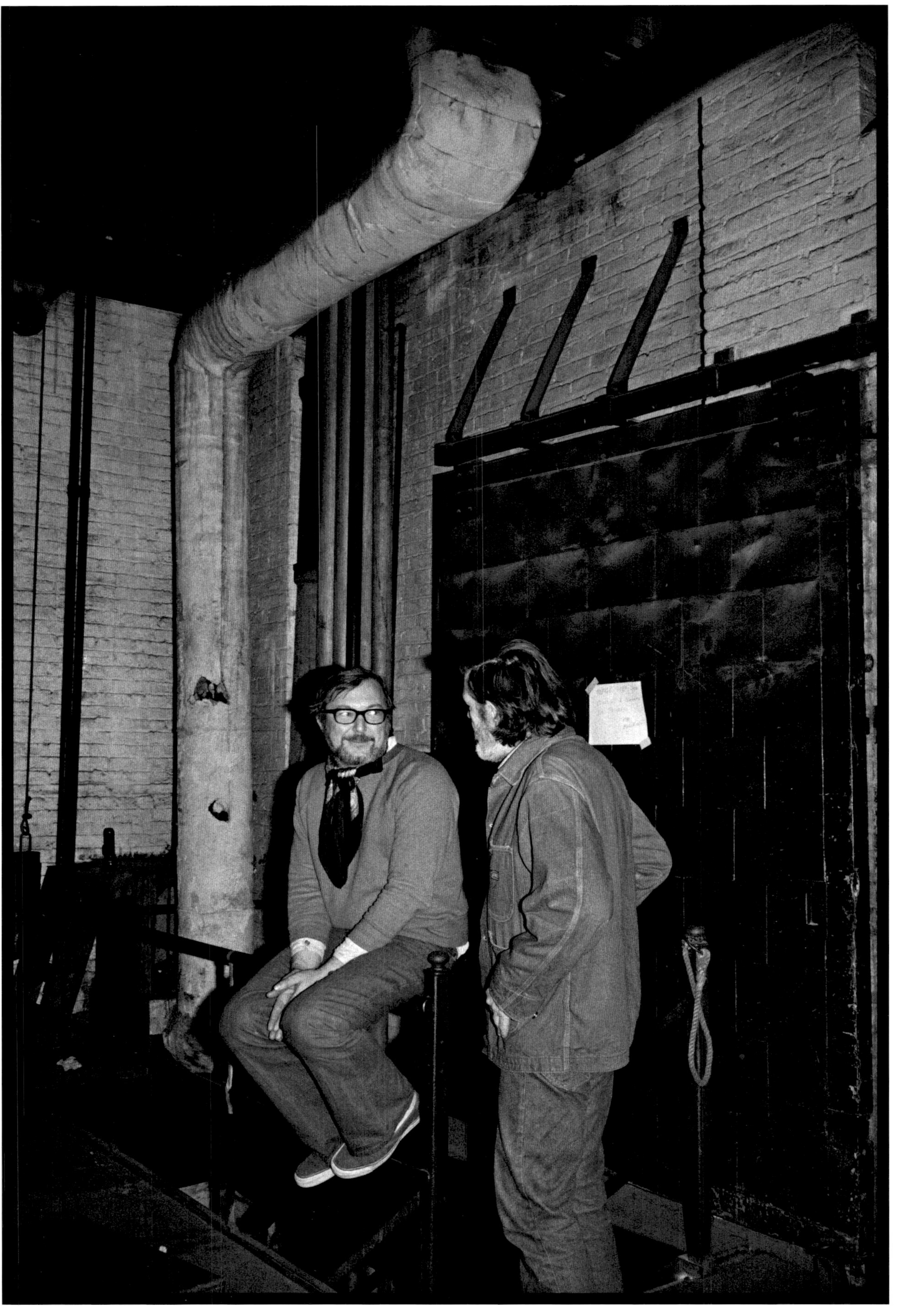

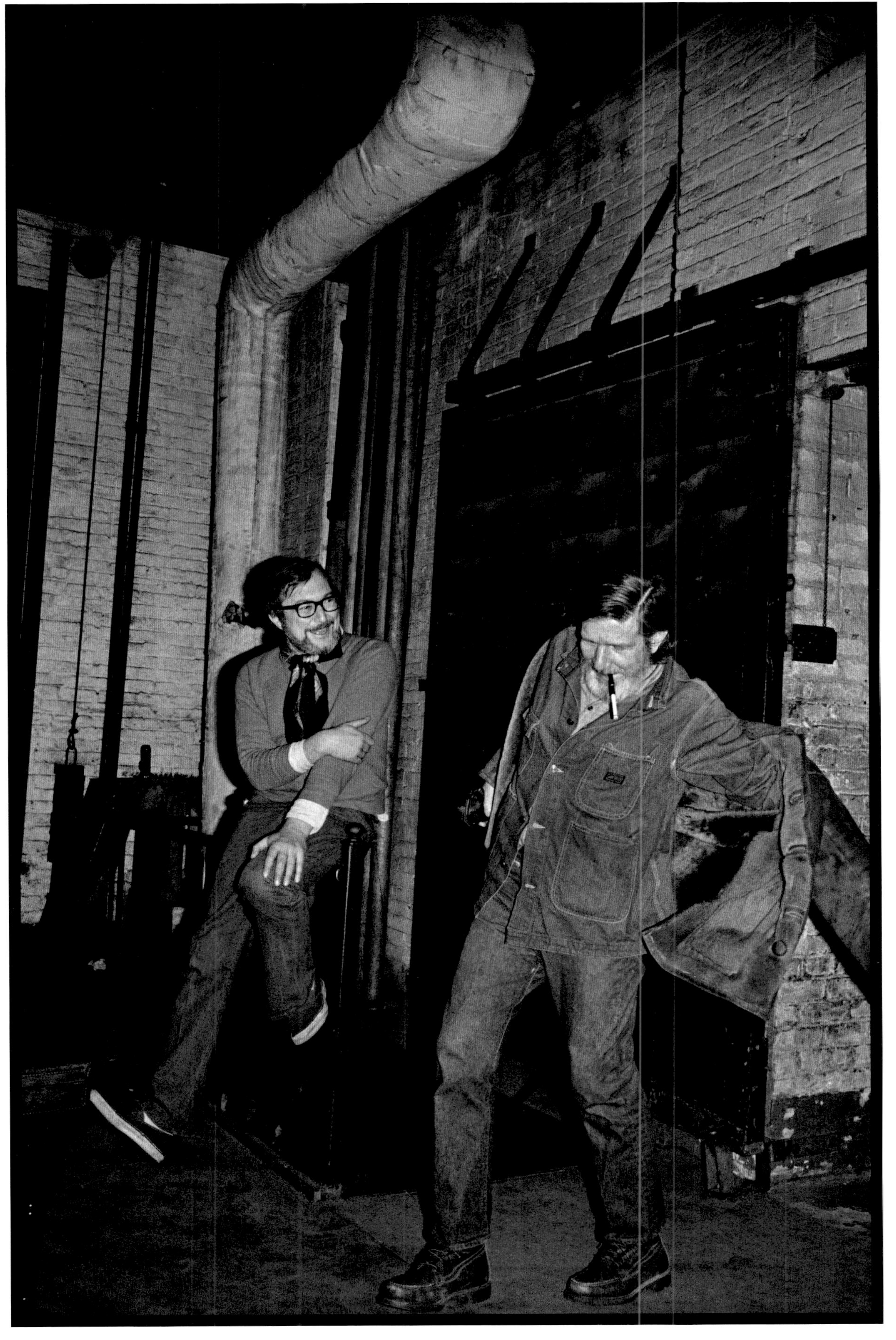

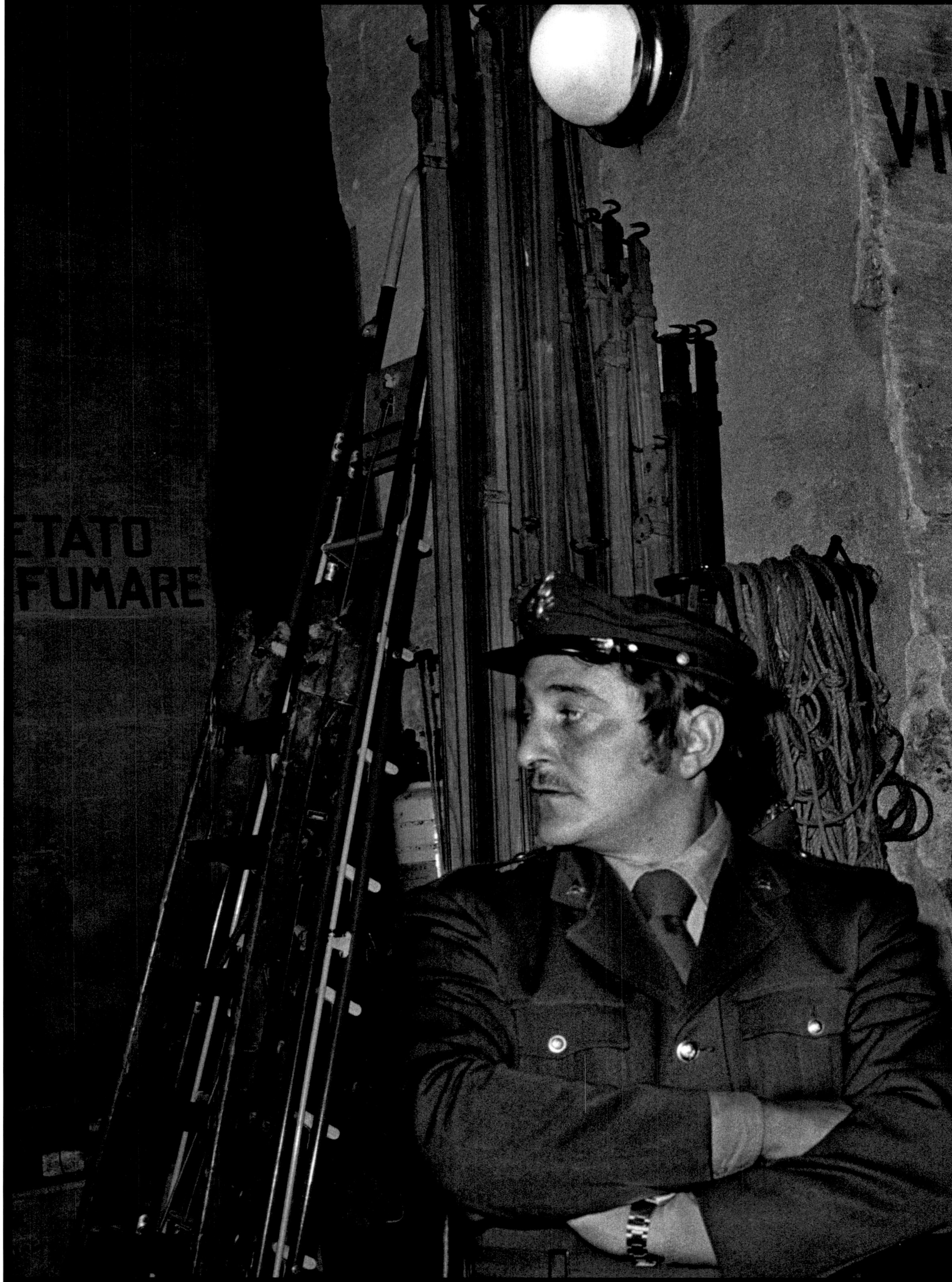
ETATO
FUMARE

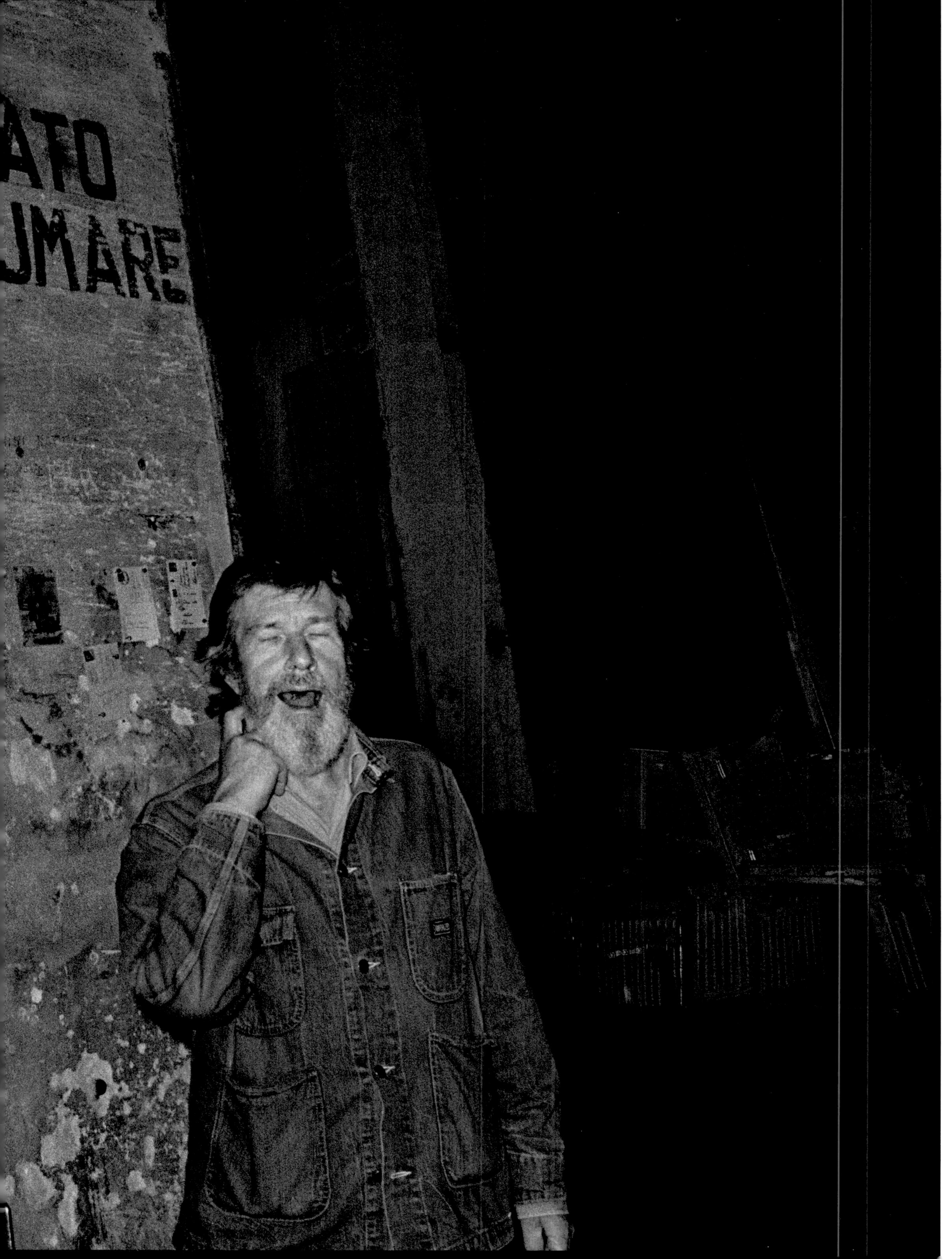
ATO
UMARE

I am sitting in a house
that is part of a 1950s development,
approachable and open,
built in the spirit of equality and
communality, postwar.
It is a house in the midst of trees
that allows me to hear the everyday around me, while the everyday
allows me to hear myself
in its midst and accords me a generative
responsibility for what I hear.
It is a house not unlike the Williams-Cage house that
surrounded Cage with his silence;
his silence was a postwar silence too
that sounded the equality and
communality of music
—John Cage was political.

— Salomé Voegelin

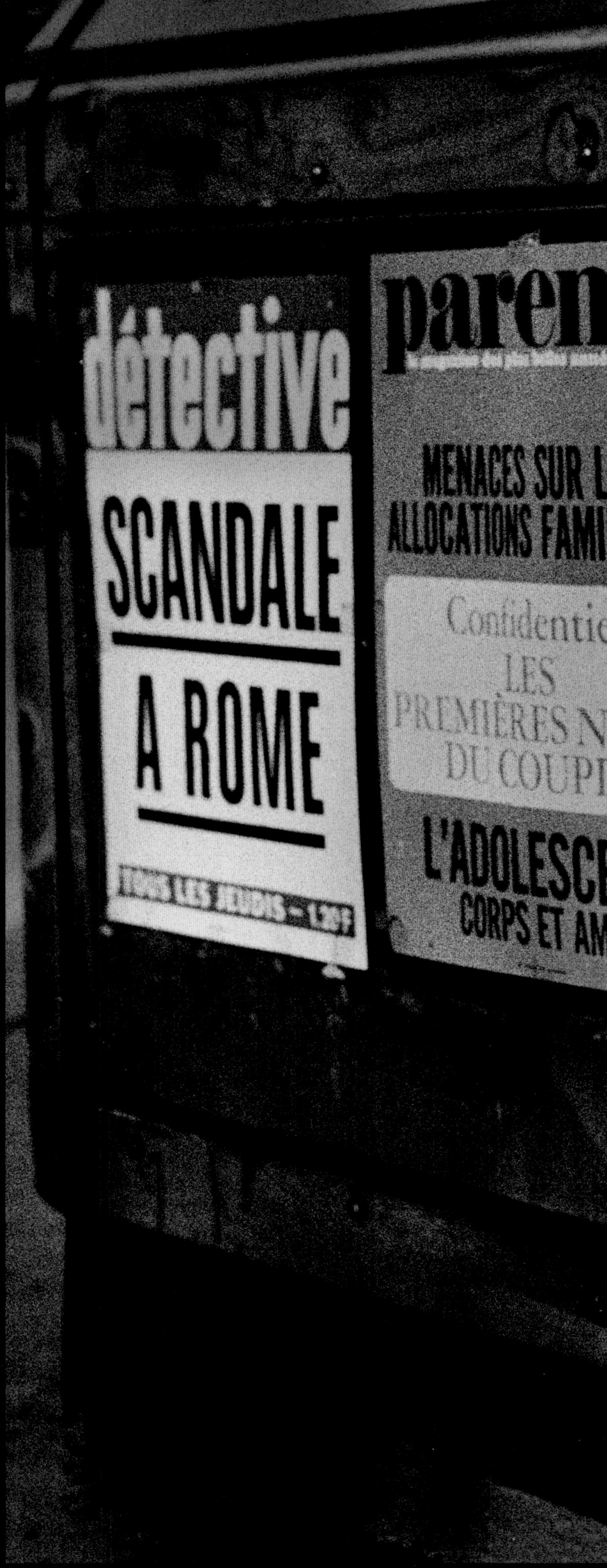

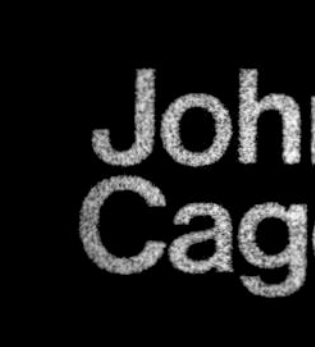
chroniques de
l'art
vivant
N° 11 Mai-Juin 1970 Prix 2,50 F abonnement 15 F
John
Cage

I could not honestly say that there was a conscious Cagean influence to my work, but I always adored him and gave thanks that such a gentle (as far as I knew) anarchist (as I often thought him) could exist in a time and space close at hand. If anything, John Cage was an influence on my conscience: things and thoughts I felt I could count on him to have and do left me free to go another direction. — Twyla Tharp

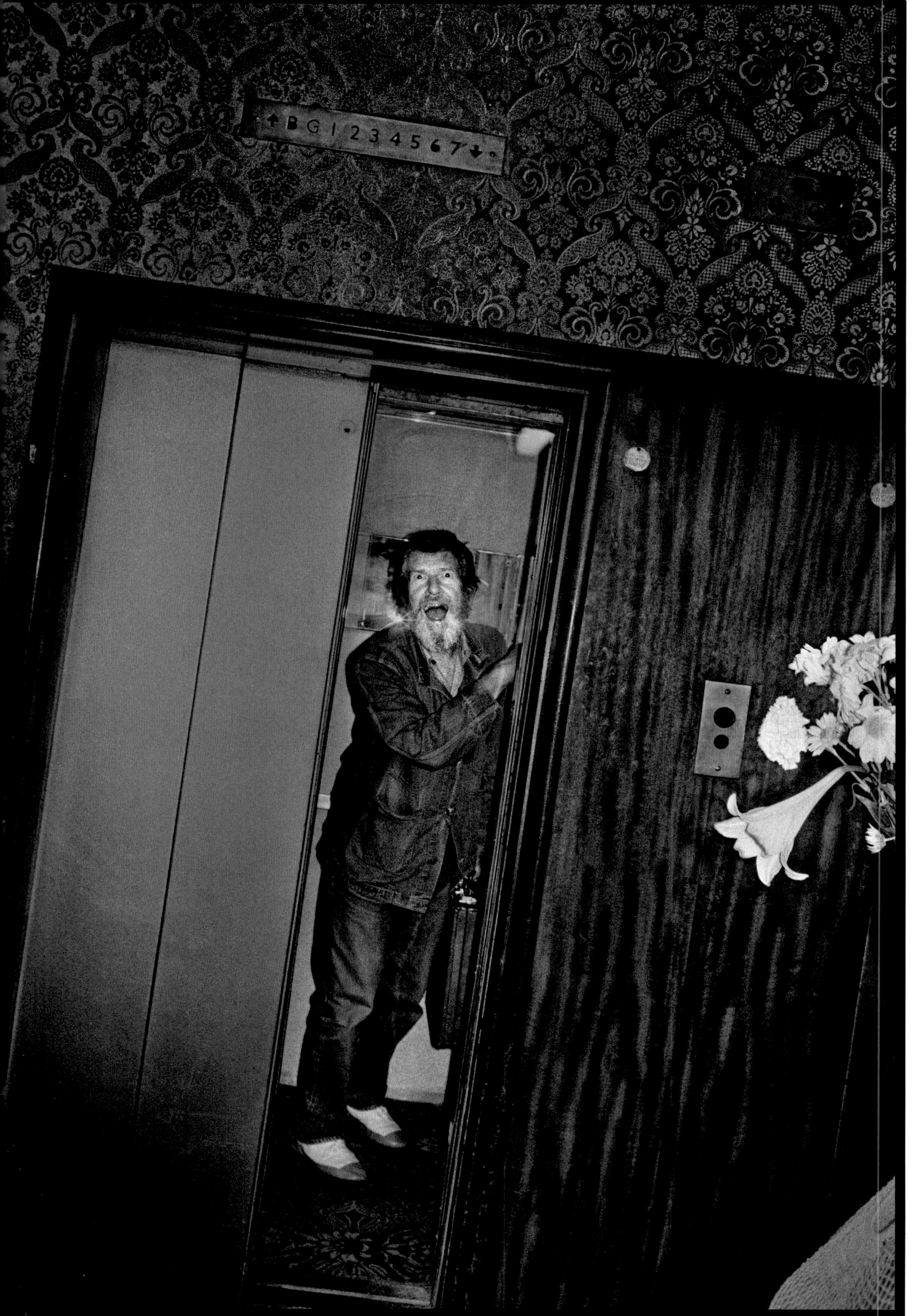
B G 1 2 3 4 5 6 7

John Cage was at home
on 18th Street in Manhattan
when I visited him one day.
I brought him a large bouquet of flowers.
John accepted the bouquet
graciously
then immediately
began to separate
the bouquet
putting each flower
in a different vase
distributed
about the room.
This brought home
the lesson
that he liked
for each sound
to be itself
existing
with
silence
around
it.

— Pauline Oliveros

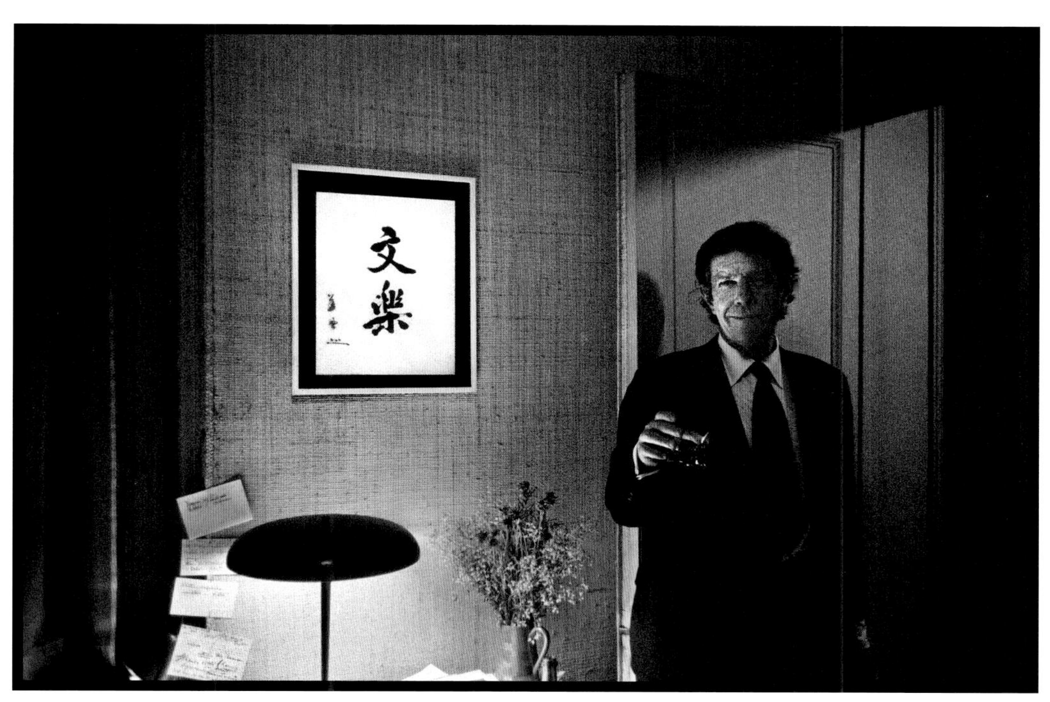
文楽

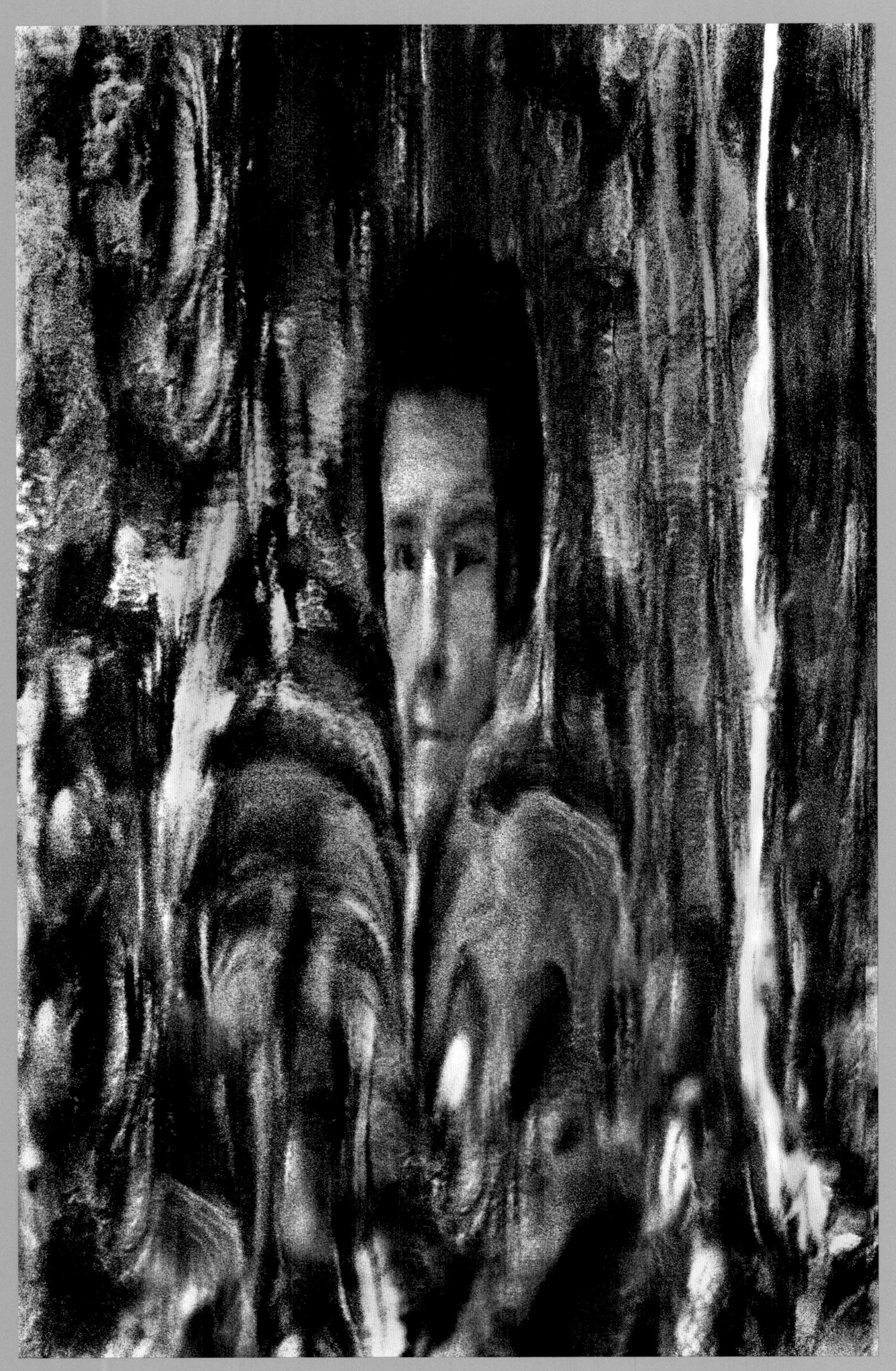

a Renaissance mind

John Cage was a teacher was my teacher John Cage was an artist, an anarchist, a writer John Cage was a music theorist, a composer an American John Cage was the most influential American composer of the 20th century. John Cage was the composer of "4'33" John Cage was a pioneer of the prepared piano. John Cage composed "Sonatas and Interludes (1946-48) John Cage was taught by Henry Cowell, Arnold Schoenberg, Indian musician Gita Sarabhai, D.T. Suzuki and Zen Buddhism, Richard Buhlig. John Cage was influenced by & knew Marcel Duchamp, James Joyce, Ananda Coomaraswamy, Igor Stravinsky, Paul Hindemith, Johann Sebastian Bach, Walt Whitman, László Moholy-Nagy, Takemitsu, Max Ernst, Peggy Guggenheim, Piet Mondrian, André Breton, Jackson Pollock, Cathy Berberian, Luciano Berio, Oliver Messian, Pierre Boulez, Iannis Xenakis, David Tudor, Allen Kaprow, Al Hansen, George Brecht, Dick Higgins, Antonin Artaud, Nam June Paik, Marshall McLuhan, Buck Fuller, Helmut Lachenmann, Earle Brown, Morton Feldman, Christian Wolf, La Monte Young, Terry Riley, Steve, Phil Glass, Gavin Bryars, Toru Takemitsu & Frank Zappa.

"Nothing has changed but now our eyes and ears are ready to hear and see" J. Cage

— Robert Wilson

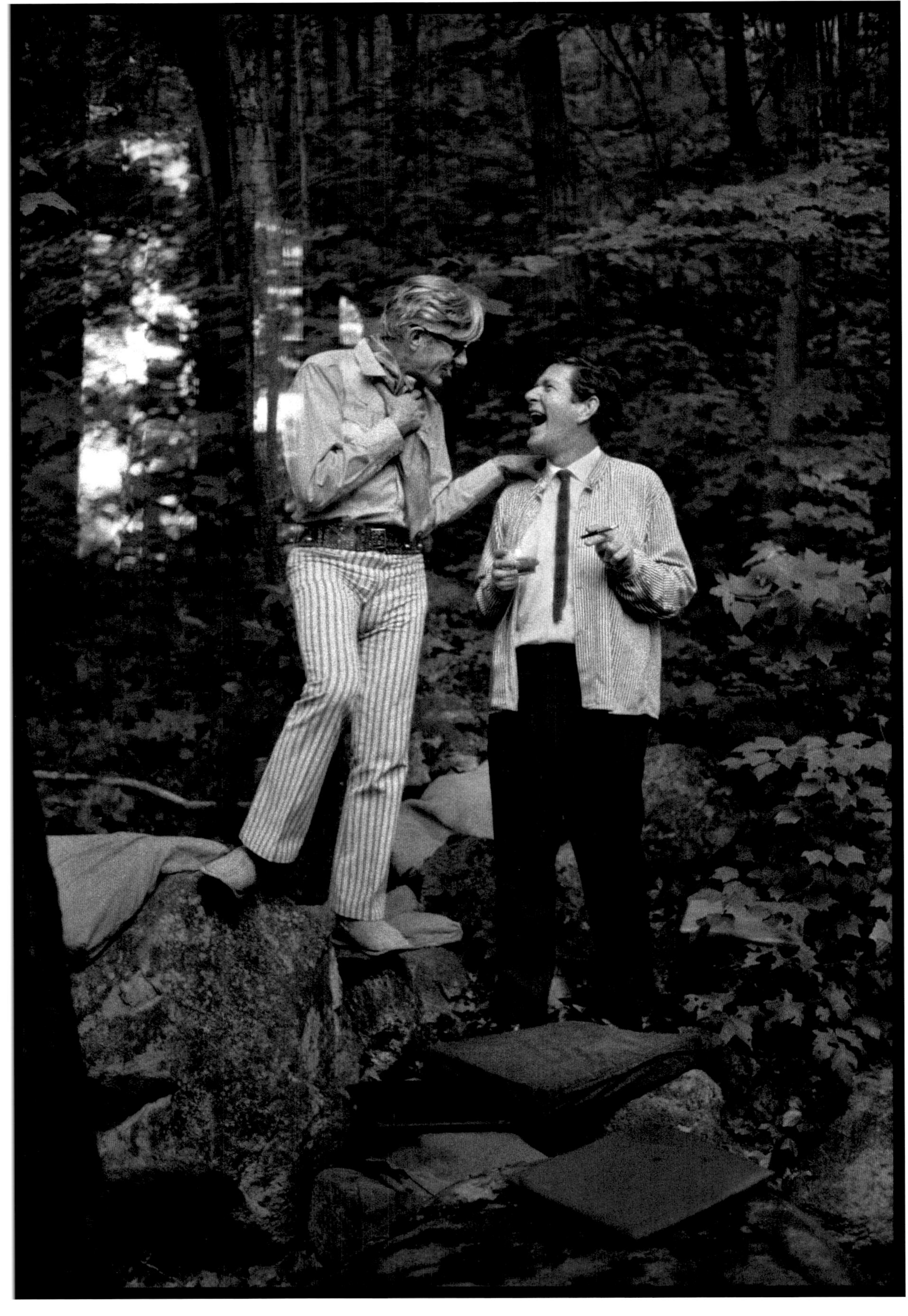

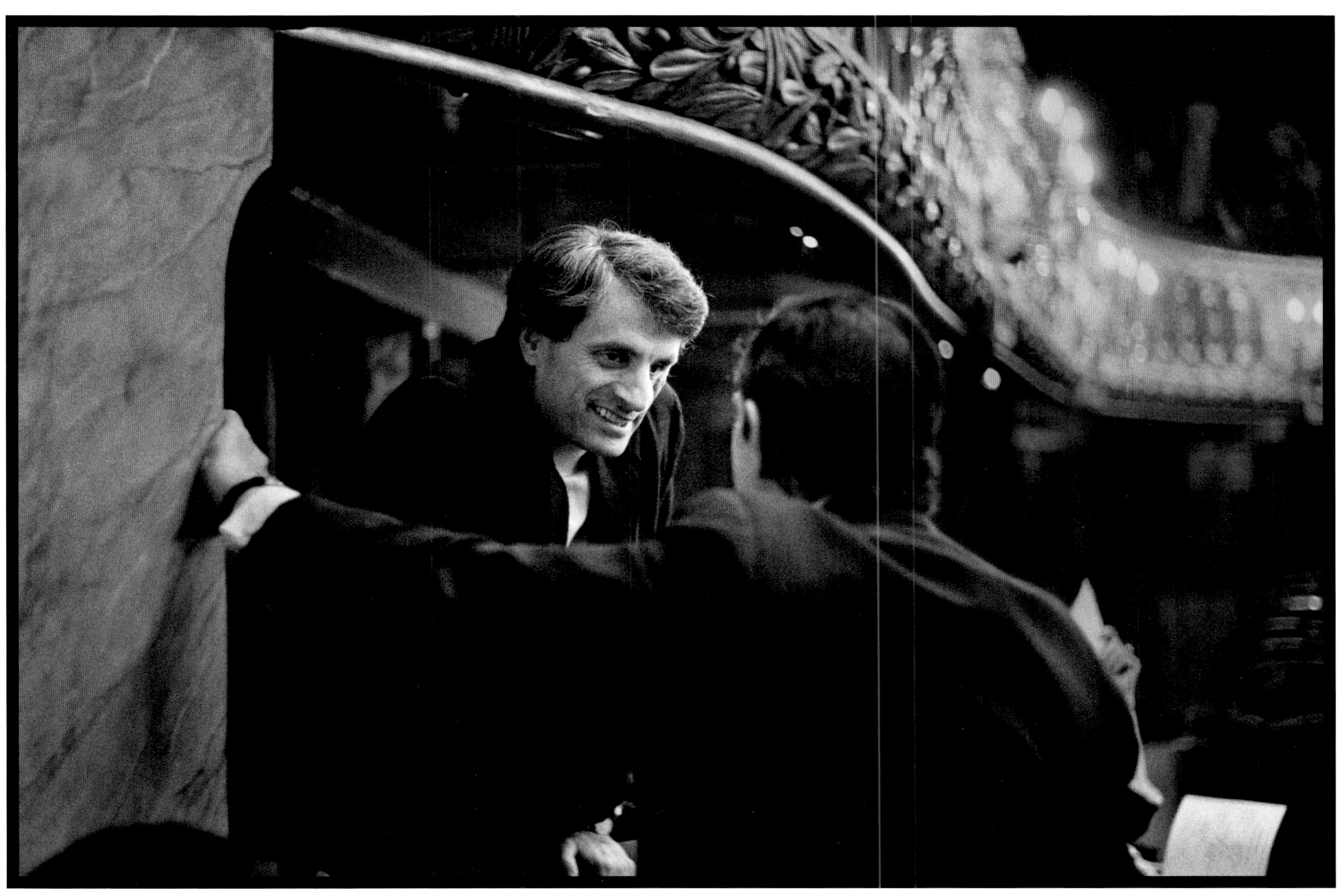

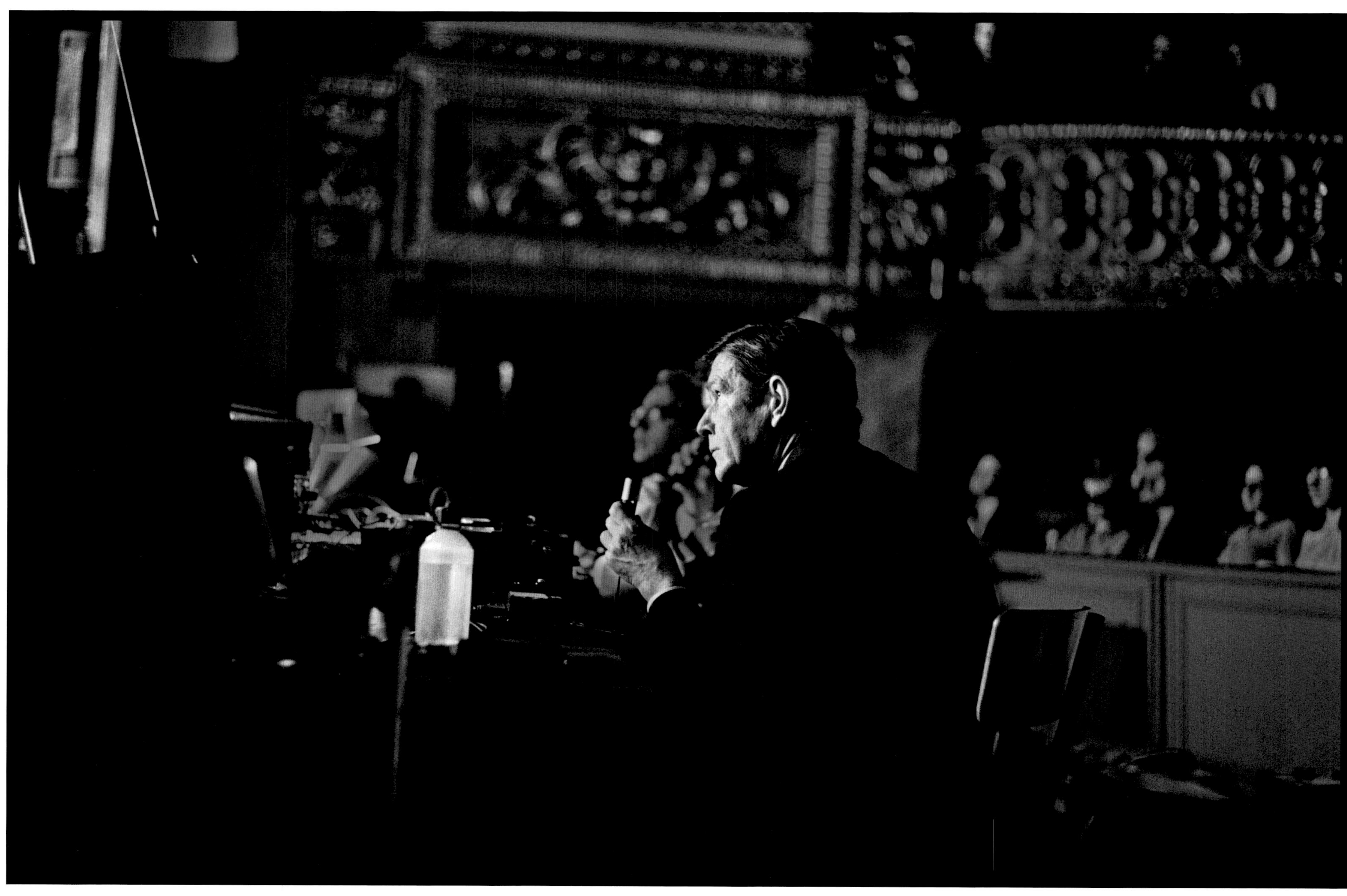

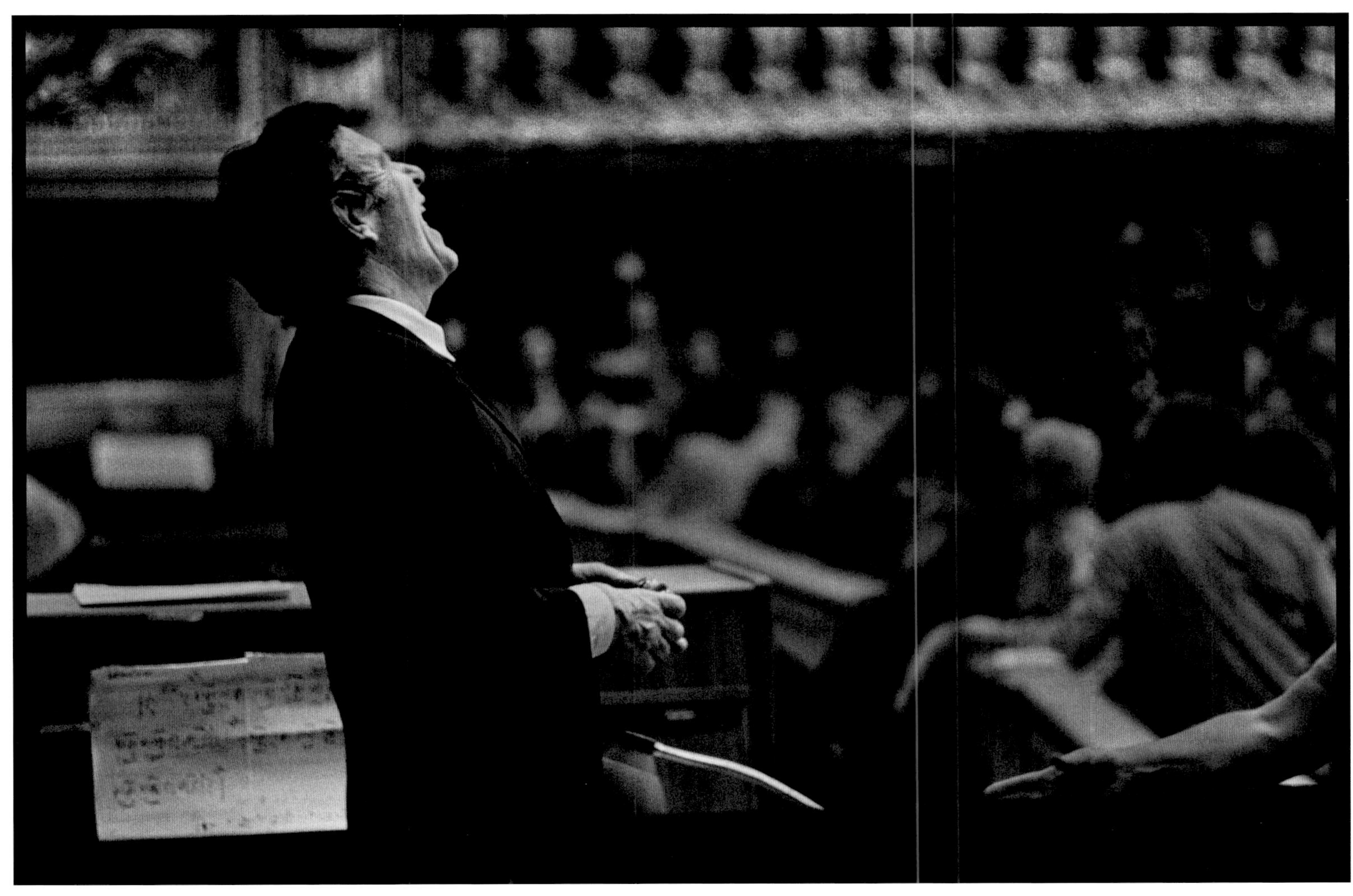

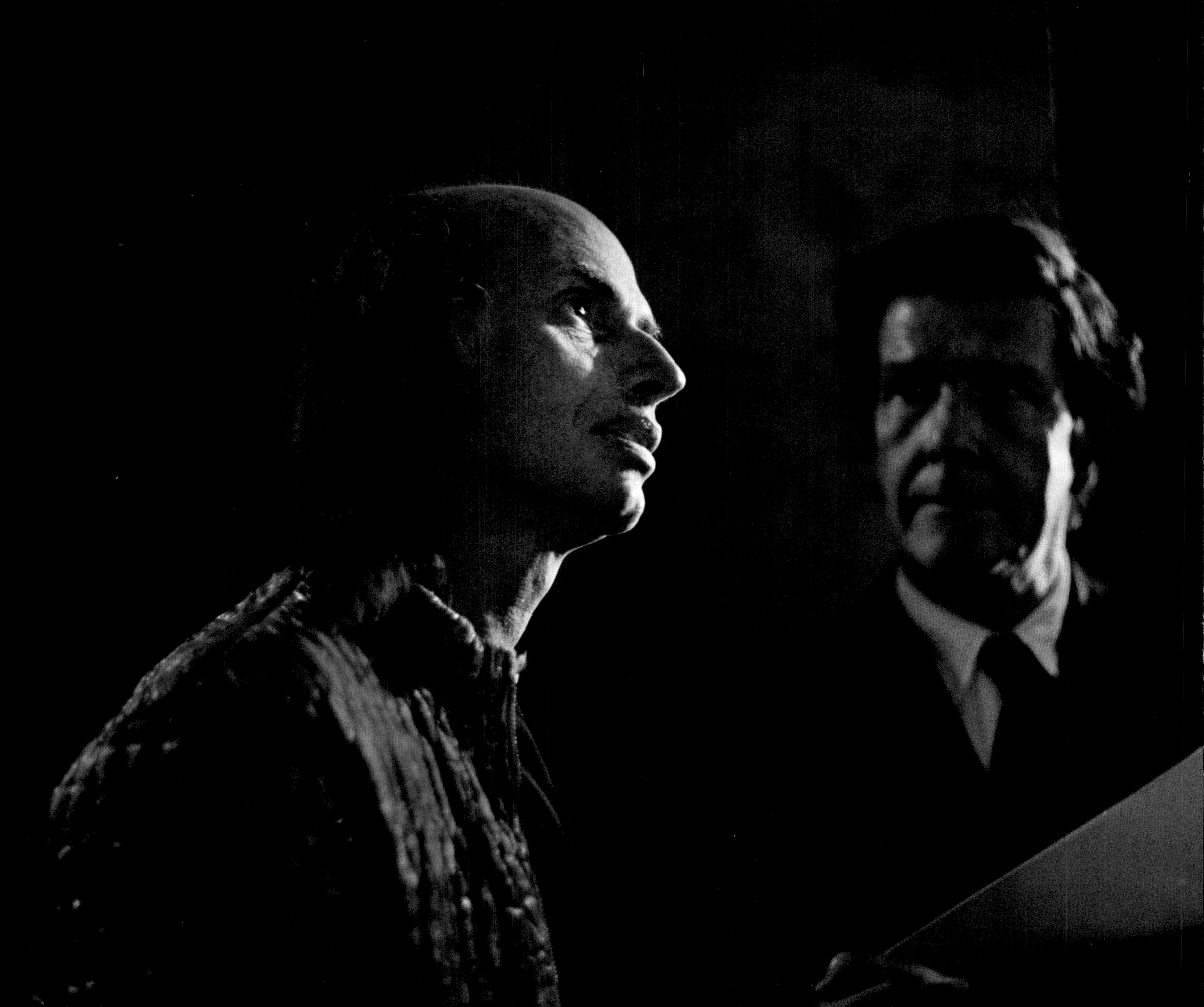

John Cage was the great innovator who turned music, literature, and theater upside down and inside out.

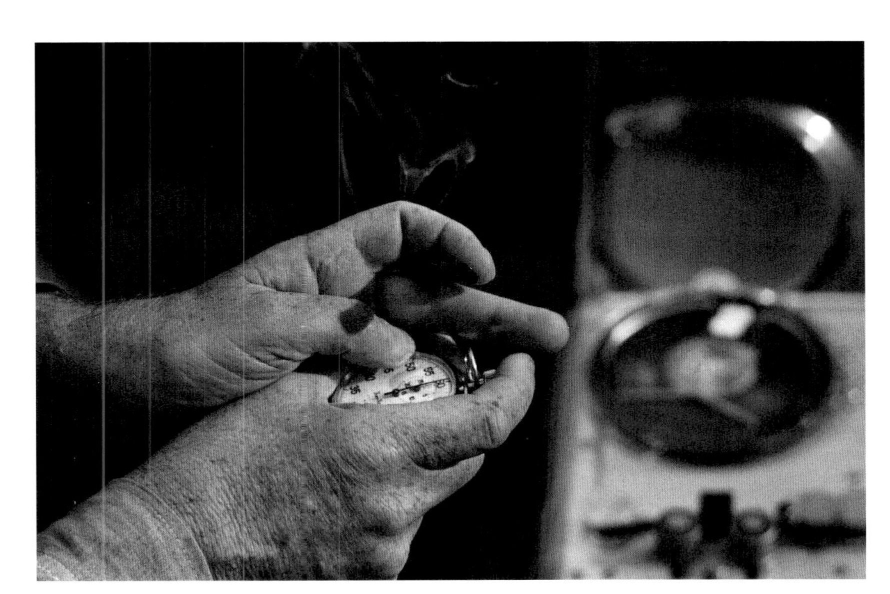

John showed that the horizons we imagined to be our limitations are only illusions. We can transcend the labyrinth of the tradition. Cage opened the gates for us. We must not abandon the Hegelian formula: "Beginning, Middle, and End." John brought music, poetry, and dance into the open arena and said: "Go forth," and we are still going forward into unlimited territory. Now we know the next step must already be left behind us because we must move forward into the Permanent Revolution.

— Judith Malina

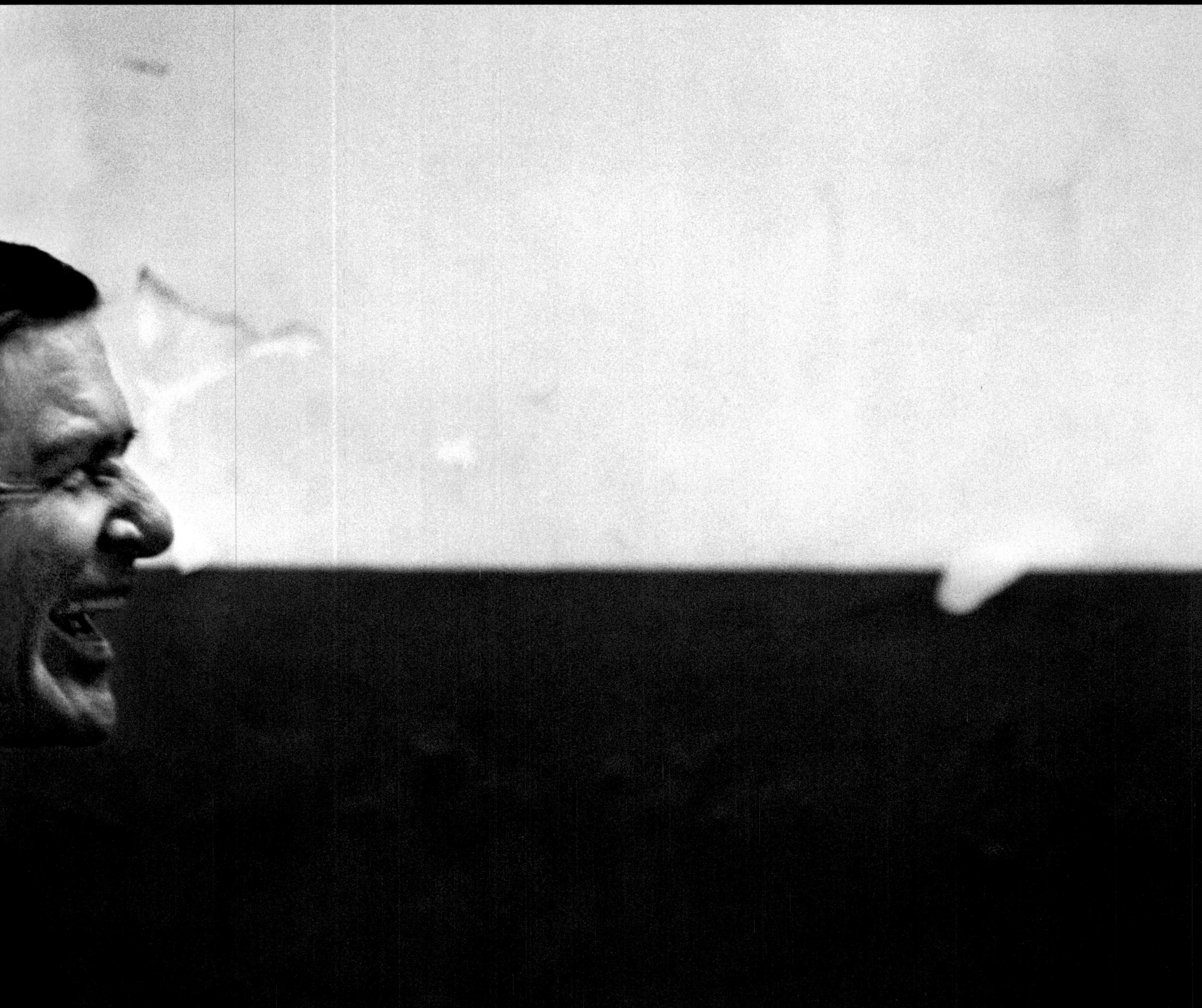

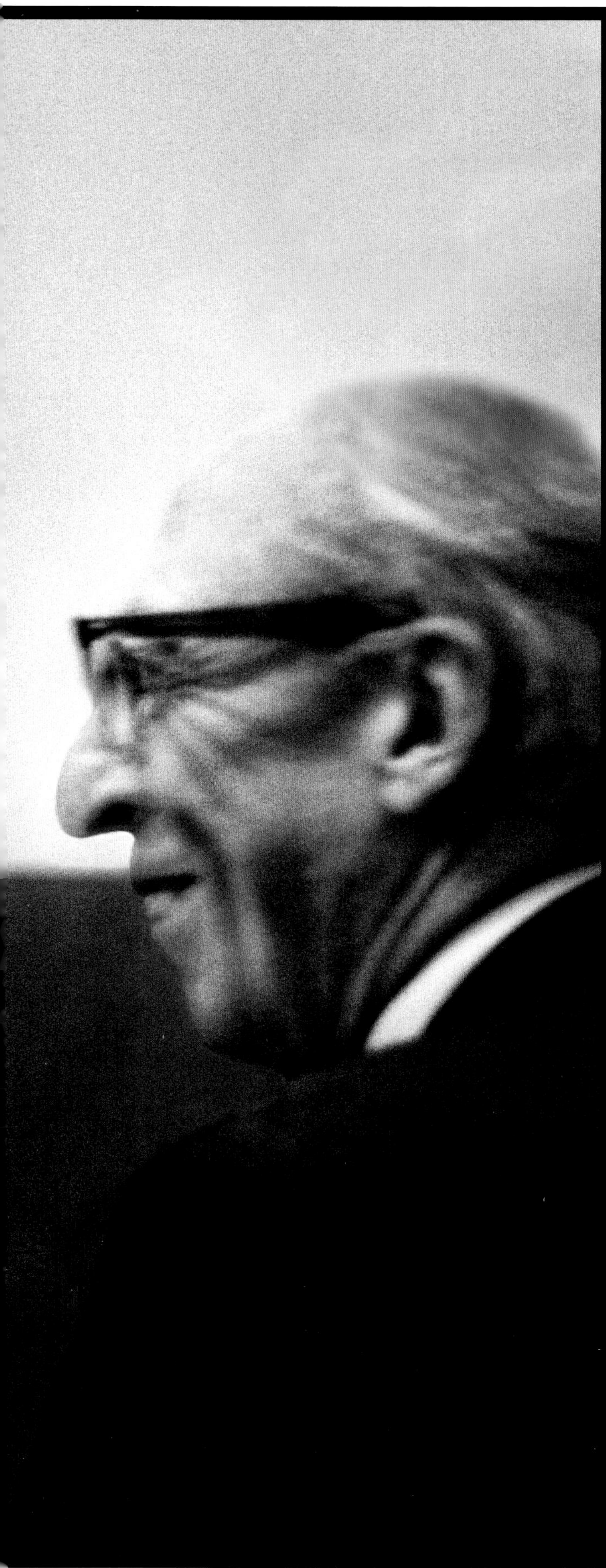

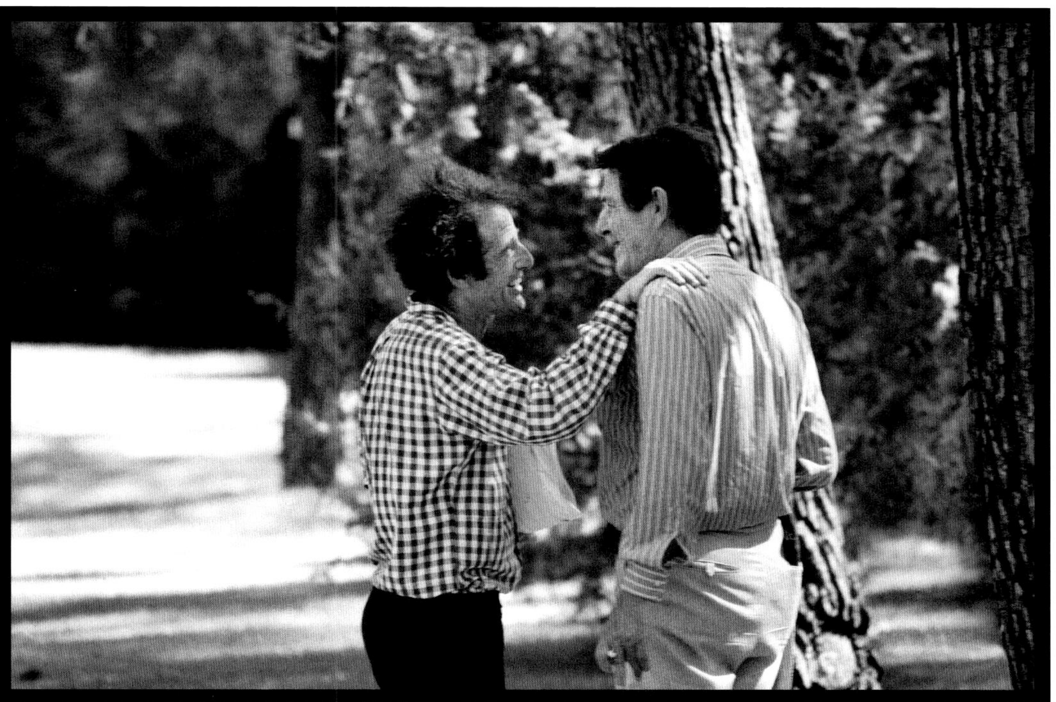

John Cage had an influence on me but more as a person . . . his philosophy more than his music. I think that's true of most composers who were influenced by John Cage. John Cage was a prophet.

— Lukas Foss

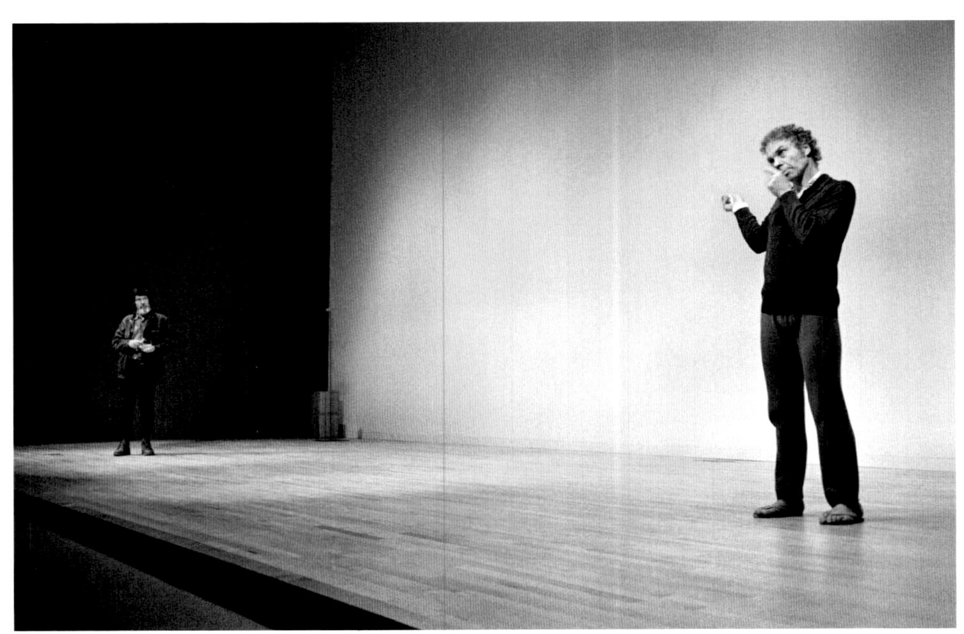

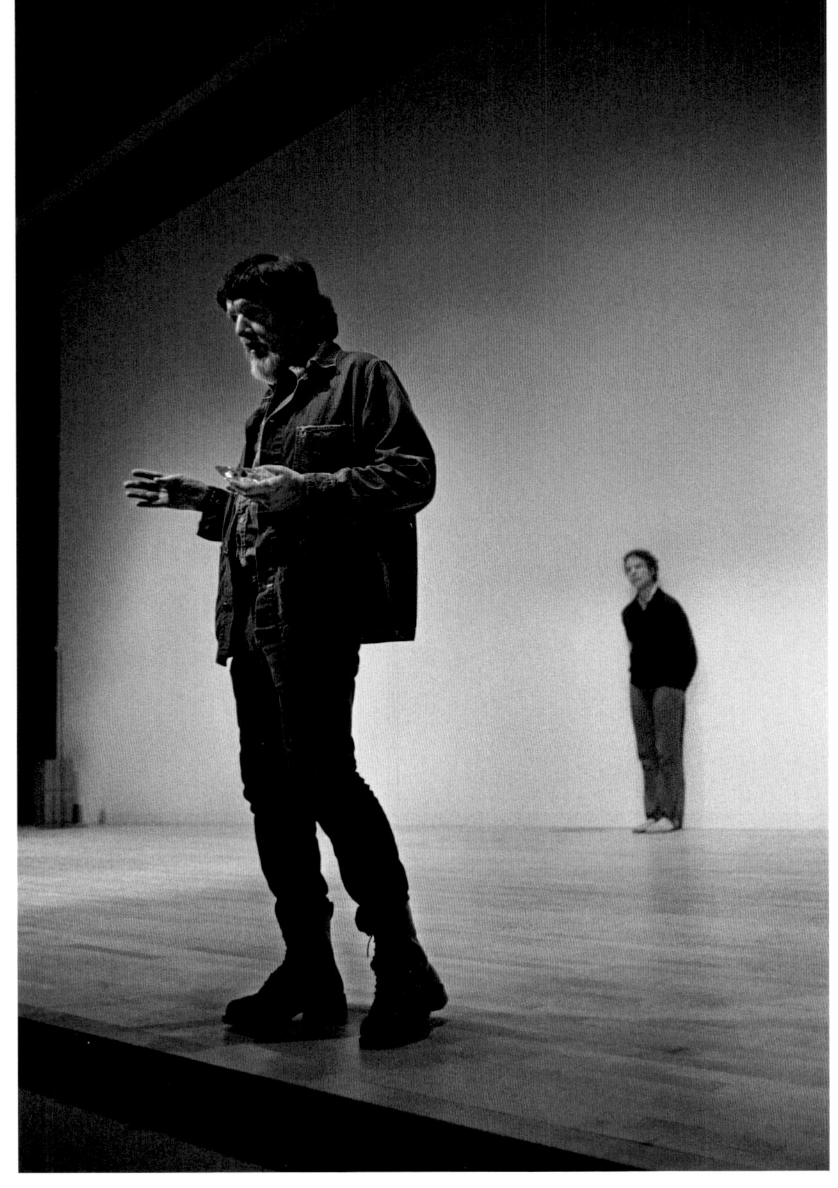

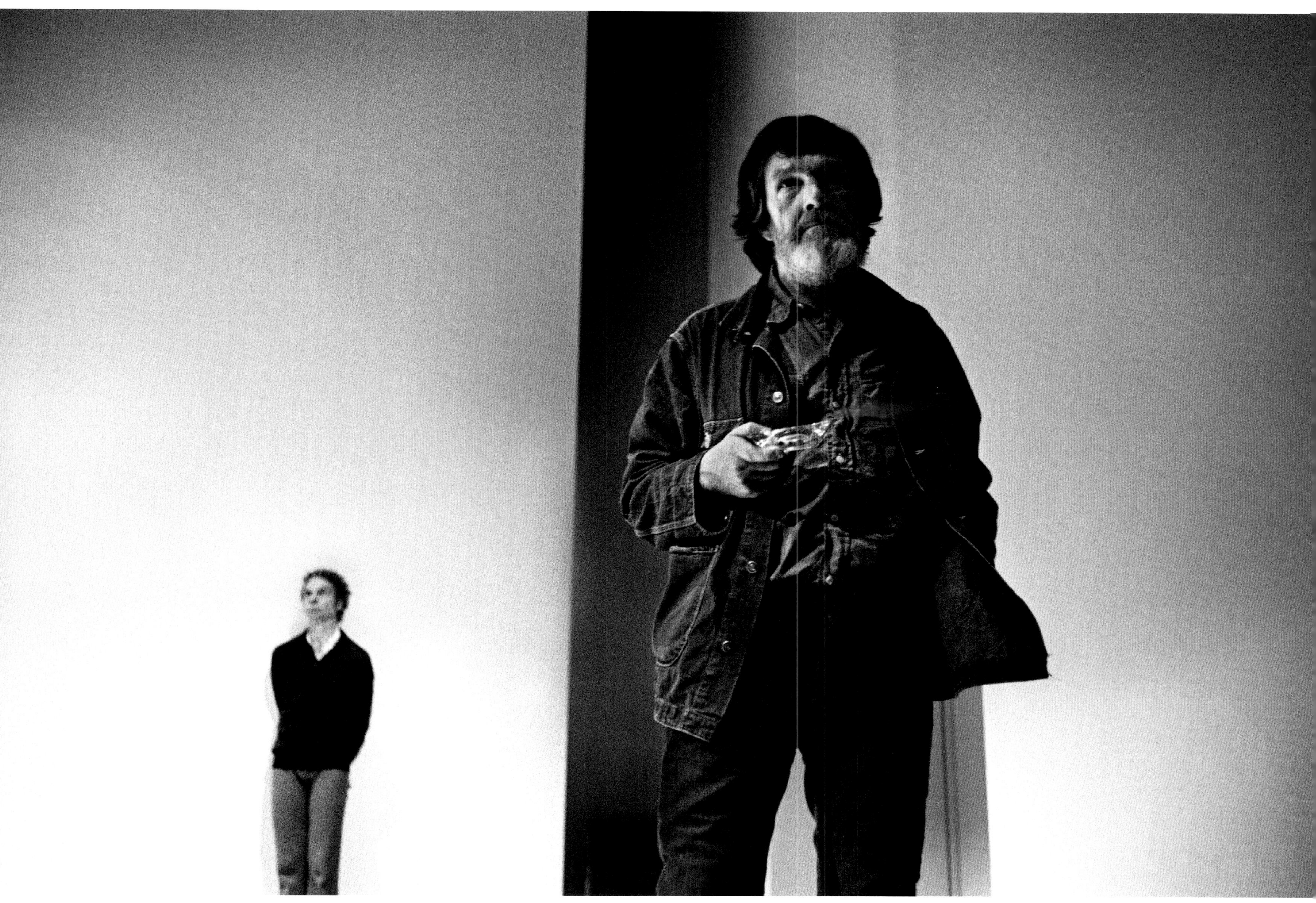

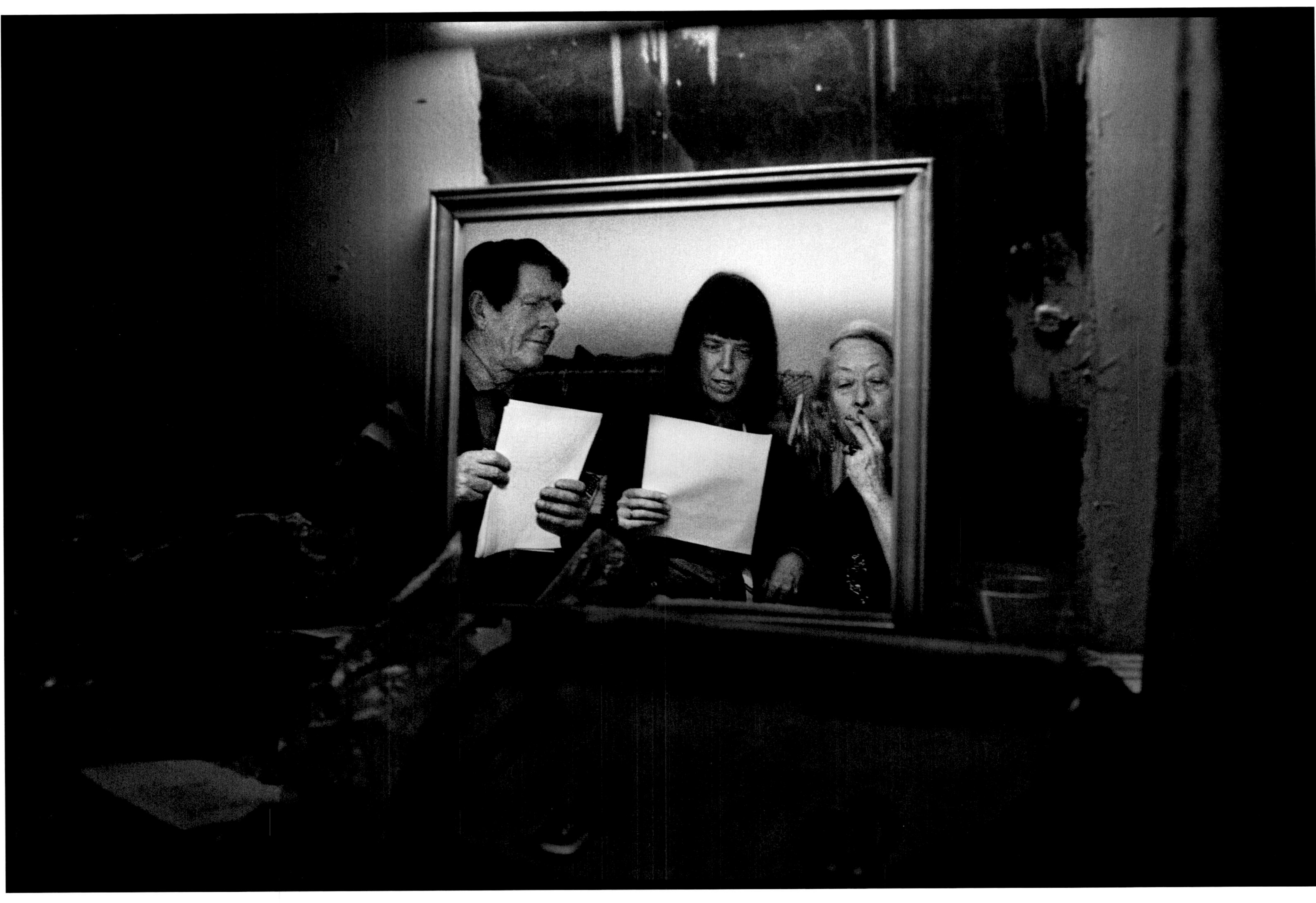

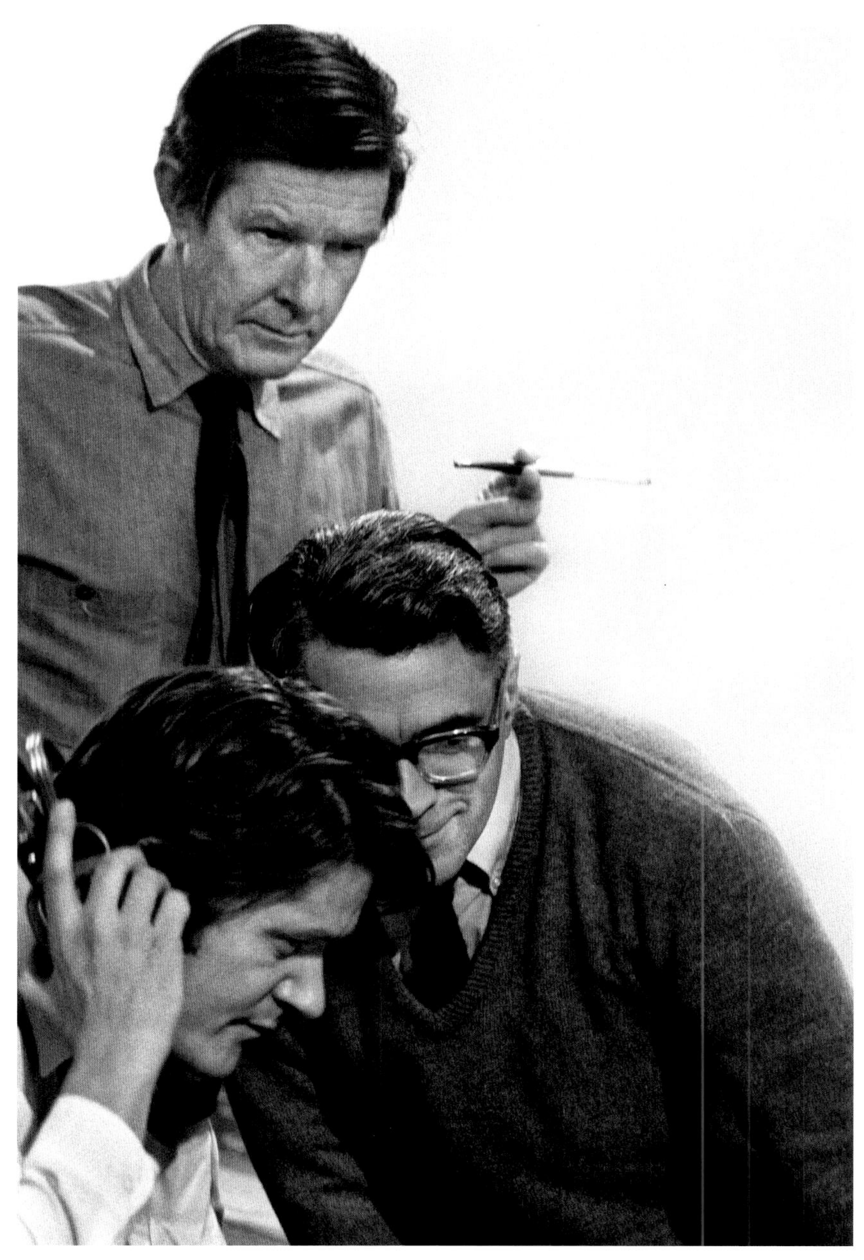

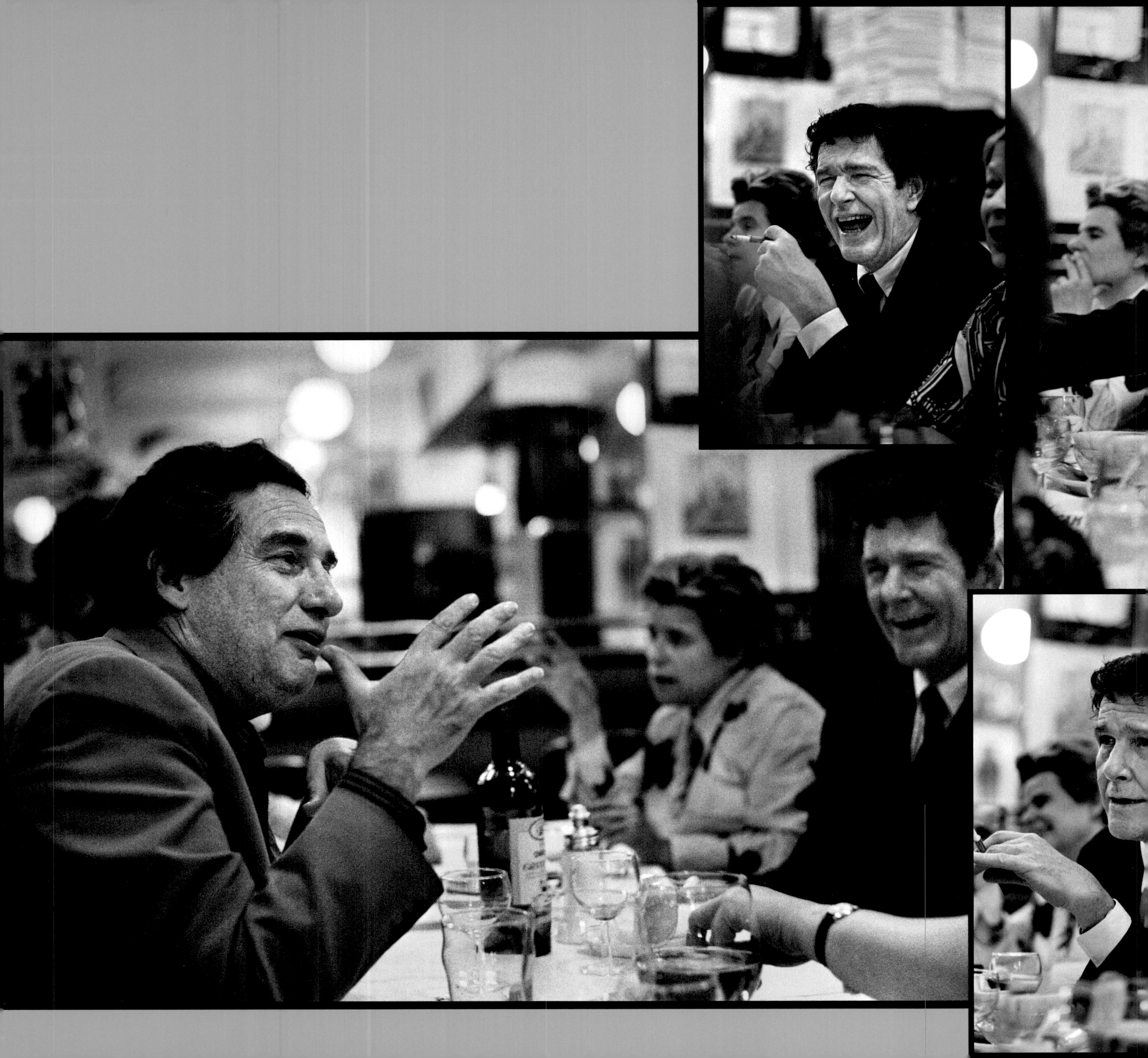

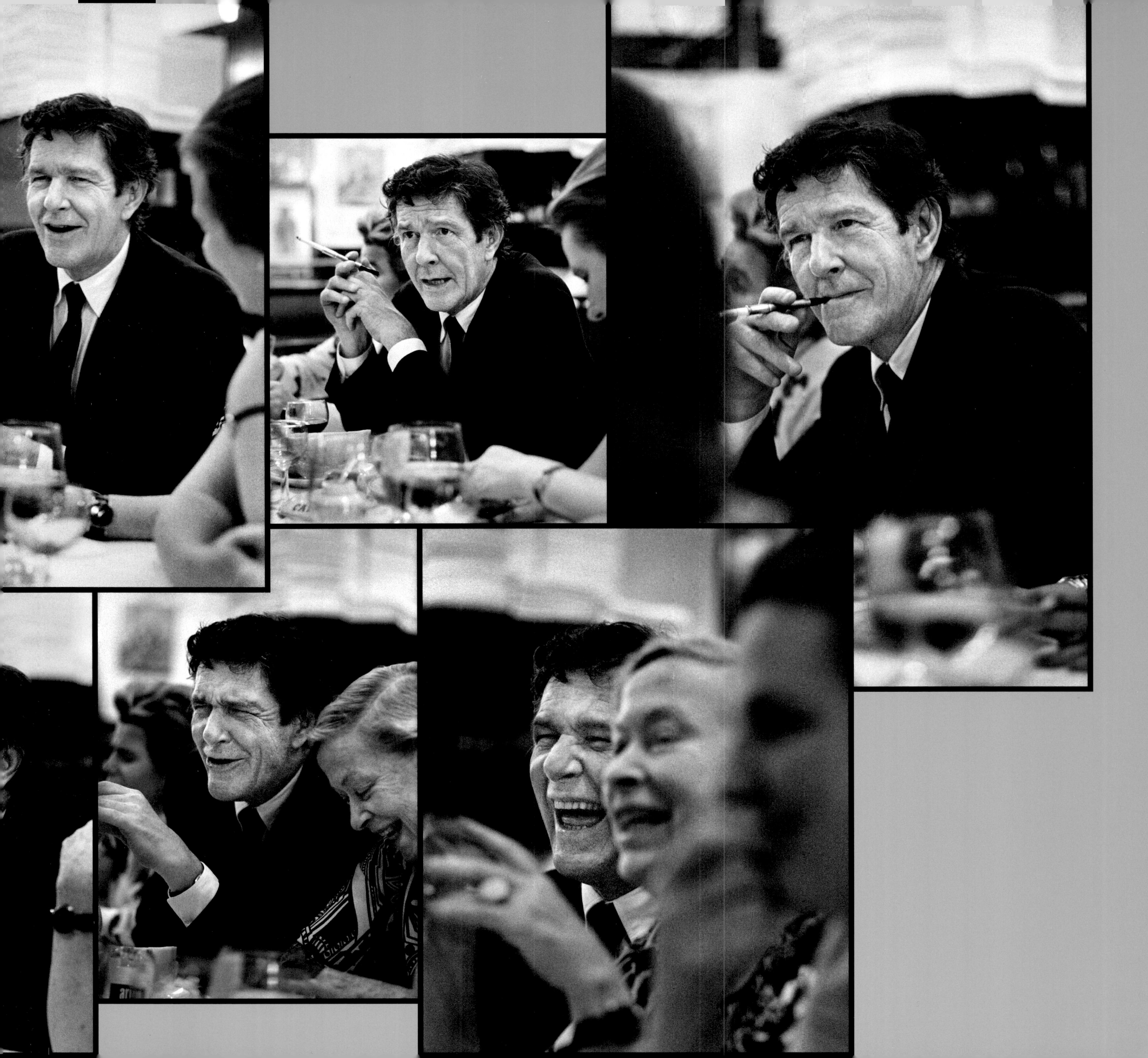

ON READING JOHN CAGE

Reading
            Flowing
Music without measurements,
Sounds passing through circumstances.
Inside myself I hear them
                                    Passing by outside
Outside myself I see them
                                    Passing by with me.
I am circumstance.
Music:
          I hear inside what I see outside
          I see inside what I hear outside
(I cannot listen to myself hearing: Duchamp).
                                                              I am

An architecture of instant
Sounds
          Over
Space disintegrating.
                              (Everything
We come across is to the point.)
                                                    Music
Creates silence.
                    Architecture
Creates space.
                    Air factories.
Silence
          In the space where music happens:
Space
          Unextended:
                              There is no such thing as silence
Save in the mind.
                              Silence is an idea
                              The one idea of music.
Music is not idea:
                    It is sound,
Sound moving over silence.
(Not one sound fears the silence
                              That extinguishes it.)
Silence is music
                      Music is not silence.
Nirvana is Samsara

Samsara is not Nirvana.
Knowing is not knowing:
Recover ignorance,
Knowing of knowing.
It is one thing to hear
Footsteps in the afternoon
Between trees and houses
And another
To see the same afternoon now
After reading
Silence.
Nirvana Samsara
Silence is music.
(Let life obscure
The difference between art and life.)
Music is not silence:
It is not saying
What silence says,
It is saying
What it does not say.
Silence has no sense
Sense has no silence.
Music slips between the two
Unheard
(Every something is an echo of nothing.)
In the silence of my room
The murmur of my body:
Astounding.
Some day I shall hear its thoughts.
The afternoon
Is standing still:
Yet–it is moving.
My body hears the body of my wife
(A cable of sound)
And responds:
This is called music.
Music is real,
Silence is an idea.
John Cage is Japanese
And it's not an idea:
It is sun over snow.
Sun and snow are not the same:
Sun is snow and snow is snow
Or conversely
Sun is not snow and snow is not snow
Or conversely
John Cage is not American
(U.S.A. is determined to keep the Free World free,
U.S.A. determined)
Or conversely
John Cage is American
(That the U.S.A. may become
Just another part of the world,
No more, no less)
Or conversely
Snow is not sun
Music is not silence
Sun is snow
Silence is music
(The situation must be Yes-and-No
Not either-or)
Between silence and music
Between art and life
Snow and sun
There is a man
This man is John Cage
(Committed
To the nothing in between)
He says a word
Not snow not sun
A word
Which is not
silence:
A year from Monday you will hear it.

The afternoon has become invisible.

— Octavio Paz
Delhi, December 14, 1967

Translation from Spanish by Monique Fong
(parentheses are quotations from Cage's *A Year from Monday*)

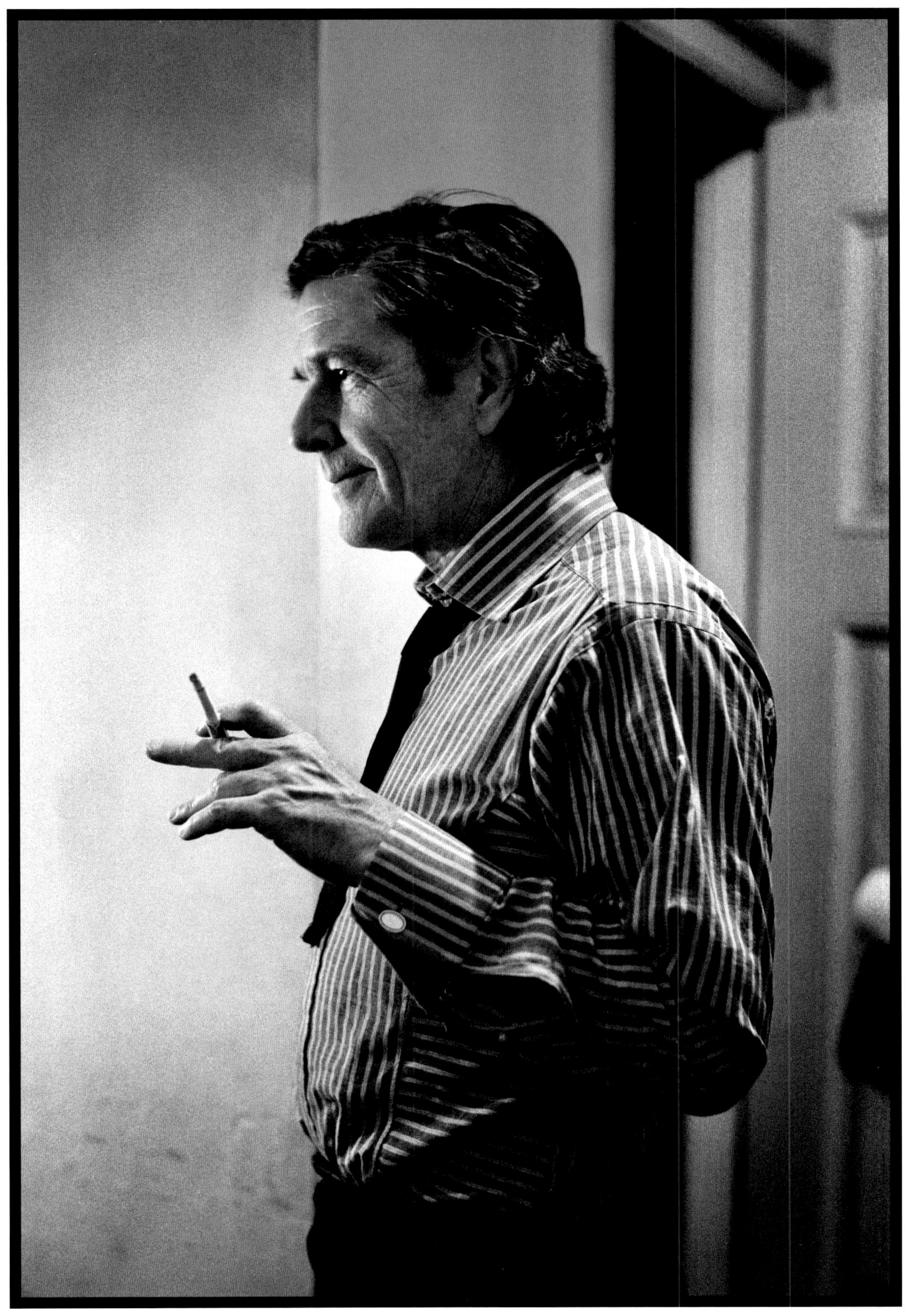

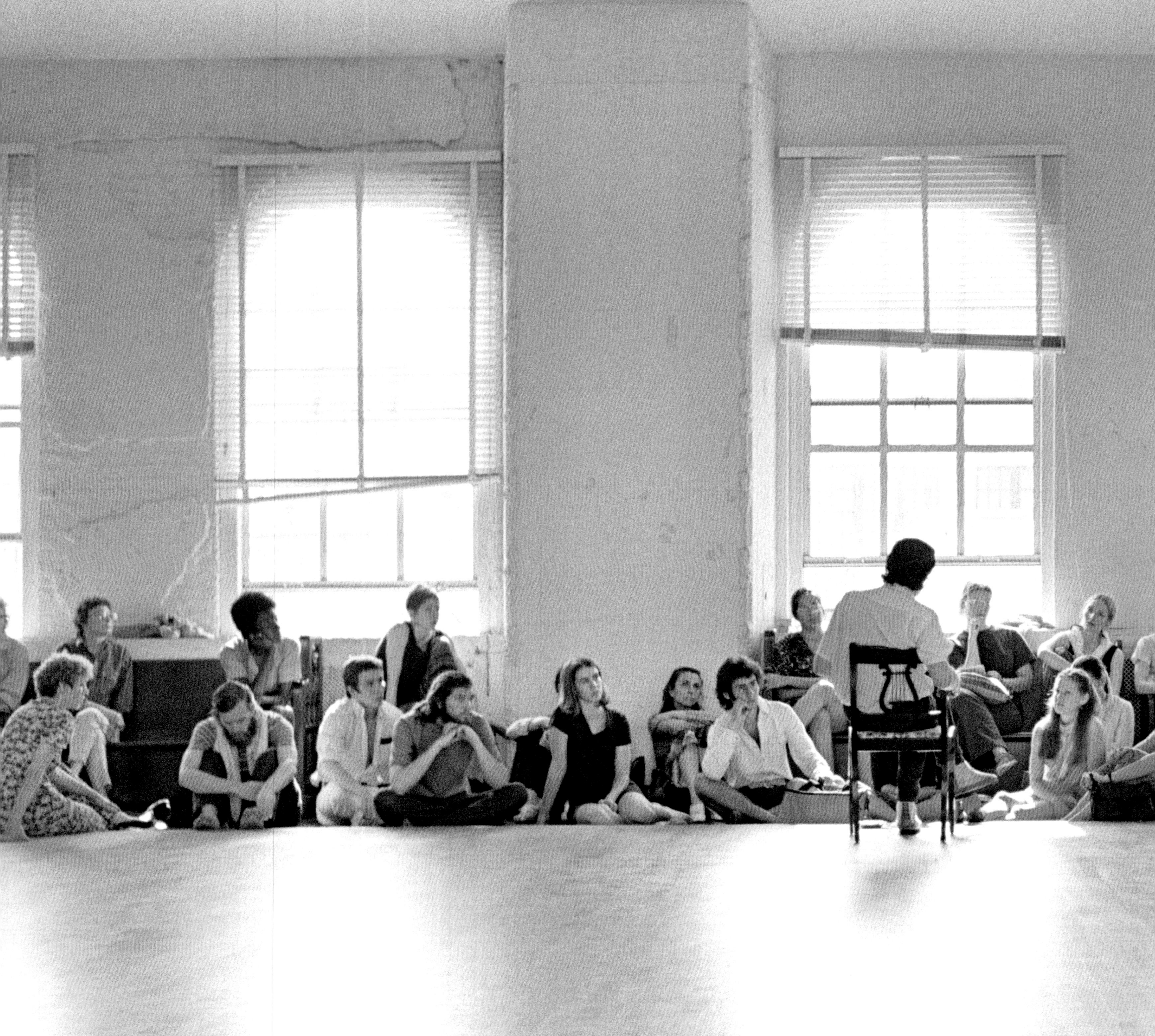

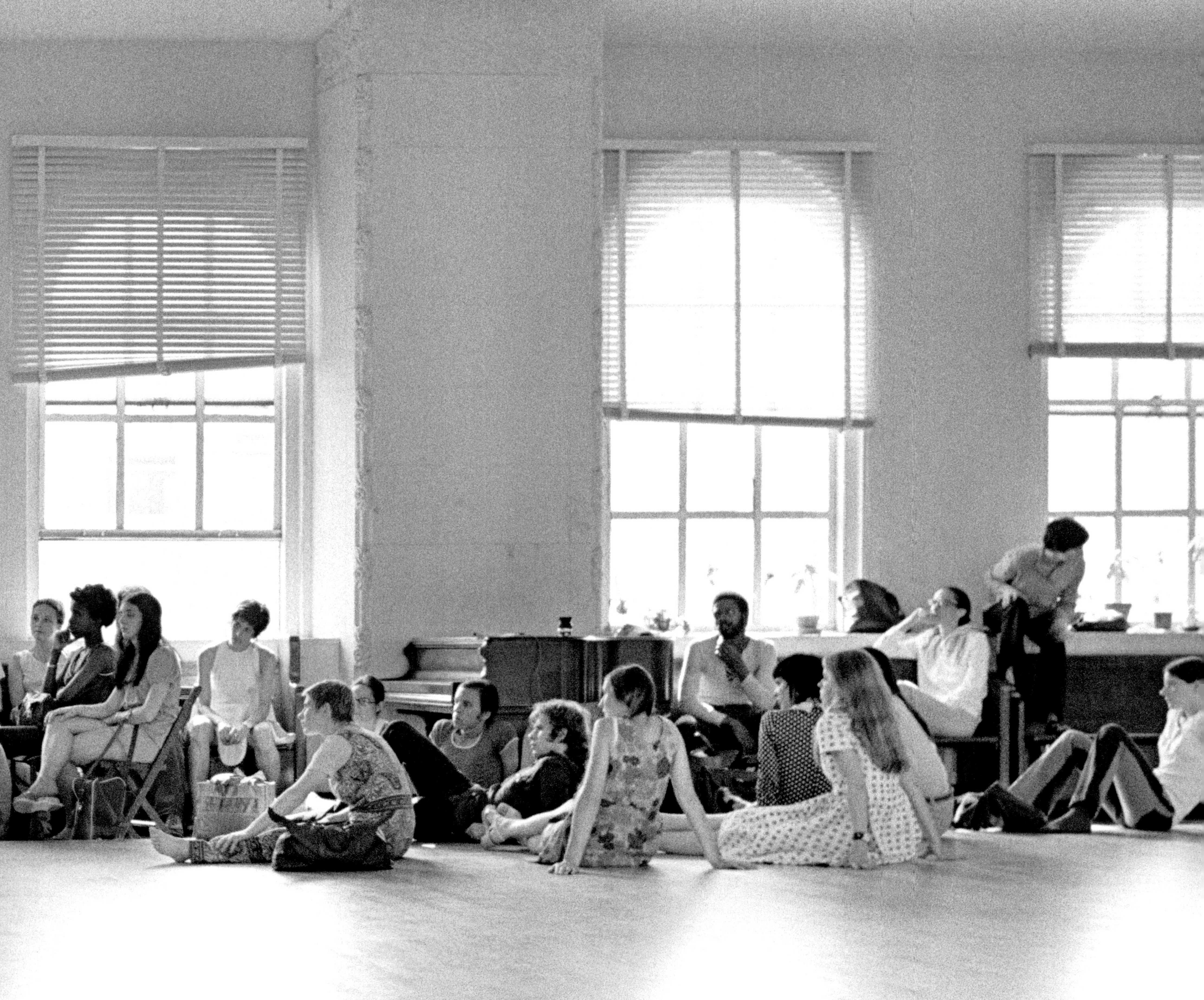

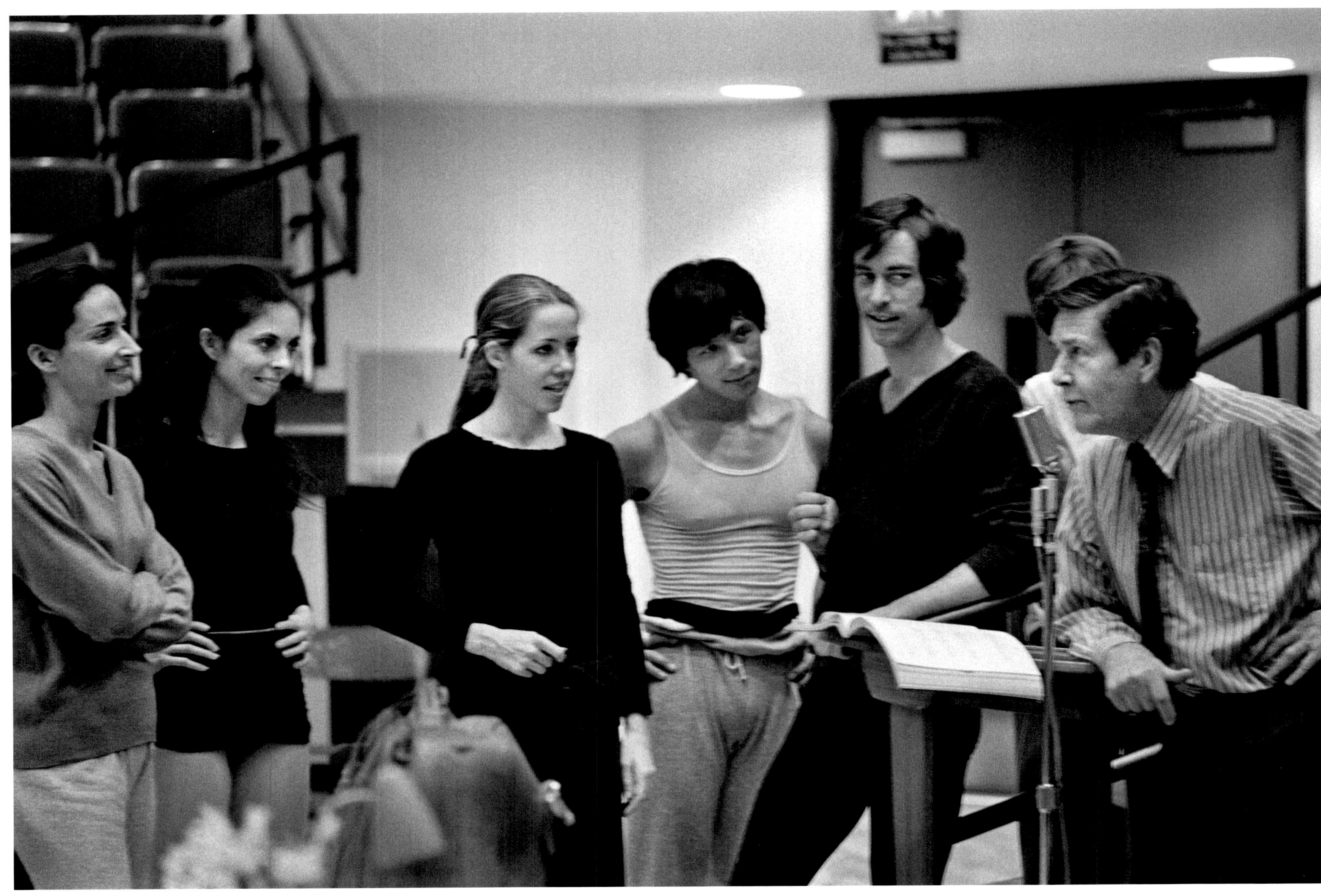

John Cage was an exemplary teacher. The night we first met—I was helping him move materials after a performance of *HPSCHD*—he needed directions to an after-party. John asked a passing gentleman for directions. The man's directions were a rapid stream of heavily accented English. I exclaimed in befuddlement. John said, "Be quiet and listen." Over the next twenty years Cage applied that lesson many ways as we prepared his music for publication. We were, he mused, seeking perfection, never reaching it but coming ever closer.

— Paul Sadowski

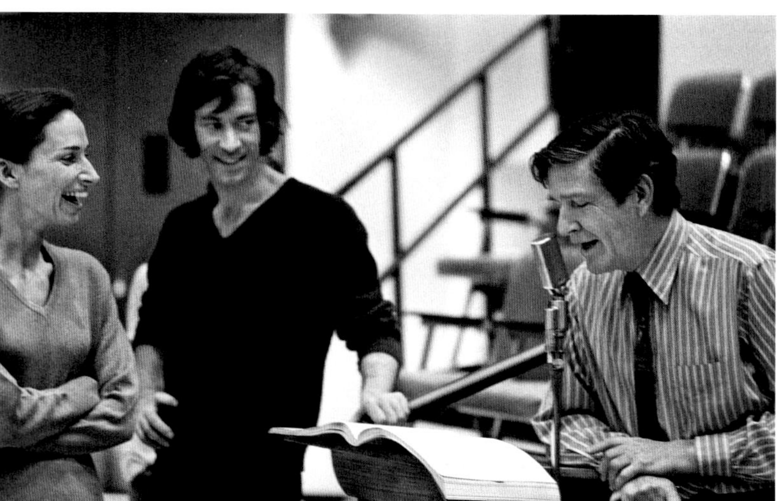

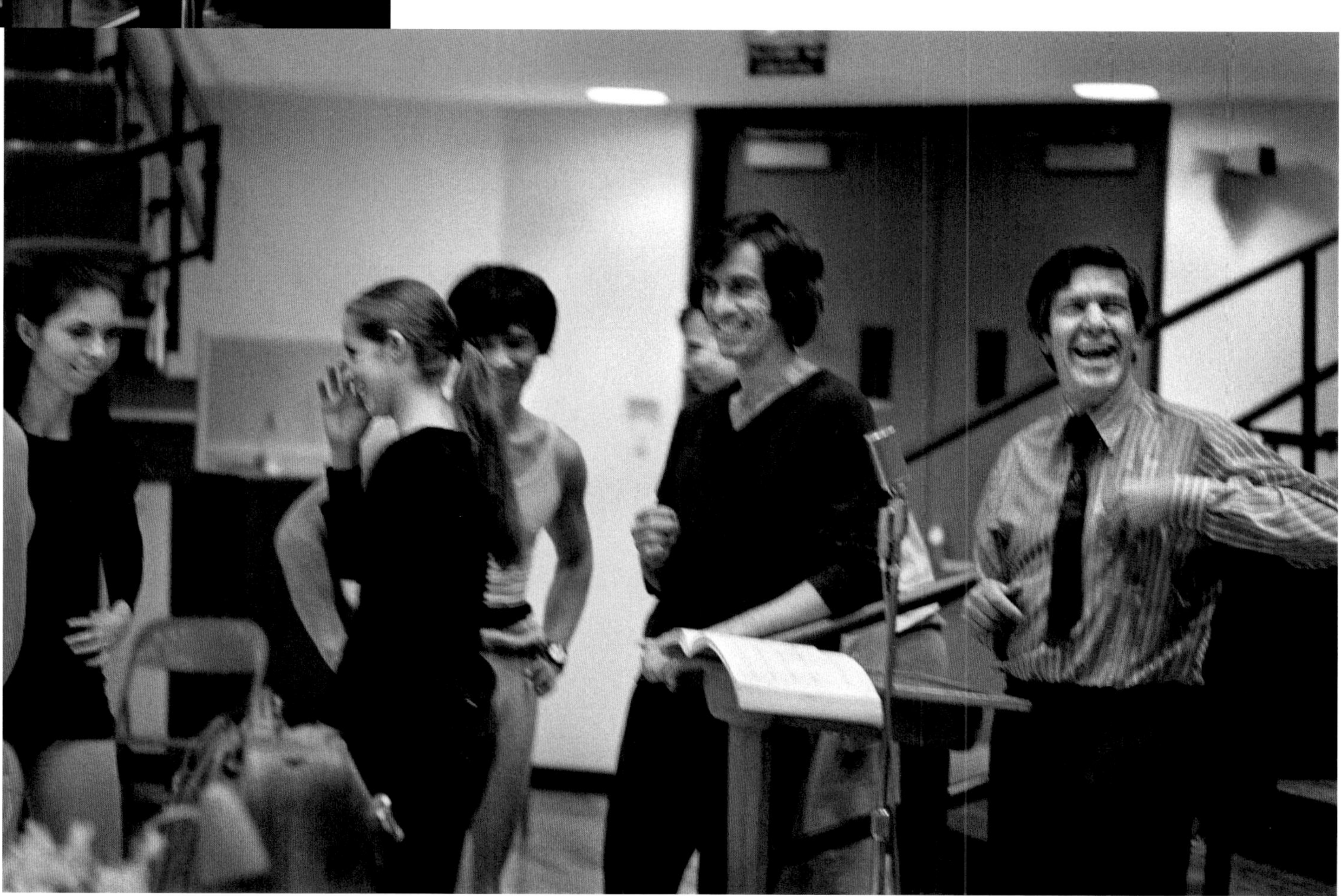

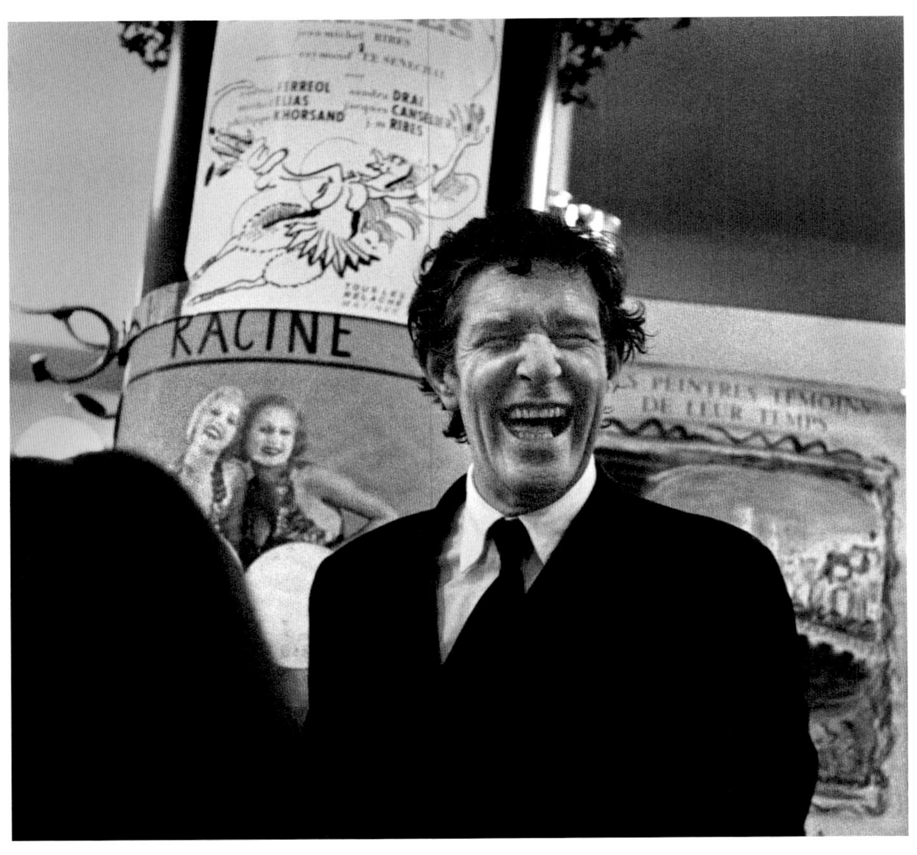
RACINE

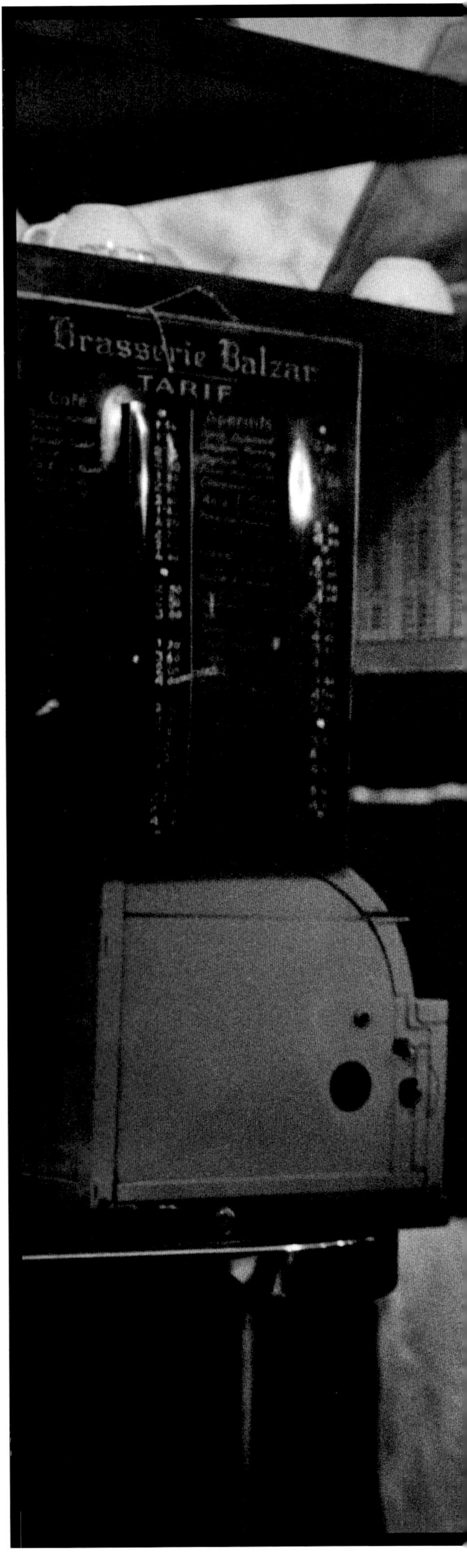
Brasserie Balzar
TARIF

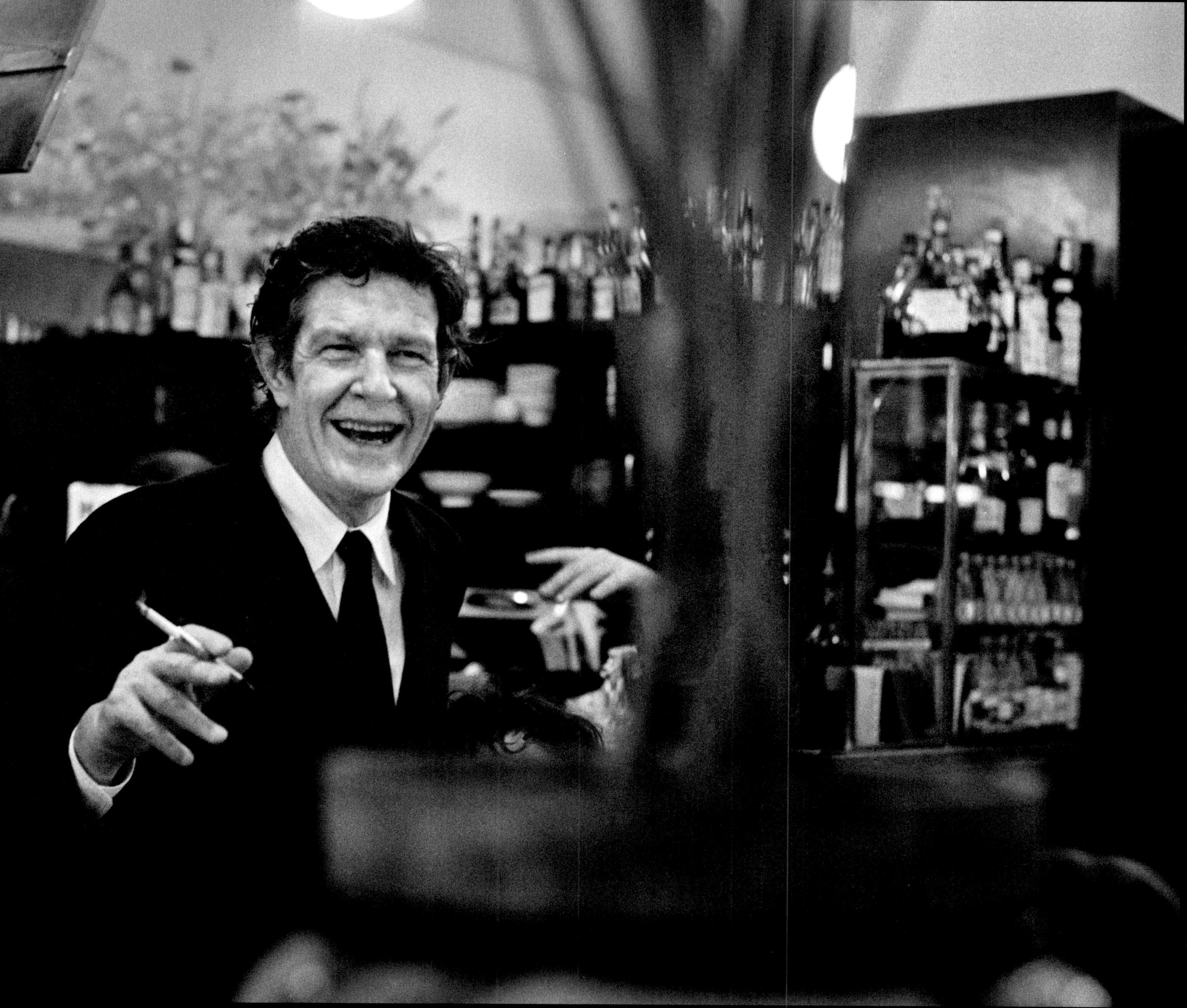

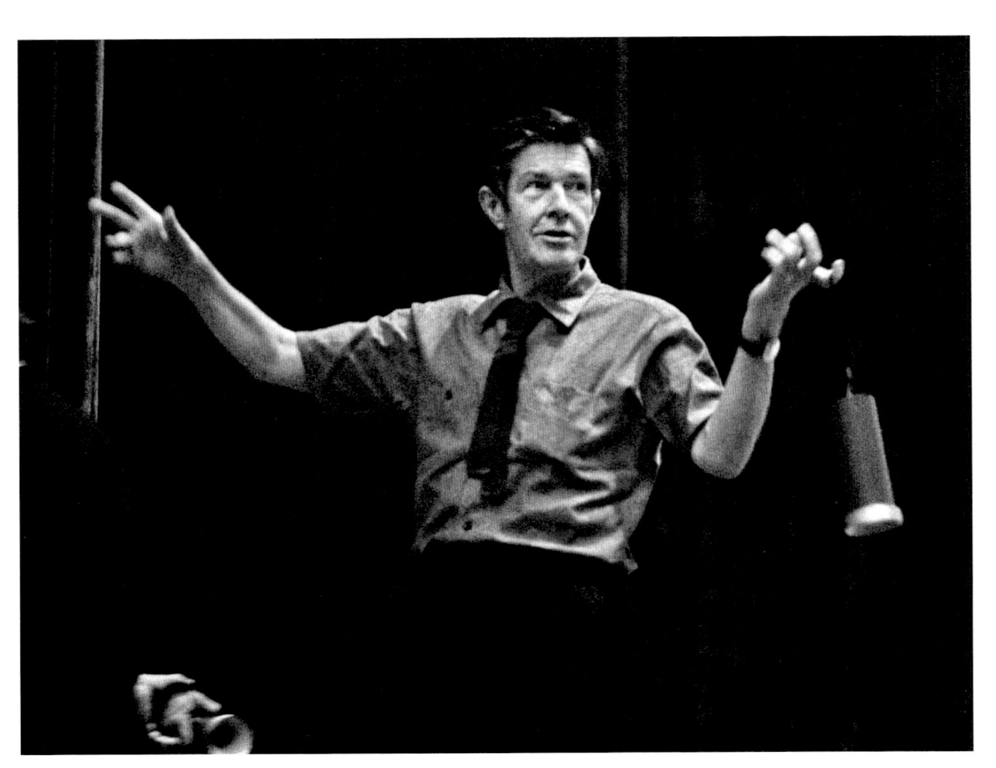

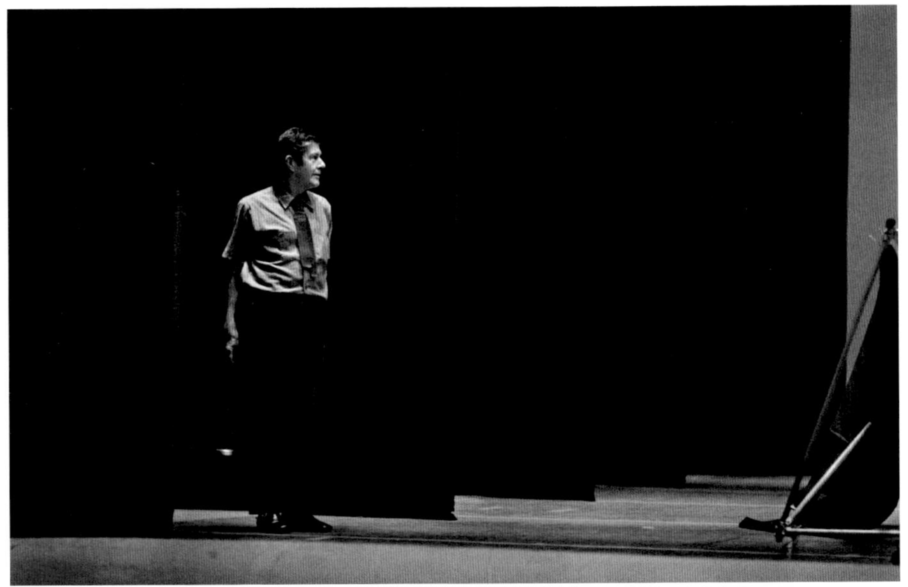

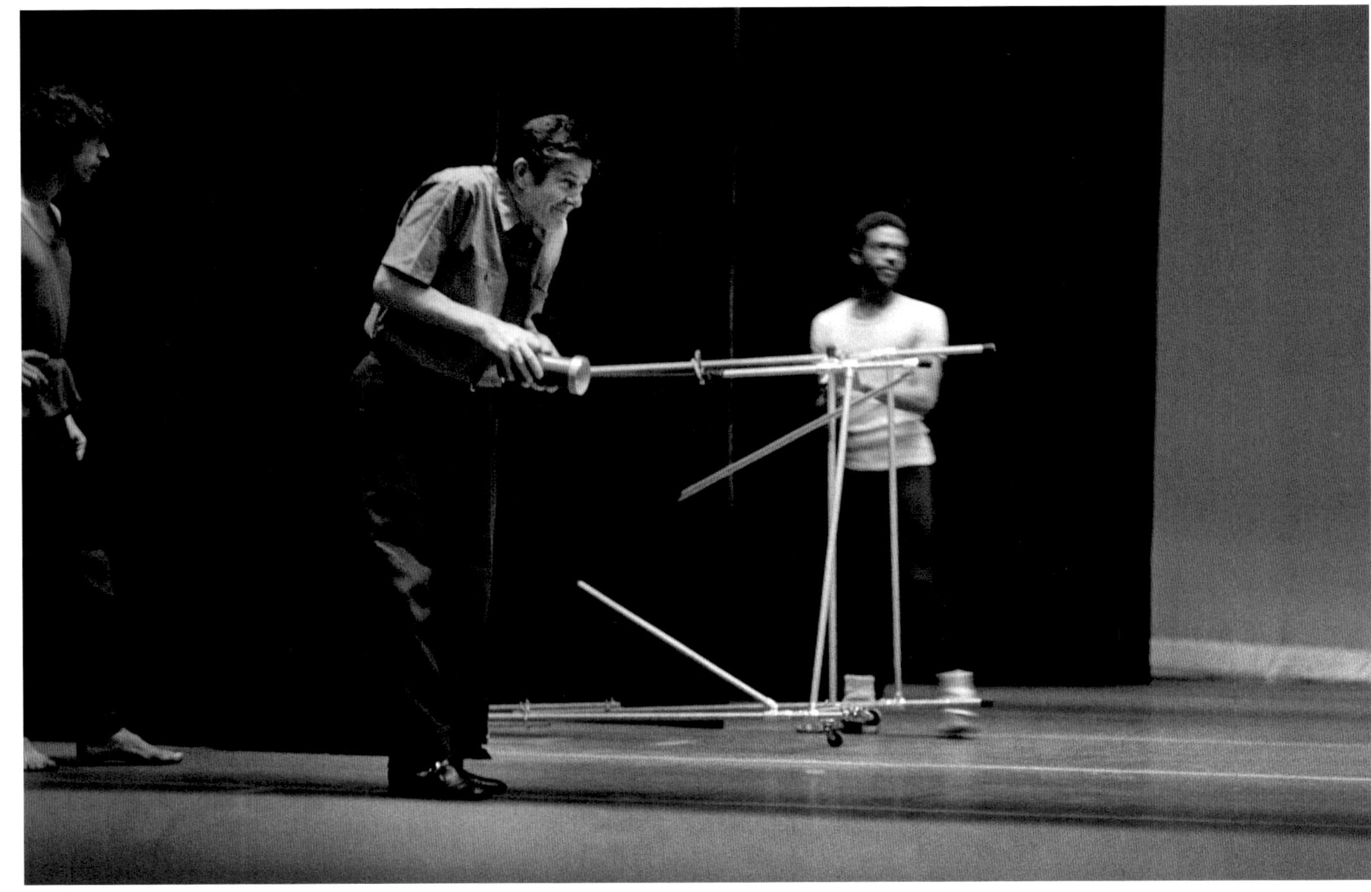

John Cage was, once.
He shone.

So new, so sane. So now.
No swan: He hews congas anew.
He how's, he hones, he nags chaos.

He chews cones, snow, as echos?

He's gone song, he saw change.

"John, when can we jog?"
"Scan an eon."
"When awns wane?"
"Wean, son, chew an ens. Wage own show."

"Caw a schwa?"
"No. Chase chaos. Gash ashen cogs."
Jaws ache when one haws,

ah's, ha's, as echo of song of John Cage.

—Douglas Dunn

Glossary
echos: Byzantine music theory mode
awn: bristle-like appendage of a plant
ens: a real thing
schwa: mid-central, neutral vowel sound

John Cage was always laughing.

“Oh, it’s going to be horrendous!” he exclaims,

laughing, at Crown Point Press in 1979.

I have this on videotape. “We could easily get up to two hundred colors!”

a printer reports, consulting John’s “score.”

Suddenly we grasp the huge amount of work required to follow “chance operations”

and the printers, John, and I are all laughing together.

Even now when I see one of our *Changes and Disappearances* etchings—

so delicate, so beautiful, so difficult—I smile.

“The most manifest sign of wisdom is continual cheerfulness,” wrote Montaigne.

John Cage was wise.

— Kathan Brown

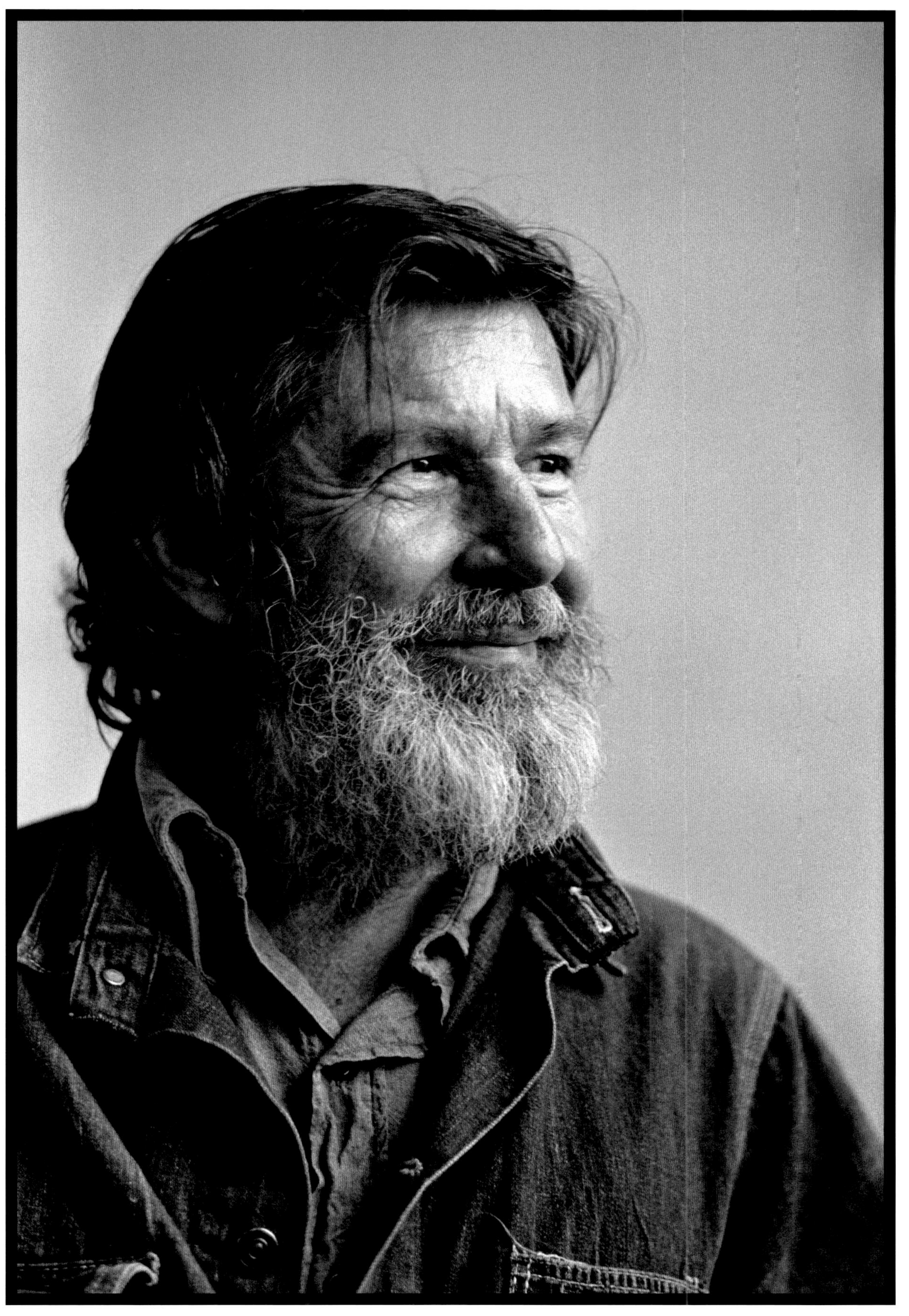

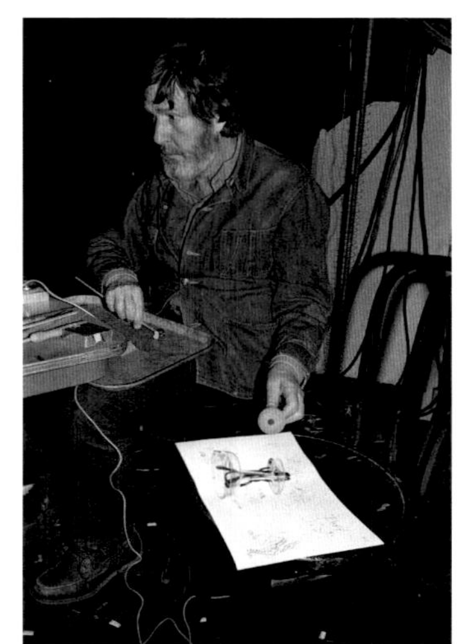

John Cage was
the man who roused me
from political
and aesthetic
sleep.
In 1949
I attended a multicultural jamboree at Vassar.
I was then studying music,
so I attended the sessions on music,
dominated by delegates from Juilliard
with strongly Stalinist views:
American composers should write symphonies
(et al.) based on American folksongs.
Eventually
John Cage spoke and said:
"If you wish to write democratic music,
write pieces that can be played
on pots
and pans,
or with tools
from the garage"
. . . changing
my own views on
the politics of music
for life.
McLuhan
in a nutshell.

— Harry Mathews

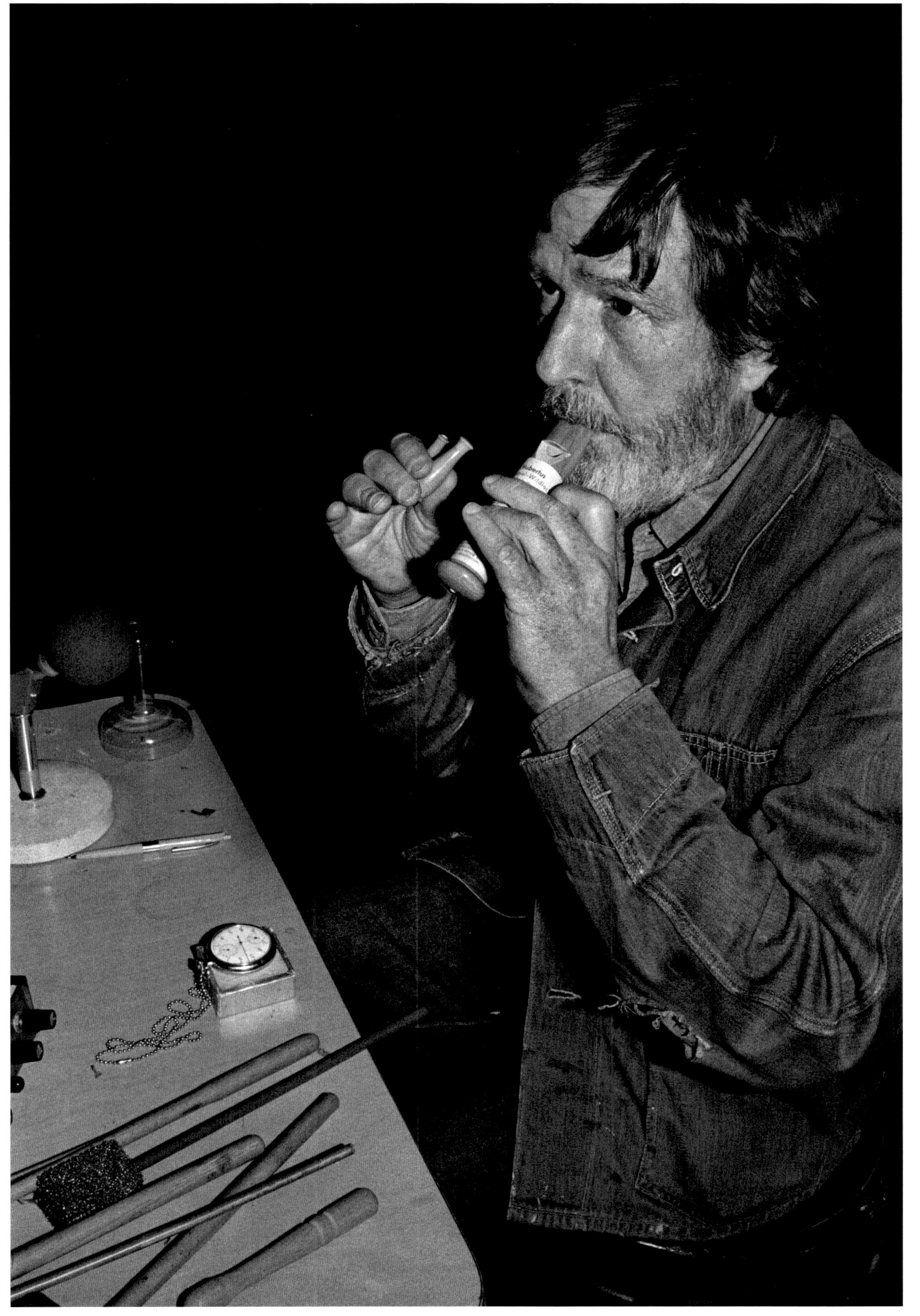

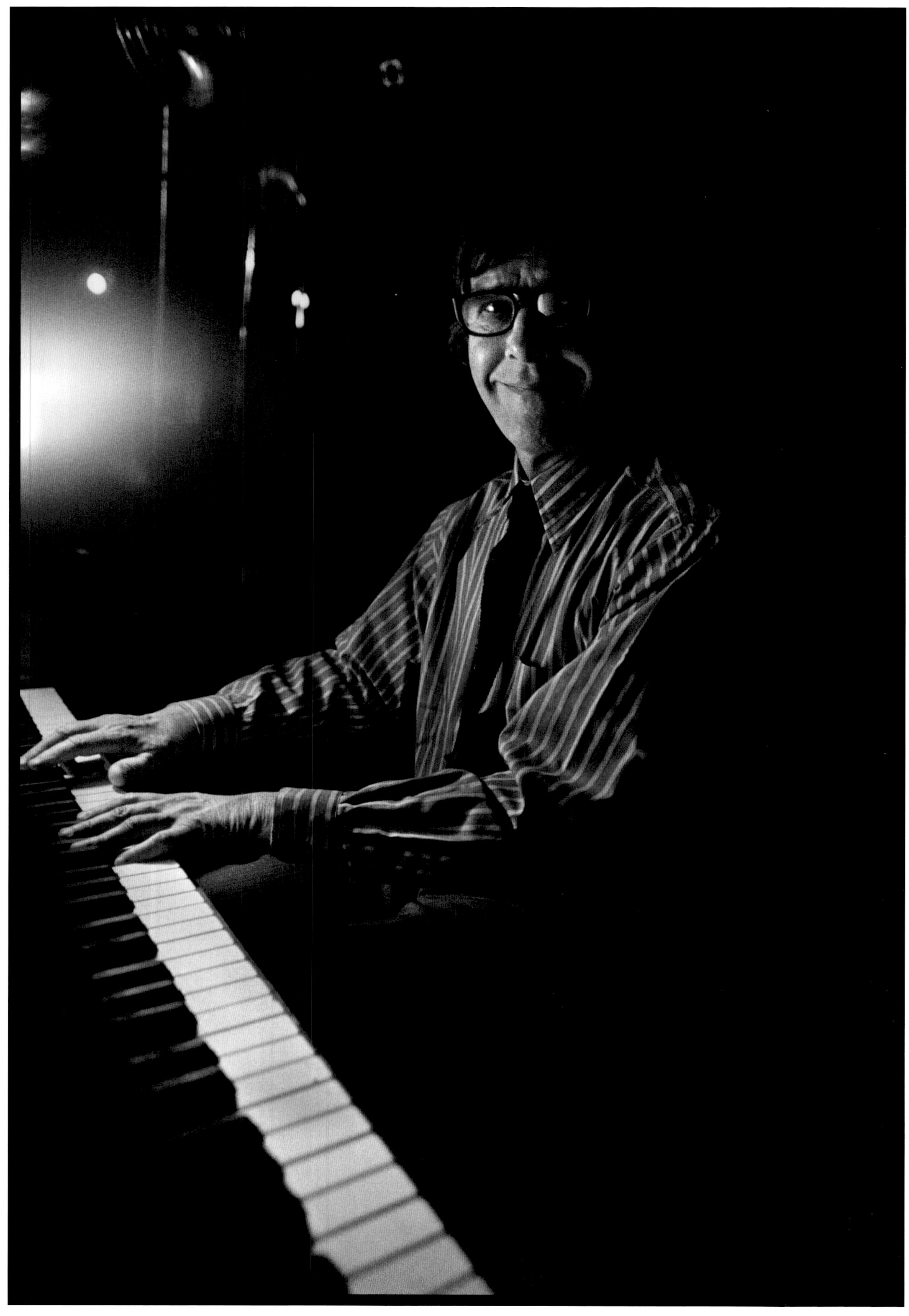

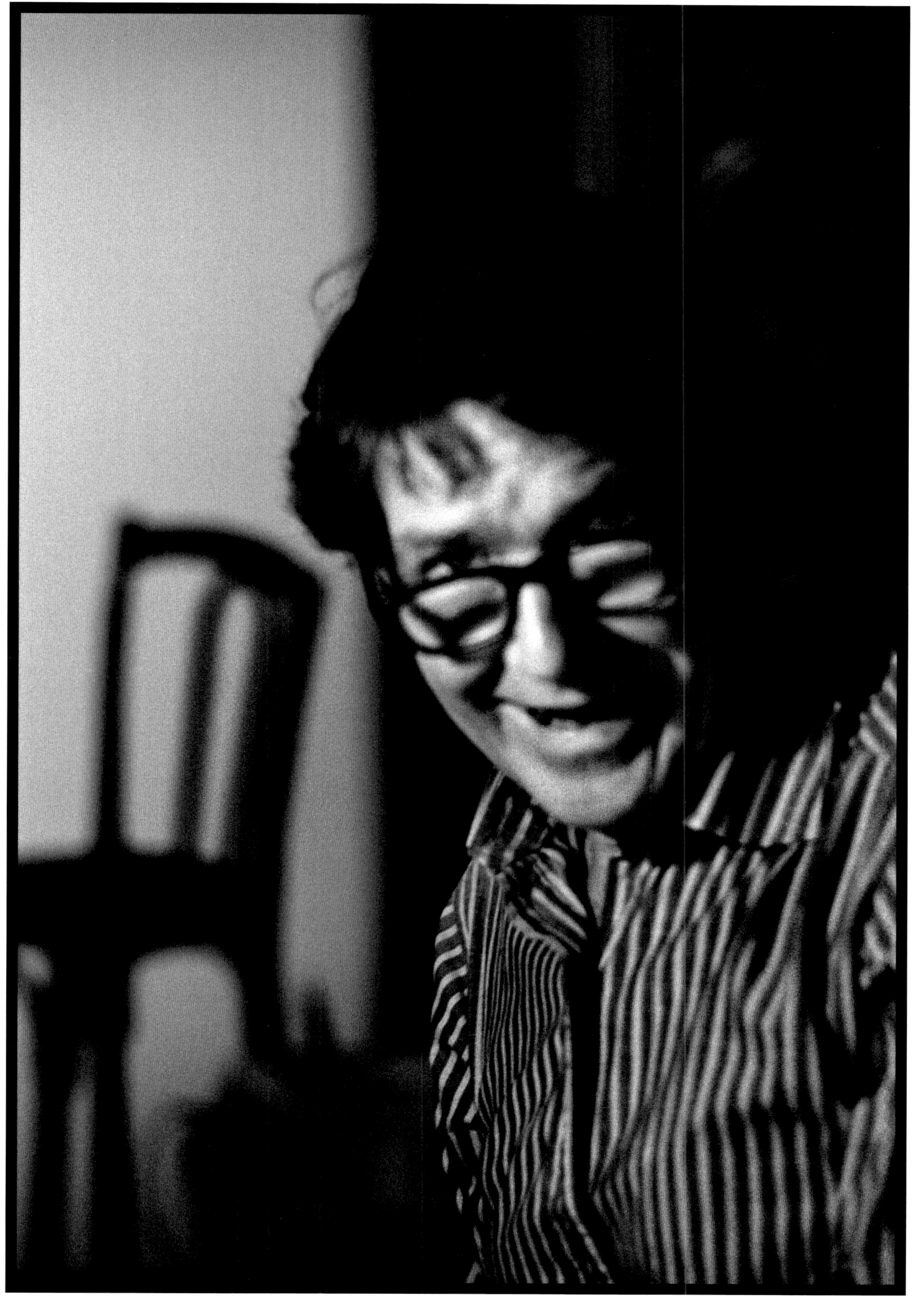

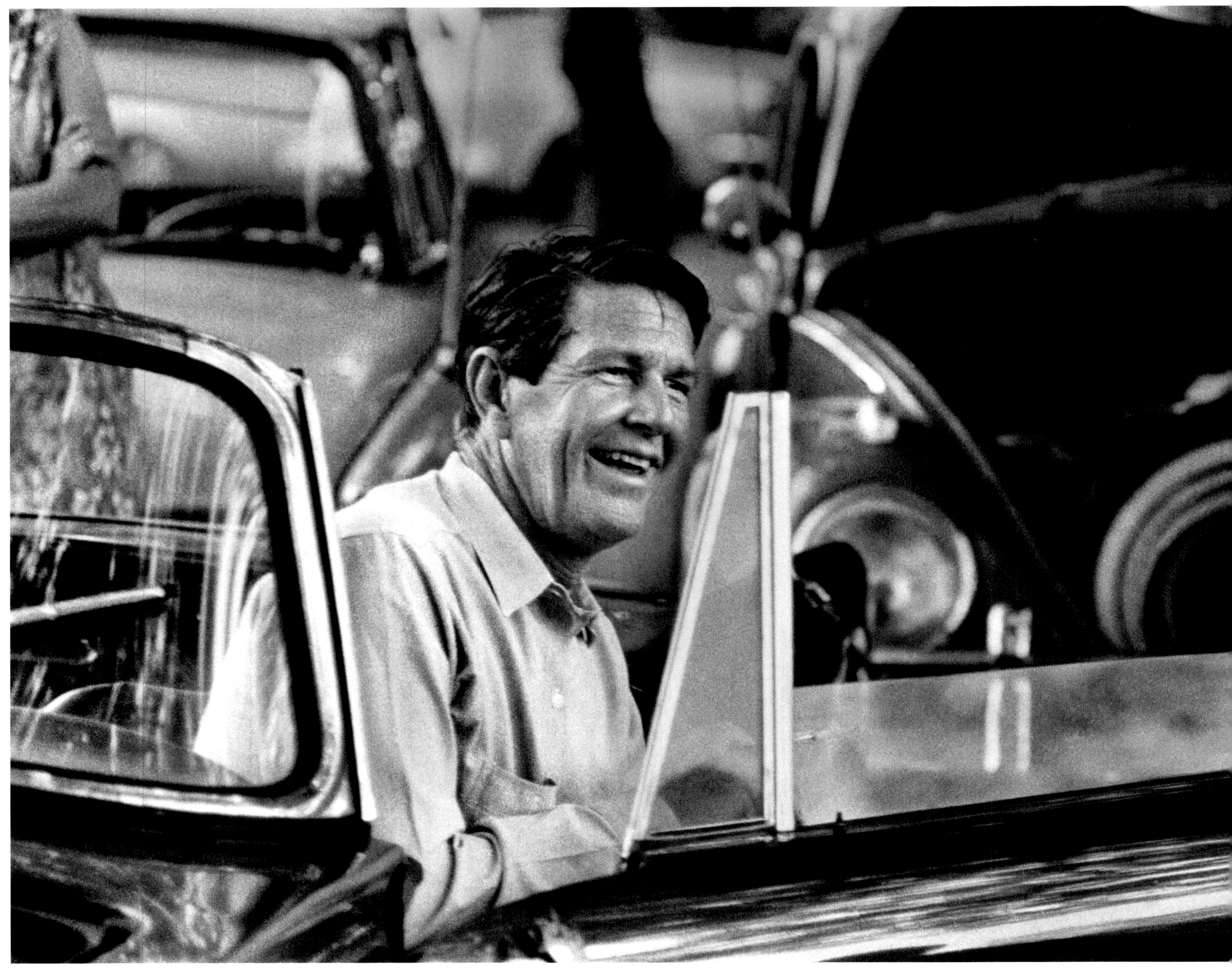

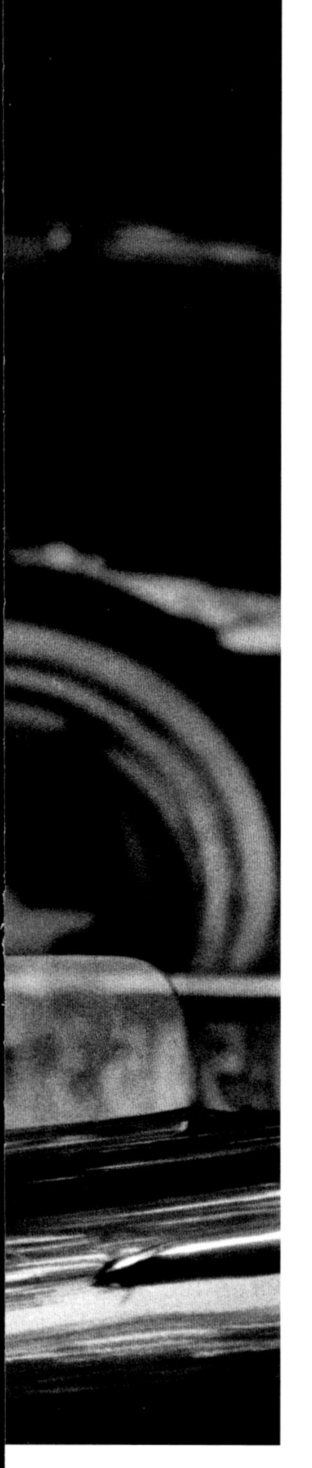

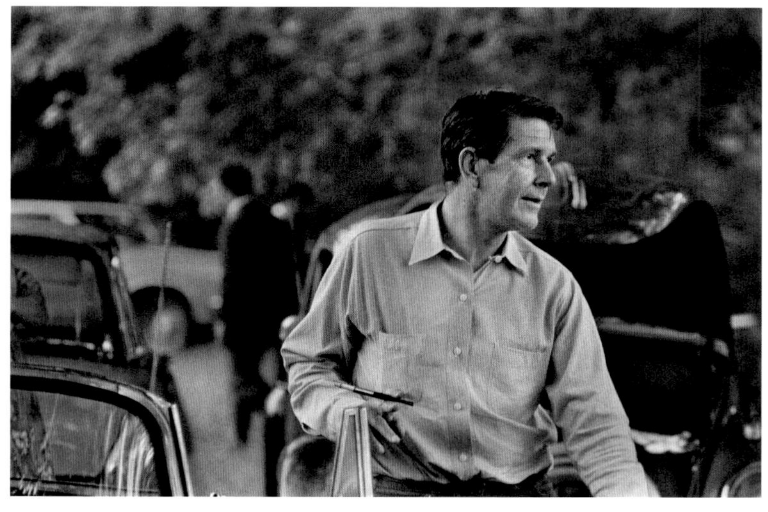

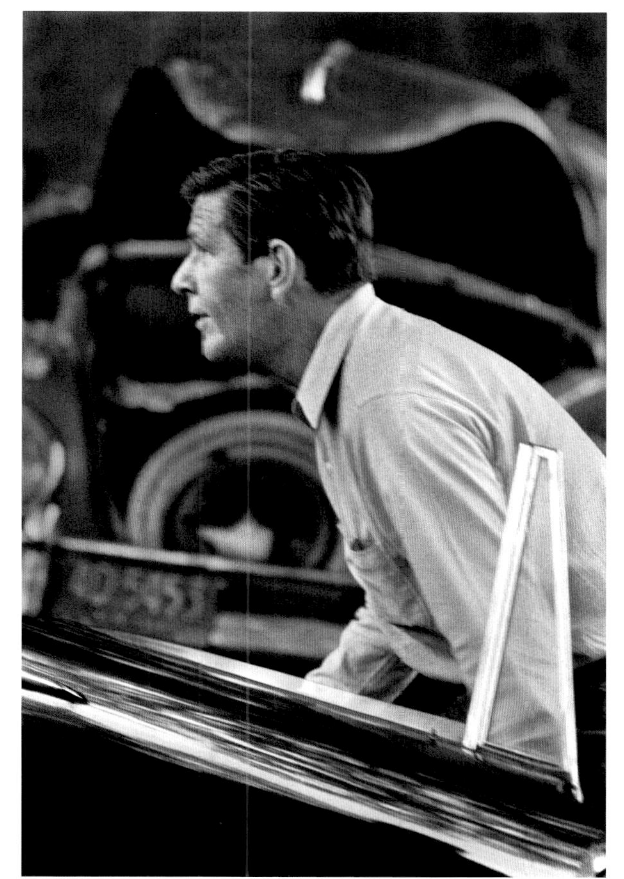

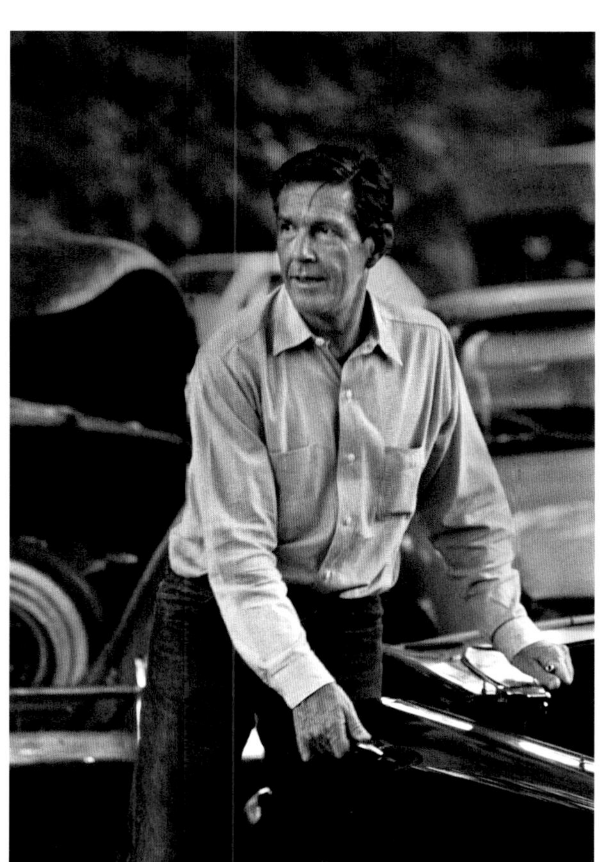

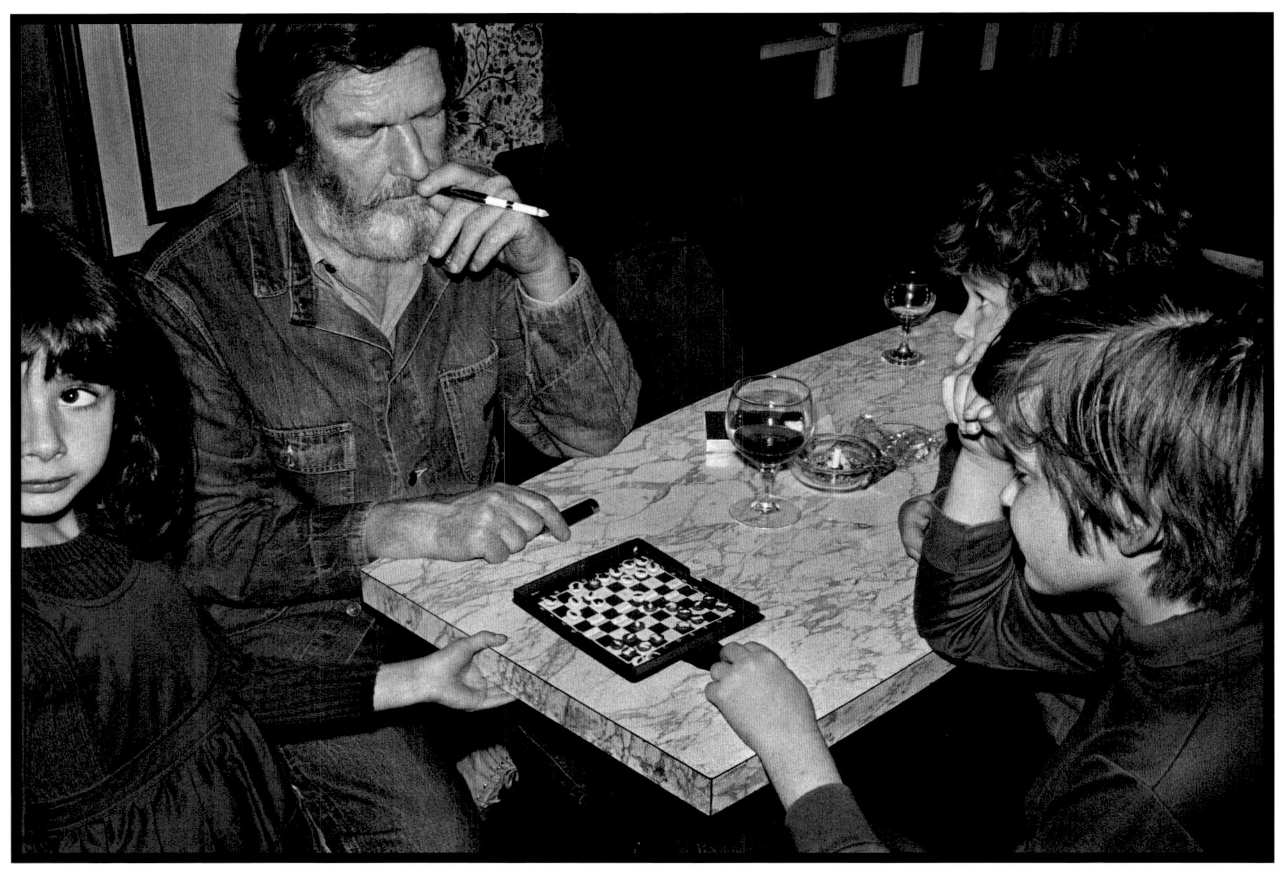

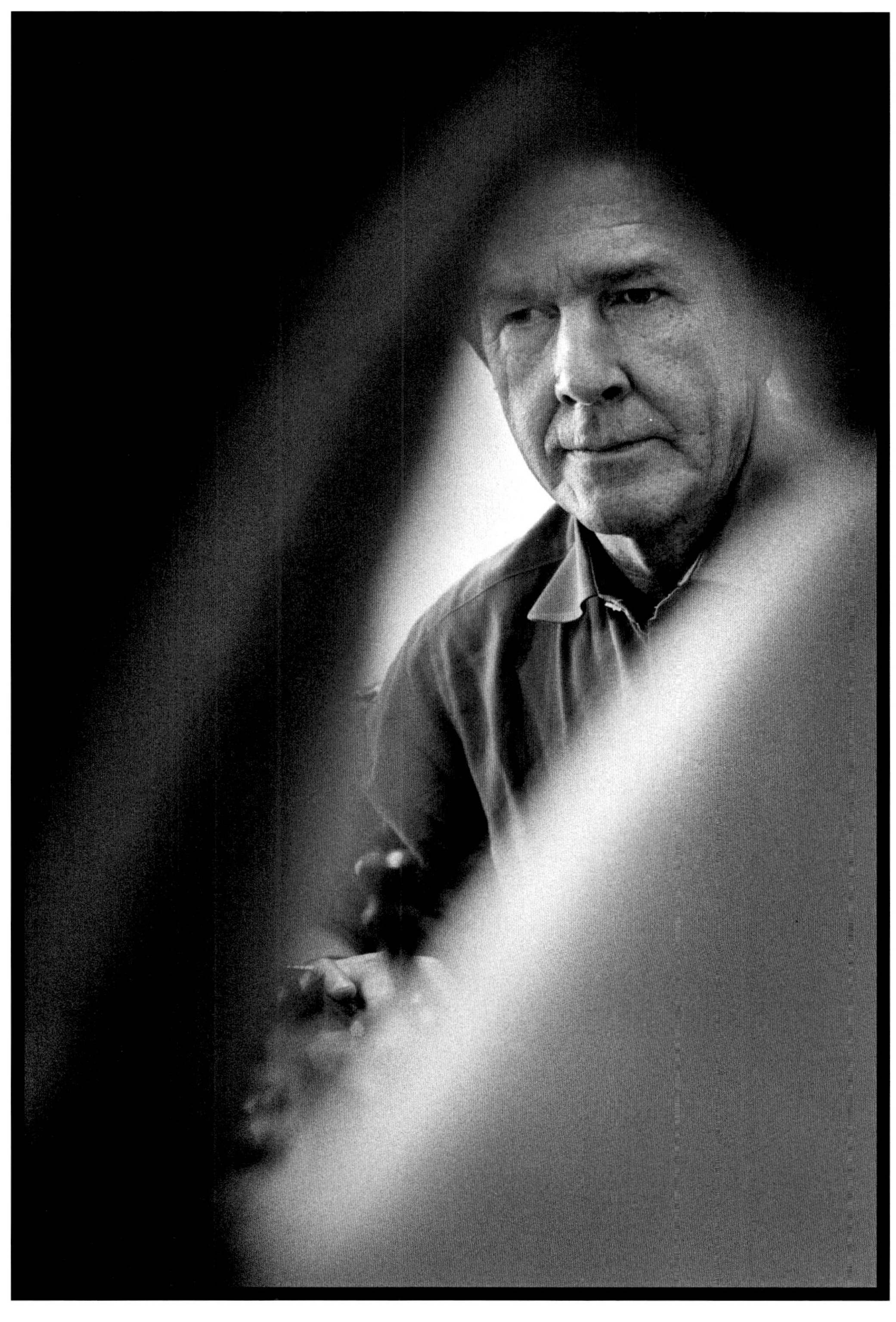

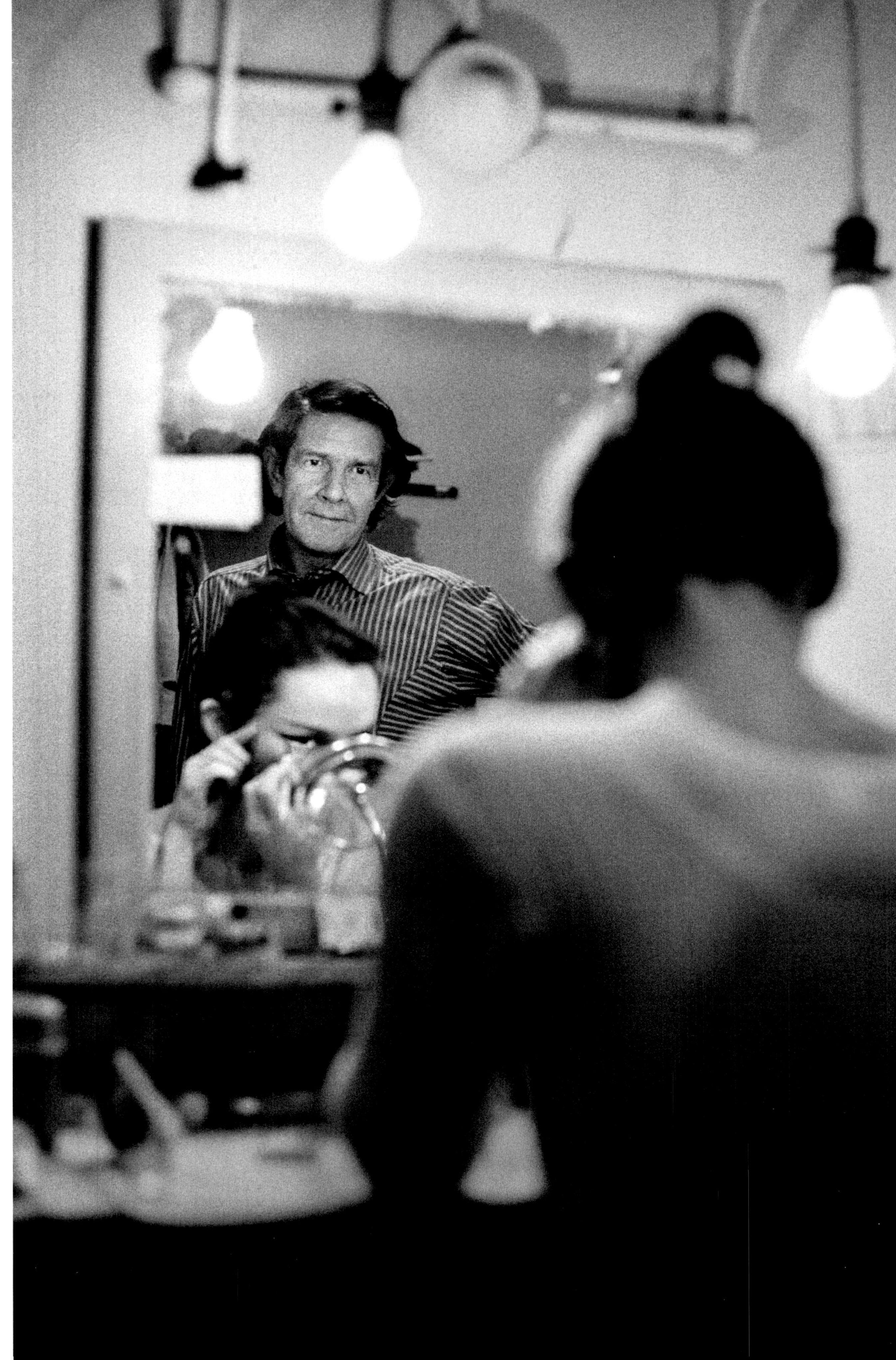

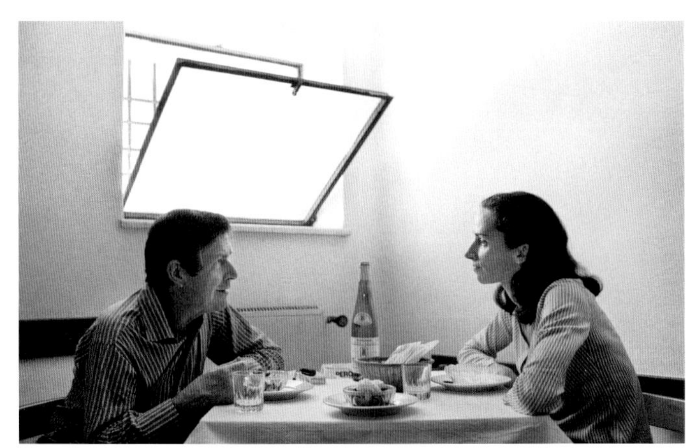

Of course John Cage was the most important influence in my life.

How could it be otherwise?

I arrived in NYC a timid New England puritan,

a Denishawn dancer raised on classical music,

a wannabe writer with nothing yet to write about,

a philosophy student in search of answers to the great questions.

John, happy to be guru,

unblinkered my eyes and mind,

opening them to an unimagined world of art and ideas.

He was, for me,

the heart and soul of the Cunningham Dance Company,

making the experience of dancing with Merce

an ever-surprising, vital,

life-changing

voyage.

— Carolyn Brown

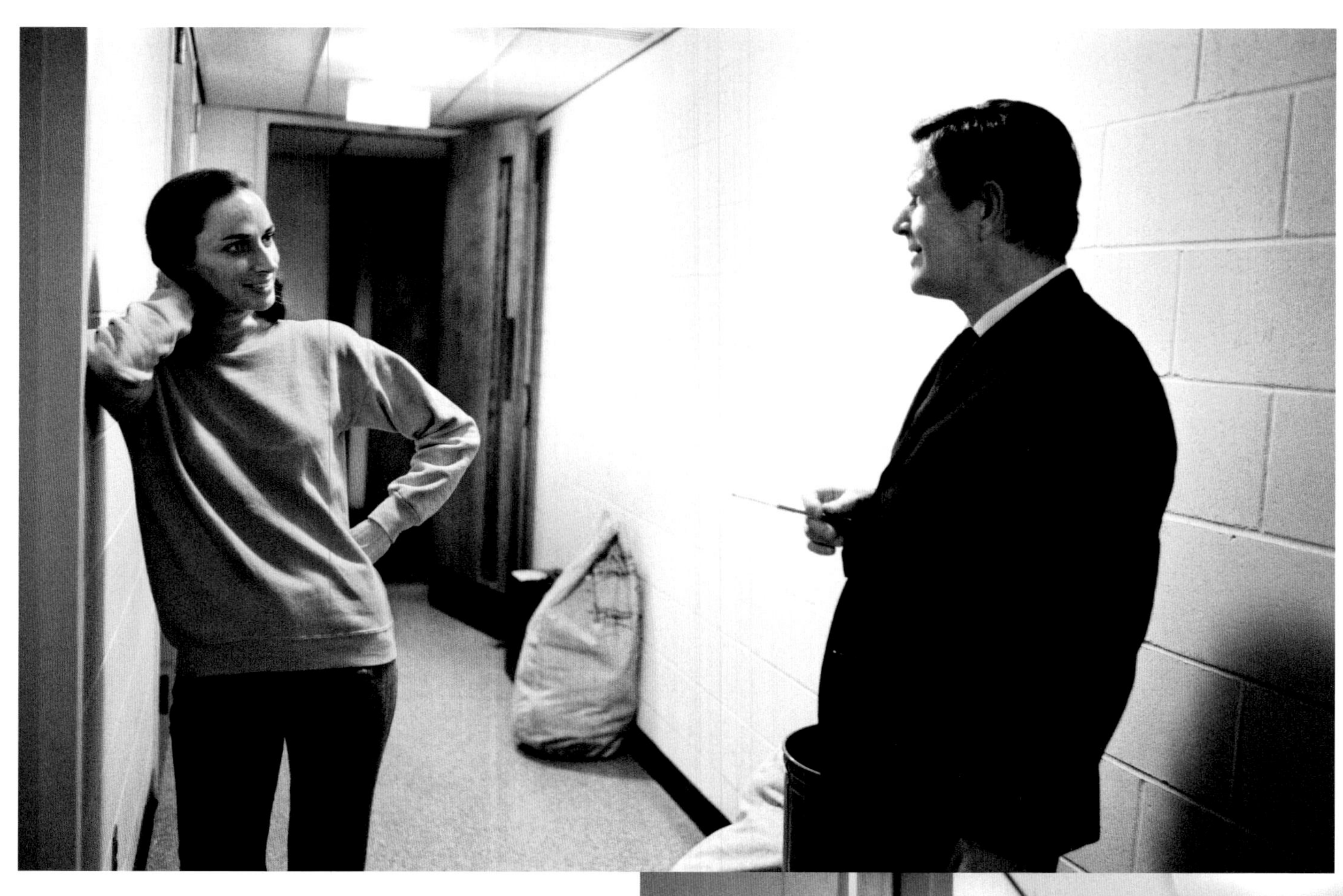

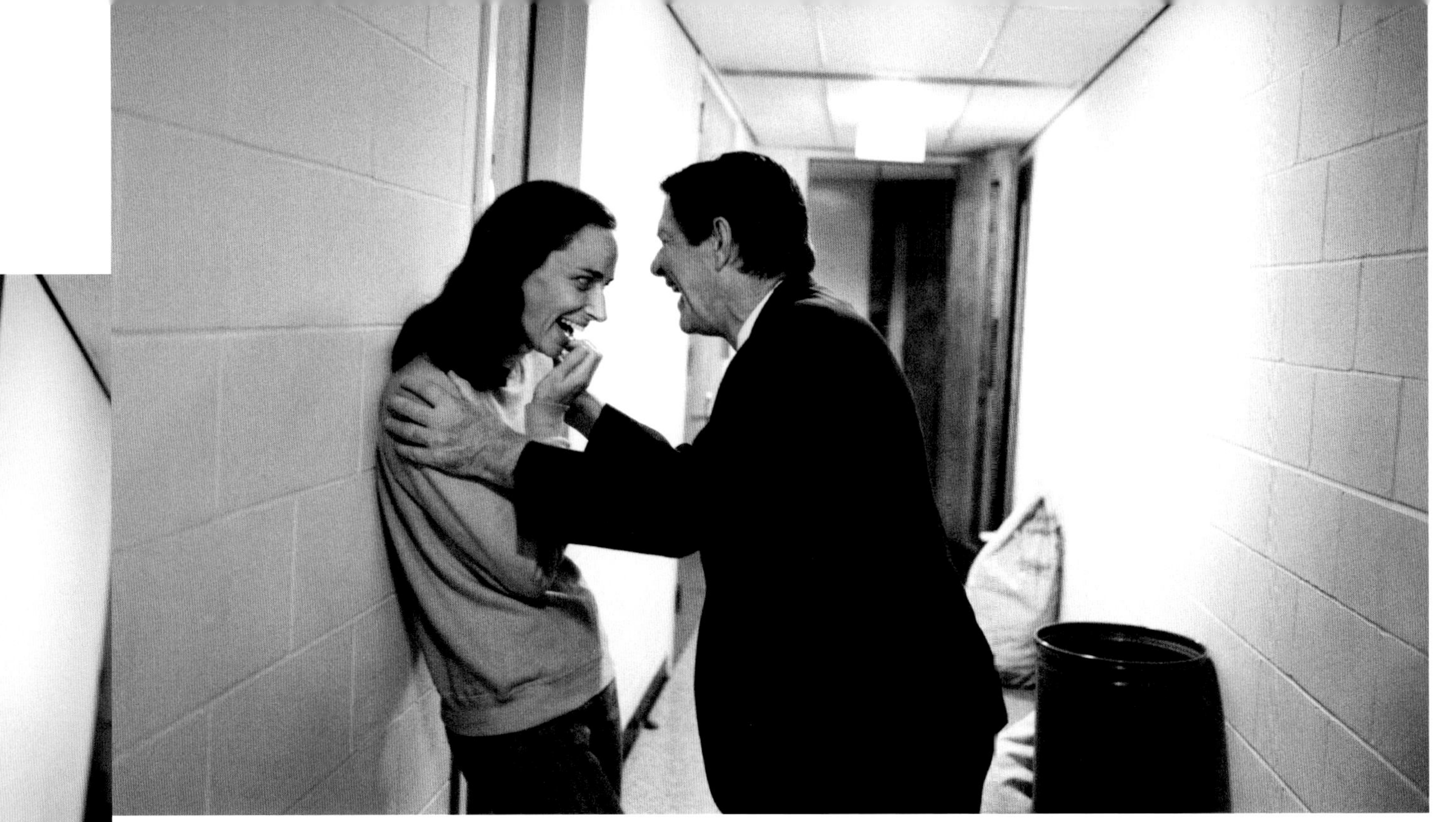

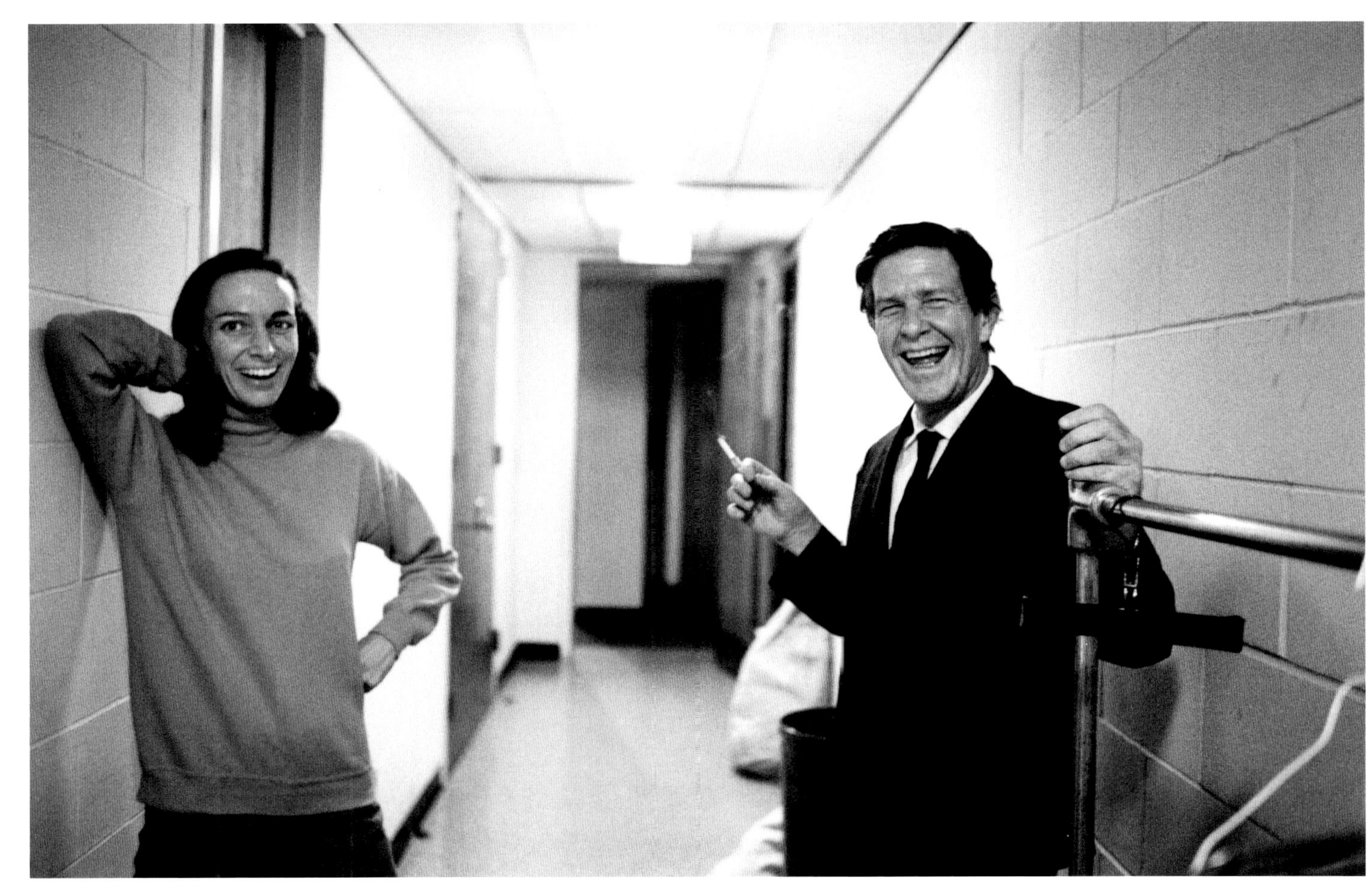

JOHN CAGE WAS A SORT
OF HAUNTING,
OVER-THE-SHOULDER FIGURE
MY ENTIRE LIFE.

FAMILIAR WITH *4'33"* AS A KID, I SUPPOSE I THOUGHT OF CAGE THE WAY MANY SEVEN-YEAR-OLDS THINK OF, SAY, THE PRESIDENT, OR MAYBE THE POPE? MY GROWNUP ATTENTION WAS FIRST HELD BY THE PREPARED PIANO PIECES AND THEN *CHILD OF TREE*, A WORK THAT USES SUCH HUMBLE, WELL, *ABSURD* MEANS, AND CREATES A BEAUTIFUL, SATISFYING COMPOSITIONAL WORLD, BASICALLY IN A DIFFERENT LANGUAGE. I WAS HOOKED. CAGE LIVED LIFE SO WELL AND SO CREATIVELY; SURFING HIS CATALOGUE IS LIKE EXPLORING ANOTHER,
UNBELIEVABLY
GORGEOUS PLANET.

— NADIA SIROTA

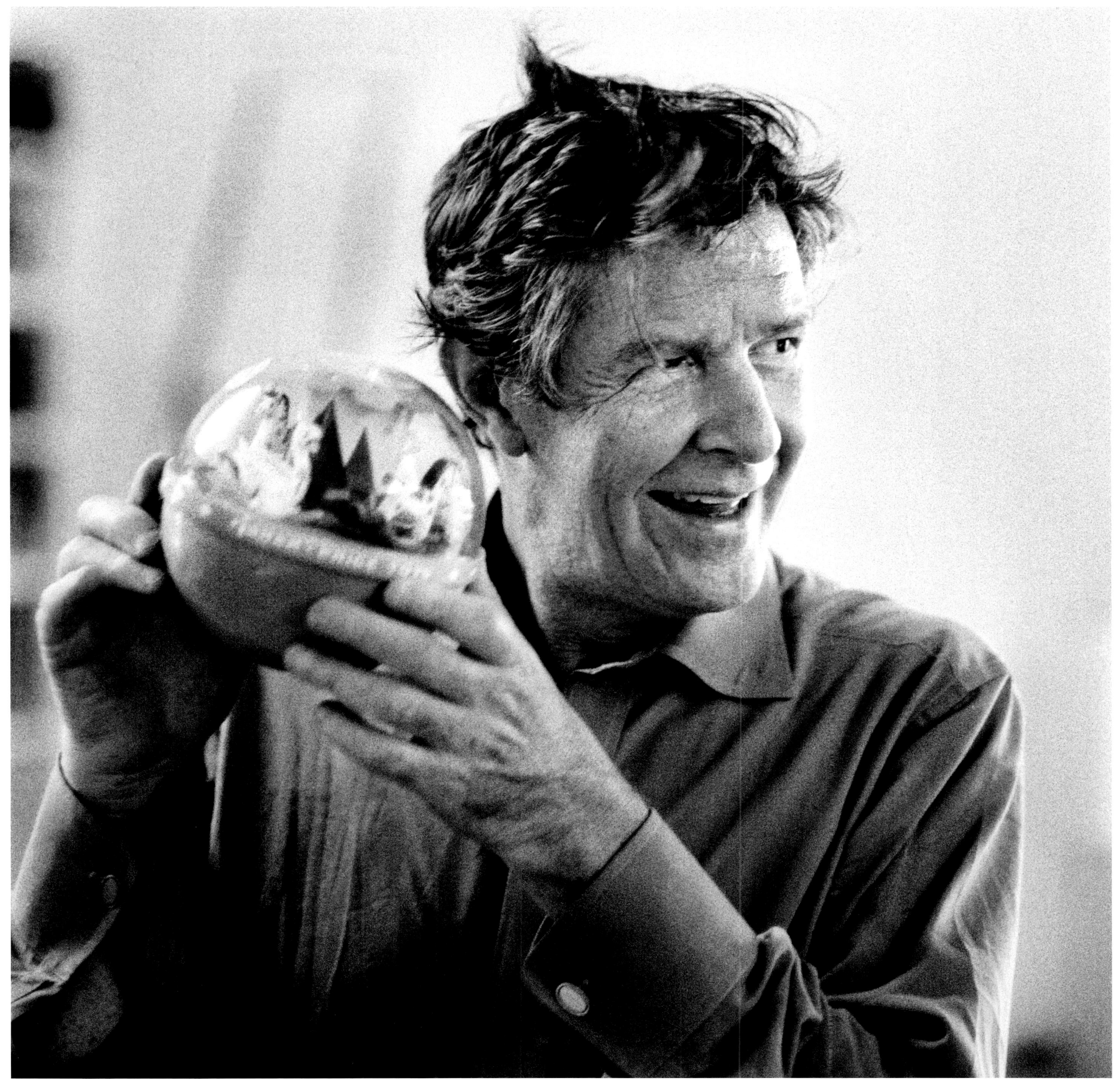

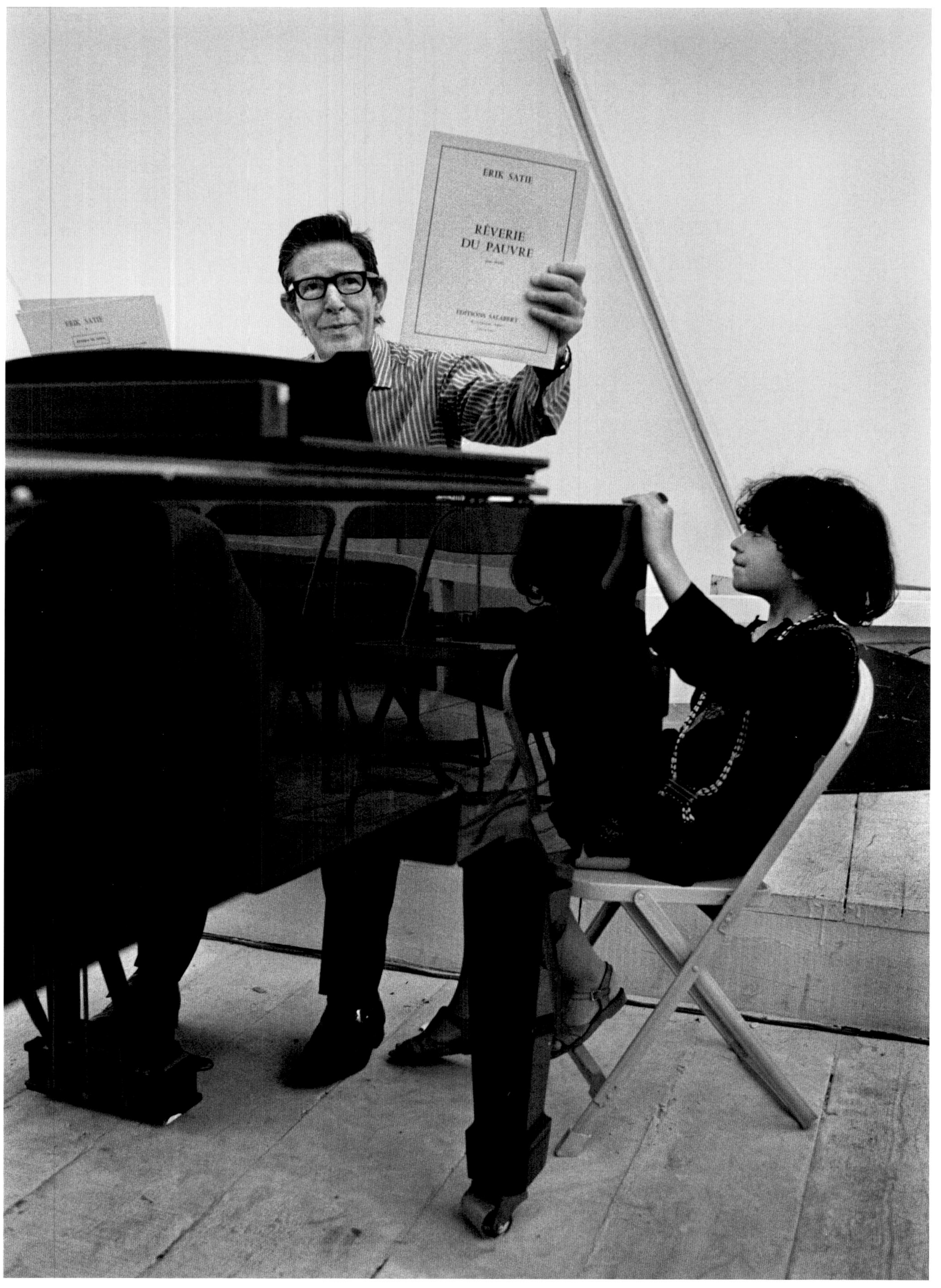
ERIK SATIE
RÊVERIE
DU PAUVRE
EDITIONS SALABERT
ERIK SATIE

Valda Setterfield danced
with Merce Cunningham for eleven years.
Valda and I had one child in 1962,
a son named Ain Heller Bern Gordon,
and John Cage was the reason
that Ain never went to private school.
Valda and I and Ain visited private schools
when he was five or six.
At one meeting the interviewer
asked Ain, "Do you have a best friend?"
Ain said, "Yes." She said,
"What's his name?" Ain said, "John Cage."
I thought Ain better go to public school.

— David Gordon

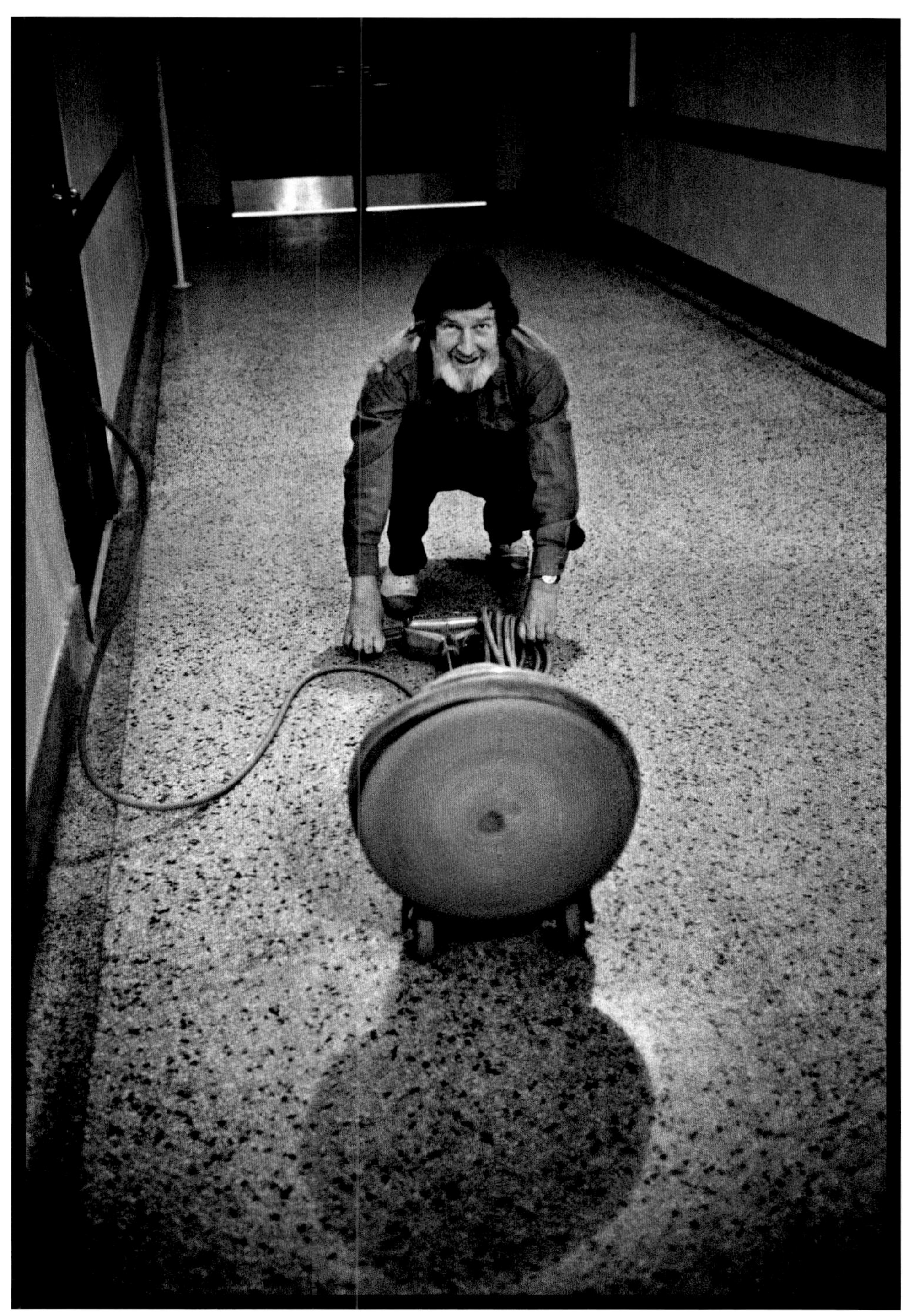

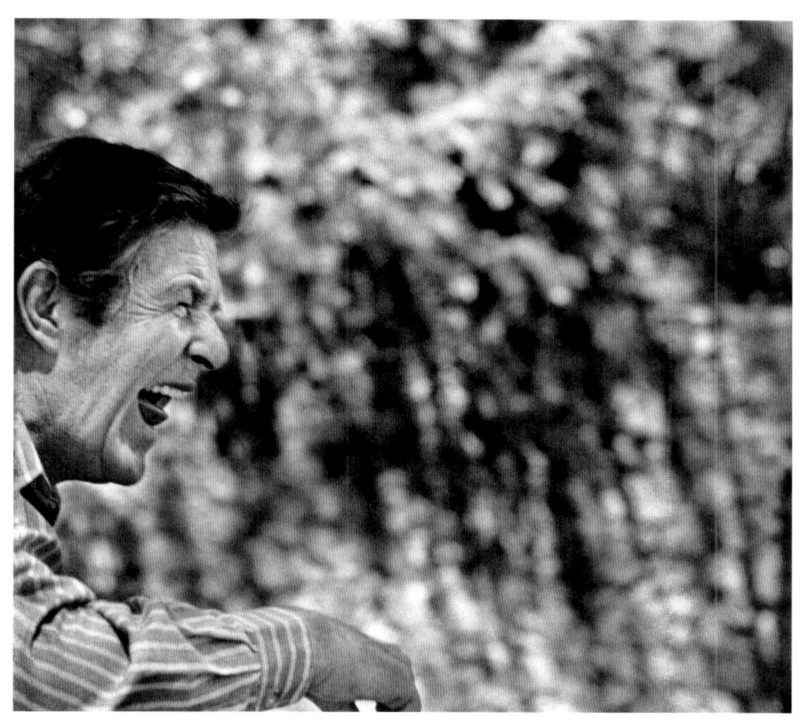

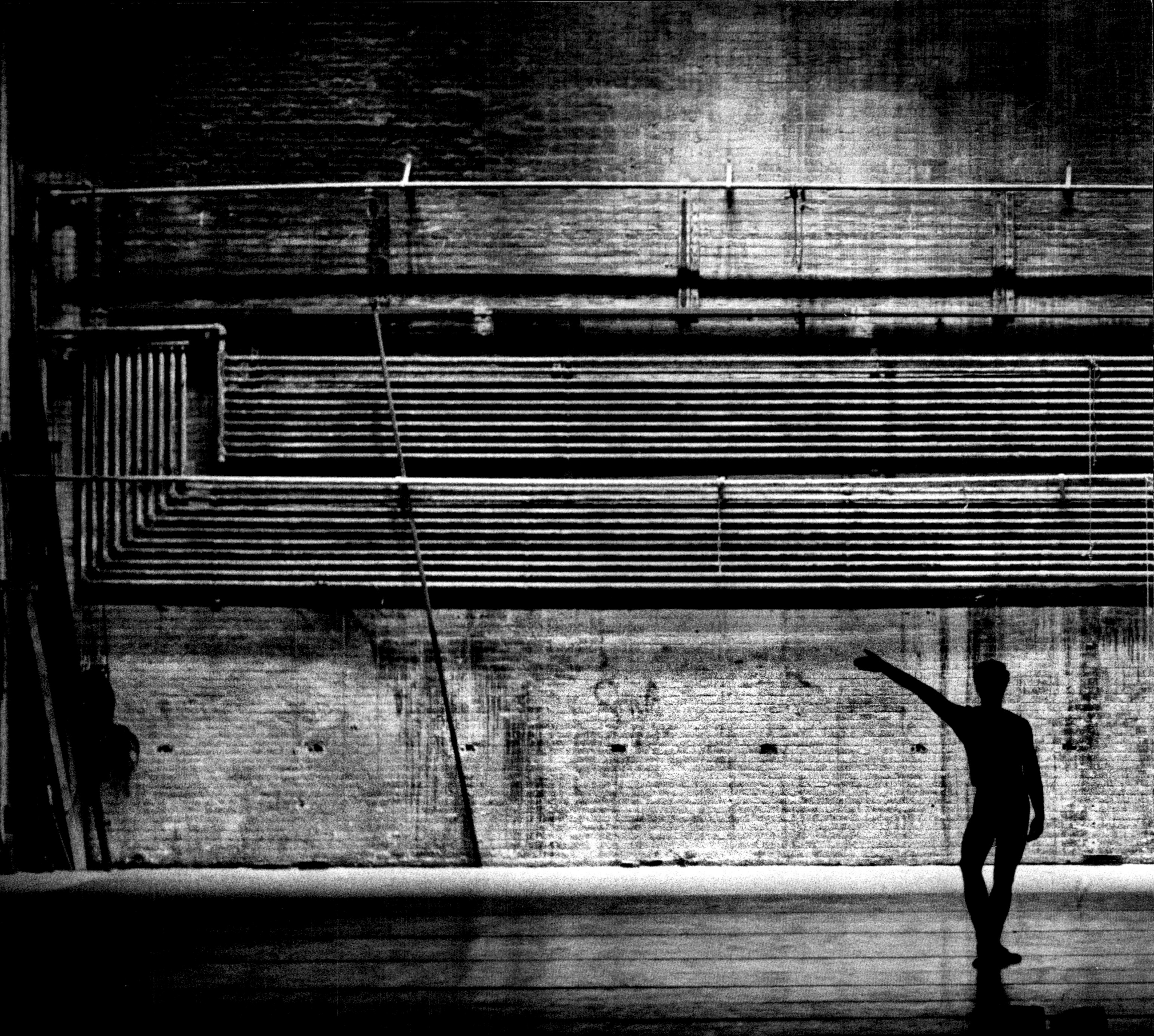

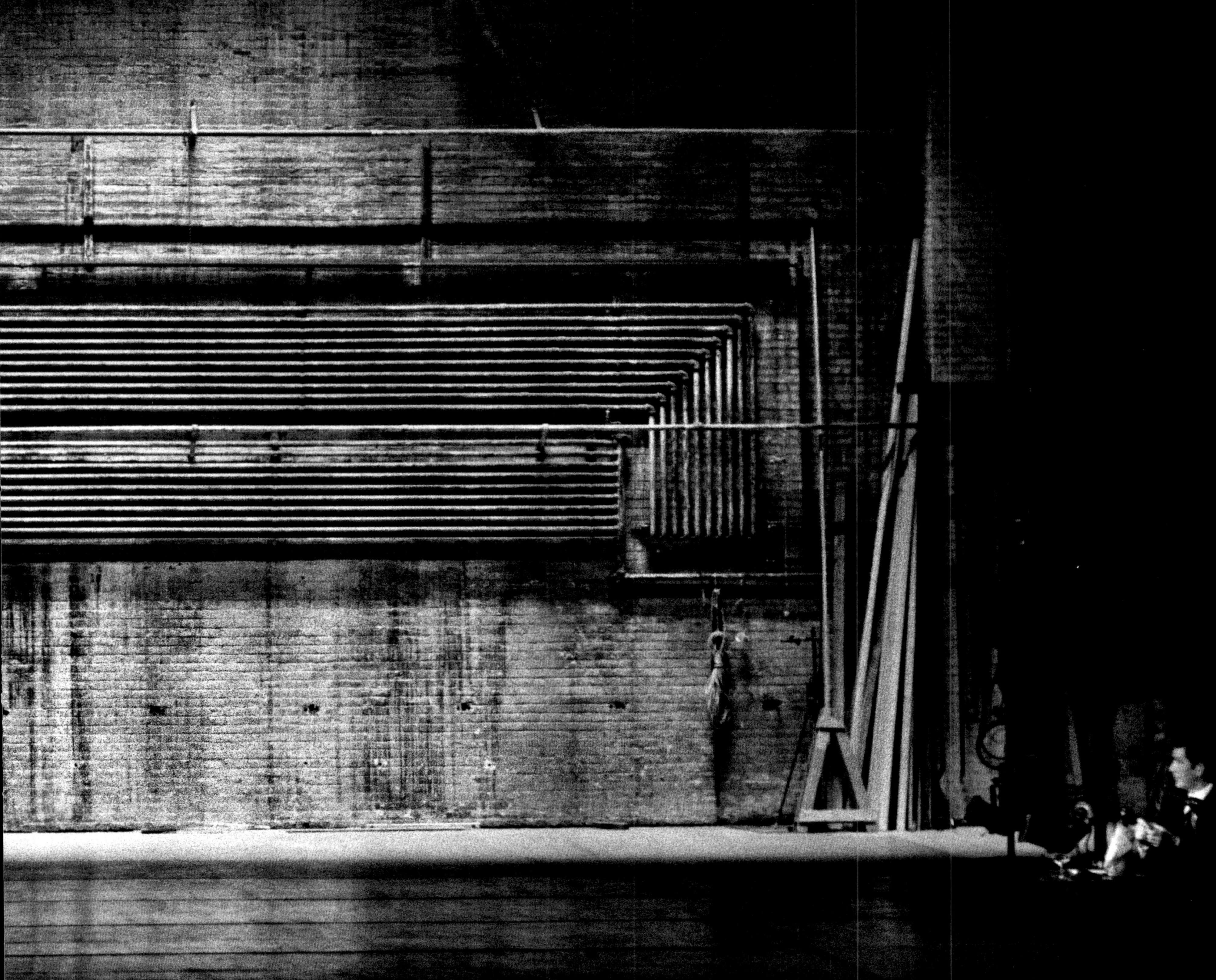

John Cage was responsible for freeing me
from a drought in my writing.
Frank O'Hara and I saw David Tudor play Cage's *Music of Changes*
at the Cherry Lane Theater on New Year's Day in 1952.
I was completely taken by surprise.
It was just arbitrary bangs on the piano over quite a long period of time.
And long pauses.
I felt like I hadn't written anything good in almost a year.
It really gave me ideas about
how to write poetry again.

— John Ashbery

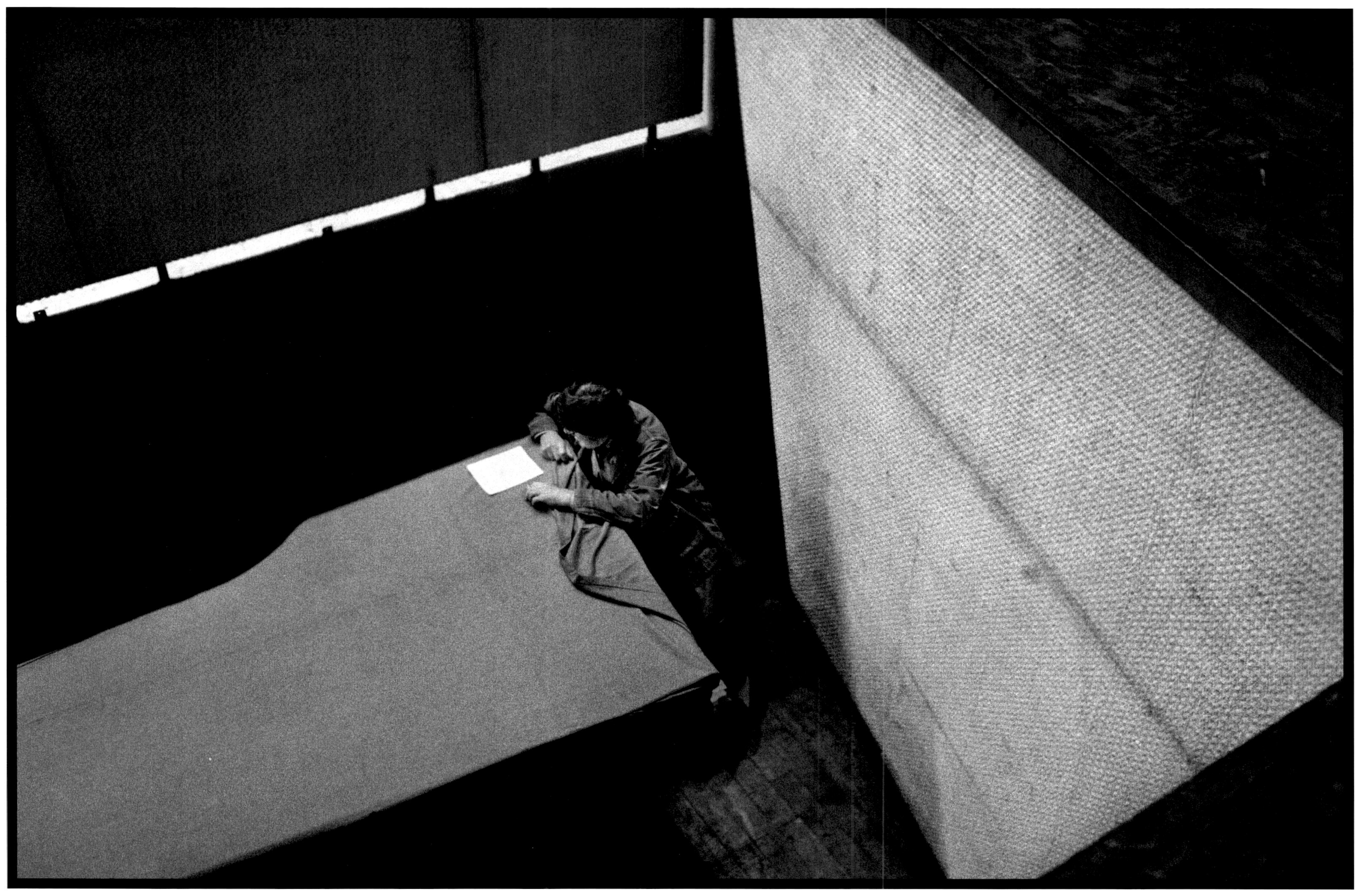

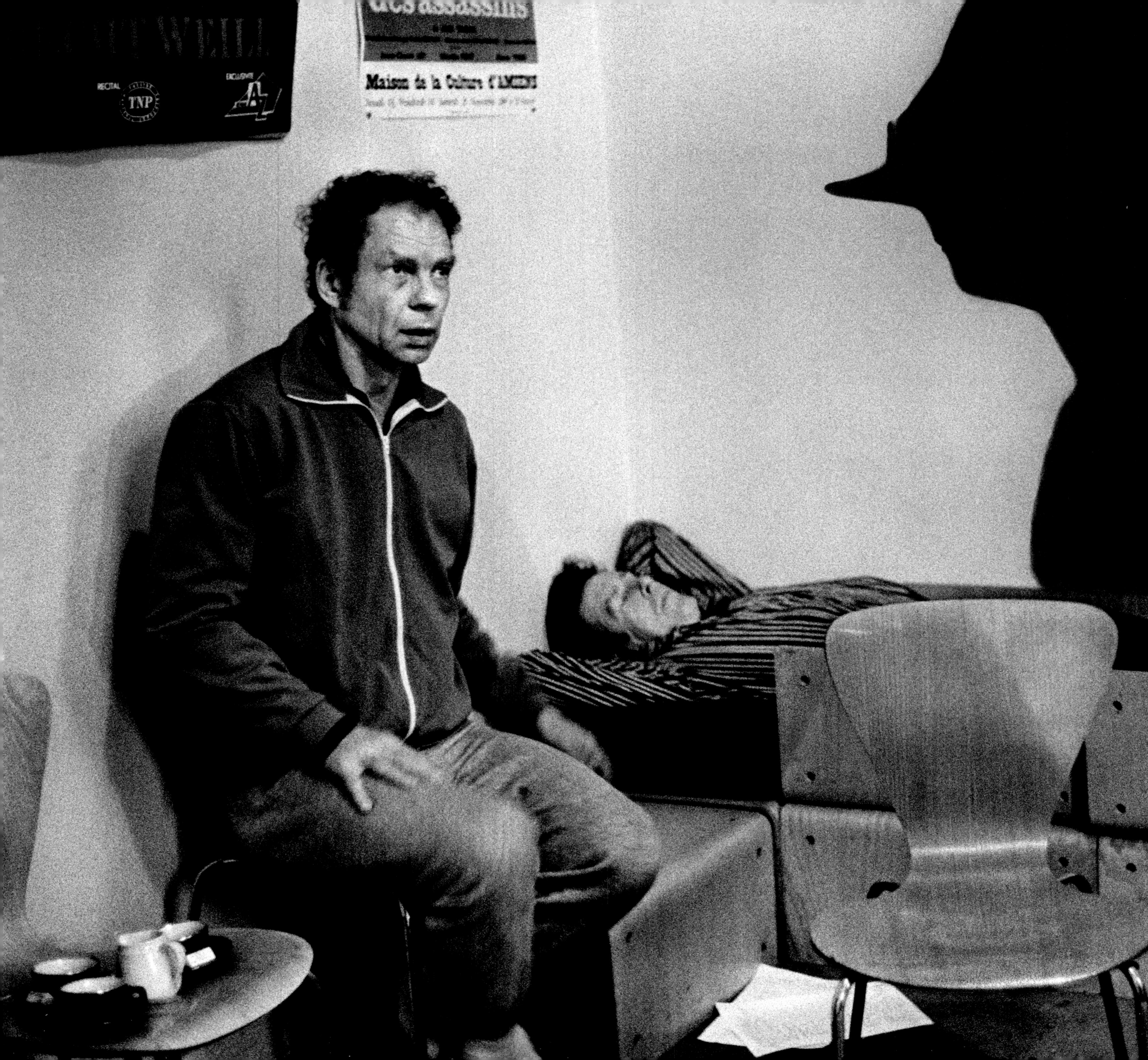
RECITAL
TNP
Maison de la Culture

Because John Cage transformed

the composer's role by creating **RECOMBINANT AURALITIES** of sound/music, language,

and **MEDIA ASSEMBLAGE**, he might also be appreciated as a neuroacoustician.

His **PRODIGAL INVENTIVENESS** catalyzed a bicameral fission

that gave us a new lease on our ears and minds.

JOHN CAGE WAS MORE INSTRUMENTAL THAN ANY ARTIST OF HIS TIME

in moving the boundaries that synergize art forms, disciplines, media,

and—Merce Cunningham's Dance Company provided

the perfect **EXPERIMENTAL HOTHOUSE**, think tank, and extended research center.

Challenged by **QUANTUM INDETERMINACY**, Cage's open-ended experiments

engineered a **PRODIGIOUS RECALIBRATION OF THE FREQUENCIES AND SONICS OF INFORMATION.**

— Kenneth King

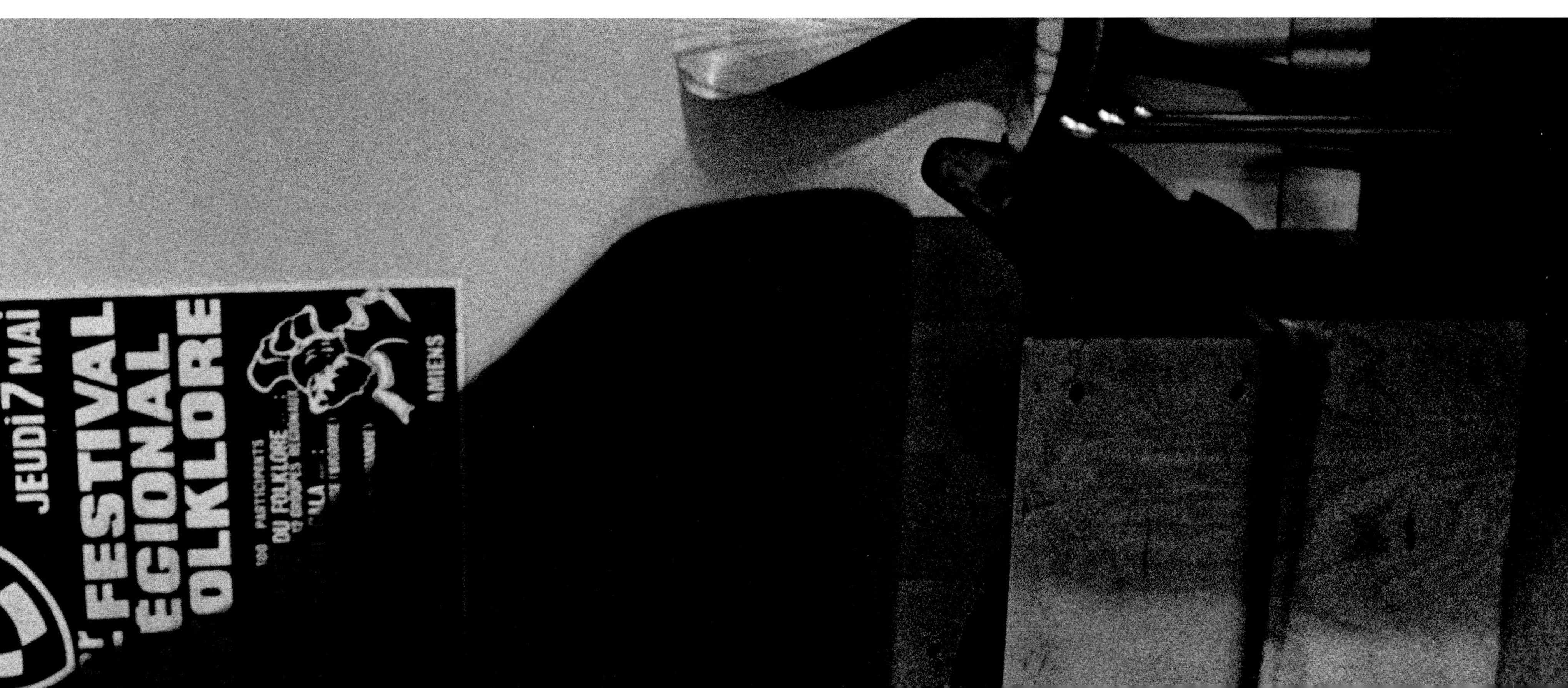

We first talked of no government and of ambiguity in Dostoevsky.

There was kindness of spirit and joy of work, reinforced at every meeting.

I learned: limits are not reasons for failure, but opportunities for creation.

John Cage was why I—a philosopher—have tried to work within discipline not under it, embodying an anarchistic sense of goodness, listening carefully to the nonintentional, silent world. A last talk was of a campus performance of his *Speech* by one hundred-plus students; he smiled and said, "Are you still allowed to teach there?" I am, with John often walking right behind me.

— Richard Fleming

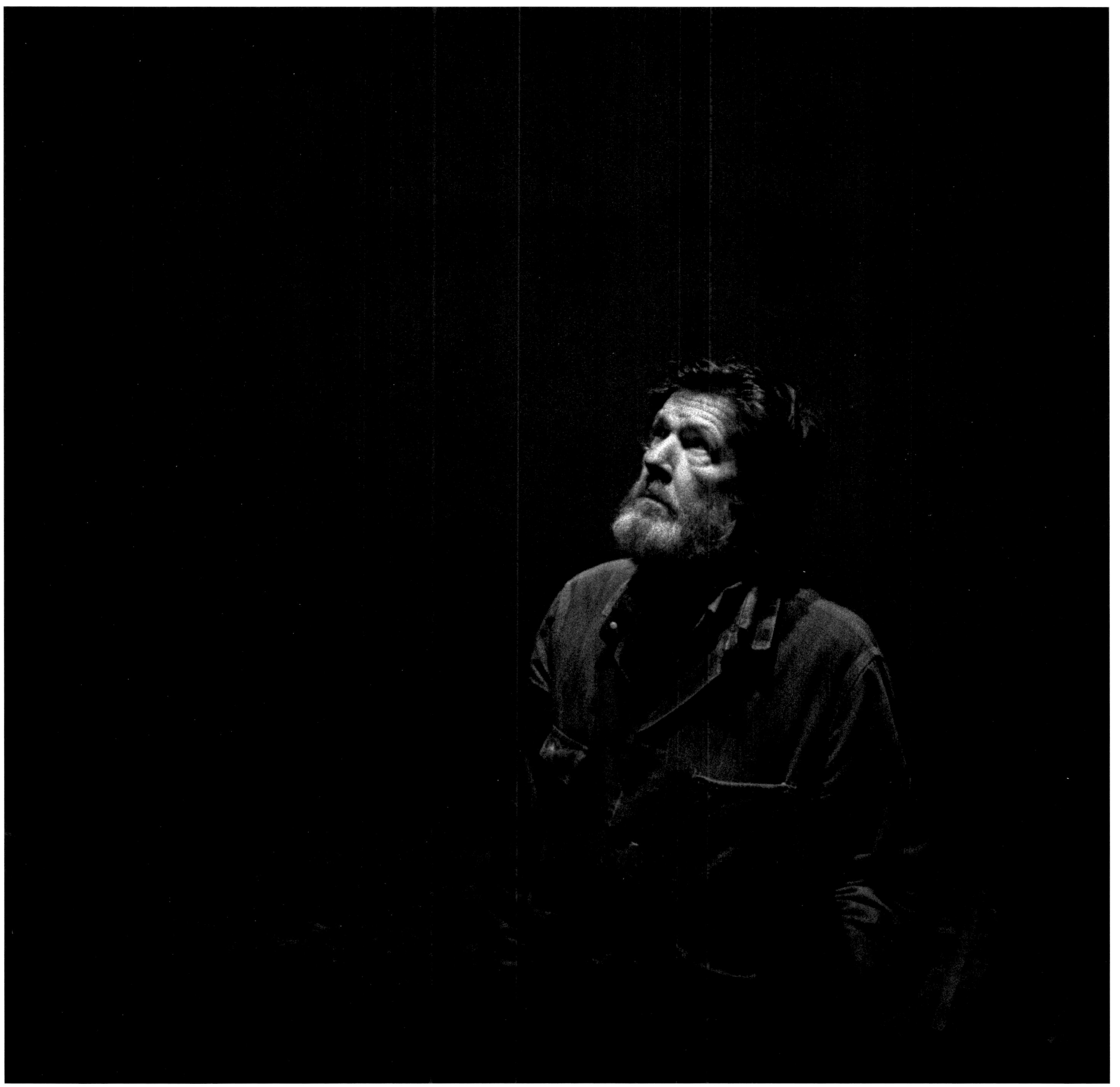

What John Cage was, was a poet

and philosopher

disguised as a composer

who taught the world
that things
are not
what they seem,

especially pianos.

I admired his apparent calm.

—Peter Schickele

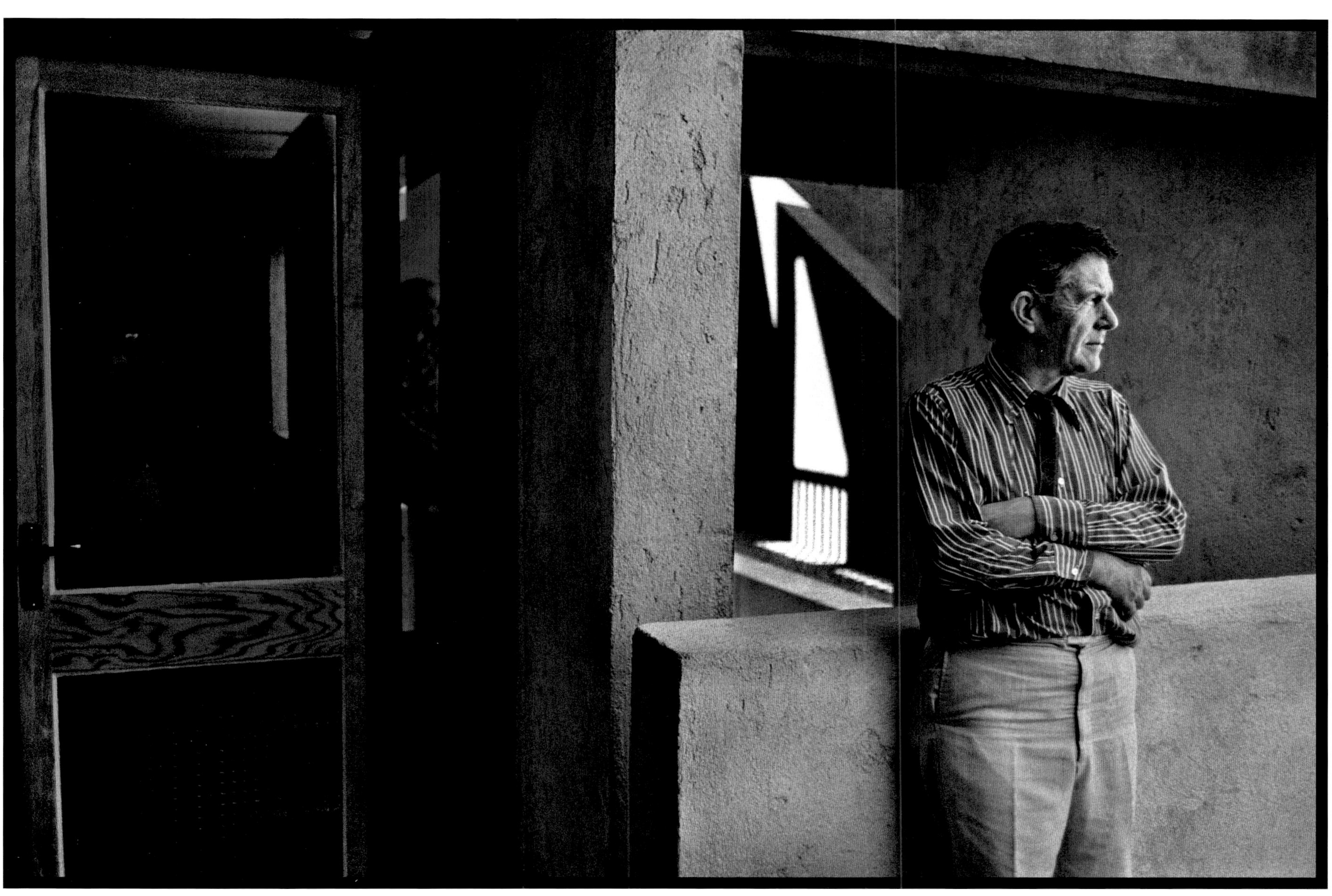

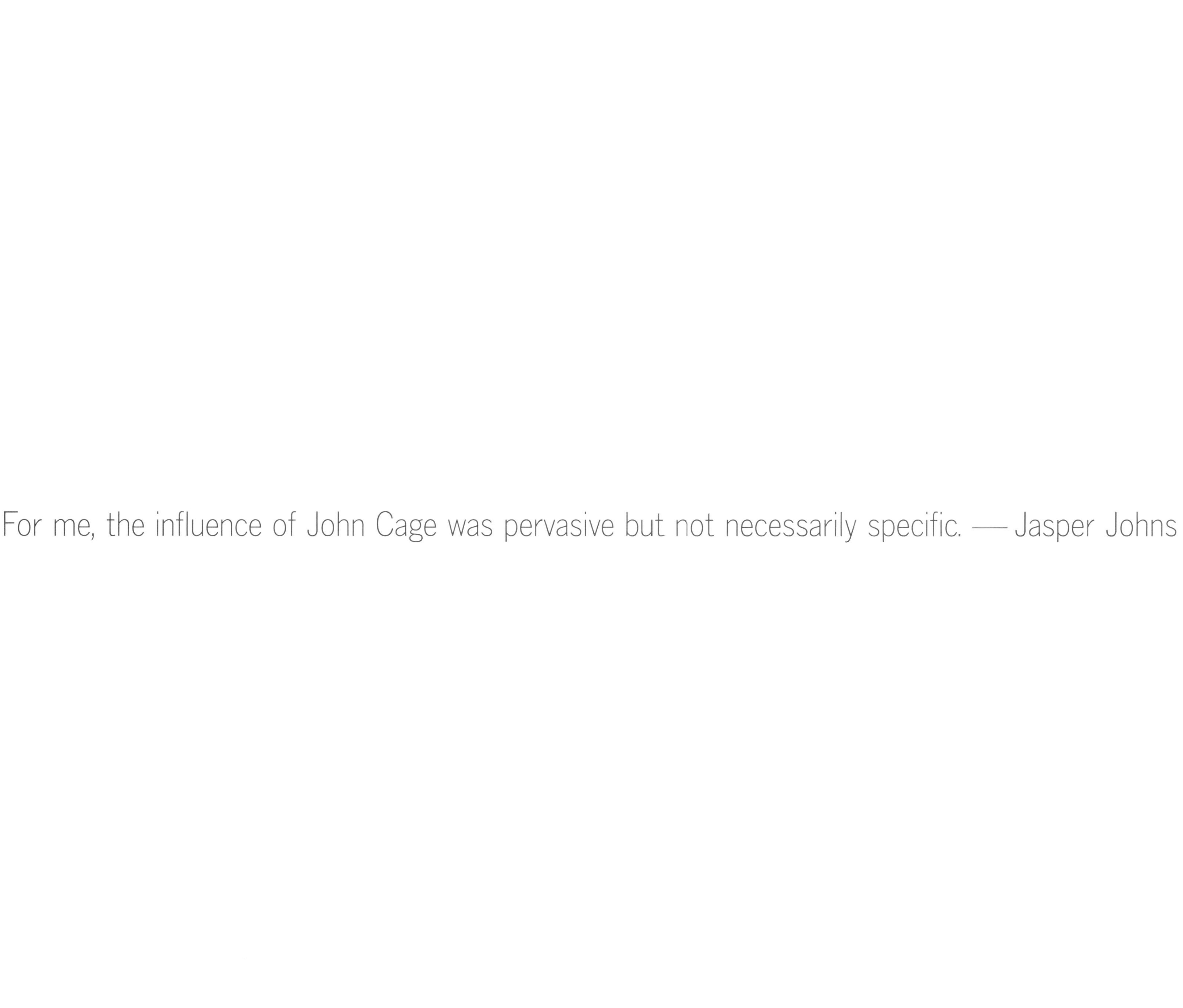

For me, the influence of John Cage was pervasive but not necessarily specific. — Jasper Johns

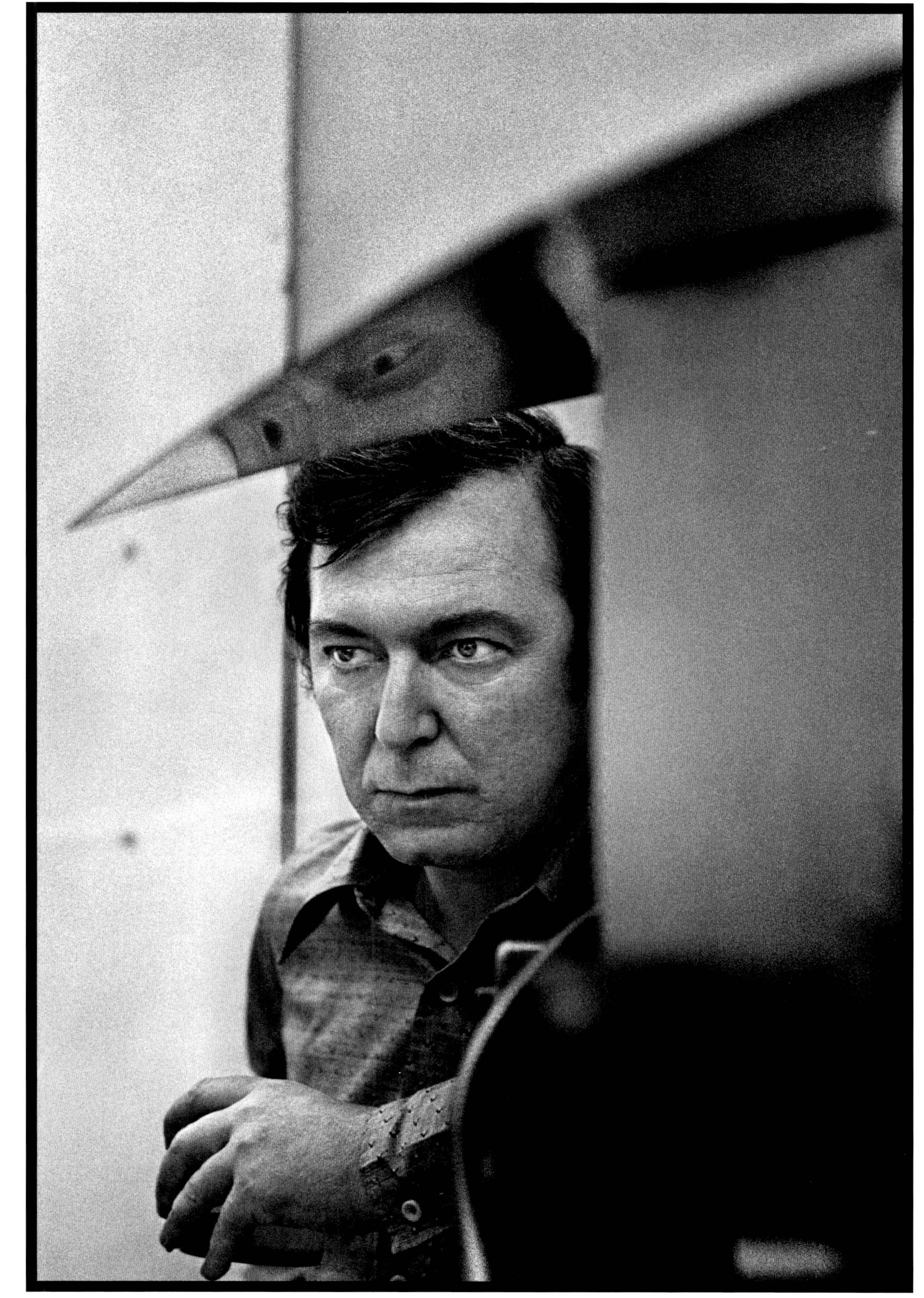

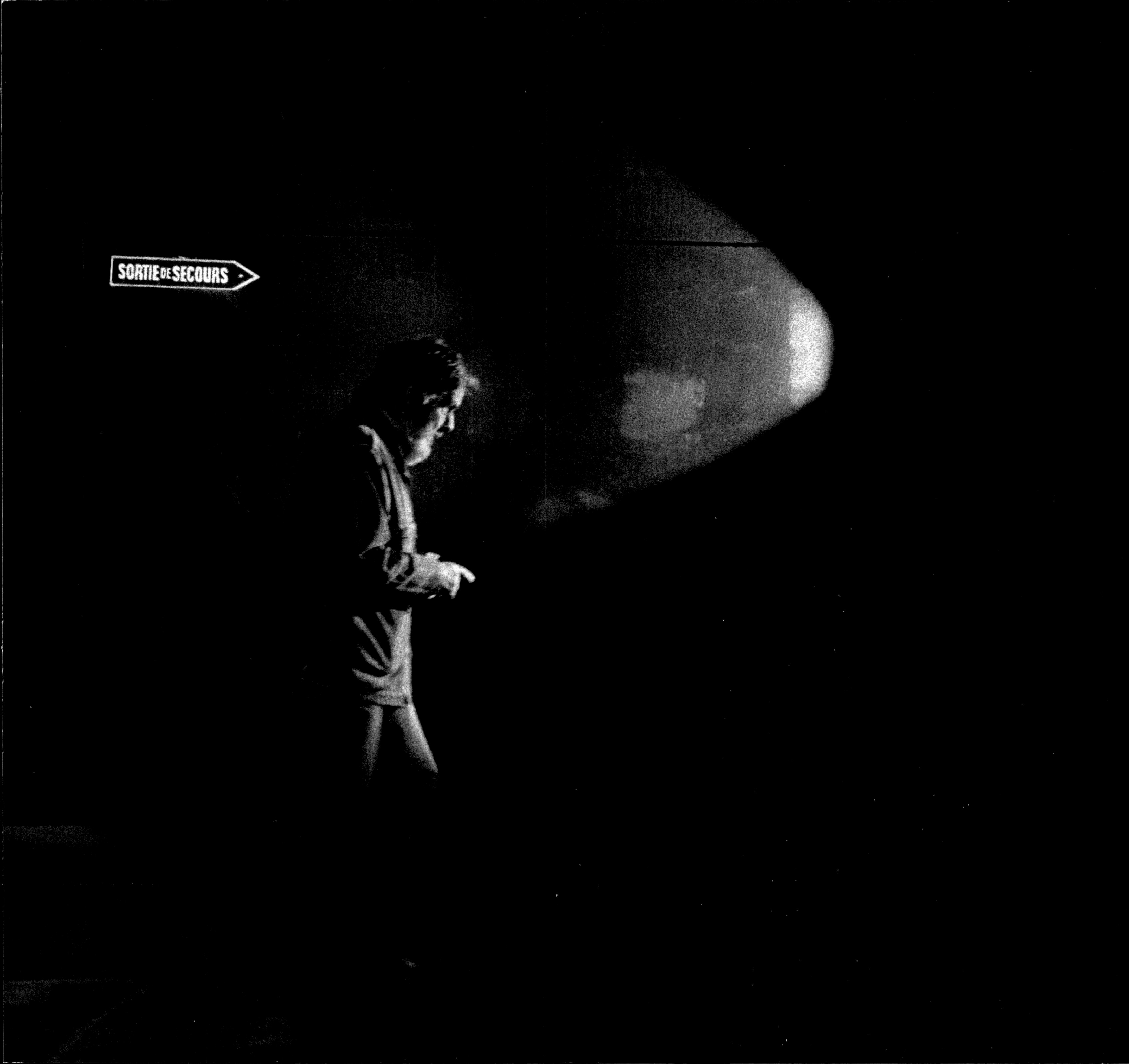

SORTIE DE SECOURS

The history of Western music
can be divided into B.C. (Before Cage)
and A.C. (After Cage).
I am a lucky girl to have bumped into him
in my roller coaster life.
John Cage was
one of the very few people
who understood my work at the time.
People in the small downtown art circles in new york
called him J.C. for Jesus Christ.
I thought everybody knew this.
We did not always meet eye to eye
but in the end, we both knew we would always be friends.
I still miss him.

— yoko ono

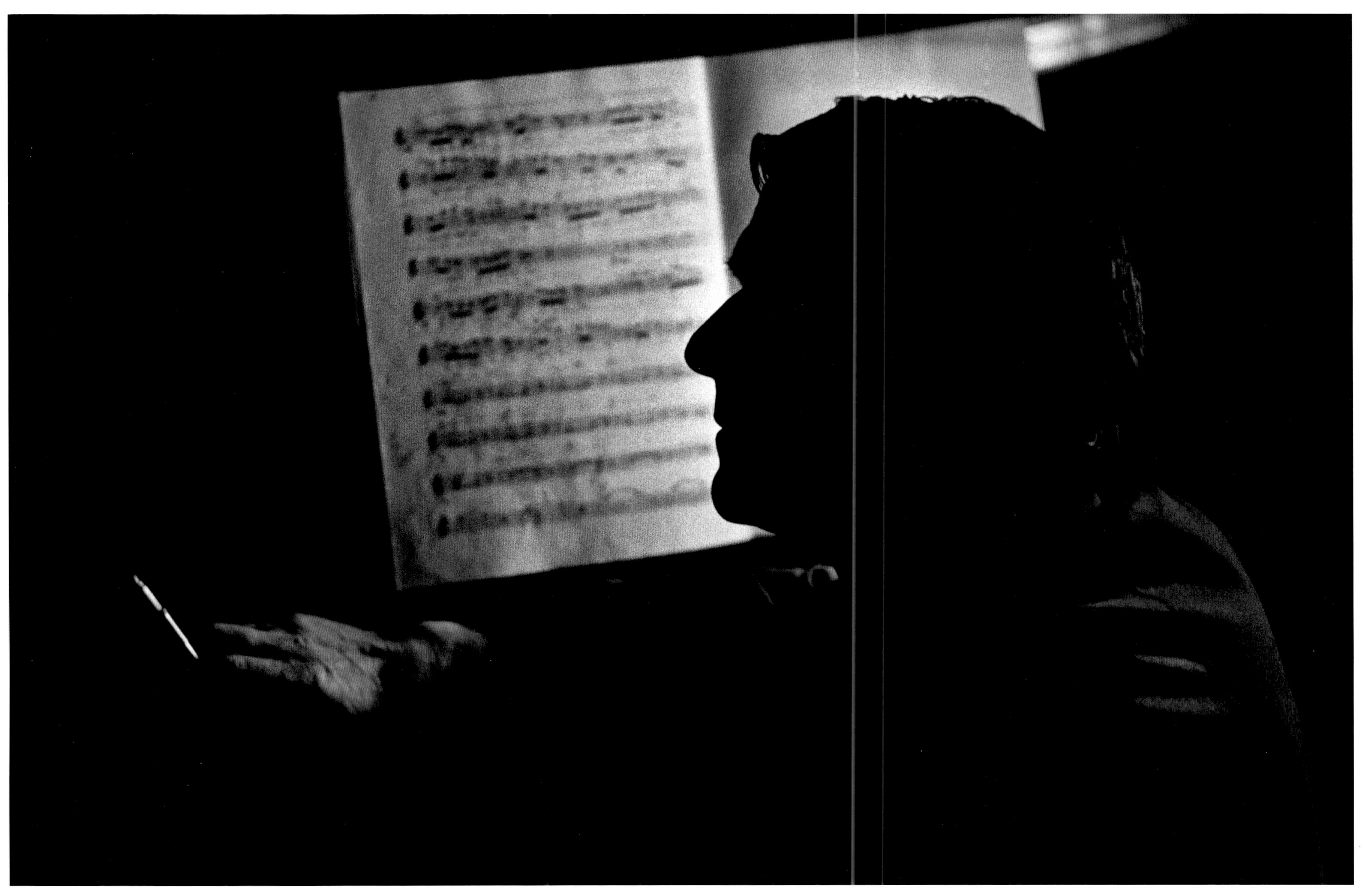

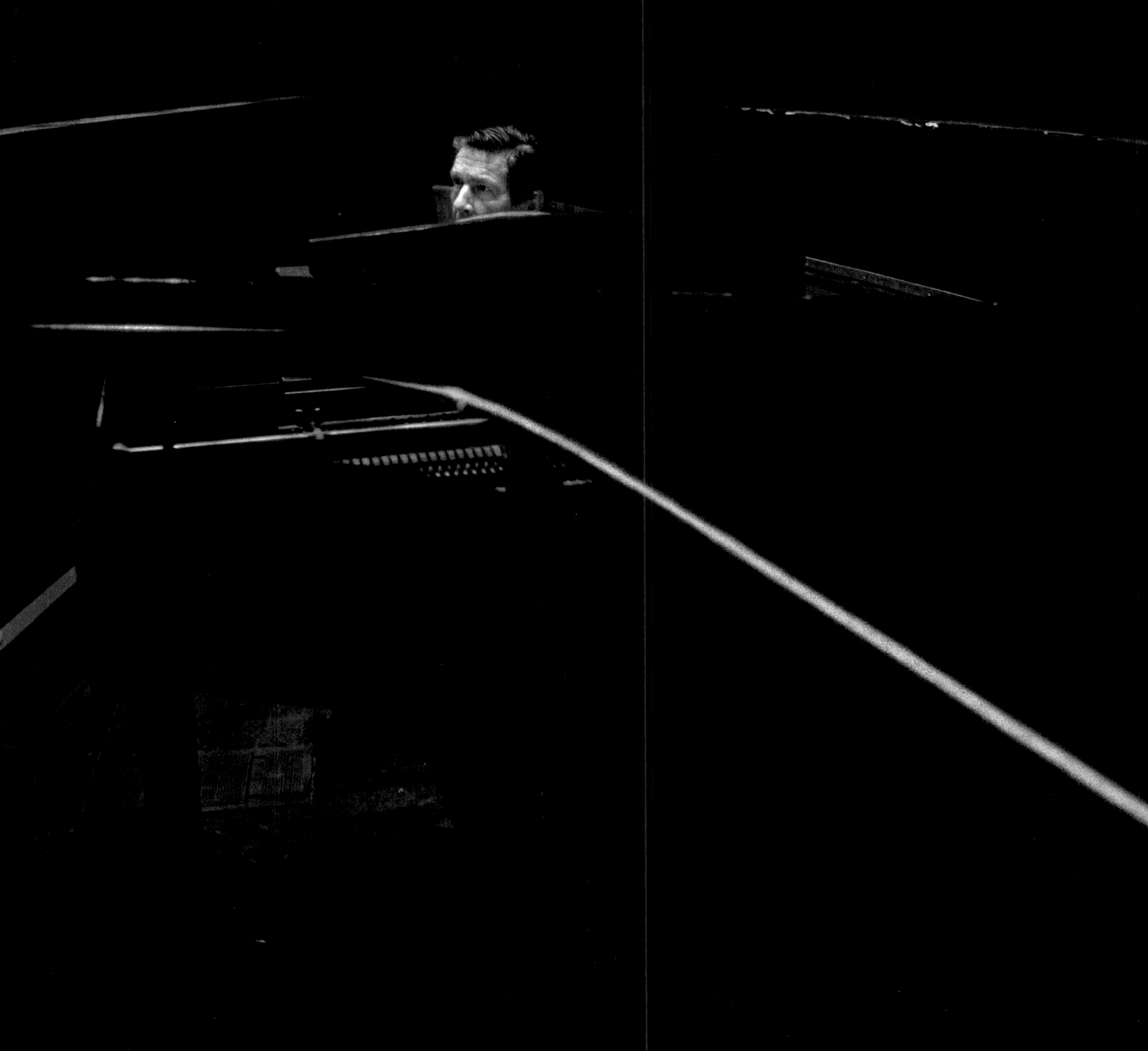

I asked Virgil Thompson once what he thought of Cage.
Answer: He was a "preacher."

He certainly held dogmatic views on many questions,
including politics.
He also had a tendency

to repeat himself, as though he were quoting sacred text.
I think of him as a thoroughly traditional classical composer,

especially in his piano music.
The notes in *Etudes Australes* may be drawn from a star atlas;

but it's clear
he went through it carefully,
eliminating everything that was unplayable.
In his working method, John Cage was a rigorous traditionalist;
unlike Brahms, a revolutionary who wore the mask of tradition.

— Frederic Rzewski

John Cage was always supportive of a new idea. In 1965 he encouraged me to present my brain wave piece, *Music for Solo Performer*, live at a concert in the Rose Art Museum at Brandeis even after I told him it probably wouldn't work. He said it was more important to try it and fail than not attempt it at all. The intention was what was important. He also insisted that we include a work of Christian Wolff who was at that time teaching at Harvard nearby in Cambridge. By the way, *Solo Performer* did work at that first concert.

—Alvin Lucier

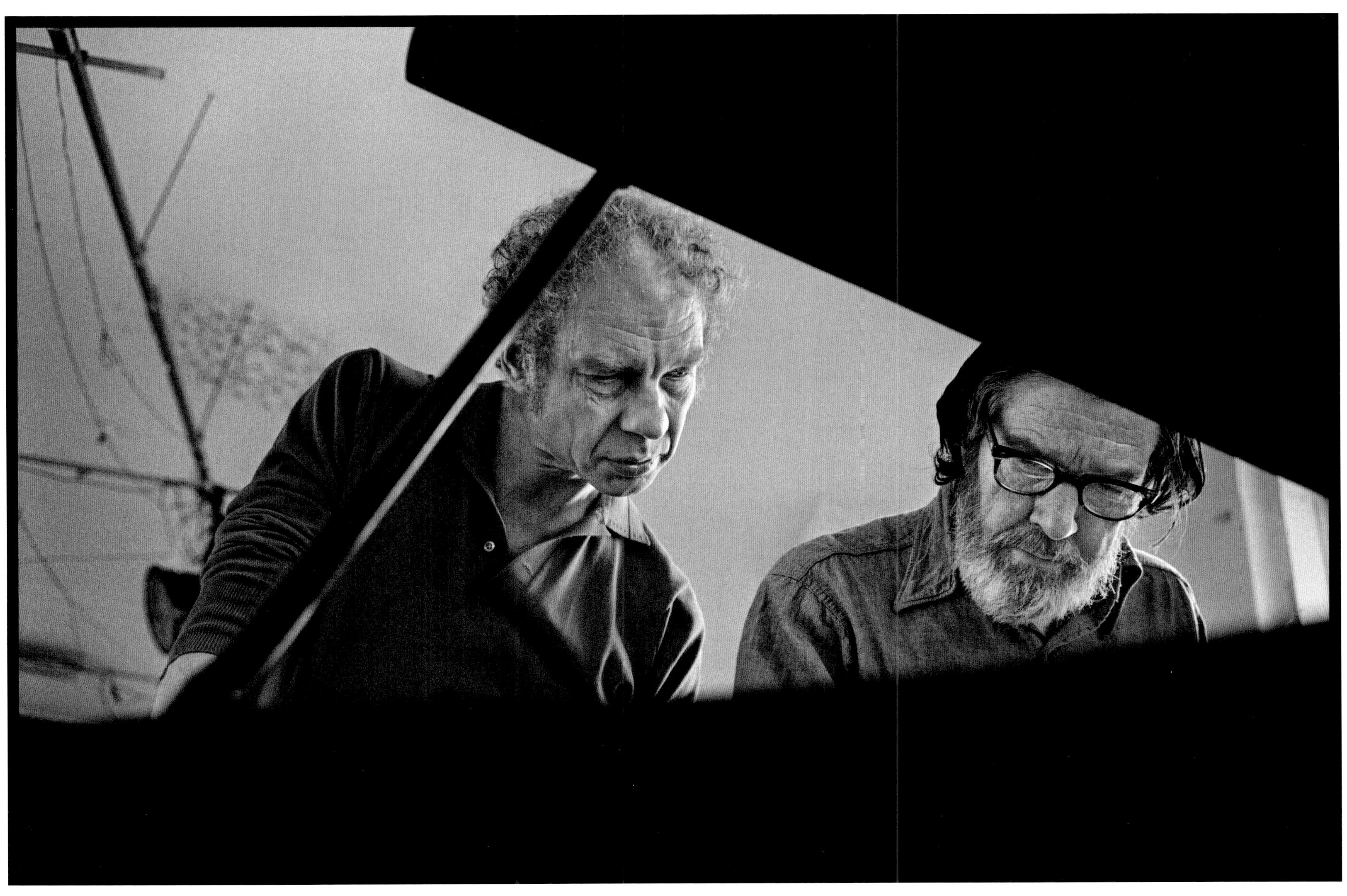

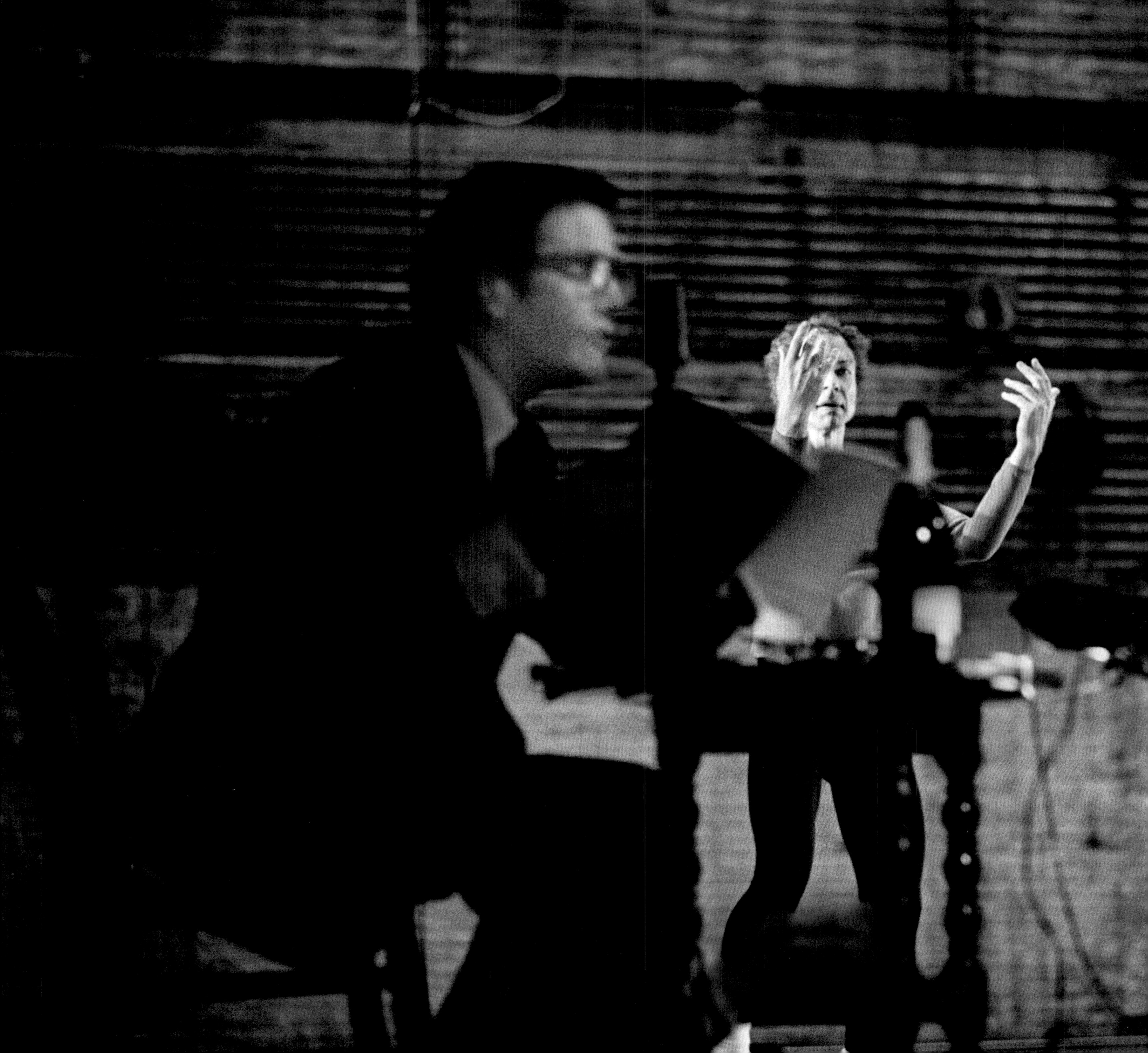

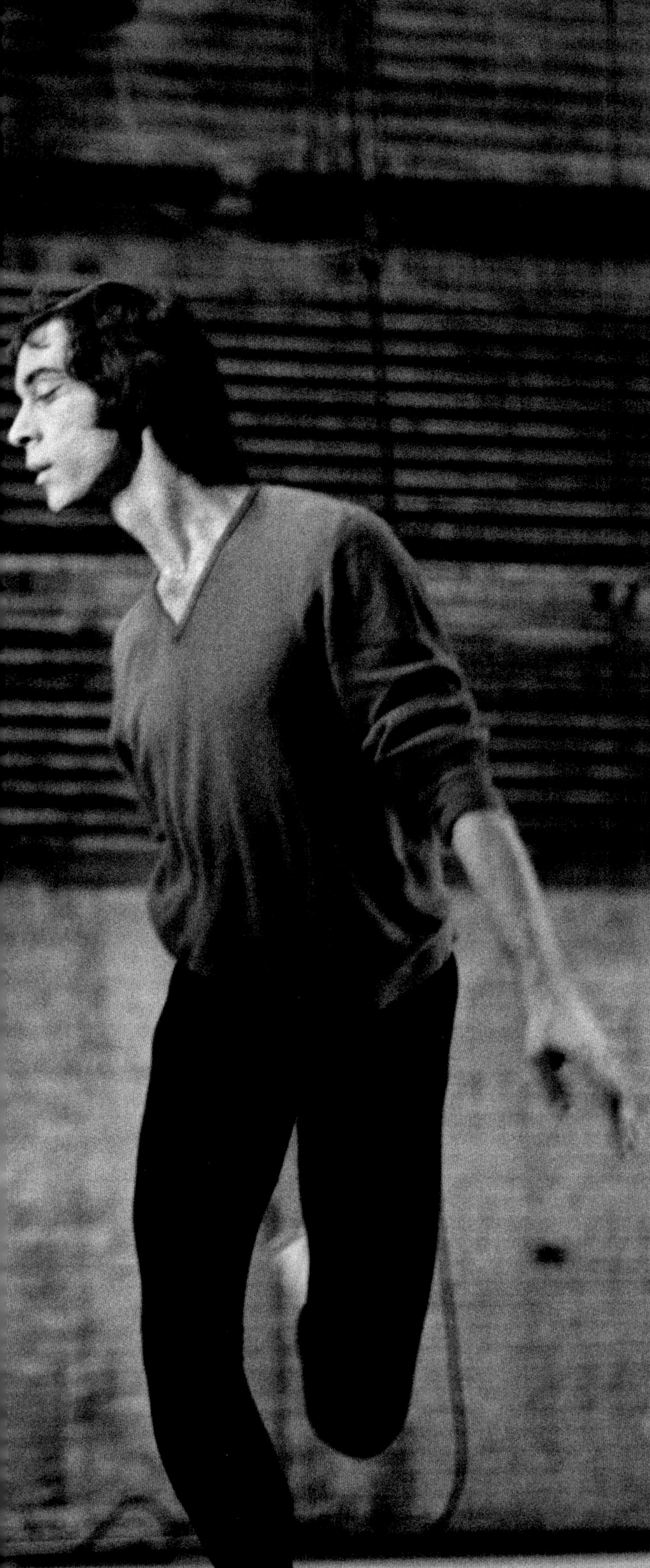

John Cage was fascinated with surprise and experiencing the unexpected. For nearly twenty years, I performed in his works presented in overlapping simultaneities with remarkable, unpredictable results. His generosity was boundless; I never knew him to back away from a situation or a question—whether simple or complex. He communicated freedom and encouragement to intrepidly continue in the face of adversity—perhaps because of adversity. His influence remains in those of us who compose or create art, reflecting his spirit of adventure. Whenever I hit a wall, I remember John's "yes" to open the window of possibilities in my work.

—Joan La Barbara

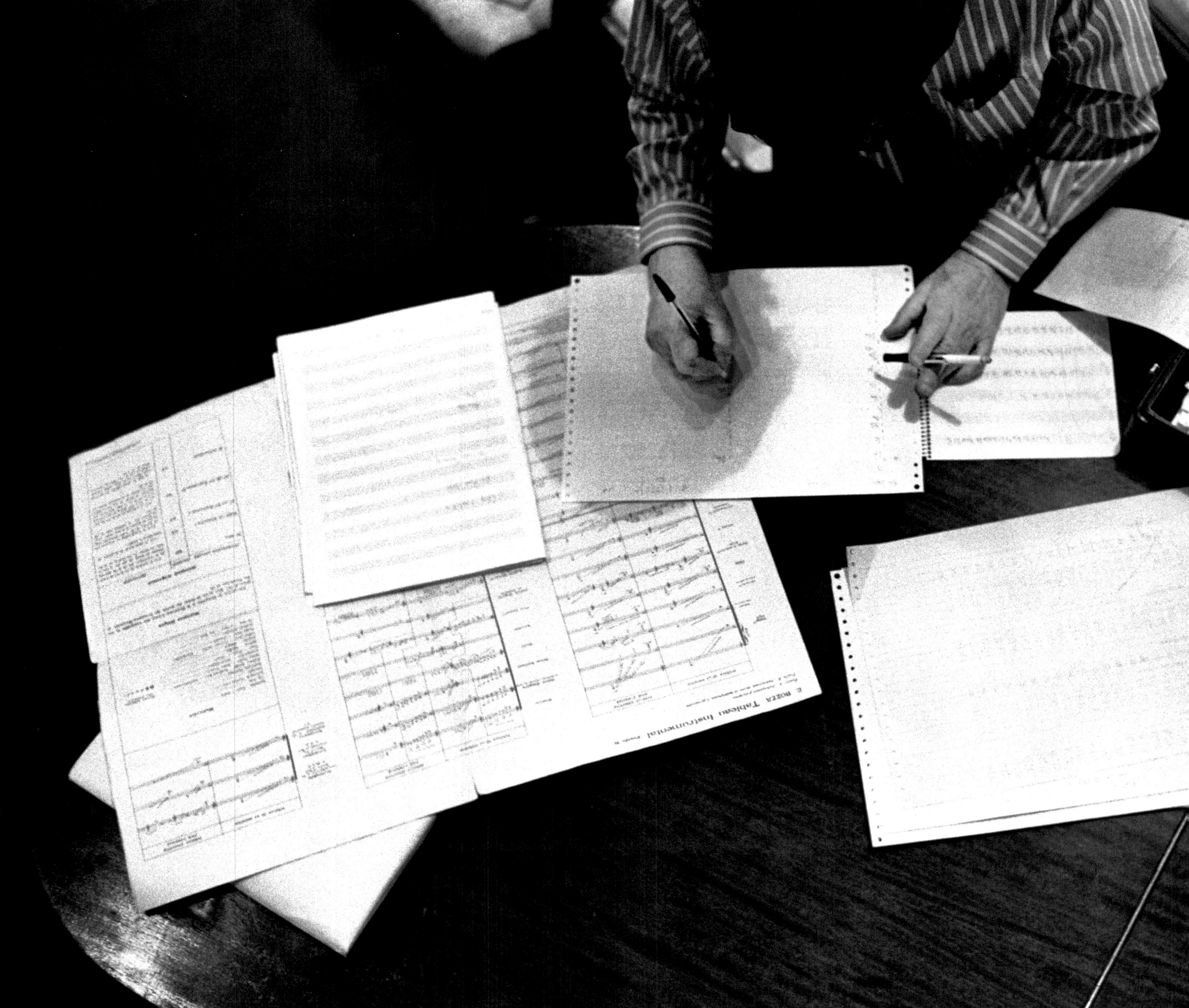
E. BOZZA Tableau instrumental

I invited Cage to Simon Fraser University
the year it opened (1965).
I remember two things about that visit.
On entering my office, John saw some graphic scores pinned on the wall.
"Oh, did you do that?" he exclaimed, and examined them in detail.
I was embarrassed and flattered.
But John Cage was unpredictable.
He was to give a lecture to the entire university.
Several philosophers and scientists attended.
They were confused and could hardly wait to ask questions.
When they did, John shuffled a pack of cards and read an answer.
They were furious and stormed out.

— R. Murray Schafer

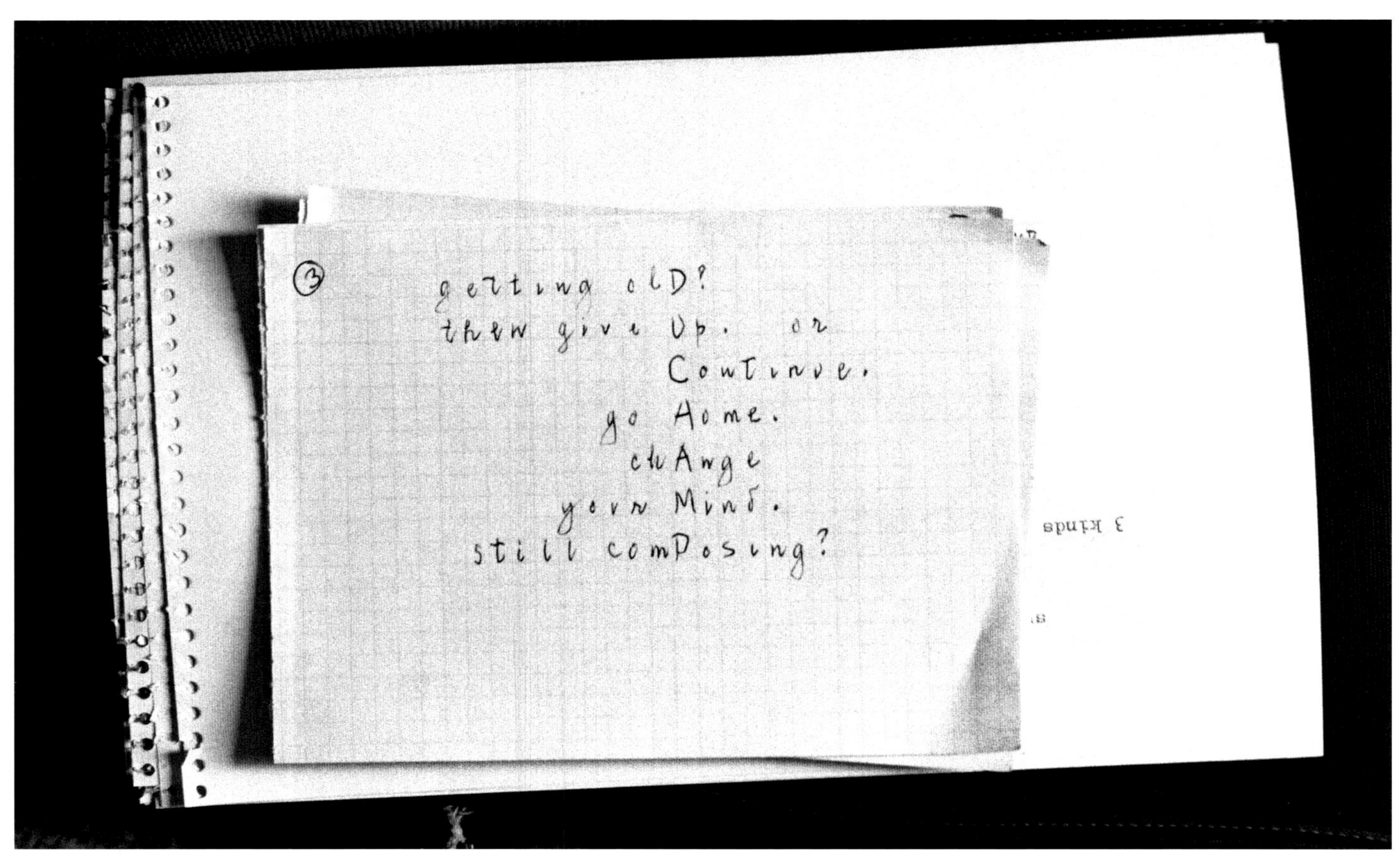
③
getting olD?
then give Up. or
Continue.
go Home.
chAnge
your Mind.
still comPosing?
3 kinds

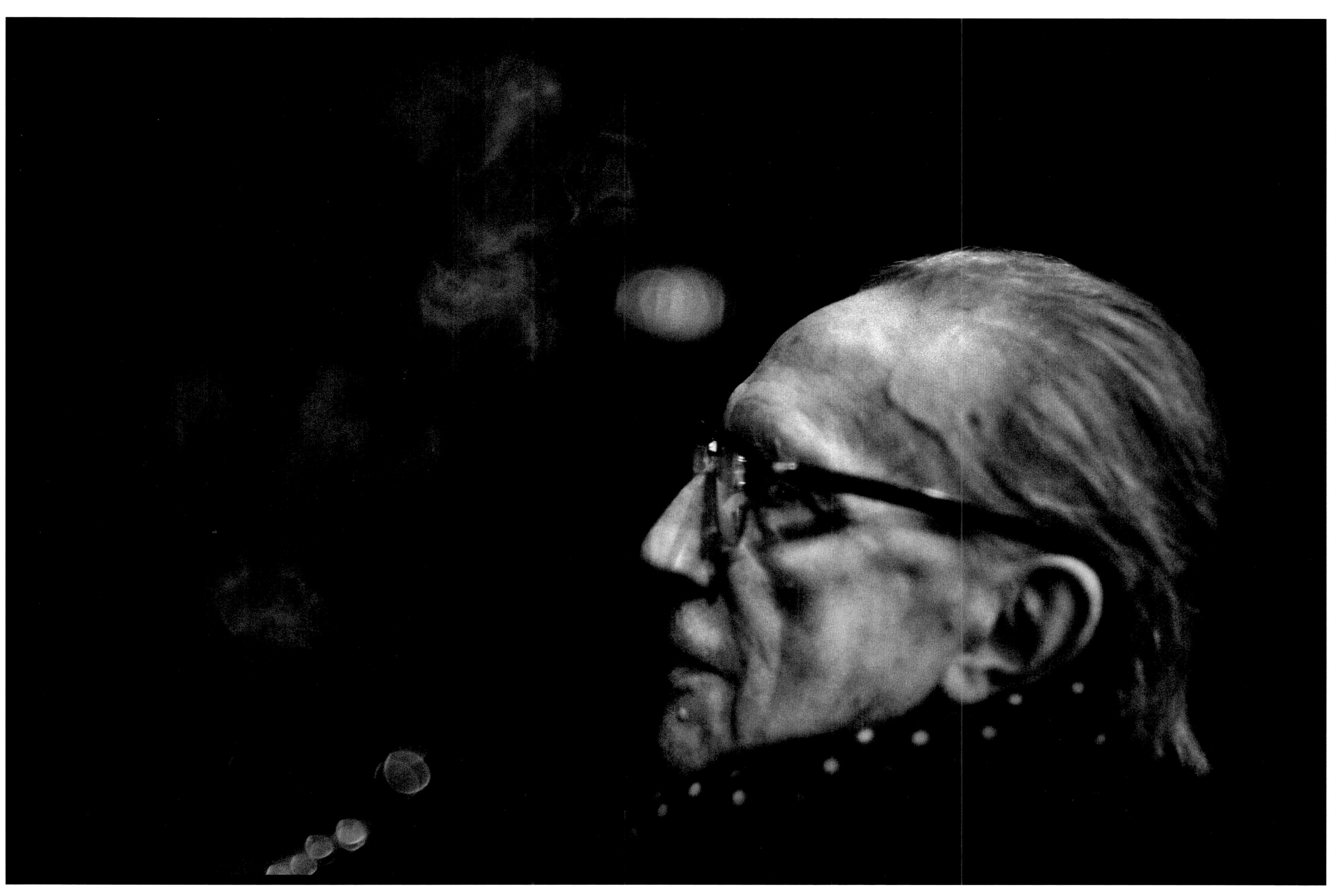

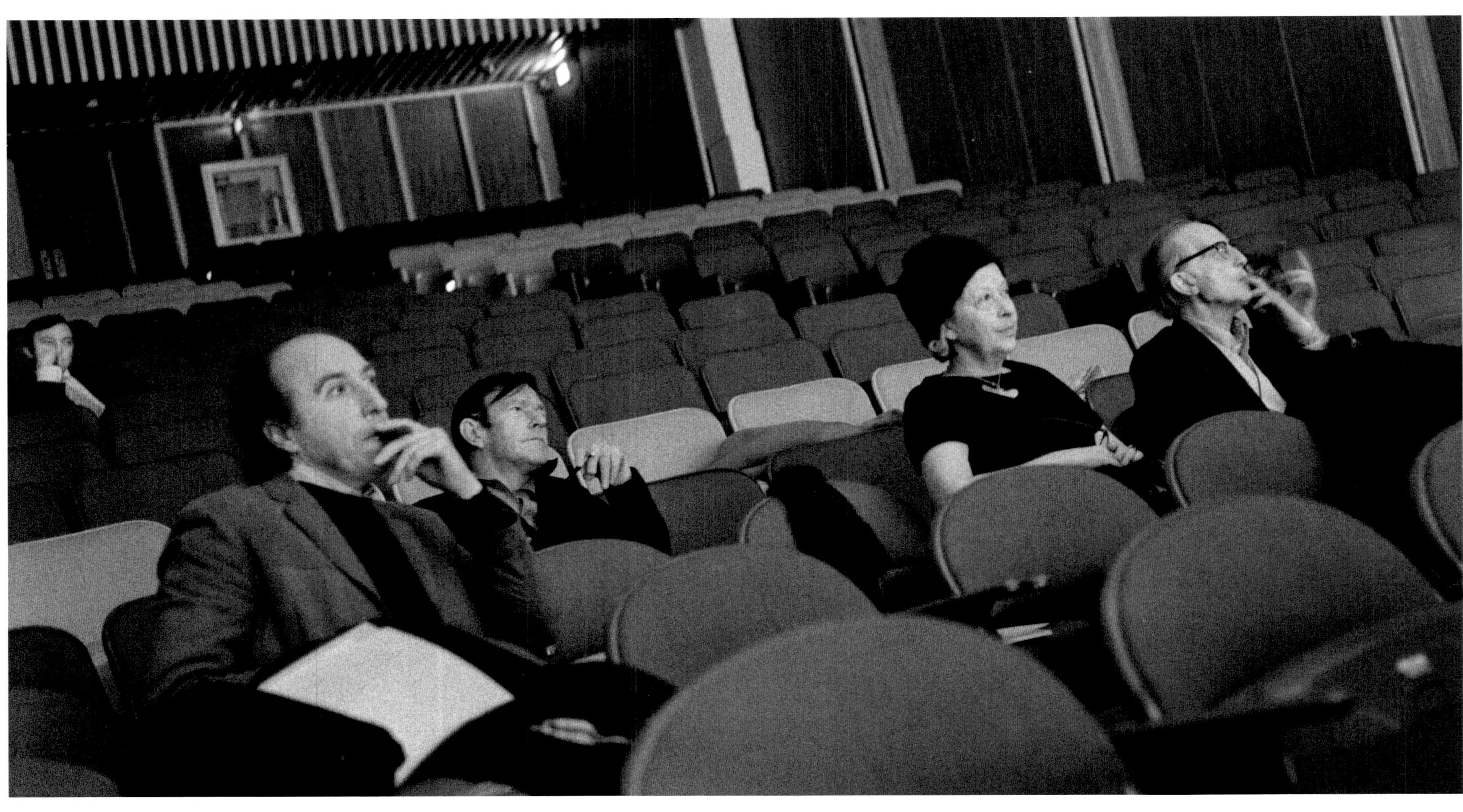

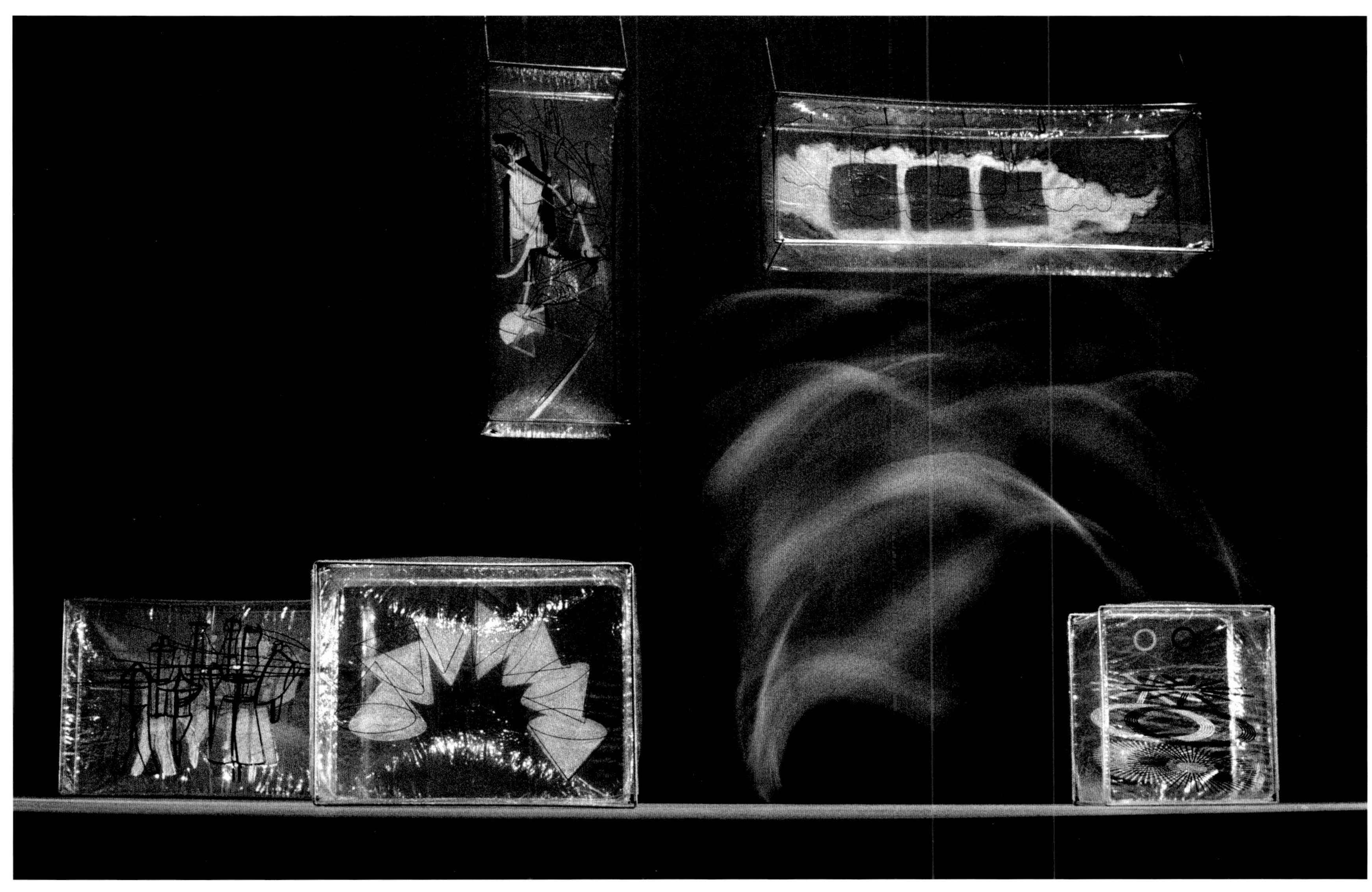

TO ORGANIZE A STUDIO PRACTICE THAT WOULD ENABLE JOHN CAGE TO PAINT WATERCOLORS,

I REEXAMINED MY USE OF THE MEDIUM.

JOHN DID NOT LIKE REPEATING HIMSELF, BUT WOULD PAINT IF SOMETHING WERE NEW.

REEXAMINING MY PAINTING CONVENTIONS CONFOUNDED MY HABITUAL MANNERISM AND LED TO NEW BEGINNINGS.

I DESIGNED A MULTI-PANELED FORMAT FOR JOHN THAT HE DID NOT LIVE TO USE.

LIKE "SMOKING" LARGE PAPERS—A PROCESS WE PERFECTED FOR HIM—

IT BECAME A DYNAMIC ELEMENT IN MY OWN WORK.

JOHN CAGE WAS AN ALCHEMIST.

MAKING HIS FINAL "SMOKED" WATERCOLORS,

HE COMMENTED HE WAS TRYING TO "CHANGE FIRE INTO WATER."

— RAY KASS

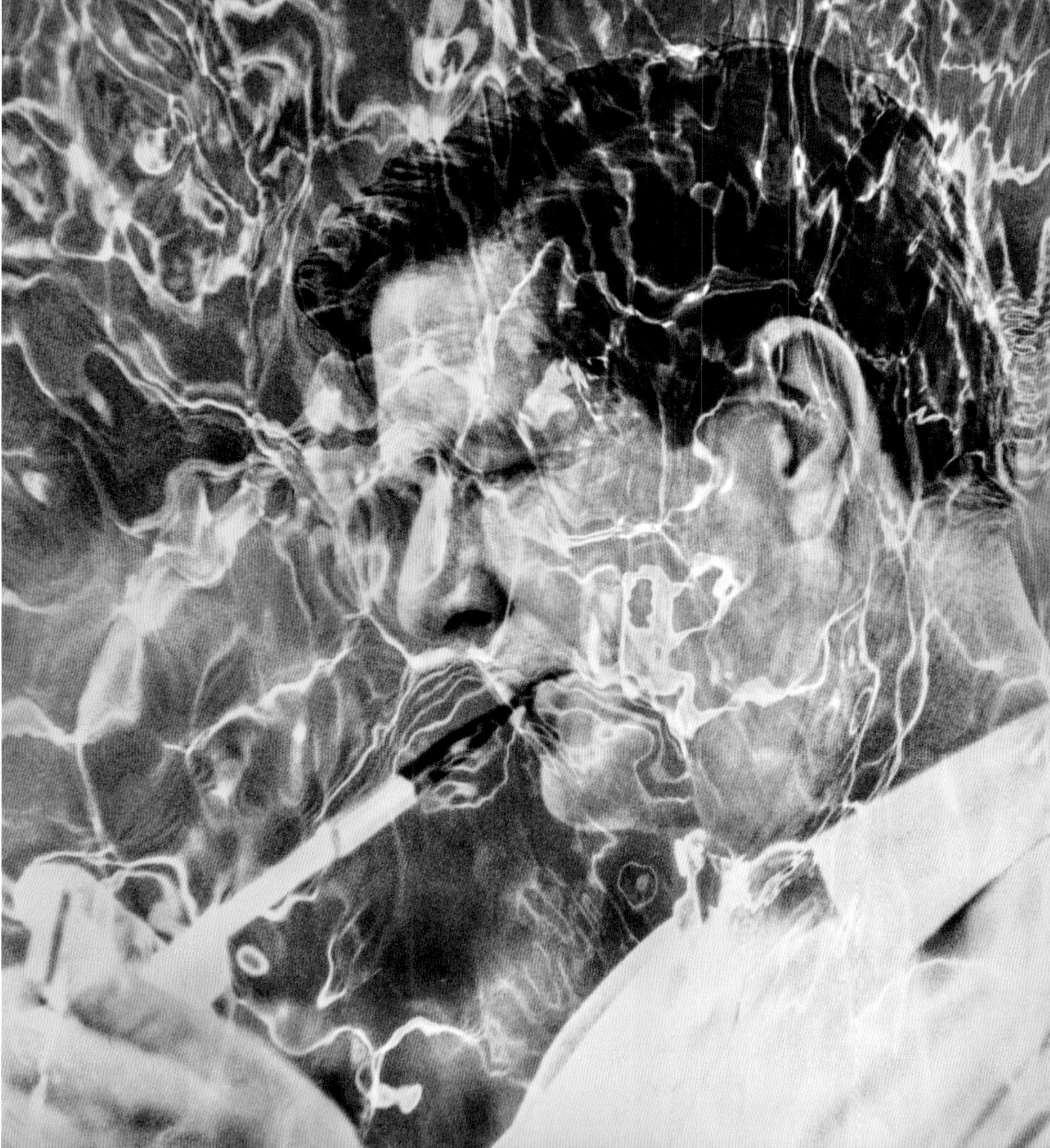

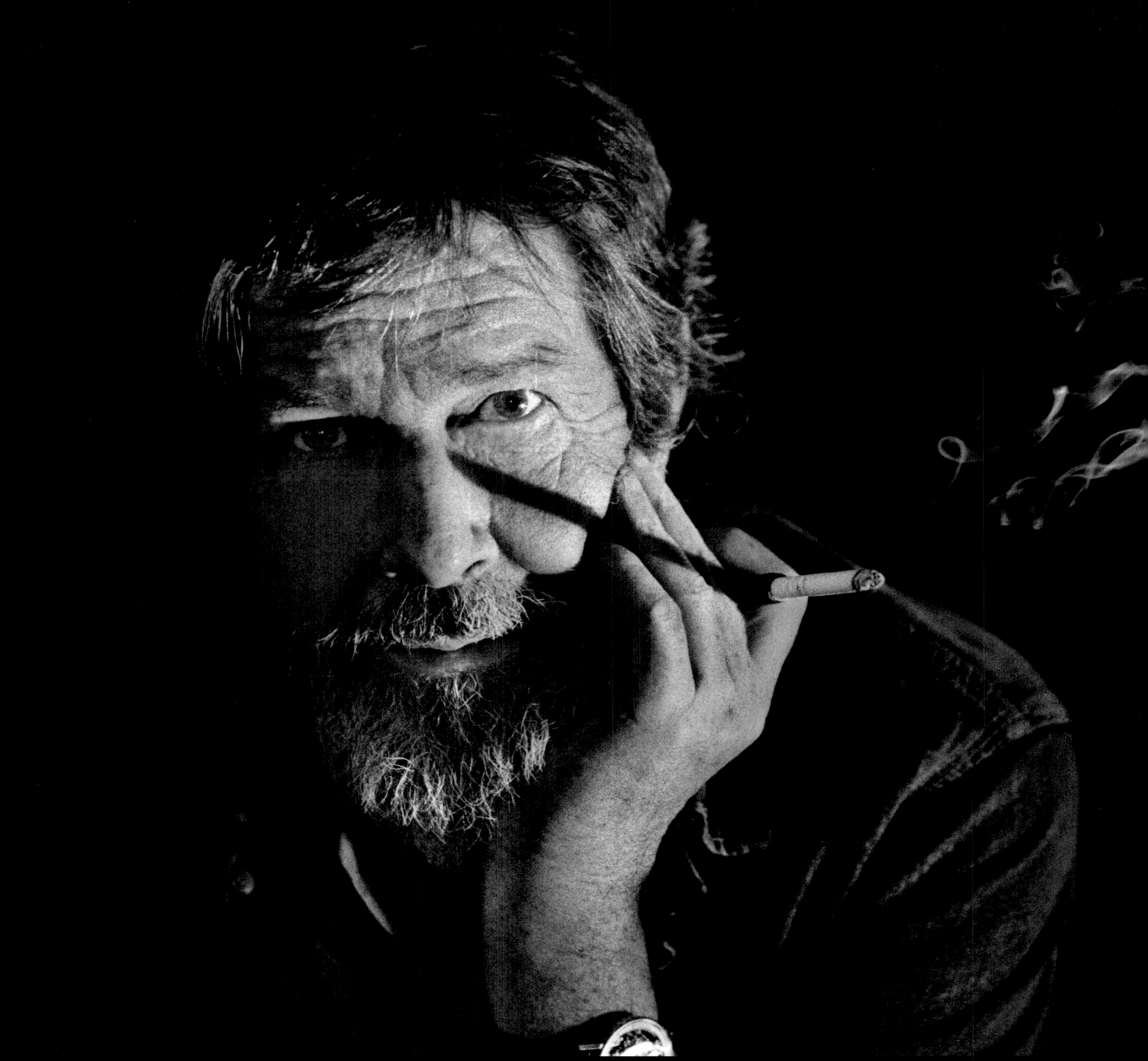

The living,

breathing,

softly unspooling image

that I carry of John

across

the years is a picture of

quiet courage.

I got to know him in college, and refer to him almost every day in my life and in my work.

I see him now sitting in the audience during a performance of Lecture on the Weather,

surrounded by hostile, furious, exasperated, bored, blank people in a state of perfect peace,

seeking and finding fulfillment and pleasure. John Cage was the image

of "Eight Verses for Training the Mind" and a powerful and delicate vector of love itself in action.

— Peter Sellars

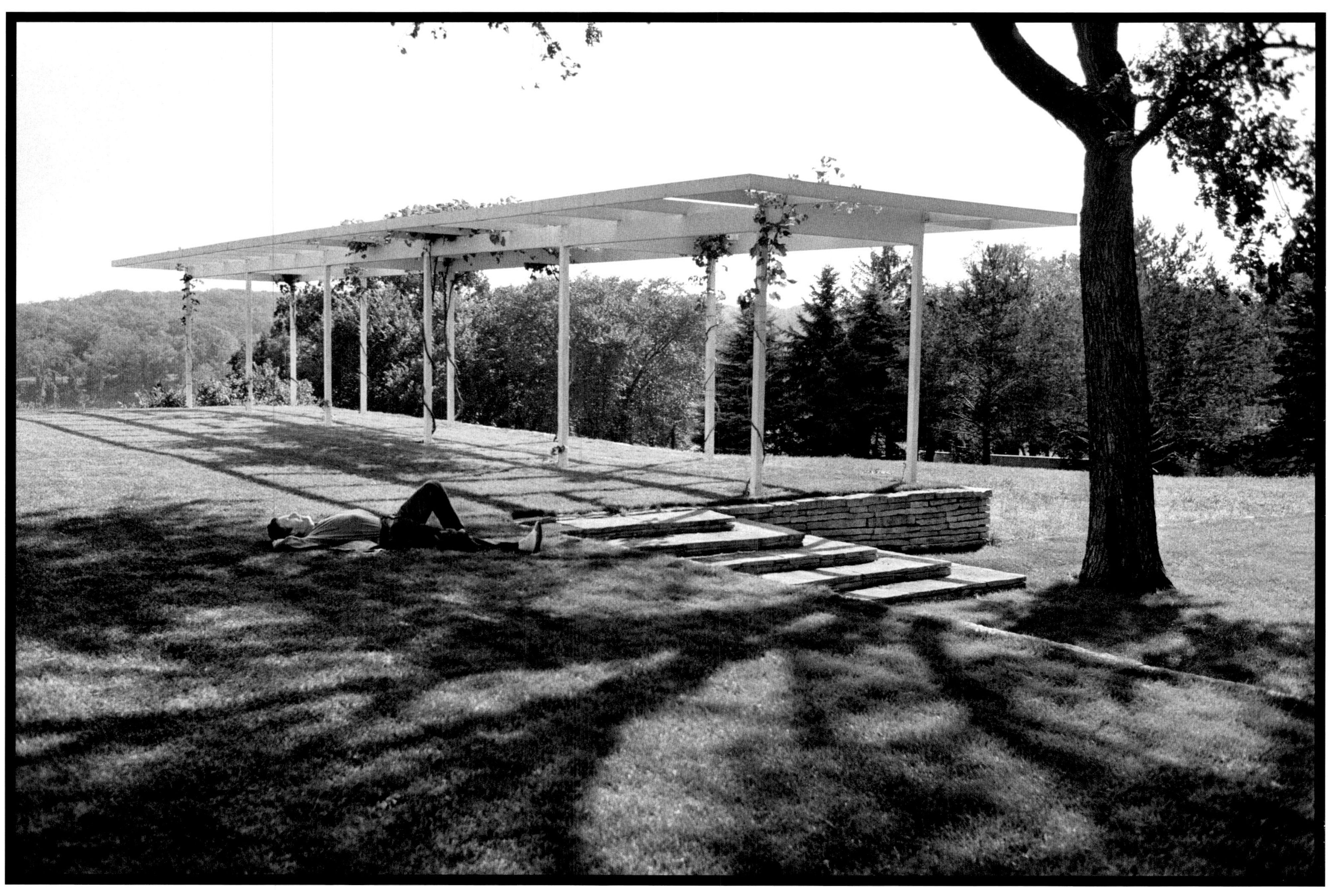

John Cage was a composer.

Cage is often misunderstood as a musical philosopher or a conceptual composer.

But he's not. John Cage is a *perceptual* composer.

Cage's music is all about listening—not the idea of listening,

but the active experience of listening.

Cage challenges us to expand our awareness,

and listen to the music all around us all the time.

If we're not listening, then we're missing the real meaning of Cage's work.

Cage reminds us that sounds in music can be as free as they are in nature.

And when we are listening, the whole world is music.

— John Luther Adams

ask
Little
art O
where it wants
to take
you.

Love,
John

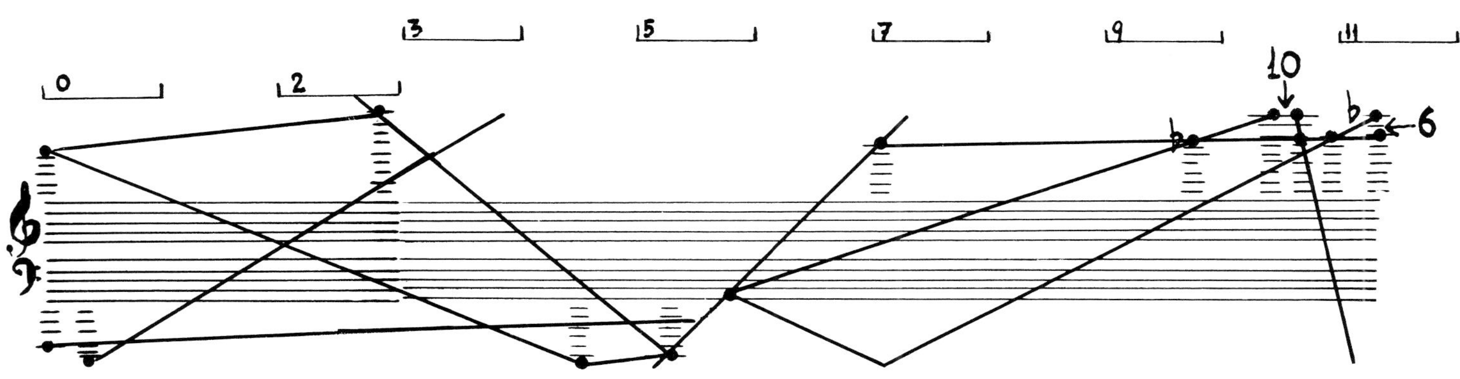

CONTRIBUTORS

JOHN LUTHER ADAMS (page 211) is a composer whose life and work are deeply rooted in the natural world. Called "one of the most original musical thinkers of the new century" by Alex Ross in the *New Yorker*, he is a recipient of the Heinz Award for his contributions to raising environmental awareness. Adams has also been honored with the Nemmers Prize from Northwestern University, "for melding the physical and musical worlds into a unique artistic vision that transcends stylistic boundaries." He is the recipient of the 2014 Pulitzer Prize for music and the author of two books, *Winter Music* and *The Place Where You Go to Listen*, and the subject of a third. His music is recorded on Cold Blue, New World, Cantaloupe, and Mode.

LAURIE ANDERSON (page 75) is one of America's most renowned—and daring—creative pioneers. She is best known for her multimedia presentations and innovative use of technology. As writer, director, visual artist, and vocalist, she has created groundbreaking works that span the worlds of art, theater, and experimental music. Her recording career, launched by "O Superman" in 1981, includes the soundtrack to her feature film *Home of the Brave* and the album *Life on a String*. Anderson's live shows range from simple spoken word to elaborate multimedia stage performances. Anderson has published seven books and her visual work has been presented in major museums around the world.

JOHN ASHBERY (page 180) was born in Rochester, New York, in 1927. He has published more than twenty collections of poetry, most recently *Quick Question*, as well as numerous translations from the French, including works by Pierre Reverdy, Arthur Rimbaud, Raymond Roussel, and several volumes of poems by Pierre Martory. Active in other areas of the arts, including theater and film throughout his career, he has served as executive editor of *Art News* and as art critic for *New York Magazine* and *Newsweek*; he exhibits his collages at the Tibor de Nagy Gallery in New York.

MARY BAUERMEISTER (page 67) is one of the most versatile figures of the German and American postwar art scene. From 1960 to 1961, her legendary "Atelier Mary Bauermeister" in Cologne presented concerts, exhibitions, and intermedia events—with Nam June Paik, John Cage, Christo, and many others—which were a crucial influence on the founding of the Fluxus movement. She moved to New York City in 1962, exhibiting her work regularly at the Bonino Gallery on 57th Street. In 1967, she married Karlheinz Stockhausen, whom she later divorced. In the 1970s, she returned to Germany where she has continued to work.

JAMSHED BHARUCHA (page 34) is the twelfth president of the Cooper Union for the Advancement of Science and Art. A cognitive neuroscientist, he has published extensively on the cognitive and neural underpinnings of music, and has been awarded grants from the National Science Foundation and the National Institutes of Health for his work. From 1993 to 1994, he was a Fellow at the Center for Advanced Study in the Behavioral Sciences at Stanford University, and is currently an Honorary Fellow of the Foreign Policy Association. Bharucha is a classically trained violinist, having received an associate's diploma in violin performance from the Trinity College of Music, London, in 1973.

CAROLYN BROWN (page 169) met John Cage in April 1951 in Denver, when Cage and Merce Cunningham were touring the country giving concerts and master classes. At a party in Cage and Cunningham's honor, she and her husband, the composer Earle Brown, sat at John's feet and listened to him speak about music, art, and chance. Life was never quite the same again. From 1953 to 1973, Brown was a member of the Merce Cunningham Dance Company. She created her part in the first performance of John Cage's *Theatre Piece* and danced in Robert Rauschenberg's first dance work, *Pelican*. After the Cunningham Company, she has been a choreographer, lecturer, teacher, as well as an artistic advisor, coaching early Cunningham works. She is the producer and director of the film *Dune Dance* and the author of *Chance and Circumstance: Twenty Years with Cage and Cunningham*.

KATHAN BROWN (page 158) is founding director of Crown Point Press in San Francisco, publisher of artists' etchings. In 2013, the press marked its fiftieth anniversary with the exhibition, *Yes, No, Maybe: Artists Working at Crown Point Press* at the National Gallery of Art in Washington, D.C. Featured in the exhibition were twenty-six etching projects that Cage completed at Crown Point, working there for a couple of weeks nearly every year from 1978 to 1992. Brown is the author of six books, including *John Cage Visual Art: To Sober and Quiet the Mind* and a memoir, *Know That You Are Lucky*.

GAVIN BRYARS (page 59) studied philosophy, but became a jazz bassist and pioneer of free improvisation with Derek Bailey and Tony Oxley. Early iconic pieces, *The Sinking of the Titanic* and *Jesus' Blood Never Failed Me Yet*, achieved great popular success. His works include four operas, a large body of chamber music, several concertos, and much vocal music. Bryars has collaborated widely with visual artists, choreographers, and theater directors, as well as writing music for the films of Anna Tchernakova. Currently, he tours and records with the Gavin Bryars Ensemble and is regent of the College of Pataphysics. He has done many recordings for ECM, Point, Philips, Naxos, Decca, and his own label GB Records.

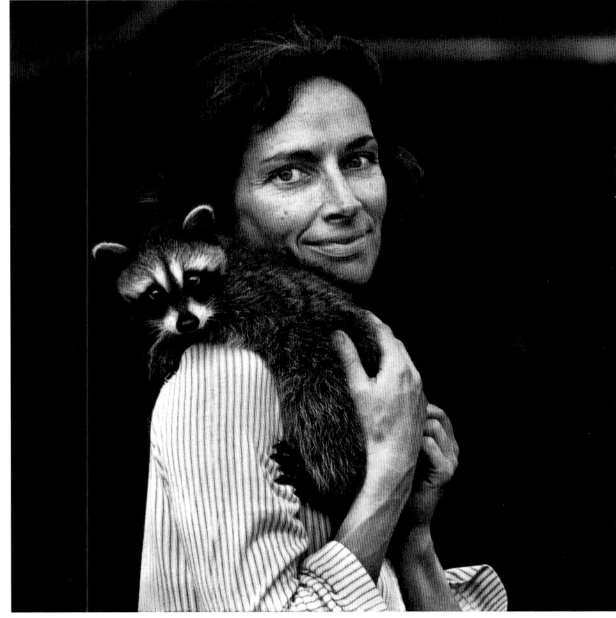

CAROLYN BROWN AND ZOOMIE THE RACCOON, 1978

SYLVANO BUSSOTTI (page 92) has enjoyed a varied and exuberant career as composer, performer, painter, poet, journalist, set and costume designer, and theater and film director. In 1965, he founded the music theater organization Bussottioperaballet. For a time he was the artistic director of the Teatro La Fenice. A flamboyant personality, his music is described as anarchic, virtuosic in its graphic style, and fiercely demanding to perform. His works abound in cross references to his personal life and to each other. He and Cage first met in Darmstadt, Germany, in 1958.

ALEXINA "TEENY" DUCHAMP (1906–1995) (page 44) was born in Cincinnati, and studied sculpture in Paris with Brancusi in the 1920s. She met Marcel Duchamp in 1923, and married Pierre Matisse, the youngest son of Henri Matisse, in 1929. Teeny and Pierre separated in 1949. Five years later, she married Duchamp in New York City, and they remained together until his death in 1968. Both were avid chess players. They summered in Cadaqués, Spain, in a house overlooking the harbor. Teeny Duchamp was an honorary trustee of the Philadelphia Museum of Art.

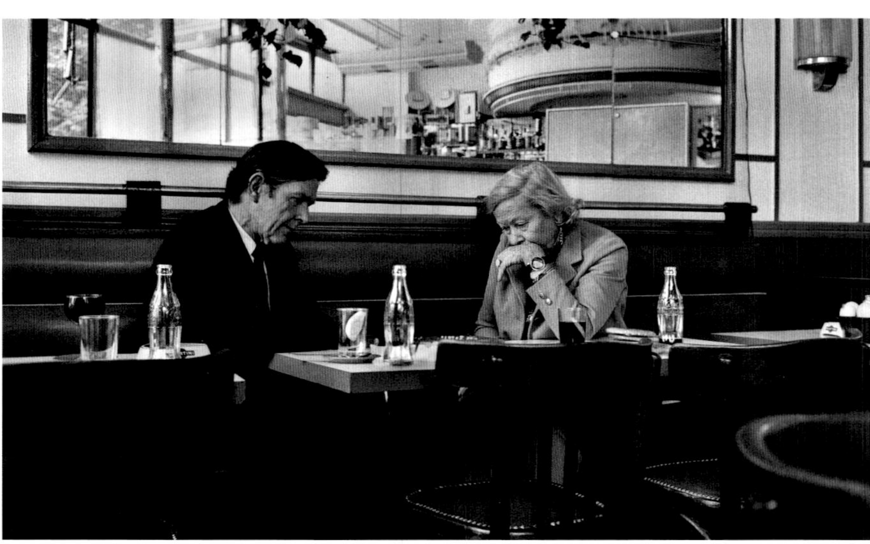

J.C. AND TEENY DUCHAMP, PARIS, 1970

DOUGLAS DUNN (page 157) dances in the Cunningham/Cage nexus from 1968 to 1973. Inspired by their silence, seriousness of daily practice, and wit, he sets out blindly to execute as dancer and choreographer whatever non-sense will come up. Formal defining of inchoate urges provides a means to overcome inherent shyness, and gradually the heart works its way toward the sleeve. Deciding to locate psychic byplay on stage, at arm's length from others, rather than in the "social sphere," doesn't forestall wonderful friendships with colleagues and dance connoisseurs. To be an acknowledged participant within the lineage of workers, lovingly shaping mind into body, is no small amenity.

RICHARD FLEMING (page 184) is an Ordinary Language philosopher and author of books in philosophy and contemporary music, including *The State of Philosophy*, *First Word Philosophy*, and *Evil and Silence: Socrates to Cage*. With the contemporary musician William Duckworth, he edited *John Cage at Seventy-Five* and *Sound and Light: La Monte Young, Marian Zazeela*. He regularly teaches philosophy and humanities courses, recently giving seminars on Wittgenstein at Duke University and Cage presentations for the Fusion Art Exchange, Northeastern University. His newest text, *Threads of Philosophy*, includes a lengthy appendix on "Listening to Cage: Nonintentional Philosophy and Music."

MONIQUE FONG (page 56) was born in Paris. She was a member of the Surrealist group, where she met Octavio Paz who became her "mentor." Coming to the United States in 1951, she made the acquaintance of Marcel Duchamp, with whom she first discovered New York City. She translated Octavio Paz's books on Duchamp into French, as well as a selection of John Cage's *Silence* and *A Year from Monday*. Later, she and Cage collaborated on a "trans-creation" into French of his *Diary: How to Improve the World (You Will Only Make Matters Worse)*. She is the author of *Duchamp des oiseaux*.

LUKAS FOSS (1922–2009) (page 139) was a composer, conductor, pianist, and educator. In 1953, he succeeded Arnold Schoenberg on the UCLA faculty. He was conductor of the Buffalo Philharmonic, the Brooklyn Philharmonic, and the Milwaukee Symphony. Foss once said, "I conduct because I love to make love to the past." A wide ranging, stylistically diverse, and witty composer, he was a great champion of his peers. His early compositions were influenced by Bach and Stravinsky, but he later became interested in controlled improvisation and chance procedures, even while employing serial techniques. Notable among his works are *Time Cycle*, *Echoi*, and *Thirteen Ways of Looking at a Blackbird*.

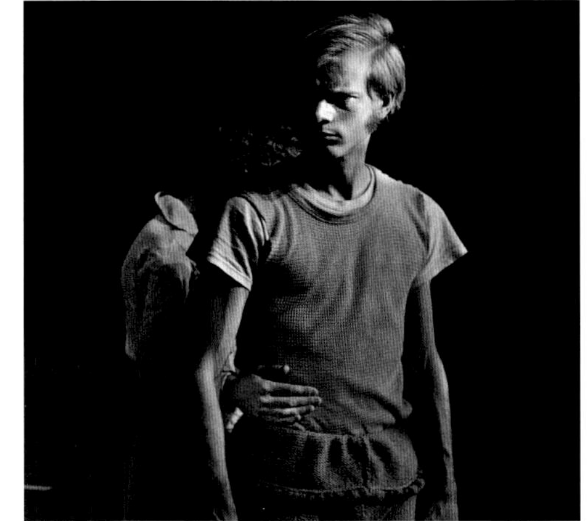

DOUGLAS DUNN, SAINT-PAUL DE VENCE, FRANCE, 1970

KYLE GANN (page 33) was born in 1955 in Dallas. He is a composer and, from 1986 to 2005, was new-music critic for the *Village Voice*. Since 1997, he has taught music theory, history, and composition at Bard College. He is the author of *The Music of Conlon Nancarrow*, *American Music in the 20th Century*, *Music Downtown: Writings from the Village Voice*, *No Such Thing as Silence: John Cage's 4'33"*, and *Robert Ashley*. He also wrote the forewords to the fiftieth-anniversary edition of Cage's *Silence* and to the new edition of Ashley's *Perfect Lives*, and is coeditor of *The Ashgate Research Companion to Minimalist and Postminimalist Music*. Gann studied composition with Ben Johnston, Morton Feldman, and Peter Gena, and his music is often microtonal.

KENNETH GOLDSMITH (page 78) is a poet living in New York City. He is the founding editor of UbuWeb, the Internet's largest site for free distribution of avant-garde materials.

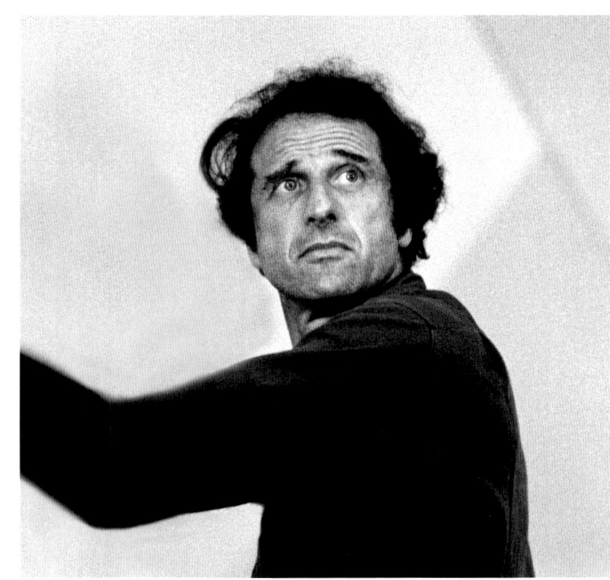

LUKAS FOSS, FRANCE, 1970

DAVID GORDON (page 175) is a writer, director, and choreographer. His commissions include Actors Studio, American Repertory Theater, BBC Channel 4, Brooklyn Academy of Music, Dance Theatre of Harlem, Danspace, New York Theatre Workshop, PBS Great Performances, Serious Fun! at Lincoln Center, Walker Art Center, and many others. His awards include two Obies, three Bessies, two Dramalogues, two Guggenheims, two Pew Charitable Trust grants, three National Endowment for the Arts' American Masterpiece grants, and a Doris Duke Performing Artist Award. He is a founding artist of the Center for Creative Research, Grand Union, and Judson Church. He has performed with Yvonne Rainer and James Waring, and currently constructs dance and theater events for Pick Up Performance Co(s).

MICHAEL GORDON (page 70) is a cofounder of Bang on a Can. His music embodies—writes the *New Yorker*'s Alex Ross—"the fury of punk rock, the nervous brilliance of free jazz and the intransigence of classical modernism." Ranging from major orchestral commissions to works conceived for the recording studio, Gordon's music has been commissioned by Lincoln Center, Carnegie Hall, the BBC Proms, and the Brooklyn Academy of Music, among others. Honored by the Guggenheim Foundation, the National Endowment for the Arts, the Foundation for Contemporary Performance Arts, and the American Academy of Arts and Letters, he and The Michael Gordon Band tour the world over.

RICHARD HAMILTON (1922–2011) (page 118) was a multifaceted British painter and collagist, who the *Guardian* called "the most influential British artist of the twentieth century." He anticipated, and some would say fathered, the Pop art movement in Great Britain. Consumer culture was a constant subject for him, as was the work and aesthetics of Marcel Duchamp, whose art he championed. Hamilton's replica of *The Large Glass* resides at the Tate Modern. His political engagement was constant, typified by a series of paintings, begun in the 1980s, on the "troubles" in Northern Ireland. Hamilton designed The Beatles' *White Album*.

MELISSA HARRIS (page 60) has been the editor-in-chief of Aperture Foundation for ten years, where she has edited Donna Ferrato's *Living with the Enemy*, Sally Mann's *Immediate Family*, Mary Ellen Mark's *American Odyssey*, David Vaughan's *Merce Cunningham: Fifty Years* and the subsequent app, *Merce Cunningham: 65 Years*, among others. In collaboration with Cunningham, she edited his book *Other Animals*. She is a visiting critic in the graduate photography program at Yale University and a past cocurator of the La Triennale di Milano.

PAUL HILLIER (page 62) is from Dorset, United Kingdom. He was director of the Hilliard Ensemble, and subsequently founded Theatre of Voices. He is the author of *Arvo Pärt*, and editor of Steve Reich's *Writings on Music, 1965–2000*, and numerous anthologies of choral music. He was awarded an OBE (Order of the British Empire) for services to choral music, two Grammies for Best Choral Recording, and received the Order of the White Star of Estonia. He lives in Copenhagen.

ALBERTO IBARGÜEN (page 62) is president of the John S. and James L. Knight Foundation. He first encountered John Cage at Wesleyan University in 1965, and was moved for life. After serving in the Peace Corps in the Amazon and Colombia, he graduated from the University of Pennsylvania Law School, practiced in Hartford, Connecticut, entered the newspaper business, moved to New York City, and then became publisher of the *Miami Herald*. He has served on the board of the Merce Cunningham Dance Company, and chaired PBS and the Newseum in Washington, D.C. He sits on the boards of PepsiCo, American Airlines, AOL, and the Secretary of State's Foreign Policy Advisory Committee. He is now a grandfather.

JASPER JOHNS (pages 100, 188) was born in 1930 in Augusta, Georgia, lived in South Carolina throughout his childhood, and moved to New York in 1949. He met John Cage in the mid-1950s and in 1963 they and a few friends established the Foundation for Contemporary Performance Arts, now the Foundation for Contemporary Arts, where he remains a director. At present, he lives and works in Sharon, Connecticut.

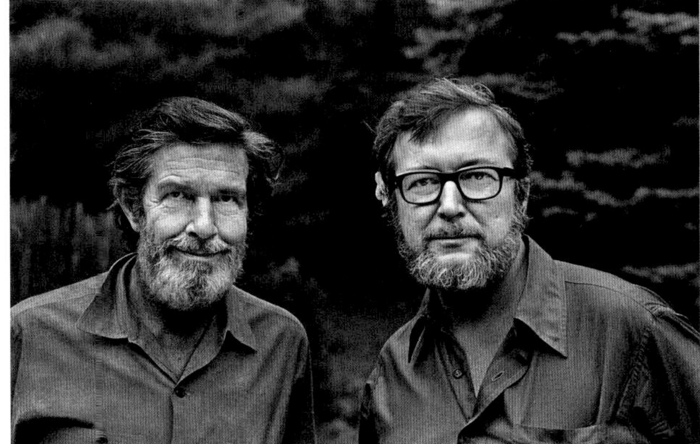

JOHN CAGE AND JASPER JOHNS, JUNE 1971

ALAIN JOUFFROY (page 22) is a French poet, publisher, creator of magazines and journals, art critic, member of the Surrealist movement, and Parisian "voyageur." Eric Rohmer cast him as "the writer" in his film *La Collectionneuse*. Jouffroy cofounded L'Union des Ecrivains during the May 1968 uprisings. He is the author of over a hundred published works—collections of poems, novels, essays, and monographs of artists. Today, he writes and develops collages/montages of objects, his "posages." Jouffroy has received the Prix Apollinaire, the gold medal from Connaissance des Arts for best art critic, and the Prix Goncourt for the body of his poetic work.

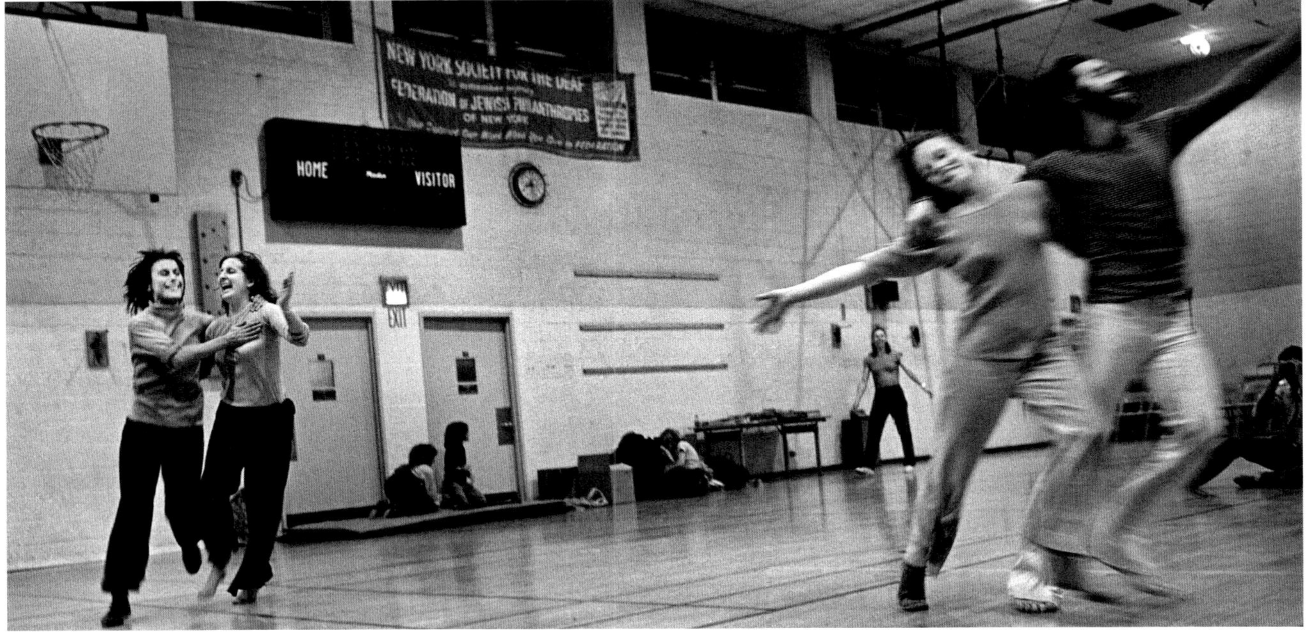

YVONNE RAINER, TRISHA BROWN, BARBARA DILLEY, DAVID GORDON, MAY 1971

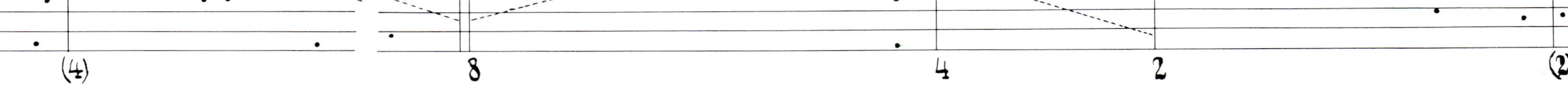

ALEX JULYAN (page 111) is a London-based visual artist and producer who makes sculptures and site-specific work from a wide variety of ephemeral media and found objects. Experimenting with the poetry of the everyday, her work focuses on transforming the mundane into the extraordinary. This ethos carries across into live performance where she collaborates across art forms and media, coproducing large-scale events involving performers, musicians, artists, scientists, and audiences. Her diverse interests have led to projects informed by language, history, architecture, and medicine. She has coproduced a number of John Cage's *Musicircuses* at major London venues.

RAY KASS (page 206) is a nationally recognized painter and writer. He is founder and director of the Mountain Lake Workshop, a collaborative, community-based art project drawing on the customs, environmental resources, and technology of Virginia's New River Valley and the Appalachian region. His paintings have been widely exhibited and are represented by Reynolds Gallery in Richmond. His publications include *Sight of Silence: John Cage's Complete Watercolors* and *John Cage: Zen Ox-Herding Pictures*, coauthored with Stephen Addiss, and *Morris Graves: Vision of the Inner-Eye*.

KENNETH KING (page 183) is a multimedia dance artist and the author of *Writing in Motion: Body—Language—Technology*. His writings have appeared in the *Paris Review*, *Chicago Review*, *Hotel Amerika*, *I nor* (*New Ohio Review*), *Art & Cinema*, *Rio Grande Review*, *Topoi: An International Review of Philosophy*, *Movement Research Performance Journal*, *PLJ/Performing Arts Journal*, *Semiotext(e)*, *Film Culture*, *Soho Weekly News*, *Dance Magazine*, and in the anthologies *Footnotes: Merce Cunningham: Dancing in Space and Time*, *Footnotes: Six Choreographers Inscribe the Page*, and *Further Steps 2: Fourteen Choreographers on What's the R.A.G.E. in Modern Dance*.

ALISON KNOWLES (page 63) was an integral part of the 1950s downtown New York artist community. By the early 1960s, Knowles was active with the circle associated with Marcel Duchamp, John Cage, Pop art, and Happenings. Her friendships with Cage and, later, Duchamp, led her to design and edit Cage's book *Notations*, a compilation of experimental composition, as well as Marcel Duchamp's last print, *Coeurs Volants*, in 1967. Both were published in partnership with Knowles's spouse, Dick Higgins, and his Something Else Press. Knowles works periodically with students in residencies all over the world, including in Berlin and Kassel, Germany, and at Radcliffe's Institute for Advanced Study at Harvard University.

LAURA KUHN (page 41) is an avid new-music enthusiast and longtime director of the John Cage Trust.

JOAN LA BARBARA (page 199) is a composer, performer, and sound artist, renowned for her unique vocabulary of experimental and extended vocal techniques, who composes for multiple voices, chamber ensembles, theater, orchestra, interactive technology, dance, video, and film. She was awarded a Demetrio Stratos Prize and a DAAD (German Academic Exchange Service) Artist-in-Residency in Berlin. She has received fellowships from Civitella Ranieri, the New York State Council of the Arts, and the Guggenheim Foundation. as well as seven National Endowment for the Arts grants and the American Music Center's Letter of Distinction for significant contributions to American music. Recordings of her music include *ShamanSong*, *Voice Is the Original Instrument*, and *73 Poems*. which was presented at Whitney Museum's *American Century Part II: Sound Works*. John Cage was her mentor. La Barbara is currently composing an opera.

JACK LENOR LARSEN (page 63) is possibly the most accomplished textile designer living, certainly one of the most innovative and influential in the second half of the twentieth century. He is the author of *Jack Lenor Larsen: A Weaver's Memoir*. Longhouse Reserve, his twelve-thousand-square-foot home in East Hampton, New York, is also an arts foundation and a sixteen-acre garden open to the public. Examples of Larsen's work are preserved in the collections of major museums around the world, and his is one of only two design houses to have been the subject of an exhibition at the Palais du Louvre.

ALVIN LUCIER (page 196) was born in 1931 in Nashua, New Hampshire. He attended Yale and Brandeis universities, and spent two years in Rome on a Fulbright Scholarship. He taught at Brandeis and, for forty-three years, at Wesleyan University, where he became John Spencer Camp Professor of Music. Since the mid-1960s he has made numerous sound installations and chamber and orchestral works, many of which explore the acoustic characteristics of sound and its natural movement in space. Lucier was awarded the Lifetime Achievement Award by the Society for Electro-Acoustic Music in the United States, and received an Honorary Doctorate of Arts from the University of Plymouth, United Kingdom.

JUDITH MALINA (page 137) is a fiercely intellectual actress, director, and writer. In 1947, she cofounded the Living Theater—the longest lived and most influential experimental theater company in the United States—with Julian Beck. In 1959, the top floor of the Living Theater's 14th Street building became home to the Merce Cunningham Dance Company. After Beck's death in 1985, Malina continued to run the company with Hanon Reznikov until 2008, and recently with a young group from the Lower East Side. Malina and the Living Theater performed throughout the world, including Brazil where, in 1971, her radical aesthetics and leftist political philosophy resulted in two months' imprisonment.

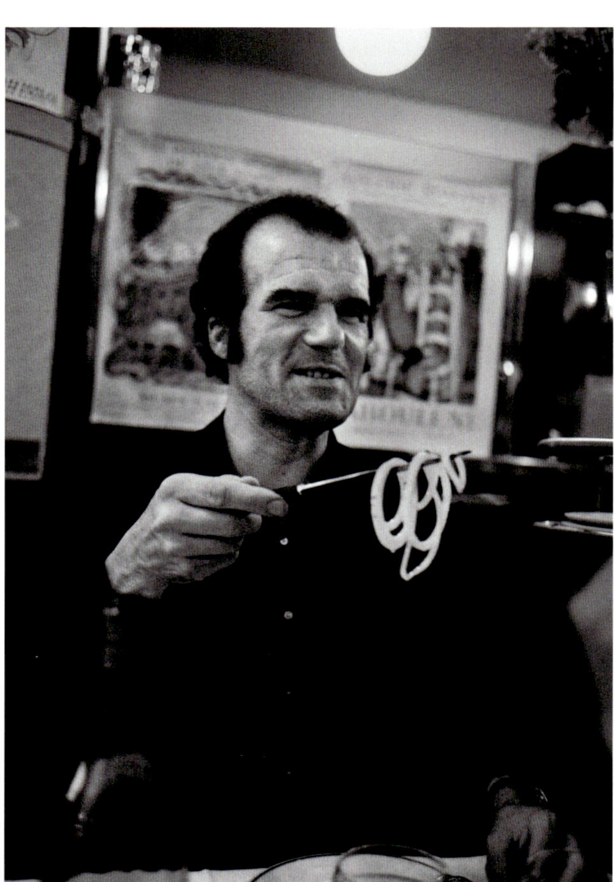

HARRY MATHEWS, PARIS, 1970

HARRY MATHEWS (page 160), a novelist and essayist, was born in New York City in 1930, and settled in Europe in 1952, living in Spain, Germany, Italy, and France. Married to the French writer Marie Chaix, he now divides his time between France and the United States. His most recent publications are *The Case of the Persevering Maltese: Collected Essays*, *My Life in CIA: A Chronicle of 1973*, and a book of poetry, *The New Tourism*.

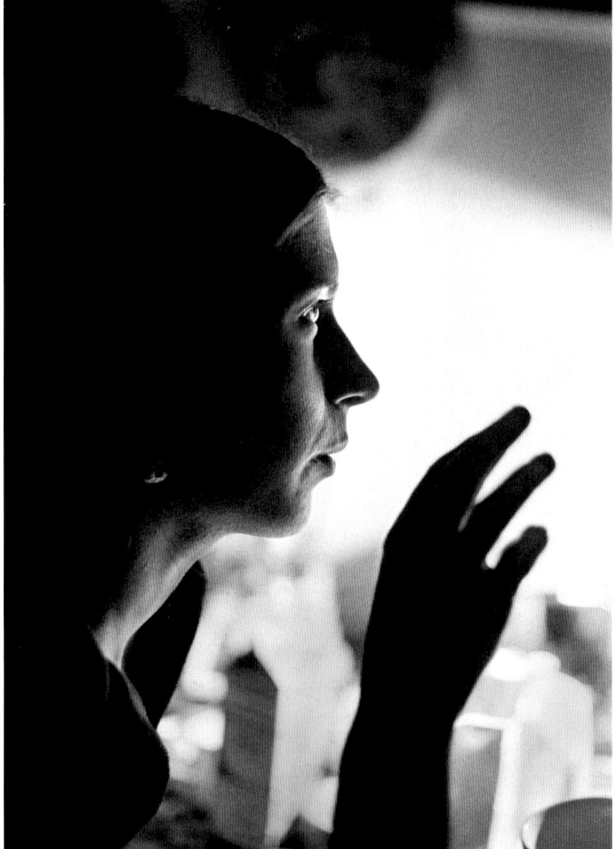

MEREDITH MONK, 1969

MEREDITH MONK (page 114) is a composer, singer, director/choreographer, and creator of new opera, music-theater works, films, and installations. A pioneer in what is now called "extended vocal technique" and "interdisciplinary performance," Monk creates works that thrive at the intersection of music and movement, image and object, light and sound. Her ground-breaking exploration of the voice as an instrument, an eloquent language in and of itself, expands the boundaries of musical composition. Monk has received a MacArthur "Genius" Award, two Guggenheim Fellowships, three Obies, and two Bessies.

STEPHEN MONTAGUE (page 106) is an Anglo-American freelance composer and pianist based in London since 1974, whose works have been performed world-wide by a range of ensembles, from the London Symphony Orchestra to Lucinda Childs Dance. He did many first recordings of John Cage's prepared piano and other works for the BBC, and performed with Cage on numerous occasions, particularly in Europe. He was in the London premiere of *Europeras 3 & 4*, touring with Cage to Berlin and Paris. Since the 1990s, Montague has organized and directed ten Cage *Musicircuses* in the United Kingdom and Europe, including a centenary tribute at the English National Opera, London.

RICK MOODY (page 55) is the author of five novels, three collections of stories, a memoir, and most recently a volume of essays entitled *On Celestial Music*. He also plays in the Wingdale Community Singers, whose most recent album is *Night, Sleep, Death*.

MARK MORRIS (page 94) is artistic director of the internationally renowned Mark Morris Dance Group and Music Ensemble. The *New York Times* has hailed him as "the most successful and influential choreographer alive, and indisputably the most musical." Morris frequently collaborates with preeminent musicians, orchestras, and opera companies, performing in the world's most prestigious dance and music venues, and remains much in demand as a ballet choreographer and opera director. His Mark Morris Dance Center, founded in 2001, provides outreach programs for local children and seniors, and is home to a school offering music and dance classes to students of all ages and abilities.

GORDON MUMMA (page 62) was born in 1935 in Framingham, Massachusetts. He has performed diverse instruments—piano, horn, voice (in classical chamber music and orchestra), musical saw, and bandoneon. Since the 1950s, he has developed his own live-electronic music instruments. His composing and performing includes participation in the historic ONCE Festivals, Sonic Arts Union, Cunningham Dance Company, and collaboration with many other diverse artists. He has lectured and written extensively on the arts and technology. A large selection of his writings is forthcoming, and includes his work with John Cage and the milieu of the Cunningham Company.

PAULINE OLIVEROS (page 128) is a composer and improviser who performs extensively, locally and throughout the world, in a variety of venues. Her music is performed widely by many notable musicians and ensembles. Her recorded works are available for download and on cassette, CD, DVD, and vinyl. She was introduced to John Cage by David Tudor when they were organizing the Tudor Fest at the San Francisco Tape Music Center in 1964.

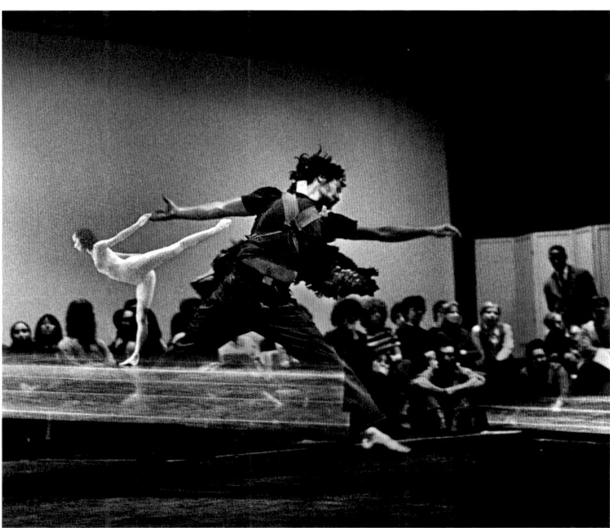

ACCIDENTAL DOUBLE EXPOSURE OF STEVE PAXTON AT THE WHITNEY MUSEUM AND CAROLYN BROWN AT BAM, 1970

YOKO ONO (page 192) was, in the 1950s and early 1960s, a central figure in the downtown avant-garde, Fluxus-oriented art scene, for which Cage was a father figure. She created, participated in, and hosted performance art of varyingly radical kinds. In the 1970s, chance processes threw her and Cage together again, when she, John Lennon, Merce Cunningham, and Cage found themselves living next door to one another on Bank Street in Greenwich Village.

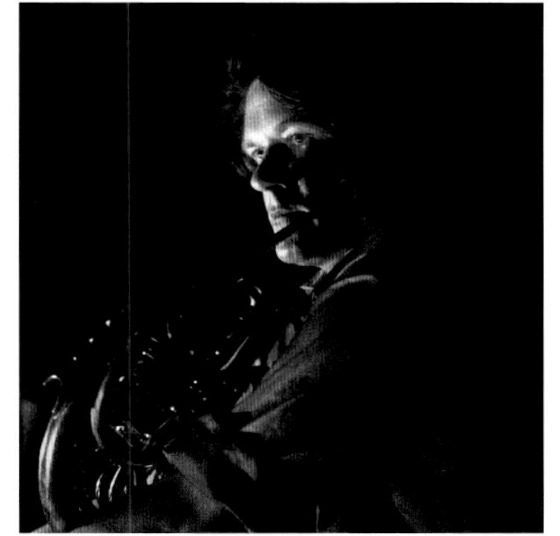

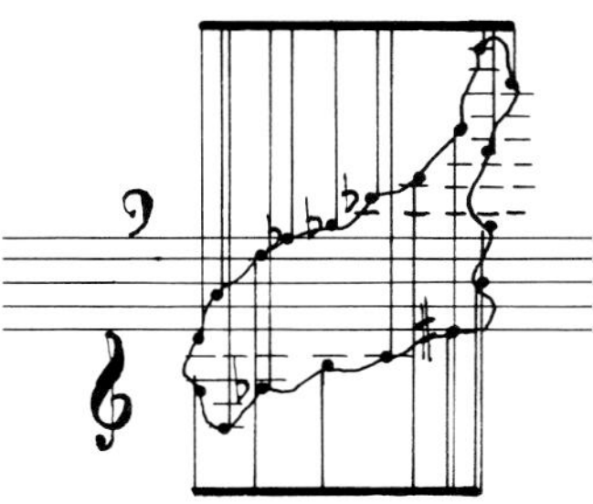

GORDON MUMMA, PARIS, 1970

RON PADGETT (page 109) is the author of the poetry collections *How to Be Perfect*, *You Never Know*, and *Great Balls of Fire*, as well as memoirs of Joe Brainard, Ted Berrigan, and the author's father. Padgett has received Fulbright, National Endowment of the Arts, Guggenheim, and Civitella Ranieri fellowships, and was named Officier Chevalier dans l'ordre des Arts et des Lettres by the French government. A Chancellor of the Academy of American Poets, he received the Shelley Memorial Award from the Poetry Society of America, and his *How Long* was a Pulitzer Prize finalist in poetry. His newest book is *Collected Poems*.

STEVE PAXTON (page 64) met John Cage at the Merce Cunningham Studio on 14th Street and 6th Avenue. He had seen Cage and David Tudor deliver a lecture at the American Dance Festival in 1958, which seemed to rewire his brain. At the Studio, however, he met the John Cage who was not the musical public intellectual but a devoted administrator and chauffer who—along with David Tudor, Robert Rauschenberg, and, of course, the amazing dancers who performed with Cunningham and were the foundation of the enterprise—created a perfect alternative to the dance world they operated within. On a shoestring. Over decades. This experience was a fundamental lesson in "what it takes" for Paxton, which he holds close to this day.

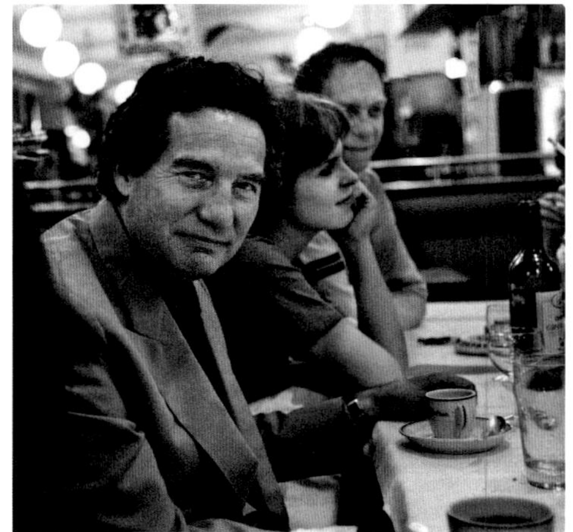

OCTAVIO PAZ, PARIS, 1970

OCTAVIO PAZ (1914–1998) (pages 146–47) is widely recognized as one of the most important poets of the twentieth century. In 1990, Paz received the Nobel Prize in Literature. He also served as a diplomat for Mexico, posted to Japan, Switzerland, France, and India. It was in 1964, in his capacity as Mexico's ambassador to India, that Paz and John Cage first met during the world tour of the Merce Cunningham Dance Company. In 1965 Paz wrote to Monique Fong, "I was completely captivated by Cage: a mixture of Satie and Bashô and terribly 'yankee' in the good (now forgotten) sense of the word."

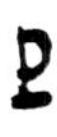

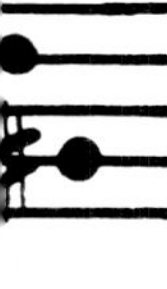

YVONNE RAINER (page 104) was a cofounding member of the Judson Dance Theater in 1962. Following a fifteen-year career as a choreographer and dancer (1960–1975), she made a transition to filmmaking. After making seven experimental feature films, she returned to dance in 2000 via a commission from the Baryshnikov Dance Foundation. Her dances and films have been shown worldwide, and her work has been rewarded with two Guggenheim Fellowships, two Rockefeller grants, a Wexner Prize, and a MacArthur Fellowship. She is the author of a memoir, *Feelings Are Facts: A Life*. A selection of her poetry was published by Paul Chan's Badlands Unlimited.

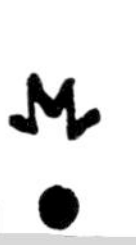

STEVE REICH (page 72) was recently called "our greatest living composer" by the *New York Times* and "the most original musical thinker of our time" by the *New Yorker*. The *Guardian* wrote: "there's just a handful of living composers who can legitimately claim to have altered the direction of musical history and Steve Reich is one of them." He has been awarded the Praemium Imperiale (Japan), the Polar Prize (Sweden), and the Pulitzer Prize (United States). He is a member of the American Academy of Arts and Letters and the Franz Liszt Academy (Budapest), and is Commandeur de l'ordre des Arts et des Lettres (France).

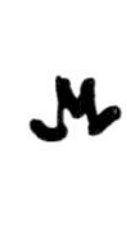

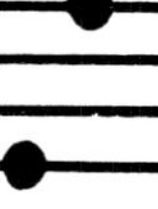

FREDERIC RZEWSKI (page 195) is an American composer and virtuoso pianist who has spent much time in Europe. Of his compositions that have political and sociological overtones, the best known is his fifty-minute set of piano variations, *The People United Will Never Be Defeated!* In the 1960s, he cofounded Rome's *Musica Elettronica Viva*. Rzewski's style and vocabulary range widely from graphic notation, improvisation, and serial techniques to more traditional forms. His classically proportioned piano concerto, which premiered in August 2013 at the Proms in Prince Albert Hall with Rzewski as soloist, was described by the *Guardian* as "cheeky."

JOEL SACHS (page 19) is an internationally performing pianist and conductor. At the Juilliard School, he conducts and directs the New Juilliard Ensemble, the school's annual Focus! Festival of nontraditional music, and its concerts at the Museum of Modern Art's Summergarden. He is a member of Juilliard's faculties of chamber music and music history. He is codirector, copianist, and conductor of the internationally acclaimed Continuum. An active historian, he is the author of a biography of Henry Cowell, a study of J. N. Hummel, and numerous articles about nineteenth- twentieth- and twenty-first century topics.

PAUL SADOWSKI (page 153) served as music copyist to John Cage shortly after graduating from SUNY Albany in 1973 until the composer's death in 1992. After Cage's passing, Sadowski joined the New York Mycological Society, which Cage founded in 1962. The activities of the Society have kept him as busy as he was getting Cage's musical oeuvre in print.

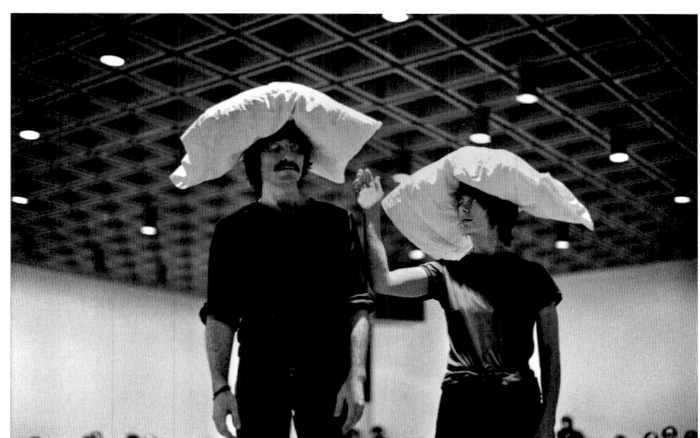

YVONNE RAINER WITH DAVID GORDON, APRIL 1970

ERIC SALZMAN (page 63) is a composer and writer in the field of new music theater and contemporary opera. He founded, directed, and codirected Quog Music Theater, the American Music Theater Festival, and the Center for Contemporary Opera, where he is composer-in-residence. He has written well-known books on twentieth-century music and the new music theater as well as many works of experimental music theater and opera. Labor Records and Naxos are putting out a series of his works in recorded form. Salzman's theater opera, *Big Jim & the Small-time Investors*, is scheduled for performances in 2014 and 2015.

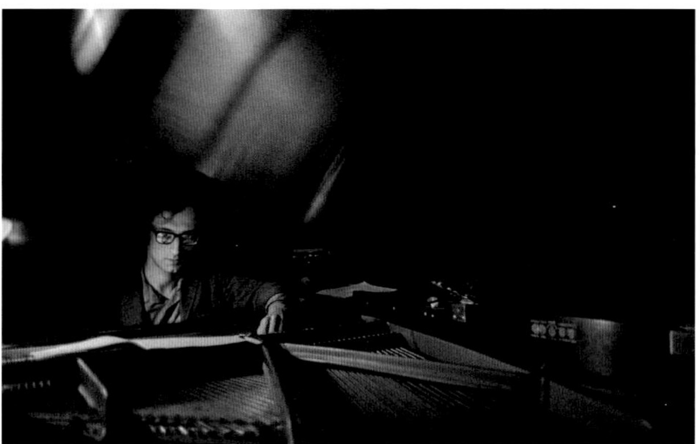

FREDERIC RZEWSKI, BAM, 1972

R. MURRAY SCHAFER (page 201), a Canadian, has achieved an international reputation as a composer, writer, educator, and environmentalist. Schafer's dramatic works employ music and theater in a manner that he calls the "theatre of confluence." His diversity belies generalizations of style, and his work could be described as a synthesis of twentieth-century avant-garde techniques with the nineteeth-century romantic spirit. He has received many awards, notably he was the first recipient of the Jules Léger Prize in 1978 and of the first Glenn Gould Prize in 1987. Recent awards include the Governor General's Performing Arts Awards for Lifetime Artistic Achievement.

PETER SCHICKELE (page 186) has received commissions from the St. Louis Symphony, the National Symphony, the Canadian Brass, and Pilobolus, as well as numerous other organizations and individual musicians. His output ranges from symphonic, choral, and chamber music to movie and television scores. As the perpetrator of the highly debatable P.D.Q. Bach, he has performed in virtually every state and province in North America, and he is the winner of five Grammy Awards. He once made a choral setting of several poems he saw on the walls of men's restrooms—like some other great works of art, the settings have since been lost.

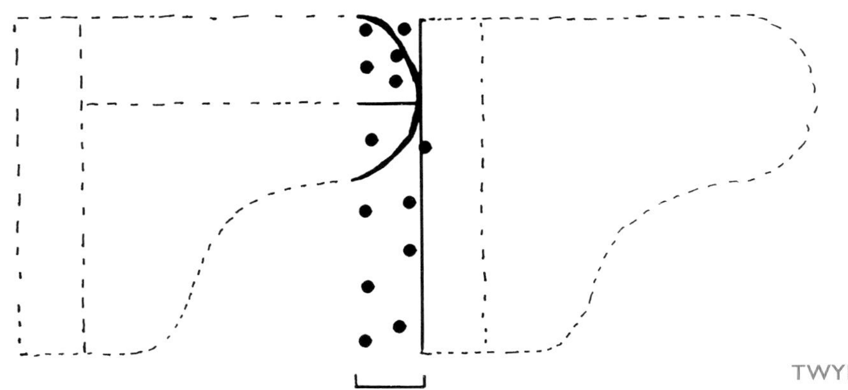

PETER SELLARS (page 209) is an opera and theater director, and an innovative and powerful force in the performing arts in the United States and abroad. A visionary artist known for groundbreaking interpretations of classics by Mozart, Handel, Shakespeare, and Sophocles, and of operas by Olivier Messiaen, György Ligeti, and especially John Adams whose *Nixon in China*, *The Death of Klinghoffer*, and *Doctor Atomic* he brought to the stage. Sellars is a professor in the Department of World Arts and Cultures at UCLA and recipient of a MacArthur Fellowship, the Erasmus Prize, the Sundance Institute Risk-Takers Award, and many other honors.

NADIA SIROTA (page 172) is a violist whom *Pitchfork* magazine has called "a one-woman contemporary-classical commissioning machine." She is known for her singular sound and expressive execution, coaxing solo works from the likes of Nico Muhly, Daníel Bjarnason, Marcos Balter, and Missy Mazzoli. In addition to her work as a soloist, Sirota is a member of yMusic, the American Contemporary Music Ensemble, and Alarm Will Sound, and has lent her sound to recordings and concert projects by such artists as Grizzly Bear, Jónsi, and Arcade Fire. She teaches at the Manhattan School of Music and is a radio host for Q2 Music in New York.

STEPHEN SONDHEIM (page 25) has single-handedly forged anew the art form we call musical theater. In the theater world he is commonly referred to, not entirely facetiously, as God. To the extent that he is mostly worshiped, even while being occasionally railed against, the description is apt.

ELIZABETH STREB (page 98) was born in 1950 and has been testing the potential of the human body ever since. The preeminent Extreme Action Architect, Streb is "a rascal," "a genius," and dance's answer to punk rock. She founded her company in 1985 and became a MacArthur Fellow in 1997. In 2003, she established the STREB Lab for Action Mechanics (SLAM) in Williamsburg, Brooklyn. Ten years later, she received a Doris Duke Artist Award. The STREB Extreme Action dance company has performed in, around, over, and on top of major landmarks, theaters, and stadiums worldwide.

TWYLA THARP (page 126) is one of America's preeminent choreographers and troublemakers. She has managed to transfer her loose-limbed but intellectually rigorous early style, forged in the small group Twyla Tharp Dance that she founded in 1965, to larger companies such as American Ballet Theater, the New York City Ballet, the Royal Ballet, the Paris Opera Ballet, and others. She has created Broadway dance musicals focusing on Billy Joel and Frank Sinatra, and is the author of the autobiography *Push Comes to Shove*. Tharp is the recipient of a MacArthur Fellowship, a National Medal of Arts, a Kennedy Center Award, and numerous other honors.

MICHAEL TILSON THOMAS (page 31) is music director of the San Francisco Symphony, founder and artistic director of the New World Symphony, and principal guest conductor of the London Symphony Orchestra. He is a Chevalier dans l'ordre des Arts et des Lettres of France, has won thirteen Grammy Awards for his recordings, received the Peabody Award for his radio series for SFS Media, "the MTT Files," and was awarded the National Medal of Arts.

SALOMÉ VOEGELIN (page 124) is an artist and writer based in London. She is the author of *Listening to Noise and Silence: Towards a Philosophy of Sound Art*. Other writings include "Ethics of Listening" in the *Journal of Sonic Studies* and "Listening to the Stars" in *What Matters Now? (What Can't You Hear?)*. Voegelin cohosts, with Daniela Cascella, a monthly radio show, "ora: voyages into listening and writing," on Resonance FM. She is currently working on a second book, *Sonic Possible Worlds: Hearing the Continuum of Sound*.

ANNE WALDMAN (page 36) has been an active member of the "Outrider" experimental poetry community, a culture she has helped create and nurture for over four decades. Her poetry is recognized in the lineage of Walt Whitman and Allen Ginsberg, and in the Beat, New York School, and Black Mountain trajectories of the New American Poetry. Author of more than forty books, Waldman is the recipient of the prestigious Shelley Memorial Award and is a Chancellor of the Academy of American Poets. Waldman was a founder and director of the Poetry Project at St. Marks's Church-in-the-Bowery, and cofounder with Ginsberg of the celebrated Jack Kerouac School of Disembodied Poetics at Naropa University.

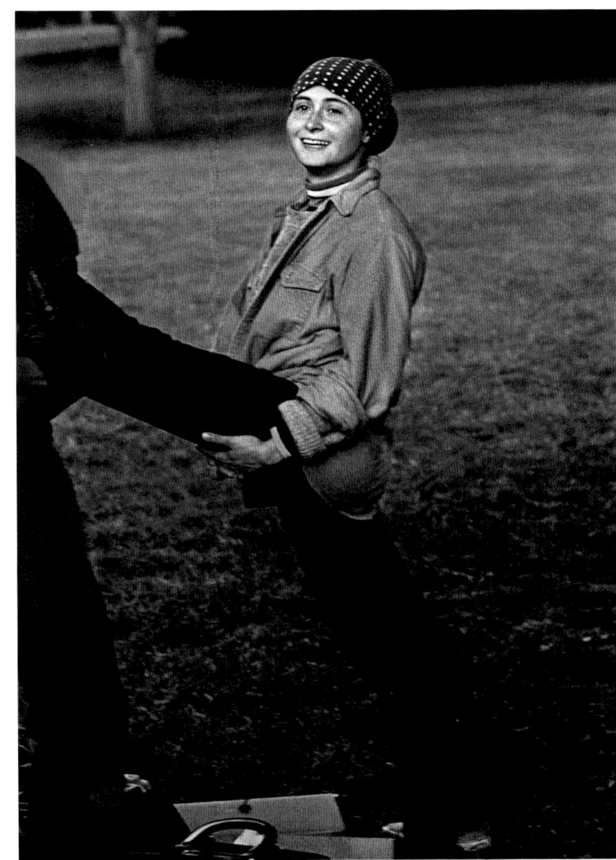

TWYLA THARP, NEW YORK CITY, JUNE 1971

ROBERT WILSON (page 131) is among the world's foremost theater and visual artists. His works for the stage unconventionally integrate a wide variety of artistic media, including dance, movement, lighting, sculpture, music, and text. His artistic collaborators include artists and musicians such as Tom Waits, Susan Sontag, Laurie Anderson, William Burroughs, Jessie Norman, and Philip Glass, with whom he wrote the seminal opera *Einstein on the Beach*. His drawings, paintings, and sculptures have been presented around the world in hundreds of solo and group showings. He is the founder and artistic director of the Watermill Center, a laboratory for performing arts.

CHRISTIAN WOLFF (page 68) was born in 1934 in Nice, France. He is a composer, teacher, and sometime performer. Since 1941 he has lived in the United States, studying piano with Grete Sultan and composition briefly with John Cage, in whose company along with Morton Feldman, then David Tudor and Earle Brown, his work found encouragement and inspiration, as it did subsequently with Frederic Rzewski and Cornelius Cardew. He also had a long association with Merce Cunningham and his dance company. Academically trained as a classicist, he taught classics at Harvard from 1962 to 1970, then music, comparative literature, and classics at Dartmouth from 1971 to 1999.

CAPTIONS

3. Westbeth, New York City, 1972
6–7. Amherst, Massachusetts, February 1970
8–9. Near Grenoble, France, October 1972
10–11. *How to Pass, Kick, Fall, and Run*, France, 1970
17. Belgrade, September 1972
18–19. Minneapolis, September 1969
20–25. Preparing a prepared piano, May 1971
26. San Francisco, 1968
27. France, 1970
28–39. Musée d'Art Moderne, Paris, May 1970
40–41. Minneapolis, September 1969
43. Grenoble, France, October 1972
45–47. Chess with Teeny Duchamp, Place de l'Odéon, Paris, June 1970
48–49. Cadaqués, Spain, July 1970
50–54. John Cage playing chess with Merce Cunningham, Teeny Duchamp observing, Figueres, Spain, July 1970
56–57. *Second Hand* rehearsal, Merce Cunningham, Carolyn Brown, John Cage, Westbeth, New York City, January 1972
58–59. *Suite for Five* duet rehearsal, Carolyn Brown, Merce Cunningham, John Cage, Westbeth, New York City, January 1972
61. Amherst, Massachusetts, February 1970
65. Fondation Maeght, Saint-Paul de Vence, France, July 1970
66. *Music for Piano 53–68*, the score for Cunningham's *Suite for Five*, January 1971
68–69. Gordon Mumma, John Cage, David Tudor; on stage: Jeff Slayton, Valda Setterfield; Chateau de Ratilly Event, June 1970
70–71. Odéon-Théâtre de l'Europe (Théâtre de France), Paris, June 1970
73–75. "Finding Music," Cunningham Event, Museum of Contemporary Art, Belgrade, September 1972
76–77. Holland, June 1970
78–79. Minneapolis, March 1972
81–83. Grenoble, France, October 1972
84. *Second Hand* rehearsal, Odéon-Théâtre de l'Europe (Théâtre de France), Paris, June 1970
85. *Second Hand* rehearsal, February 1970
86–87. Fondation Maeght, Saint-Paul de Vence, France, July 1970
88–89. Teeny Duchamp, John Cage, Carolyn Brown, Merce Cunningham, El monasterio de Sant Pere de Rodes, Catalonia, Spain, July 1970
90–91. Collecting wild greens, Rockland County, New York, May 1971
92–95. Collecting mushrooms, Grenoble, France, October 1972
96–97. *The Mushroom Book*, with illustrator Lois Long, Hollander Workshop, New York City, Spring 1972
98–99. Paris, June 1970
101. John Cage with Merce Cunningham, Heathrow, London, September 1972
102. Belgrade Airport, September 1972
103. At "The Land," Stony Point, New York, June 1969
104. Scheveningen, Holland, 1970
105. Holland, 1970
106–7. Post performance, Sadler's Wells Theatre, London, September 1972
108–9. Westbeth, New York City, Spring 1972
110–11. Piazza San Marco, Venice, September 1972
112. Charles Atlas, John Cage, Françoise Prouvoyeur, Meg Harper, Venice, 1972
113. Sandra Neels, John Cage, Brooklyn Academy of Music, November 1970
115. Scheveningen, Holland, June 1970
116. France, Summer 1970
117. Airport, Paris, June 1970
119. With Richard Hamilton, London, September 1972
120–21. Jasper Johns, John Cage, Brooklyn Academy of Music, February 1972
122–23. Teatro La Fenice, Venice, September 1972
124–25. Paris, June 1970 (photograph of John Cage by Jack Mitchell)
127. Tavistock Hotel, London, September 1972
129. Backstage, Odéon-Théâtre de l'Europe (Théâtre de France), Paris, June 1970
130. Reflection in entrance door to the inflatable theater (*théâtre gonflable*), Fondation Maeght, Saint-Paul de Vence, France, July 1970

132. Richard Lippold, at "The Land," Stony Point, New York, June 1969
133. Iannis Xenakis, John Cage, Odéon-Théâtre de l'Europe (Théâtre de France), Paris, June 1970
134–35. Odéon-Théâtre de l'Europe (Théâtre de France), Paris, June 1970
136–37. Julian Beck, John Cage, Paris, June 1970
138–39. John Cage, Aaron Copland, Brooklyn Academy of Music, 1970
139. Lucas Foss, John Cage, Fondation Maeght, Saint-Paul de Vence, France, July 1970
140–41. Lecture/demonstration, Walker Art Center, Minneapolis, March 1972
142. John Cage, Jill Johnston, Teeny Duchamp, Brooklyn Academy of Music, November 1970
143. John Cage, David Tudor, Gordon Mumma, San Francisco, 1968
144–45. Dinner with Octavio Paz, Paris, 1970
149. Brooklyn Academy of Music, January 1970
150–51. Westbeth, New York City, June 1971
152–53. The raconteur—Carolyn Brown, Sandra Neels, Susana Hayman-Chaffey, Mel Wong, Chase Robinson, John Cage, January 1971
154–55. Paris, June 1970
156. Rehearsal, with Chase Robinson, Ulysses Dove, Brooklyn Academy of Music, November 1970
159. New Year's Eve party, 1971
160–61. Performing *Burdocks* by Christian Wolff, the score which accompanies Cunningham's *Borst Park*, Brooklyn Academy of Music, February 1972
162. Le Fou I, Amherst, Massachusetts, February 1970
163. Le Fou II, Odéon-Théâtre de l'Europe (Théâtre de France), Paris, June 1970
164–65. Making automobile music on the infamous Sunbeam Alpine for a Cunningham Event, Philip Johnson Estate, New Canaan, Connecticut, June 1967
166. John Cage playing chess with children, Sadler's Wells Theatre, London, September 1972
167. Wayzata, Minnesota, September 1969
168. Carolyn Brown's dressing room, Brooklyn Academy of Music, 1970
169. With Carolyn Brown, Spoleto, Italy, July 1970
170–71. "Tall Tale," Carolyn Brown, John Cage, Minneapolis, September 1969
173. Wayzata, Minnesota, September 1969
174. With Ain Gordon, Fondation Maeght, Saint-Paul de Vence, France, July 1970
175. Minneapolis, March 1972
177. Fondation Maeght, Saint-Paul de Vence, France, July 1970
178–79. Merce Cunningham, John Cage, *How to Pass, Kick, Fall, and Run*, Brooklyn Academy of Music, 1970
181. Pit, La Grande Salle, Maison de la Culture, October 1972
182–83. With Merce Cunningham, Maison de la Culture, Amiens, France, June 1970
185. Grenoble, France, October 1972
187. Saint-Paul de Vence, France, July 1970
189. Jasper Johns, Gemini G.E.L., Los Angeles, January 1971
190–91. Grenoble, France, October 1972
193. UC Irvine, California, January 1971
194–95. UC Irvine, California, January 1971
197. Westbeth, New York City, January 1972
198–99. *How to Pass, Kick, Fall, and Run*, with Chase Robinson, Brooklyn Academy of Music, November 1970
200–201. Boston, February 1970
202. France, Summer 1970
203. Marcel Duchamp, Buffalo, New York, March 1968
204. Jasper Johns, Richard Hamilton, John Cage, Teeny and Marcel Duchamp, watching dress rehearsal prior to the premier of Merce Cunningham's *Walkaround Time*, Buffalo, New York, March 1968
205. *Walkaround Time*, decor by Jasper Johns after *The Large Glass* by Marcel Duchamp
207. Watersmoke, June 1967
208–9. Grenoble, France, October 1972
210. Wayzata, Minnesota, September 1969
213. Saint-Paul de Vence, France, July 1970
228. Scheveningen, Holland, June 1970

Thank You To:

Gene Caprioglio and Edition Peters for their generous permission regarding reproduction of excerpts from John Cage's *Concert for Piano and Orchestra* on the endpages and pages 215–21.

American Public Media's "American Mavericks," the source of the quote from Lukas Foss.

New Directions for permitting use of a different translation of "On Reading John Cage" than that which appears in their volume SELECTED POEMS OF OCTAVIO PAZ, edited by Eliot Weinberger.

John Ashbery's text, © John Ashbery 2013, is used by arrangement with George Borchardt, Inc.

Steve Reich's text is based on an extract (c.100w) from p. 165 from *Writings in Music 1965–2000* by Steve Reich. Used by permission of Oxford University Press, Inc.

Thank you to Yolanda Cuomo and Bonnie Briant for the heady mix of expertise and openness which they brought to the table in equal measure, turning the making of this book into both a true collaboration and an adventure. Thank you also to Carolyn Brown, Alison Granucci, and Melissa Harris for their ideas, encouragement, and support and, finally, to Wesleyan University Press.

A Special Thank You To:

In the introduction I refer to my limited technical abilities in the digital realm. This, it turns out, was being kind. The photographs—which looked fine to my eyes—were actually filled with invisible digital "artifacts" which rendered them useless for the duotone printing process to come. To have a book meeting Yolanda Cuomo's standards every image would have to be rescanned from the original negative, then reprinted by lab technicians to match my photographs. This was somewhat like being informed one's children must be raised all over again from birth by someone else! But apparently we had no choice. Test negatives were sent out, rescanned and reprinted, but the resulting photographs looked like someone else's work, not mine. I was simply unable to accept them and was on the verge of abandoning the whole project when a young man in Yolanda's studio, Jonno Rattman, volunteered his services. He seemed quite certain he could reproduce the images as I had originally conceived them. Something about him inspired my confidence, and, to make a long story short, although some images proved a struggle, he did it. This book exists. It would not have without him. So thank you, Jonno Rattman!

John Cage Was

Cover image: Grenoble, France, October 1972
Endpaper illustrations by John Cage, taken from the score for *Concert for Piano and Orchestra*

Wesleyan University Press
Middletown, CT 06459
www.wesleyan.edu/wespress

Manufactured in the United States of America

BOOK DESIGN BY YOLANDA CUOMO DESIGN/NYC
Associate Designers: Bonnie Briant and Kristi Norgaard
Production Management: Luke Chase
Reproduction and Print Preparation: Jonno Rattman
Duotone Separations and Printing: Meridian Printing, East Greenwich, RI
Packaged by Paper Cinema, LLC

10 9 8 7 6 5 4 3 2 1

Library of Congress Cataloging-in-Publication Data

Klosty, James.
John Cage was / James Klosty.
228 p. 30.5 x 28 cm.
ISBN 978-0-8195-7504-3 (cloth : alk. paper)
1. Cage, John—Pictorial works. 2. Composers—United States—Pictorial works.
I. Title.
ML410.C24K46 2014
780.92—dc23
2014007892

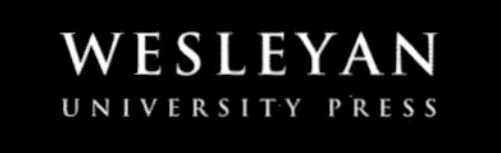

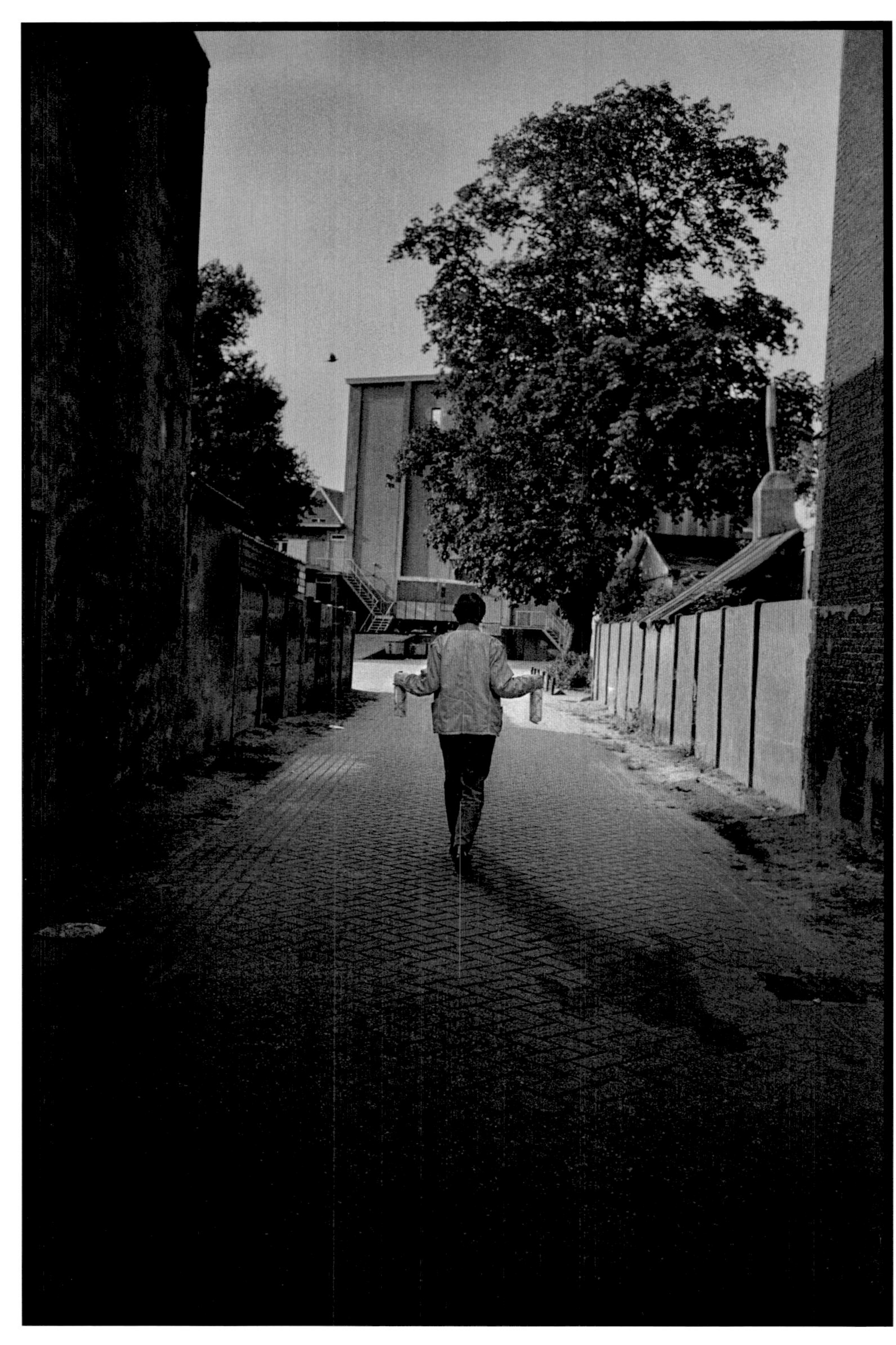

CE

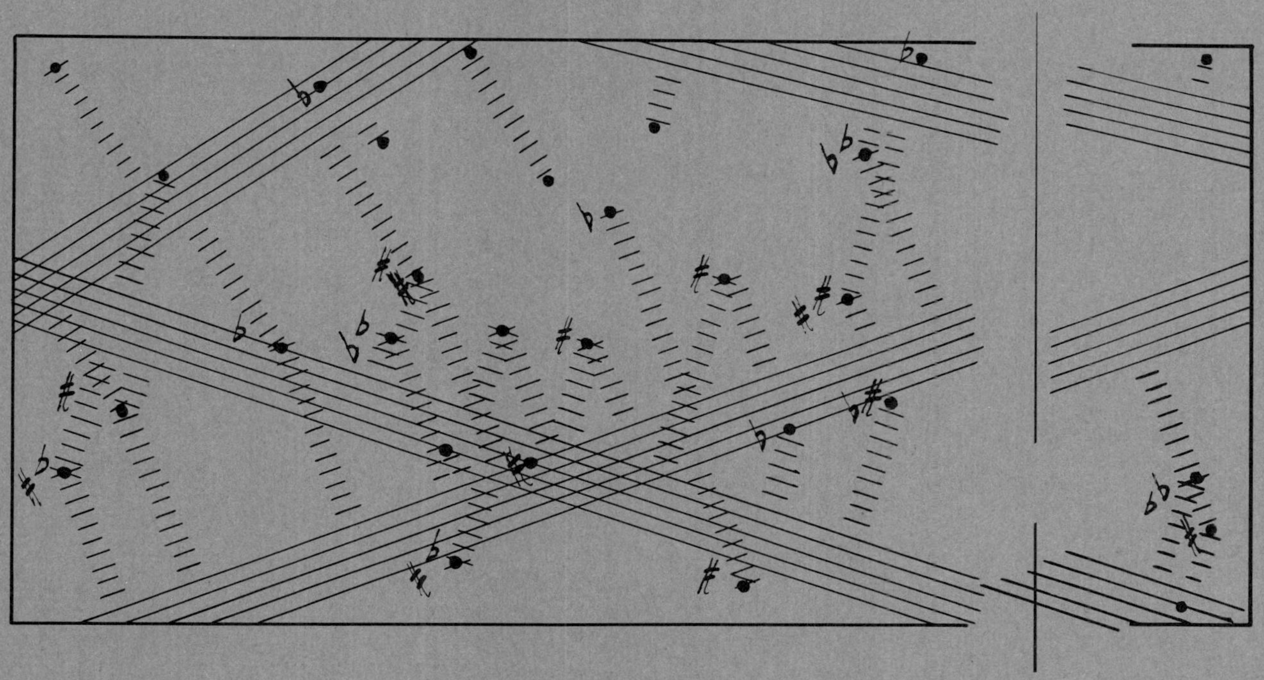

BM

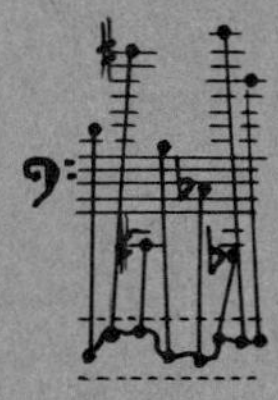

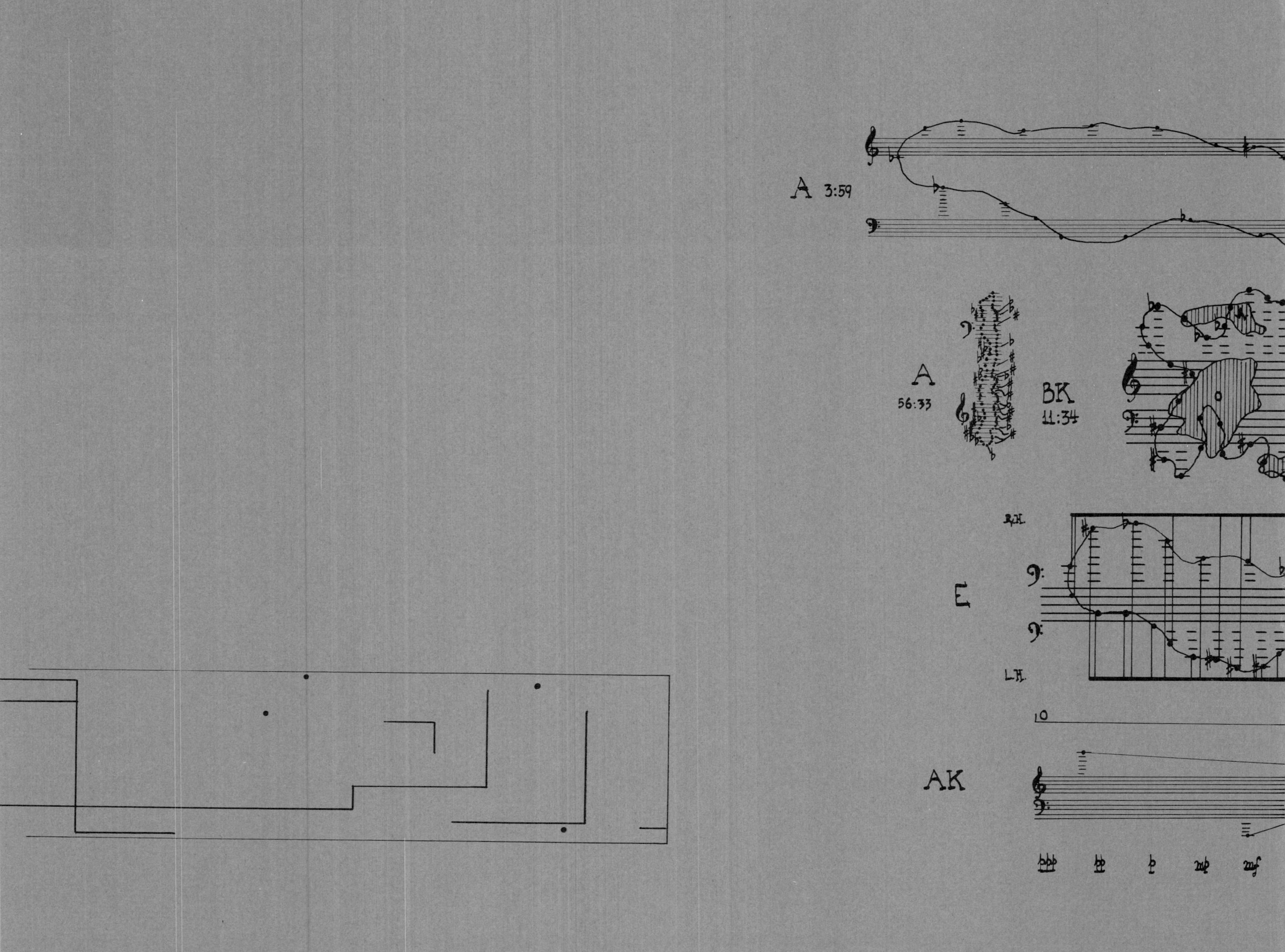
A 3:59
A
56:33
BK
11:34
R.H.
E
L.H.
10
AK
ppp
pp
p
mp
mf